The Scarlet Woman
and the Red Hand

The Scarlet Woman and the Red Hand

*Evangelical Apocalyptic Belief
in the Northern Ireland Troubles*

Joshua T. Searle

PICKWICK *Publications* · Eugene, Oregon

THE SCARLET WOMAN AND THE RED HAND
Evangelical Apocalyptic Belief in the Northern Ireland Troubles

Pickwick Publications
An Imprint of Wipf and Stock Publishers
199 W. 8th Av.e, Suite 3
Eugene, OR 97401

www.wipfandstock.com

ISBN 13: 978-1-62564-623-1

Cataloging-in-Publication data:

Searle, Joshua.

The scarlet woman and the red hand : evangelical apocalyptic belief in the Northern Ireland troubles / Joshua T. Searle.

xx + 256 p. ; 23 cm. Includes bibliographical references.

ISBN 13: 978-1-62564-623-1

1. Political violence—Northern Ireland. 2. Northern Ireland—History. 3. End of the world. 4. Millennialism. 5. Bible, Revelation—Criticism, interpretation, etc. I. Title.

BT892 S217 2014

Manufactured in the U.S.A.

To my parents, Roy and Shirley Searle

Cursed are the peacemakers
For they might compromise
Cursed are those who mourn
For they might apologise
Cursed are the poor in spirit
For they might confess and regret
And cursed are the merciful
For they might forgive and forget
And cursed are the meek
For they won't ride their high horse
But blessed are the arrogant
For they will maintain this curse

—STEVE STOCKMAN, "THE BELFAST BEATITUDES"

Contents

Preface

APOCALYPTIC ESCHATOLOGY SETS US questions that lead us into the heart of the relationship between ideas and their expression in culture. The significance of apocalyptic eschatology becomes apparent upon a brief consideration of its immense existential scope. Human beings seem to possess an extraordinary capacity to rise above present adversity by looking forward to future possibilities out of which to create new horizons of hope. Apocalyptic-eschatological language furnishes the human imagination with a munificent array of conceptual possibilities through which to envision an "ideal world."[1] These conceptual possibilities can be directed towards the transfiguration of present circumstances through hope. Such hope is predicated on the power of the apocalyptic-eschatological imagination to conceive of the future as the realm of "realised possibility."[2] Apocalyptic eschatology postulates an earth-shattering vision of hope by providing an overarching conception of reality and cosmic purpose through which to surmount the tragedy, irony and apparent contingency of human experience. The ubiquity of the utopian impulse throughout history in diverse religions and cultures testifies to the notion that the hope for a better world is an ineradicable fact of the human condition.[3]

Apocalyptic eschatology is the language of human hope.[4] As such it supplies the conceptual resources through which utopian impulses are articulated and enacted in human life and history. Although often associated specifically with Christian theology, apocalyptic eschatology,

---

1. Ernst Bloch alluded to the notions of "Tagträume" and "Wunschbilder", which he posited as the preconditions of artistic creation. See Kesser, *Ernst Blochs Ästhetik*, 70–72.

2. Bloch, *Literary Essays*, 342.

3. Levitas, "The Imaginary Reconstitution of Society," 53.

4. Hayes, *Visions of a Future*, 93–95.

as "an inherent . . . component of the human condition,"[5] is a matter
of decisive historical significance that extends beyond particular denominations and theological perspectives. A proper phenomenology
of the human condition recognizes that hope, as a primary conviction
involving the will as well as reasons and feelings, inhabits every aspect
of human motivation and action.[6] Hope, in the words of Ernst Bloch, is
"a basic feature of human consciousness."[7] Hope initiates a process of
existential transformation through which human subjects are endowed
with the capacity to engage in creative acts of self-surpassing and self-
transcendence and thereby to elevate themselves to new levels of being.

Yet far from being confined to existential conceptions of individual development, hope has social consequences that can transform
cultures and alter the course of world history. The shaping power of
apocalyptic-eschatological hope as a change-agent of cultures consists
in the imaginative vision it sets forth for social reconciliation and cosmic consummation. Theologians have alluded to the notion of a "messianic idea," which denotes a gradual yet inexorable spiritual resolution
in human history.[8] The culmination of this idea is described as a utopian
golden age in which "all that is in heaven and under the earth flows
together in one laudatory voice."[9]

The principle of a messianic resolution perceives in the historical
process not a chaotic improvisation of unrelated accidents but a dynamic unfolding development which moves towards a determined *telos*
of "a fuller disclosure and realisation of life's essential meaning."[10] In the
Christian understanding, this resolution is manifested in the eschatological metaphor of the kingdom of God and the conviction that history
is orientated according to a messianic purpose. History is under the control of a benevolent, sovereign Lord who will ultimately save the world
and its inhabitants from sin, death, persecution, fear, angst and every
other kind of existential impediment to human flourishing. According
to this interpretation, the messianic resolution of history will culminate

---

5. Gardiner, "Bakhtin's Carnival: Utopia as Critique," 44.

6. Macquarrie, *In Search of Humanity*, 244.

7. Bloch, quoted in Amsler, "Pedagogy Against 'Dis-Utopia,'" 305.

8. Klausner, *The Messianic Idea in Israel*, 7–12.

9. Dostoyevsky, *The Brothers Karamazov*, 319.

10. Niebuhr, *The Nature and Destiny of Man*, ii, 2.

in a "glorious appearing" (Titus 2:13) of the "Son of man sitting on the right hand of power, and coming in the clouds of heaven" (Matt 26:64).

Far from being confined to the dusty monographs of erudite, eso-teric theological scholarship, apocalyptic eschatology is, and has been throughout history, an integral and universal part of human history and experience, reaching into the hidden depths of both popular and elite cultural production.[11] "Apocalypse," asserts Thomas Altizer, "is at the very center of an original Christianity, just as it has been a primal ground of a uniquely Western and Christian history and culture, and has even been reborn in our contemporary world."[12] Recent scholarship in millennial studies has reinforced the notion that "apocalyptic and millennial ideas are far more central to western historical conscious-ness than was previously recognized."[13] The apocalyptic-eschatological narrative of hope has the power to shape nations and to change the course of world history. For the Marxist-atheist thinker, Ernst Bloch, to be human meant to exhibit the capacity to hope. Thus arose Bloch's formulation of the dynamic *spero ergo ero*[14] as an inversion of Descartes' static *cogito ergo sum*. Out of this primary conviction arose his notion of a "utopian impulse," which he posited as the main driving force behind all of the great creative artistic, cultural and political achieve-ments of humankind.[15] Likewise, for Nikolai Berdyaev, the messianic idea of eschatological fulfilment was nothing less than the "basic theme of history."[16] Theologians have also recognized the visionary power of the apocalyptic-eschatological narrative on the course of world history. "The religious and secular enactments of this narrative," notes Catherine

11. For a general historical overview, see Himmelfarb, *The Apocalypse: A Brief History*. An example of a work which effectively uncovers the subtle yet pervasive ways in which apocalyptic ideas inhabit modes of popular cultural production is Dark, *Everyday Apocalypse*. For an overview of the ways in which apocalyptic motifs prevail in American popular culture, see Rehill, *The Apocalypse Is Everywhere*.

12. Altizer, *Genesis and Apocalypse*, 9.

13. Shantz, "Millennialism and Apocalypticism," 42.

14. "*Ich hoffe, also werde ich sein*" (I hope, therefore I will be); Bloch, *Atheismus im Christentum*, 332. My thanks to Kurt Seidel for giving me this reference.

15. Bloch, *The Principle of Hope*, ii, 624 (originally published as *Das Prinzip Hoffnung* between 1954 and 1959). Bloch regarded his philosophy of hope as a genuine contemporary expression of the apocalyptic tradition of the biblical prophets. See Migliore, *Faith Seeking Understanding*, 333; see also Jameson, *Archaeologies of the Future*, 3.

16. Berdyaev, *The Beginning and the End*, 200.

Keller, "have generated . . . much of the dynamism of Western history."[17] In his radical theological appropriation of Ernst Bloch's *Das Prinzip Hoffnung* (1954–59), Jürgen Moltmann made a decisive contribution to our understanding of the power of this narrative in world history. Rejecting deterministic conceptions of historical progress, Moltmann opts for the notions of creativity and freedom that inhere in the idea of the fulfillment of the divine promise in history.[18] Moreover, according to Paul Ricoeur's commentary on Moltmann, this fulfilment signifies not an end or definitive closure but "an increase, a surplus, a 'not yet' which maintains the tension in history."[19]

History furnishes countless examples of the epoch-making dynamism of apocalyptic-eschatological convictions. "History from Abraham to Marx," observes John Howard Yoder, "demonstrates that significant action, for good or for evil, is accomplished by those whose present action is illuminated by eschatological hope."[20] Every major world religion, including Judaism,[21] Islam,[22] Hinduism,[23] and Buddhism[24] (notwithstanding conspicuous differences both within and among these religions) has retained an apocalyptic-eschatological consciousness. Thus, despite fundamental differences in conceptions of historical development,[25] each variation manifests a certain commonality on the point of its orientation towards the transcendence of death and the possibility of the transfiguration of present circumstances into a greater state of existence. These notions have been a wellspring of hope for countless millions throughout world history. The focus of this study,

17. Keller, *Apocalypse Now and Then*, x.

18. Moltmann, *Theologie der Hoffnung*, 98.

19. Ricoeur, "Freedom in the Light of Hope," 405.

20. Yoder, *The Original Revolution*, 71.

21. Idel, "On Apocalypticism in Judaism," 40–74; Scholem, *The Messianic Idea in Judaism*.

22. Zakzouk, "The Islamic Doctrine of the Eschatological Completion," 89–100; see also, Kehl, *Eschatologie*, 81–90; Kabbani, *The Approach of Armageddon? An Islamic Perspective*; Kenney, "Millennialism and Radical Islamist Movements," 688–715.

23. Knipe, "Zur Rolle des provisorischen Körpers," 62–81.

24. Upton, *Legends of the End*, 29–31.

25. Wessinger argues that millennial thinking does not necessarily presuppose a linear view of history, noting that forms of apocalypticism have prevailed in Asian contexts in which history was understood in terms of cyclical patterns. See Wessinger, "Millennialism with and without the Mayhem," 51.

however, is upon a certain conception of apocalyptic eschatology that is associated specifically with Christian theology.

This distinctive contribution to our understanding of the underlying meaning of world history and human destiny was inaugurated two thousand years ago through the proclamation of a radical young Jewish preacher from the town of Nazareth who was destined to change the course of world history.[26] He began by announcing that the "kingdom of God" was "now at hand" (Mark 1:15). Towards the end of his life, before he was put to death by crucifixion, he declared that there would be a fearsome ordeal, a period of unprecedented adversity, known as "great tribulation", which was to presage the end of the world (Matt 24:21).[27] According to the Gospel accounts, Christ, following his resurrection from the dead and before his ascension into heaven, left his followers with the reassurance that he would be with them "to the end of the age" together with an earlier promise that he would return again one day in glory and send his angels to gather up his chosen people "from the four winds" (Matt 28:20; 24:31).

This vision of hope finds its definitive expression in the final book of the Bible, the Revelation of John, in which a heavenly city, the New Jerusalem, is depicted. Many have regarded this distinctive depiction of cosmic consummation, in which a redeemed humanity is to enjoy perpetual bliss in this ultimate arena of human fulfilment and flourishing, as one of the most creative conceptions of human destiny ever to have been produced by the human imagination. Countless myriads down through the centuries of church history have been inspired by the depiction of the effulgence of the heavenly city, which will be such that God's people will have "no need of the light of the sun or moon for the Lord their God will be radiant in their midst" (Rev 22:5). Despite the lapse of nearly two thousand years since these prophecies were first transcribed, the Christian vision of apocalyptic-eschatological hope has inspired innumerable generations and remains the basis of hope for millions throughout the world today.

26. In saying this it is important to note the indebtedness of Christian conceptions of apocalyptic eschatology to the preceding prophetic tradition of ancient Hebraic texts and the great extent to which Christ himself draws on the imaginative apocalyptic-eschatological visions depicted in earlier Jewish scriptures. This will be acknowledged in more detail in chapter 2.

27. Cf. Mark 13:10; Luke 21:23; Acts 7:11.

But apocalyptic eschatology, in common with all major historical change-agents, has its dark sides. On this point Paul Ricoeur's remark is particularly lapidary: "evil and hope are more closely connected than we will ever think them."[28] Twentieth-century history testifies to the diverse manifestations of apocalyptic eschatology and to the catastrophic consequences of misplaced millennial optimism.[29] Beneath the maniacal fantasies of Adolf Hitler and the callous brutality of Joseph Stalin's purges there lay varying degrees of an apocalyptic-eschatological conception of history.[30] Many studies have demonstrated that Hitler believed that he was engaged in an apocalyptic struggle against the Jews and Communists on behalf of Christian civilization.[31] As an important part of the programme of its brazen and systematic campaign of falsification of German history, the Nazi propaganda machine seized upon the notion of the "Third Reich" which was made to correspond with the "age of the Holy Spirit" alluded to by the medieval apocalyptic seer, Joachim of Flora.[32] Moreover, the apocalyptic undertones of the Nazi conception of the "Final Solution" (*die Endlösung*) are unmistakably apparent.[33] As historians, theologians, and literary theorists have pointed out, the Nazi's conception of the thousand-year Reich was inspired explicitly by the millennial reign of the saints prophesied in Revelation 20.[34] Similar claims have also been made with regard to Communism,

---

28. Ricoeur, "Freedom in the Light of Hope," 423. For a contemporary literary appropriation of this apparent link between evil and hope, see Shalom Auslander, *Hope: A Tragedy*.

29. Moltmann, *Das Kommen Gottes*, 167–68.

30. This thesis is powerfully articulated by John Gray in his *Black Mass*; cf. Cohn, *The Pursuit of the Millennium*.

31. Idinopulos, "Nazism, Millenarianism and the Jews," 298; Michael Burleigh's work, *The Third Reich*, devotes considerable attention to the millennial aspects of Nazi ideology. For a detailed account of the roots of Nazism in popular millennialism, see Redles, *Hitler's Millennial Reich*. See also Rhodes, *The Hitler Movement*. Moreover, the anti-Semitic invectives contained in Hitler's own *Mein Kampf* are laden with apocalyptic overtones.

32. Frank Kermode makes this connection in his *The Sense of an Ending*, 12–13. Joachim's vision of the "Third Age" has surfaced in various other forms throughout history and can be discerned in the millennial programmes of Thomas Müntzer, Girolamo Savonarola, G. E. Lessing, Auguste Comte, Karl Marx and Pierre Teilhard de Chardin among others.

33. Moltmann, *Das Kommen Gottes*, 11.

34. Robbins and Palmer, *Millennium, Messiahs and Mayhem*, 9; Moltmann, *Das Kommen Gottes*, 193; Cohn, *Pursuit of the Millennium*. Cohn refers to such beliefs as

which some have argued was just as much a messianic, apocalyptic religion as it was a political ideology.[35] The important point to draw from this in terms of the present study is that apocalyptic belief has its dark sides. Although utopian visions can inspire human agents to heroic acts of compassion and self-sacrifice, their implied hermeneutic of absolute commitment also render them vulnerable to dehumanizing ideologies. Put to the service of such ideologies, millennial belief can exacerbate what one theologian calls "the self-destructive potentialities of human creativity."[36] Future endeavors in millennial studies must thus be aware of a central paradox of apocalyptic belief: that is, the extent to which millennialism provides an auspicious ideological habitat in which the most extravagant affirmations of human hope can coexist with the most fearsome expressions of inhuman terror and brutality.

Moreover, the blood-curdling rhetoric of many biblical apocalyptic-eschatological texts have frequently provoked strenuous objections on account of their alleged inhumanity and brutality which, it is claimed, have been seized upon by religious fanatics as a warrant for their militant and violent agendas.[37] It would be impertinent to reject such criticisms as mere idle remonstrations, for, as Harry O. Maier rightly points out in his following list of thought-provoking questions:

> Who ... does not pale at Revelation's two-hundred-mile-long river of human blood, as high as a horse's bridle, pouring out from the winepress of God's wrath (Rev. 14:20)? Whose stomach

aspects of a pathological condition, which he identifies as "revolutionary millennialism." This belief, according to Cohn, manifested clear destructive tendencies and Cohn claims to identify instances of it in the Crusades and National Socialism.

35. This claim was made by Fritz Gerlich, in his book, *Der Kommunismus als Lehre vom Tausendjährigen Reich,* in which he described Communism as *"ein Kind des neueren Chiliasmus."* Nikolai Berdyaev likewise maintained that the Soviet communism of his time was "a transformation and deformation of the old Russian messianic idea." See Berdyaev, *The Origin of Communism,* 228. For a more recent account of the religious dimensions of Communism, see Crossman, *The God that Failed: Six Studies in Communism.* Alistair Key focuses specifically on the messianic aspects of Marx's eschatological conception of history in his article, "Marx's Messianic Faith," 101–13.

36. Alves, *A Theology of Human Hope,* 44.

37. A example of such criticisms is D. H. Lawrence's *Apocalypse,* which condemned Revelation in particular as "the most detestable book" of the Bible and the product of a "second-rate mind." George Bernhard Shaw likewise condemned the book, describing the text as "a curious record of the visions of a drug addict which was absurdly admitted to the canon under the title of Revelation"; quoted in Phelan, "Revelation, Empire and the Violence of God," 66.

does not turn at that vision of birds gorged on the flesh of the dead (19:17–18)? Who can warm to the damned thrown into lakes of burning fire (19:20; 20:14–15)? Who does not cover their eyes in horror upon witnessing this text's history in culture? . . . Who can estimate the apocalyptic sum of all those gulags and concentration camps designed to usher in a Revelation-inspired millennium?[38]

The texts of biblical apocalyptic eschatology, in particular the book of Revelation, have also been indicted on account of their alleged militant content which is said to provide ideological fuel for the hell-fire sermonising and irresponsible psychological manipulation of religious communities by pathological egomaniacs. The unimaginable terror of the Jonestown episode of 1978 which resulted in the mass "suicide" of 918 people provides us with a vertiginous example of the calamitous consequences which can ensue when a perverted utopian ideology, derived largely from esoteric readings of apocalyptic-eschatological texts, is abused by a charismatic leader.[39] The tragic deaths of the Branch Davidians in 1993 likewise illustrate the catastrophic ramifications which can arise from the misuse of apocalyptic eschatology. This deadly altercation at Mount Carmel in Waco, Texas, arose when another charismatic leader, David Koresh, declared himself to be the Lamb of the Apocalypse and gathered together a band of followers who were convinced by his proclamation of the imminent fulfilment of the opening of the seven seals of Revelation 5. The result was a conflagration between Koresh's supporters and federal agents that led to an inferno in which seventy-six men, women, children, and infants were incinerated.[40] Jonestown and Waco were both (to varying degrees) underpinned by utopian, esoteric interpretations of apocalyptic-eschatological biblical texts, which transpired in tragedy.

The rich and diverse landscape of Northern Ireland evangelicalism during the Troubles is ideally suited to this study of the ways in which apocalyptic eschatology can transform cultures. Like all cultural contexts in which apocalyptic-eschatological themes retained a compelling

38. Maier, *Apocalypse Recalled*, 165.

39. According to some accounts, the circumstances of many of these deaths might be more accurately categorized as murder. The theological convictions of Jones and the People's Temple are explicated in Chidester, *Salvation and Suicide*.

40. For a detailed, perceptive and sympathetic account of these events and the beliefs of Koresh and his supporters see Newport, *The Branch Davidians*.

contemporary relevance, the history of Northern Ireland during the late twentieth century, although avoiding the same kind of conflagrations as Jonestown and Waco, nevertheless manifested both the light and dark sides of apocalyptic eschatology. For some the biblical apocalyptic-eschatological texts engendered a sense of foreboding and insecurity which manifested itself as cultural pessimism, social exclusion or sectarian violence. For others apocalyptic eschatology was interpreted as a vision of hope and a prototype of the redeemed community and, as such, was used to promote a core ethic of inclusive humanity and compassion in order to surmount the conventional distinctions between "Protestant" and "Catholic."

The ways in which a community's interpretation of apocalyptic-eschatological texts illuminates important characteristics of the community itself is one of the issues addressed in the following study. Thus I shall examine the ways in which these texts became embodied in the various evangelical communities. The aim will be to portray the apocalyptic-eschatological beliefs and basic theological convictions of the much-misunderstood cultures within Northern Ireland evangelicalism. My hope is that what follows will contribute to a better understanding of how apocalyptic eschatology influences culture—for better or worse—through an original analysis of its application to Northern Ireland during the Troubles.

Acknowledgments

ON MY WAY TOWARDS the completion of this work, I have accumulated many intellectual debts. To Crawford Gribben I am extremely grateful for supervising the PhD thesis out of which this book arose. His supervision was conducted with characteristic diligence and attention to detail, which, I hope, has ensured that any notion of apocalyptic chaos has been restricted to my primary sources and has not spilled over into my own argument and method. Professor Gribben personifies the judicious balance between academic rigor and good humor and I have been hugely impressed from the outset by his commitment not only to the thesis but also to my broader intellectual development. I am very grateful to the staff and students of the world-class School of English at Trinity College, including the undergraduate students in my Literary Theory tutorials, for creating an auspicious intellectual environment so amenable to our collective aspirations to produce creative scholarship commensurate to the highest standards of academic rigor.

I owe a profound debt of gratitude to my teachers and friends at the International Baptist Theological Seminary (IBTS) in Prague. In particular, I thank Dr. Keith Jones, Dr. Parush Parushev, Dr. Ian Randall, Dr. Lina Andronoviene, Dr. Peter Penner, and Dr. Tim and Dr. Ivana Noble for their encouragement and inspiration. It was a particular blessing to have had Dr. Parushev as my supervisor and mentor during those formative years in Prague.

I must express my sincere thanks to the following people and institutions which offered invaluable assistance along the way: the librarians at Trinity College Dublin for their courtesy and patience, especially in relation to the inordinate bombardment of stack requests I have put to them over the past few years; the Orange Lodge on Cregagh Road, Belfast, for providing me with free and unfettered access to the complete collection of the *Orange Standard* and other important archival materials; the staff and students at the Belfast campus of the Irish School of

Ecumenics for providing a research base in Belfast during several research trips north of the border; Stephen Gregory of Union Theological College, Belfast, who directed me towards useful sources and gave generously of his time and archival expertise to ensure that I was able to make the most of the extensive collections kept in the excellent library at Union. I also profited from two extended study trips to Germany, firstly to the Johann-Adam-Möhler Institut für Ökumenik in Paderborn and then to the Theologische Hochschule in Ewersbach. I am grateful to Johannes Oeldemann, Wolfgang Thönissen and Michael Schröder for their generous hospitality and for allowing me to use their well-stocked libraries. I also thank the following people who read and commented on the work, offering valuable and perceptive feedback: Professor John Briggs, Dr. Brian Cliff, Professor Paul Fiddes, Dr. Andrew Holmes, Dr. Patrick Mitchel, Dr. Andrew Pierce, David Pott, Professor Robert Schreiter, and Dr. Sam Slote.

Most of all I must acknowledge my parents, Roy and Shirley Searle, to whom my gratitude is and always shall be boundless. Although he would not consider himself an academic theologian, my father is endowed with one of the most creative theological minds I have ever encountered. His example has taught me more than anyone else about the imperative expressed in the motto (attributed to the Northumbrian saint, Aidan): "to love God and live generously." My mother, although she too would not consider herself to be a literary scholar, still less an academic theologian, has, through her near-lifetime of selfless devotion to our family, taught me more about the Christian virtues of humility, compassion, self-denial, and generosity than I could ever have learned from spending a lifetime ploughing through the hefty tomes of Aquinas, Calvin, Barth, or even Kant. Good parents are a blessing indeed. This work is dedicated to them as a small token of acknowledgement of this blessing and of their constant love and support.

Introduction

Nature, Scope, and Structure of the Book

This book examines how evangelicals in Northern Ireland read the Troubles (1966–2007) in the light of how they read the Bible. Notwithstanding its rootedness in the Northern Ireland context, this work is more than yet another addition to the existing articles and monographs that constitute the historiography of the Troubles. By considering the ways in which evangelical readings of the Bible inform their interpretations of society, this work supervenes on issues that reach out beyond this specific field of scholarly debate and makes sustained critical incursions into the much larger academic provinces of critical theory, hermeneutics and biblical studies. This study will demonstrate that biblical apocalyptic-eschatological language was a decisive presence (albeit often an inconspicuous and subtle presence)[1] in evangelical discourses concerning the turbulent events that characterized this dark yet fascinating period in the history of Northern Ireland. The very fact that the Northern Ireland conflict has become known in the popular mind as the "Troubles" could be seen as an implicit acknowledgement of the decisive role of apocalyptic eschatology in the crisis associated with the violent events of 1967–2007. The word, "Troubles", possesses connotations that resonate with the biblical notion of "tribulation," particularly the apocalyptic conception of the "great tribulation" (θλίψιν μεγάλην— Matt 24:21; Rev 2:22; 7:14).[2] This work aims to shed important new

---

1. Landes, a leading figure in contemporary millennial studies, notes that "most of the time . . . apocalyptic beliefs remain dormant or concealed." See Landes, *Heaven on Earth*, 41.

2. In what has become known as his "Olivet Discourse," Christ spoke of a time of

1

light on the issue of how the interpretation of certain texts can affect the hermeneutical horizon of evangelical experience in a context of crisis and conflict. The analysis will be directed throughout towards providing innovative ways of conceptualizing the relation between texts and social events and processes.

Despite the vast range of primary and secondary materials and the eclectic diversity of disciplinary approaches employed in this study, the unity of this work is established by the central notion of the text as an active agent rather than a passive object in the hermeneutical process. Much of the scholarship in the field of millennial studies has underlined the great extent to which apocalyptic-eschatological texts can be adapted to suit the changing contexts of differing ages according to the convictions and aspirations of a particular people for whom apocalyptic categories become formative of their identity.[3] My aim is to overturn this understanding by positing the notion of the text as an active hermeneutical agent in the interpretive process in relation to Northern Ireland evangelical interpretations of biblical apocalyptic-eschatological texts.

Although millennial studies has undergone a decisive break with the so-called "deprivation thesis,"[4] even the most recent scholarship continues to take for granted the notion that apocalyptic discourse[5]

---

tribulation, "such as was not since the beginning of the world to this time, no, nor ever shall be," which would accompany the end times. This period would be marked by natural disasters such as "famines, and pestilences, and earthquakes in divers places" and disruptions in the firmament, as well as man-made calamity such as war, and a profusion of false prophets who will deceive many people into their ruin (Matt 24).

3. Weber, *Apocalypses,* 32; Farmer, *Beyond the Impasse,* 145; Schüssler-Fiorenza, "The Phenomenon of Early Christian Apocalyptic," 313–14.

4. This notion, which dominated early millennial scholarship in the wake of Norman Cohn's *Pursuit of the Millennium* (1957), asserted in its crudest form that millennial ideas were little more than ideological by-products of the social context that produced them. See chapter 1 for a more detailed summary of this notion in the history of millennial studies and a sustained refutation of its central assumptions.

5. In using this word, I should note that this study introduces a subtle distinction between the terms "text" and "discourse." My use of these terms in this study corresponds to the notion that biblical texts generate discourses, which includes the interpretation of the reading community. "Text" thus refers to language that pre-exists a particular interpretive community, whereas "discourse" refers to the use of such language in context by communities which interpret these texts. However, this distinction is not clear-cut and there is considerable overlap in the use of these terms. For instance, as Ricoeur argues, texts can be understood as extending to phenomena "not specifically limited to writing, nor even to discourse." See Ricoeur, *Hermeneutics and the Human Sciences,* 37. For a useful discussion of the formal distinctions between the two terms and an account

emerges out of social contexts. Seeking to critically interrogate this assumption, this book aims to identify ways in which millennial writing itself can become constitutive of the contexts against which it is read. This study will demonstrate that far from responding to prevalent social conditions, apocalyptic language became formative of evangelical perceptions of their context. But the relationship between text and context is not a simple "either/or" issue. Context was important in determining how apocalyptic-eschatological language was used for particular purposes and why it acquired a particular influence at certain points in the history of the Troubles. Although there is no evidence to support the notion of a direct correlation between political contexts of crisis and the emergence of apocalyptic thought, it is nevertheless the case that, in some instances, the sense of crisis contributed to an increase in the use of apocalyptic language. In other words, it will be shown that although a context of crisis does not create apocalyptic thought, it can amplify its influence. Rather than positing either/or arguments for text and context, I will argue that the theory that language shapes social reality supports the notion of a dialectical relationship between text and context, since context is itself a confluence of texts.

Therefore, in acknowledging the importance of context in this respect, it is equally important not to overlook the ways in which apocalyptic-eschatological language of the biblical texts actively shaped evangelical perceptions of their historical context. In other words, apocalyptic language was more than simply a response to a historical crisis or a feeling of deprivation or persecution among evangelical interpreters. This point underlines the complexity and polyvalence of the relation between text and context which lies at the heart of this book. Pursuing the implications of these claims I will argue that the analysis of apocalyptic-eschatological language during the Troubles can be used to illuminate some of the theoretical arguments which have occupied philosophers of language concerning the relationship between texts and contexts in interpretive processes.[6]

---

of how theorists have used the terms, see Georgakopoulou and Goutsos, *Discourse Analysis*, 1–8.

6. Jacques Derrida has argued that the "text" overruns contextual limits. A text is best understood as "a differential network, a fabric of traces referring endlessly to something other than itself, to other differential traces"; Derrida, "Living on," 84–85. See also Derrida, *Spurs*, 123–43.

This study is thus a discursive analysis of evangelical uses of apocalyptic-eschatological language in relation to the conflict and crisis of the Northern Ireland Troubles between 1966 and 2007. The aim is to outline an original approach to the relationship between the interpretation of apocalyptic-eschatological texts and contextual crises. By setting out this relationship this study brings a new perspective to millennial studies that has the potential to open new paths towards a proper conceptualization of the interaction between apocalyptic-eschatological texts and social crisis. Part of the aim will be to illustrate and account for the different interpretative responses of evangelicals to apocalyptic-eschatological texts through an innovative analysis of the relations among the texts, contexts and cultures of evangelicalism in Northern Ireland during this period.

This book is written with two distinct reading audiences in mind. Firstly, I hope to reach those with an interest in the Troubles. Many of the arguments in this book are original and offer new and creative perspectives from which to comprehend the dynamics of the conflict, particularly with regard to the supposed biblical warrants for ideologically-inspired sectarian violence. The second audience is much broader and includes all those in search of fresh and imaginative ways of understanding how people interpret formative texts (such as the Bible) determines how they form and interpret culture. This work thus aspires to develop creative ways of conceiving the relationship between hermeneutics (in particular biblical hermeneutics) and the interpretation of culture. Although this present work is a study of a particular phenomenon in a specific setting, it aims to provide a constructive way of understanding the engagement between biblical texts and their effect on readers. As such I hope that despite its contextual rootedness, this work will make a genuinely original contribution to the broader ongoing debates concerning the cultural expressions of biblical interpretations.

Guiding Presuppositions

Undergirding this book is a core conviction that human existence, as an emerging reality rather than something fixed or static, is inherently orientated towards eschatology.[7] Human life, remarks John Macquarrie

---

7. In the words of one German theologian, Claus Schwambach, commenting on Leonard Boff's theology, "Human existence is from the beginning nothing other than eschatological existence." See Schwambach, *Rechtfertigungsgeschehen und Befreiungsprozess*, 224 (my translation).

commenting on Heidegger, is necessarily eschatological in so far as it can be considered as "Being-toward-death" and aware of "the urgency and responsibility of living before the imminent end."[8] Moreover, if we share with Karl Rahner the conviction that eschatological assertions are invariably assertions concerned with human existence,[9] it follows that the study of how eschatological language is negotiated by human interpreters has the potential to shed new light on the most difficult yet most important question of what it means to be human. Since it is concerned with potentiality just as much as with actuality, apocalyptic eschatology issues a salutary reminder that the study of human nature must go beyond existing empirical "facts" and take seriously the role of dreams, visions and the imagination as basic realities governing human volition.[10] Ernst Bloch claimed that to be human is to hope and that volition is determined primarily not (*pace* positivism) by empirical calculations based on an inherent inclination to make the most material gain out of present circumstances.[11] Human beings are governed above all not by calculation but by vision, by an underlying will to hope, *eine Leidenschaft für das Mögliche* ("a passion for the possible").[12] This "will to hope" manifests itself in a desire to work creatively towards the realization of deeply-held, almost inarticulable aspirations for the future.[13] In the Christian tradition, it is in apocalyptic-eschatological texts that such hopes find their ultimate collective manifestation and definitive culmination. The vision of hope applies to every aspect of human life, both individually and corporately; it is a vision in which "the usurped creation will be restored; the corrupted universe will be cleansed [and] the created world will be recreated."[14]

This study also proceeds from another core conviction: namely, that interpretation matters. The central place of interpretation in every aspect of human life has been acknowledged and pursued by some of the greatest philosophical minds down through the centuries. "Our ex-

---

8. Macquarrie, *Martin Heidegger*, 31.

9. Rahner, "Hermeneutics of Eschatological Associations," 337.

10. Macquarrie, *Humanity*, 3–4.

11. Bloch, "Zur Ontologie des Noch-Nicht-Seins," 41.

12. Moltmann, *Theologie der Hoffnung*, 15. This phrase is attributed originally to Søren Kierkegaard. See Ricoeur, "Freiheit im Licht der Hoffnung," 205.

13. Parushev, "Walking in the Dawn of the Light," 60–120.

14. Russell, *Method & Message*, 280.

perience of things, indeed even of everyday life . . . also of the sphere of our vital concerns," insists Hans Georg Gadamer, "are one and all hermeneutic."[15] Gadamer recognized that every attempt we make to understand something will invariably involve us in an act of interpretation.[16] Interpretation is not merely an academic matter of exegetical method nor an issue to do with "mere ideas" but a matter that lies at the heart of what it means to be human. It thus follows that any sustained philosophical analysis of hermeneutical phenomena is at the same time an anthropological reflection on the basic issues pertaining to human life in general. Interpretation matters.

This maxim applies with particular truth and contemporary relevance to the subject of this book—the controversial issue of biblical interpretation. Of all the textual battlegrounds on which the hermeneutical conflicts of modernity have taken place, there has been none more bitterly fought over than the Bible.[17] Despite the secularization of culture, which sociologists allege has been one of the salient trends of Western society since the Reformation, the Bible remains in the front line of the hermeneutical wars that rage in our culture today. "Debates about postmodernity," observes Garrett Green, "have focused, for good reason, on the interpretation of texts—especially culturally authoritative texts, among which the Scriptures represent the most authoritative of all."[18] The way the Bible is interpreted by particular communities or individuals can determine how one relates to every issue of ethical concern. In the sphere of social ethics, when the issues concern vital questions of war, peace, violence, sectarianism, racism, euthanasia, or other decisive matters of contemporary controversy, interpretation becomes literally a matter of life and death. Many of the contemporary conflicts over which today's churches and Christian cultures contend most bitterly can be shown to be to some extent attributable to issues of biblical hermeneutics; that is, they are conflicts generated in large part by disagreements concerning how biblical texts ought to be read.

15. Gadamer, quoted in Ward, *Cultural Transformation*, 65.

16. "*Alles Verstehen ist Auslegung*" (all understanding is interpretation), as Gadamer put it in his greatest work, *Wahrheit und Methode*. See Gadamer, *Gesammelte Werke*, I:392.

17. Sawyer, ed., *Blackwell Companion to the Bible and Culture*.

18. Green, *Theology, Hermeneutics, and Imagination*, 18.

A notable example of such a conflict was the Northern Ireland Troubles. Although this assertion does not amount to the claim that the complex dynamics of the Troubles can be reduced to hermeneutics (still less biblical hermeneutics), it does give due precedence to the decisive influence of interpretive issues in evangelical perceptions of the conflict. In an article written in response to the unrest and division generated by the Good Friday Agreement in 1998, David Porter, Director of the Evangelical Contribution on Northern Ireland (ECONI), made the following succinct and telling observation: "The current problems with the peace process in Northern Ireland are, at one level, a problem of hermeneutics."[19] This was a remarkable insight, which attests to the acute attentiveness of certain evangelicals in Northern Ireland during the Troubles to the issues underlying the conflict. The following study will seek to develop the implications of this insight by considering the evangelical interpretations of biblical apocalyptic-eschatological texts during the Northern Ireland Troubles, all the time keeping in view the larger issue of how evangelicals interpret the Bible.

Outline Structure of the Argument

On the way to the conclusion concerning the notion of an active text in the hermeneutical process, it will be demonstrated that Northern Ireland expressions of apocalyptic eschatology were characterized by a juxtaposition of contradictions, an apparently chaotic mingling of hope and fear, pessimism and optimism, activism and quietism, assurance and uncertainty. Although the variety of expressions of Northern Ireland apocalyptic-eschatological convictions necessitates a wide-ranging discussion, the key stages in the development of the argument can be clearly delineated. Chapter 1 situates the main arguments and approaches of this study within the context of other scholarly attempts to understand religion and apocalyptic in the Troubles. The second chapter will set out with an account of the methodological premises together with a definition of the key strands of the argument—the texts, cultures, and contexts of Northern Ireland apocalyptic eschatology. Northern Ireland evangelical apocalyptic eschatology may be said to follow a threefold pattern, each strand corresponding to the notions of hope, fear, and uncompromising rhetoric, which manifested dualistic

19. *lion & lamb* (Winter, 1998), 3.

tendencies by postulating rigid distinctions between heaven and hell, the present age and the age to come, the elect and the reprobate, good and evil, light and darkness, and victory and defeat. The issue of how these themes—hope, fear and apocalyptic dualism—found expression in the apocalyptic-eschatological discourses of Northern Ireland evangelicalism, will be taken up in chapters 3, 4, and 5 respectively.

Defining the Key Terms

The initial difficulty encountered by anyone wishing to understand the diverse discourses of Northern Ireland evangelicalism is the wide variety of semantic associations to which its dominant characteristics have been affixed. The existing scholarship reflects both the semantic heterogeneity and the multiplicity of applications of such terms as "evangelicalism," "fundamentalism," "apocalyptic eschatology" and "Protestantism." Thus it is necessary to introduce certain general considerations of the key terms before entering upon a closer examination of their meaning in the Northern Ireland Troubles.

Evangelicalism and Fundamentalism

This book focuses specifically on evangelical uses of apocalyptic eschatology.[20] The term "evangelicalism" has been used in numerous contexts with varying degrees of accuracy to denote a primary theological conviction that "truth is constituted by what God has done for his world and for humankind in Jesus Christ."[21] Evangelicalism goes beyond this basic Christian conviction by manifesting a range of further characteristic ethical, religious, and political beliefs. Recent historians of the Northern Ireland Troubles have generally followed the British historian David Bebbington who identifies the four convictions of biblicism, crucicentrism, conversionism, and social activism as the salient manifestations common to British evangelical worldviews.[22] This classification

---

20. This is not to suggest that there were not other expressions of apocalyptic eschatology in Northern Ireland during the Troubles apart from evangelical ones. These included beliefs of other groups such as Catholics, Jehovah's Witnesses and Muslims, all of which would make for an interesting study. Nevertheless, in the interests of specificity and the constraints of time and space, this study shall focus on evangelical expressions of apocalyptic eschatology in Northern Ireland.

21. O'Donovan, *Resurrection and the Moral Order*, ix.

22. Bebbington, *Evangelicalism in Modern Britain*, 1–19. For examples of histori-

is to be found not merely in the scholarly contributions to Northern Ireland evangelicalism but also in Northern Ireland evangelical primary texts themselves.[23] George Marsden, who has focused more upon the American context, has identified five marks of evangelicalism, which he enumerates as the Reformation emphasis on the Bible as the ultimate authority in matters of faith; the historical reality of God's salvation plan; eternal life made possible by the death and resurrection of Christ; mission and evangelism; and an emphasis on holiness and spiritual growth.[24] Given its significance as a place in which evangelicals constitute such a high proportion of the general population (relative to other parts of the UK), it is noteworthy that neither Marsden nor Bebbington has written a sustained analysis of evangelicalism in Northern Ireland.[25] Both Bebbington and Marsden have highlighted important aspects of evangelicalism, all of which could be applied to the context of this inquiry into Northern Ireland evangelicalism. Nevertheless, since historians are now coming to recognize that evangelicals in Ireland "have frequently understood their world in millennial and apocalyptic terms,"[26] it may be necessary to include an emphasis on apocalyptic eschatology as a central aspect of evangelicalism in the Northern Ireland context.[27] A typical expression of this attitude is found in an article in a 1966 edition of the Northern Ireland fundamentalist evangelical publication, the *Protestant Telegraph,* in which the writer remarked, "I cannot classify Christians who reject prophecy . . . as Evangelicals."[28] This is an illuminating example of an apocalyptic-eschatological category being used by a particular evangelical to determine the semantic parameters of what

---

ans of Northern Ireland evangelicalism who have used Bebbington's classification, see Hempton and Hill, *Evangelical Protestantism,* 14; Gribben, "Antichrist in Ireland," 2.

23. Examples include the following ECONI publications: Thompson, *The Fractured Family,* 17–18; ECONI, *A Future with Hope,* 9–10.

24. Marsden, *Understanding Fundamentalism,* 4–5.

25. In a 1977 essay, Marsden does make passing reference to Northern Ireland. See Marsden, "Fundamentalism as an American Phenomenon," 215–32.

26. Gribben, "Antichrist in Ireland," 2.

27. In his survey of evangelical belief in Northern Ireland, Patrick Mitchel claims that Bebbington overlooks the significance of personal piety in evangelicalism; Mitchel, *Evangelicalism,* 106.

28. *Protestant Telegraph,* 17 December, 1966, 4. Readers may be interested to learn that in 1967 the *Protestant Telegraph* claimed to circulate 100,000 copies to subscribers and newsagents each week; *Protestant Telegraph* (18 March 1967), 4.

constitutes an "evangelical." By making the acceptance of "prophecy" a precondition of evangelical identity, this evangelical author was able to restrict the definition of "evangelical" to those who were interested in or at least accepting of prophecy.

This example highlights the point that the term "evangelical" in Northern Ireland was a hotly contested concept. Thus, when a group emerged in Northern Ireland in the 1970s calling themselves "evangelical Catholics," many fundamentalist evangelicals responded with criticism and derision at what they saw as a meaningless contradiction in terms. According to one of the early leaders of the evangelical Catholic movement, the term referred to those Catholics who "came into a deeper, or first-time, personal relationship with Jesus as Lord and Saviour and were baptised in the Holy Spirit."[29] Given that there is no evidence of this group stating its eschatological position or even commenting on apocalyptic-eschatological material, this study will focus exclusively on evangelicals who would self-identify as Protestants, from Paisleyite fundamentalism to the more moderate evangelicalism of ECONI.

The strong criticism of the "evangelical Catholic" movement and the insistence upon an acceptance of "prophecy" as a necessary corollary of evangelical identity highlight the important distinction between "evangelicals" and "fundamentalists" in Northern Ireland. The distinctive emphasis upon prophetic speculations of an apocalyptic-eschatological nature has been identified by historians as one of the major points of divergence between British evangelicals and their more fundamentalist counterparts in Northern Ireland. Gribben explains that in the late twentieth century,

> British evangelicals grew increasingly suspicious of apocalyptic rhetoric, which was increasingly identified with the horrors of sectarian conflict in Northern Ireland and the perceived anti-intellectualism of American Fundamentalists. It was a sign that

---

29. Monaghan, "What Is an Evangelical Catholic?" This essay was originally published on the (now extinct) website of the Evangelical Contribution on Northern Ireland (ECONI). A version of the essay remains online on the website of an Irish Free Presbyterian, complete with a scathingly critical commentary. The critic writes, "Evangelical Catholics endorse the concept of the Pope being another Christ on earth. They endorse the Calvary denying error of the mass. They endorse salvation by a sacrament and not by grace alone. Sorry, but we can't run with this and be faithful to the word of God." Online: http://www.corkfpc.com/evangelicalcatholics.html.

> the British evangelical mainstream was beginning to position
> itself at a critical distance from that of the United States.[30]

This remark highlights the apparent gap between "evangelicals" and "fundamentalists." The term "fundamentalism" is derived from a set of twelve books published by a group of American Protestants which were collectively entitled, *The Fundamentals: A Testimony of the Truth* (1910–15).[31] Although many theologians and social scientists conflate Christian, Jewish, and Islamic fundamentalism into a single "mass movement,"[32] Christian fundamentalists have distinguished themselves historically both from other faiths as well as their liberal Christian counterparts in their affirmation of the indispensability of five doctrines: Biblical Inerrancy, the Deity of Christ, the Virgin Birth, Penal-Substitutionary Atonement, and the Physical Resurrection and Bodily Return of Christ to Earth.[33] Historians have uncovered the extent to which these theological principles of the early fundamentalists were birthed in millennial thinking and how they provided a focal point of unity upon which radical millenarians and traditional conservatives could converge.[34]

What can be said, therefore, of the main points of divergence between evangelicalism and fundamentalism in relation to the present inquiry? Such has been the depth of evangelical convictions in Northern Ireland that it is often difficult to maintain a clear distinction between these two terms. Historians and theologians have come to different conclusions as to whether the difference between the two is one of essence[35]

---

30. Gribben, *Evangelical Millennialism*, 120.

31. *The Fundamentals*.

32. Odermatt, *Der Fundamentalismus*, 8–9. Odermatt, writing from the perspective of psychology, contends that fundamentalism across these three religions constitutes a mass movement (*Massenbewegung*) and claims that fundamentalism thrives only in cultures in which monotheistic religion is prevalent. Fundamentalism, however, is by no means confined to monotheistic religions, as demonstrated by the phenomenon of Hindu fundamentalism. See Teltumbde, "Hindu Fundamentalist Politics," 247–61.

33. Cole, *The History of Fundamentalism*, 34. Although these five fundamental beliefs were amplified in the series of pamphlets called *The Fundamentals*, which appeared between 1910 and 1915, they were first defined at the Bible Conference of Conservative Christians at Niagara in 1895.

34. Sandeen notes that *The Fundamentals* arose out of an "alliance between millenarians and conservatives." See Sandeen, *The Roots of Fundamentalism*, 189.

35. McGrath, *Christian Theology*, 112–13; Ward, *What the Bible Really Teaches*, 2–3 and *passim*.

or degree.[36] Others have commented on the widespread perception of fundamentalism as "anti-intellectual, reactionary, and authoritarian,"[37] which purportedly distinguishes this phenomenon from evangelicalism, which in turn, it is claimed, offers a more hospitable environment for intellectual engagement.[38] In relation to the Troubles, Gladys Ganiel highlights the extent of the overlap between evangelical and fundamentalist positions in Northern Ireland and argues that "evangelicals in Northern Ireland who could be classified as fundamentalists often call themselves evangelicals" and thus concludes, that the distinction between "evangelicalism" and "fundamentalism" is less significant than the differences that exist within evangelicalism.[39]

In light of such diverse views among scholars concerning the nature and historical significance of evangelicalism, it is important to remain focused on the issue of how the differences are manifested on the point of apocalyptic eschatology. The key point is that fundamentalism in Northern Ireland has usually been associated with premillennial worldviews. This notion corresponds to Harriet Harris' remark that one of the key differences in outlook is the "siege mentality and a narrow commitment to premillennial dispensationalism" which often distinguishes fundamentalism from evangelicalism.[40] Although fundamentalists in the Troubles tended to be premillennialists, not all were committed to dispensational premillennialism. Others, most notably, Ian Paisley, were historic premillennialists.[41]

---

36. Thus he proffers the rather tongue-in-cheek, sound-bite definition of a fundamentalist as "an evangelical who is angry about something"; Marsden, *Understanding Fundamentalism*, 1.

37. Boone, *The Bible Tells Them So*, 6.

38. Barr, *Fundamentalism*, 329. Thatcher makes a similar point in his *Savage Text*, 169.

39. Ganiel, *Evangelicalism and Conflict*, 4. This argument is supported by the findings of attitude surveys of Northern Ireland evangelicals in which respondents argued that the two terms are practically synonymous. For example, see MacIver, "A Clash of Symbols in Northern Ireland," 364.

40. Harris, *Fundamentalism and Evangelicals*, 7.

41. Premillennialists hold that the second coming of Christ will occur *before* the millennium rule of the saints, as prophesied in Revelation 20. Premillennialists can be divided into those who believe that the second coming will take place after the great tribulation (historic premillennialism) and those who maintain that the return of Christ will precede the great tribulation (dispensational premillennialism). These perspectives have thus been known as "post-tribulational" and "pre-tribulational" respectively.

Despite the different opinions among scholars of evangelicalism and fundamentalism, the primary texts of Northern Ireland evangelicals appear to substantiate Ganiel's notion of the essential similarity between the two positions.[42] Consider, for instance, a definition of evangelicalism offered by the Evangelical Contribution on Northern Ireland (ECONI):

> Evangelicalism, like all movements, is diverse in its expression and embraces a wide spectrum of Christians, *including those who are commonly referred to as fundamentalists.* It is characterised by four central tenets [biblicism, crucicentrism, conversionism and activism].[43]

As well as the explicit and acknowledged use of Bebbington's model, this definition seems to imply that the difference between evangelicals and fundamentalists in Northern Ireland consisted not in the essence of theological convictions but rather in the militancy with which such convictions were held. In the context of the crisis of Northern Ireland evangelicalism during the Troubles, the distinction between "evangelicals" and "fundamentalists" can be seen in the rhetoric employed by exponents of each position, particularly in regard to apocalyptic-eschatological beliefs. This notion is also to be found in Northern Ireland fundamentalist publications, such as Ian Paisley's magazine, *Battle Standard,* launched in October 1997, whose editors maintained unashamedly that they were "dedicated to Bible fundamentalism."[44] In a passage from the debut publication of this magazine the editors reassured their readers that,

> Wherever sin's taint or Satan's trail is to be found the *Battle Standard* will be found busily engaged for God in Holy Warfare. The difference between us and other evangelical periodicals will be that they most often use a tin-tack mallet while we will employ the sledge hammer.[45]

---

42. Alywn Thompson, writing for ECONI, maintained that evangelicalism and fundamentalism exist on the same spectrum; see Thompson, *The Fractured Family*, 16. Thompson draws on both Bebbington and Marsden in his definition of evangelicalism.

43. ECONI, *A Future With Hope*, 9 [emphasis added].

44. *Battle Standard* 1/1 (October, 1997), 7.

45. Ibid., 1.

The "warfare" metaphor and the militant "sledge-hammer" approach distinguish the rhetoric of fundamentalism from the more moderate critical sentiments of evangelicalism.[46]

Despite being situated within the broader worldwide emergence of fundamentalism in the twentieth century, Northern Ireland fundamentalism has a number of notable distinctive qualities. Northern Ireland fundamentalism was distinguished not by its antipathy towards the traditional challenges of modern liberal theology and "Higher Criticism"— such aversion was a common feature of fundamentalism worldwide.[47] The distinctiveness of the fundamentalism of Northern Ireland evangelicals consisted in its inveterate antagonism towards Roman Catholicism.[48] Although anti-Catholic tropes are to be found in other contexts in which fundamentalism has been prevalent, such antipathy was not nearly as preponderant or decisive as in the case of Northern Ireland. Another crucial difference, which is not sufficiently emphasized in the secondary literature, consists in the different approaches to apocalyptic-eschatology exhibited by evangelicals and fundamentalists. In Northern Ireland it is perhaps at the level of apocalyptic-eschatological convictions that the distinction is most conspicuous.[49] Whereas evangelicalism can accommodate a broad spectrum of eschatological thinking[50]—including pre-,[51]

46. Harris, in her comparative study of evangelicalism and fundamentalism, argues that militancy is one of the characteristic manifestations of a fundamentalist mentality; Harris, *Fundamentalism and Evangelicals*, 7.

47. Anderson, "Fundamentalism," 229–33.

48. Barr, *Fundamentalism*, 329.

49. Writing about the eschatological convictions of Northern Ireland evangelicals, Crawford Gribben notes that, "Differences between evangelicals and fundamentalists were most obvious in their eschatological preferences." See Gribben, "Protestant Millennialism," 52.

50. As Harriet Harris notes in *Fundamentalism*, 6.

51. For a definition of premillennialism and its historical and dispensational varieties, see footnote 41 above.

post-[52] and a-millennial[53] perspectives[54]—fundamentalism in Northern Ireland has been associated with premillennial interpretations of biblical prophecy.

Apocalyptic Eschatology

The confusion of the "evangelical" and "fundamentalist" categories has raised considerable doubts among scholars concerning the applicability of the term "evangelical" to the Northern Ireland context. One means towards the further elucidation of the term, "evangelicalism" in relation to this inquiry is to consider the salient characteristics of evangelical "apocalyptic eschatology" and the application of the term to the Northern Ireland context. The adjectives "apocalyptic" and "eschatological" have been used to describe a wide variety of texts, cultures, individuals and worldviews. The word "apocalypse," derived from the Greek word ἀποκάλυψις, signifies "unveiling" or "disclosure." Eschatology, derived from the Greek word εσχατος, means "end," "last," "edge," and can also mean "uttermost." The concern of the following study is not to uncover the etymological origins of these words and the seemingly arbitrary meanings which theologians have chosen to confer upon these concepts; rather, our task is to examine the ways in which Northern Ireland evangelicals understood apocalyptic eschatology during the Troubles.

The idea that certain biblical texts could be isolated and classified according to a particular literary genre known as "apocalyptic" first emerged from nineteenth-century biblical criticism.[55] Under the influ-

---

52. Postmillennialism is the belief that the second coming of Christ will occur only *after* the era of the millennium has substantially transformed life on the earth. Among adherents of postmillennialism there is some variety of opinion on the point of whether the millennium signifies a gradual process of transformation or a decisive apocalyptic event. Postmillennialists also exhibit a variety of views regarding the extent to which the coming of the millennium can be advanced through their own efforts.

53. Amillennialism posits the notion that the period of one thousand years in Revelation 20 refers not to a specific event in the end times but constitutes a metaphorical description of the whole period between Christ's incarnation and the second coming.

54. For a useful summary of the leading tenets of each position, see Clouse, ed., *Meaning of the Millennium*.

55. One of the pioneering works in this regard was Friedrich Lücke, *Versuch einer vollständigen Einleitung* cf. Koch, "The Rediscovery of Apocalyptic," 18–35.

ence of theologians such as Johannes Weiss[56] and Albert Schweitzer[57] eschatology ceased to be, as Karl Barth remarked in ironical jest, "a harmless little chapter at the conclusion of Christian Dogmatics,"[58] and became instead a central theme at the heart of theological studies in the first decades of the twentieth century.[59] According to Rudolf Bultmann, writing at the beginning of the twentieth century, it was becoming "more and more clear that the eschatological expectation and hope are the core of the New Testament preaching throughout."[60] Eschatology became regarded not so much as a branch of theology as an all-pervasive perspective which should undergird all theological discussion.[61] After the devastation and carnage of the First and Second World Wars, eschatological themes began to emerge in the works of leading thinkers, such as Jean-Paul Sartre,[62] Karl Jaspers,[63] Theodore Adorno,[64] and Martin Heidegger.[65] In the second half of the twentieth century apocalyptic eschatology was subjected to sustained and detailed analysis of sociologists and historians as well as biblical scholars.[66] In the early 1980s,

56. Weiss, *Die Predigt Jesu.*

57. Schweitzer, *Von Reimarus zu Wrede.*

58. Barth, *Romans,* 500.

59. The origins and development of this trend are discussed in Fastenrath, *"In Vitam Aeternam."* Hans Schwarz also helpfully elucidates the decisive influence of Weiss and Schweitzer in particular as figures central to the reconfiguration of theology towards eschatology in his *Eschatology,* 107–15.

60. Bultmann, *Jesus Christ and Mythology,* 13.

61. This notion was taken up and vastly elaborated upon by Moltmann in *Theologie der Hoffnung,* first published in 1964.

62. See in particular Sartre's discussion of the apocalyptic aspects of his dialectical materialism in his *Notebooks for an Ethics,* 414, in which Sartre calls for a "return to the Apocalypse" as a means towards "the liberation of oneself and of others in reciprocal recognition."

63. Jaspers, *Die Atombombe.*

64. For an account of the apocalyptic-eschatological undertones of Adorno's negative dialectics, see Theunissen, "Negativität bei Adorno," 53–55.

65. For instance Heidegger's 1951–52 essay, "Was heißt Denken?," is pervaded by apocalyptic motifs pertaining to the "manifestation of Being" (die Offenbarung des Seins). Apocalypse was a key theme of post-war existentialist philosophy and literature as McElroy points out in, *Existentialism and Modern Literature,* 35.

66. There are many theories that purport to explain the resurgence of interest in apocalypticism in terms of social or cultural transitions. For example, in 1979 the Harvard scholar, Paul Hanson commenced and concluded his study of Jewish apocalypticism with references to the disrepute into which the modernist vision of scientific

Paul Hanson described the "new impetus in apocalyptic research"[67] and maintained that "concrete textual studies and more hypothetical efforts at definition and reconstruction must go hand in hand if further insight were to be gained into the mysteries of apocalypticism."[68]

Hanson's call has since been answered by a recent "explosion of scholarly writing on apocalyptic themes."[69] Since then apocalyptic concepts such as the millennium have "come to be seen as a major category of social analysis."[70] Thus there is now a broad consensus across a range of disciplines that, for better or worse, apocalyptic eschatology is an important force in the shaping of cultures.[71] Nevertheless, it could be argued that the application of scholarly methods to the interpretation of apocalyptic-eschatological biblical material has in fact contributed to the diversification of hermeneutical appropriation by opening up these texts to multiple meanings.[72] The issue is particularly complex in relation to the disputed concepts of "apocalypticism" and "eschatology." Many of the scholarly disagreements surrounding these terms have focused on the tension between immanence and transcendence.[73] In an effort to formulate a conception of apocalyptic that would facilitate interdisciplinary dialogue, John J. Collins defined "apocalyptic" as "a genre of revelatory literature with a narrative framework, in which a revelation is mediated by an otherworldly being to a human recipient, disclosing a transcendent reality which is both temporal, in that it envisages eschatological salvation, and spatial, in that it involves another, supernatural world."[74] "Apocalypse," according to Collins, is a particular expression

---

progress has allegedly fallen. See Hanson, *Dawn of Apocalyptic.*

67. Hanson, *Visionaries and their Apocalypses*, 6.

68. Ibid., 11.

69. Shantz, "Millennialism and Apocalypticism," 20.

70. Barkun, ed., *Millennialism and Violence*, 1.

71. Shantz, "Millennialism and Apocalypticism," 43.

72. Mühling, *Grundinformation Eschatologie*, 32.

73. This tension is apparent in even the most recent works in millennial studies, most notably in Catherine Wessinger, *Oxford Handbook of Millennialism*, 5.

74. Collins, "Introduction: Towards the Morphology of a Genre," 9. This statement was adopted by the *Society of Biblical Literature* as their official definition of "apocalyptic." Recent revisions criticize Collins' definition on account of its broadness and lack of reference to the means of revelation. For a recent alternative definition based on Collins' formulation but integrating these critical comments, see Reynolds, *The Apocalyptic Son of Man*, 16.

of a more general eschatological mindset, which is orientated towards transcendence. Thus Collins maintains that salvation, from an apocalyptic perspective, involves "a radically different type of human existence in which all the constraints of the human condition, including death, are transcended."[75] In contrast to Collins' emphasis on transcendence, others have insisted that the apparent apocalyptic other-worldliness of biblical prophecy must be understood in terms of its impact on the "temporal" world. On this issue, Liberation Theologians challenged the allegedly detached transcendence of Jewish apocalyptic literature, which, it is claimed, "often got lost in otherworldly and cosmic speculations, drawing it away from the historical responsibility of the believer within the world."[76] Making a similar point, but arguing from a different theological perspective, John Howard Yoder reminds us that apocalypse "is a way of thinking critically about *this* world."[77] L. L. Thompson aptly observes that the purpose of apocalyptic writing is "not to reveal another world," but to uncover "dimensions of the world in which humans live and die . . . an apocalypse is not world-negating but, rather, world-expanding: it extends or expands the universe to include transcendent realities, and it does this both spatially and temporally."[78] Stanley Hauerwas captures the tension between the immanent temporality and transcendent otherness of apocalyptic eschatology with an adroit paradox: "Apocalyptic means that there is another world, another time, than the one in which we live; but it turns out to be the same world in which we live."[79] The impor-

75. Collins, *Apocalyptic Imagination*, 10.

76. Richard, *Apocalypse*, 15. Marxist historians have likewise tended to emphasize the temporal aspects of millennial belief. According to Eric Hobsbawm the basic essence of millennial thinking consists in "the hope of a complete and radical change in the world." See Hobsbawm, *Primitive Rebels*, 57.

77. Yoder, *For the Nations*, 137. Fiorenza likewise argues that far from despairing from history, Christian apocalyptic eschatology seeks to redeem history by identifying salvation as something which occurs within its course. See Fiorenza, "The Phenomenon of Early Christian Apocalyptic," 303.

78. Thompson, *The Book of Revelation*, 31.

79. Hauerwas, *Matthew*, 24. Interestingly, the archival records of the Evangelical Contribution on Northern Ireland (ECONI) shows that Hauerwas had some involvement in the Northern Ireland peace process in the lead up to the 1998 Good Friday Agreement. His influence came not only indirectly through his writings (which seem to have been influential among the ECONI leadership) but also through personal participation in ECONI's peace and reconciliation initiatives. In 1998 Hauerwas spoke at a major ECONI conference. See ECONI's publication, *lion & lamb* (Autumn, 1998), 16.

tant point to draw from all these various scholarly perspectives for the present study is that, notwithstanding its emphasis on transcendence, apocalyptic eschatology posits a world that is at once beyond human comprehension and yet an integral part of our humanity. By insisting that "God is both radically other and yet present to us,"[80] apocalyptic eschatology offers a potential point of creative conceptual convergence between the ostensibly irreconcilable notions of the alterity of divine being and the immanence of divine presence.

In addition to the tension between immanence and transcendence in millennial discourses, a further ambiguity is the differing conceptions of when the apocalypse can be expected. A notable recent reaffirmation of the importance of imminence in millennial thinking is the *Oxford Handbook of Millennialism* (2011), edited by Catherine Wessinger. In her introductory chapter, Wessinger offers the following definition of millennialism as

> belief in an imminent transition to a collective salvation, in which the faithful will experience well-being, and the unpleasant limitations of the human condition will be eliminated. The collective salvation is often considered to be earthly, but it can also be heavenly. The collective salvation will be accomplished either by a divine or superhuman agent alone, or with the assistance of humans working according to the divine or superhuman will and plan.[81]

This formulation is not without its difficulties, for, as Crawford Gribben notes, this insistence on immanence as an integral aspect of all millennial belief does not correspond to Wessinger's equation of premillennialism and postmillennialism with what she calls "catastrophic millennialism" and "progressive millennialism" respectively.[82] The latter perspective, as noted even by some of the contributors to the *Oxford Handbook of Millennialism*,[83] does not anticipate an imminent millennium.[84]

80. Dolejšová, *Accounts of Hope*, 284.

81. Wessinger, "Millennialism in Cross-cultural Perspective," 5.

82. Gribben, "The Future of Millennial Studies."

83. See, for instance, Ashcraft's discussion of the millennial beliefs of the New England puritans in his chapter, "Progressive millennialism," in Wessinger, ed., *The Oxford Handbook of Millennialism*, 44–65.

84. In his important new work in millennial studies, Richard Landes likewise focuses on imminence as a major constitutive element of apocalyptic belief, but unlike Wessinger, offers a more nuanced and qualified definition of what the term "immi-

Millennial scholarship has also emphasized different aspects of apocalyptic eschatology, such as the centrality of the disclosure of divine mysteries[85] or the notion of reversal and restoration.[86] The Italian scholar Paolo Sacchi has sought to explain apocalypticism as an attempt to come to terms with the question of theodicy and the origins and nature of evil by appealing to its supernatural agency.[87] Still others have denied the existence of a single common characteristic of apocalyptic texts.[88] Recent historians have used conceptual models which treat "apocalypse" as an aspect of eschatology, alongside other "eschatologies" such as "immortality" and "resurrection."[89] Bernard McGinn, by contrast, contends that apocalypticism is best understood as a branch of eschatology which "covers any type of belief that looks forward to the end of history as that which gives structure and meaning to the whole."[90] History is thus perceived to progress according to an overarching messianic design until the historical process reaches its Omega point of eschatological consummation. The apocalyptic schema posits a worldview in which individual events are thus bound together to give the impression of "an inevitable progression towards a predetermined end."[91]

---

nence" means in an apocalyptic context, noting that "there are all kinds of intensities to that feeling [of imminence], from immediate to "within my lifetime" and along that spectrum a large gamut of emotions, from quiet determination to delirium, exalted or panicked." See Landes, *Heaven on Earth*, 29.

85. Rowland, *The Open Heaven*, 49–61.

86. Sanders, "Genre of Palestinian Jewish Apocalypses," 447–59.

87. Sacchi, *Jewish Apocalyptic*.

88. This view is especially prevalent among continental scholars. See Jean Carmignac, "Qu'est-ce que l'Apocalyptique?" 3–33; H. Stegemann, "Die Bedeutung der Qumranfunde," 495–530.

89. This conceptual framework is used in Bynum and Freedman, *Last Things: Death and the Apocalypse in the Middle Ages*.

90. McGinn, ed., *Apocalyptic Spirituality*, 5. Hanson departs from McGinn in this respect by positing an alternative distinction between what he terms "Prophetic Eschatology" and "Apocalyptic Eschatology." See, Hanson, *Dawn of Apocalyptic*, 10–12. Although the notion of a trans-historical process underlying the apparent contingency of events is at the heart of apocalyptic eschatology, this idea on its own is insufficient to speak of the worldview as "apocalyptic" or "eschatological." The Hegelian vision of the "End of History," although maintaining a comprehensive conception of history as infused with meaning and purpose, is devoid of the notion of human actions and natural processes being subjected to the intervention and judgment of powers or beings outside of the historical realm.

91. Hanson, "Old Testament Apocalyptic Reexamined," 57.

In the context of Northern Ireland, this conviction has often given rise to the notion that the prophetic oracles of the Scriptures were foreshadowed in significant social or political events, which were sometimes supposed to prognosticate end time events such as the tribulation and the rise and defeat of the Antichrist and the False Prophet.[92] Thus, as Patrick Mitchel observes, Ian Paisley's interpretation of prophetic Scripture presupposed "the ability to discern exact prophetic fulfilment in contemporary political events."[93] Biblical passages were perceived to have a present-day relevance and application to the extent that many were read as symbolic descriptions of the situation faced by contemporary evangelicals. Such passages were read as ominous warnings of an indeterminate yet ineluctable eschatological future which threatened "at any time to break into the present, and therefore call for an urgent response on the part of its readers."[94] This notion was often rooted in the conviction held by a significant minority of Northern Ireland evangelicals that the book of Revelation ought to be interpreted as "a record of historical events following in logical, chronological sequence from John's day in 96 AD until the present time."[95]

In a pioneering work on the social origins of the early Jewish apocalyptic writings, the scholar of the Hebrew Bible, Paul Hanson, maintained a distinction between "eschatology" and "apocalyptic eschatology" in terms of history (which pertains to the former) and myth (which relates to the latter).[96] This distinction has been challenged by others" scholarly probing into the nature and origins of apocalyptic eschatology and its relation to apocalypticism and eschatology.[97] J. J. Collins has maintained that the distinction consists in the generality (apocalyptic eschatology) and specificity (eschatology) of divine judgment.[98] David C. Sim helpfully distinguishes between the socio-religious phenomenon of "apocalypticism" and the religious conviction of "apocalyptic eschatology."[99]

---

92. Ladd, *A Commentary on the Revelation*, argues that the basic tenet of the apocalyptic worldview is the awareness that "eschatological events are foreshadowed in historical events" (156).

93. Mitchel, "Unionism and the Eschatological fate of Ulster," 208.

94. Boxall, *Revelation*, 106.

95. Campbell, *Scarlet Woman of the Apocalypse*, 4.

96. Hanson, *Dawn of Apocalyptic*, 11.

97. Roberts, "Myth versus History," 1–13; Collins, "Apocalyptic Eschatology," 43–44.

98. Collins, "Apocalyptic Eschatology as the Transcendence of Death," 61–86.

99. Sim, *Apocalyptic Eschatology*, 12.

Although such distinctions have clarified the scholarly applications of these contested terms, it seems that one of the main differences has been relatively neglected, namely that eschatology, unlike apocalypse, is indubitably a theological concept. Apocalypticism can be a matter of irredeemable disaster and has associations in the popular mind with violent endings either in the form of a suicide cult or a peril of other-worldly origins, such as that posed by an interstellar asteroid collision with the earth or even invasion by malevolent extra-terrestrial beings. Apocalyptic scenarios likewise do not entail a concomitant belief in divine or supernatural agency in causing a catastrophic end to human existence.[100] In an age of global warming, a diminishing ozone layer, and chemical, biological, and most of all nuclear weapons, the prospect of an entirely secular apocalyptic meltdown can be just as pertinent and menacing as the fear of being annihilated by the fire and brimstone of an irascible Deity consumed with fulminating wrath.[101] The only difference is that whereas theistic apocalypses usually entail some kind of ultimate consolation (albeit sometimes for only a very small remnant who profess the doctrines belonging to the cult), the secular apocalypse jettisons any hope in such deliverance and in the face of cosmic catastrophe succumbs with despairing resignation to an inevitable fate, which is invariably shrouded in doom.[102]

For the Northern Ireland Baptist pastor, L. E. Deens, eschatology was "the doctrine of the last things. Eschatology has to do with human destiny. It is a subject of tremendous fascination, shrouded in mystery, about which all covet light."[103] This study builds on this conception, adding that the eschatological component of apocalyptic eschatology introduces the notion of human destiny and its sub-themes of justice, judgment, divine condemnation, salvation and reward to apocalypticism. Whereas apocalypticism says, "the end of all things is at hand"

100. Giddens, *Modernity and Self-Identity*, 183.

101. Thompson, *The End of Time*, 133–34. Landes, *Heaven on Earth*, 19–21.

102. Travis, *Christian Hope*, 25. Despite the prevailing sense of foreboding invariably associated with apocalyptic scenarios, some have maintained that the notion of apocalypse does not rule out the possibility of hope entirely. Frank Kermode for instance distinguishes apocalypse and tragedy, the difference being that while "tragedy assumes the figurations of apocalypse, of death and judgement, heaven and hell," apocalypse leaves open the possibility that "the world goes forward in the hands of exhausted survivors." See Kermode, *The Sense of an Ending*, 82.

103. *Irish Baptist* 98 (December, 1975), 3.

(1 Pet 4:7), eschatology adds to this by saying either, "come, ye blessed of my Father, inherit the kingdom prepared for you from the foundation of the world" (Matt 25:34) or, "Depart from me, ye cursed, into the everlasting fire, prepared for the devil and his angels" (Matt 25:41). Apocalyptic eschatology combines these two ideas of catastrophic ending and divine judgment by saying, for instance, "the heavens shall pass away with a great noise, and the elements shall melt with fervent heat, the earth also and the works that are therein shall be burned up" (2 Pet 3:10). In its most hopeful and exuberant expression, apocalyptic eschatology declares that, "The kingdoms of this world are become the kingdoms of our Lord, and of his Christ; and he shall reign for ever and ever" (Rev 11:15). By stressing divine agency in the inauguration of the end times, eschatology (unlike apocalypticism) is an exclusively theological concept[104] and can be conceived only within a theistic worldview. Eschatological doctrines can be professed only by those with faith convictions, such as evangelicals.

Since Northern Ireland evangelicals from across the denominational spectrum have retained a firm conviction in the ultimate triumph of good over evil and a hope in the final vindication and salvation of God's people, the concept of apocalypticism on its own would not be adequate to our investigation. In order to encompass the diversity of opinion regarding the end times that exist within the various cultures of Northern Ireland evangelicalism, it is necessary to retain both the apocalyptic and eschatological aspects. The apocalyptic apprehension of evangelicals regarding the rise of "the beast" and the coming tribulation was counterbalanced by an equally ardent belief in his inevitable downfall and the hope that God would vindicate and reward the faithfulness of his people in the midst of great adversity—as well as punish their enemies in a sulphurous lake of unquenchable fire. Since this book considers the end-times thinking of Northern Ireland evangelicals under both apocalyptic and eschatological aspects, the concept of apocalyptic eschatology is better suited to the present study than either "apocalypticism" or "eschatology" as isolated categories.

---

104. Despite the ubiquitous use of the terms "apocalypticism" and "millennialism" in the writings of many social scientists, the related word, "eschatology" is conspicuously absent from contemporary sociological analysis. In contrast, theologians continue to make widespread use of the term "eschatology."

Despite the considerable scholarly efforts to understand both the meaning of apocalyptic eschatology and the social contexts out of which it supposedly arose, it has been said as recently as 2002 that "the study of biblical apocalypticism remains in its infancy."[105] Despite the flurry of monographs and articles since then, there remains an evident need for a study which, although focused on a particular context, aims to juxtapose disciplines in the examination of apocalyptic-eschatological language in such a way as to open up new lines of inquiry which will contribute to the broader field of millennial studies.

Protestantism

As well as "evangelicalism" and "apocalyptic eschatology" another equally contested term in relation to the Northern Ireland Troubles has been that of "Protestantism." Some historians and social scientists have argued that "Protestantism" in Northern Ireland during the Troubles was a relatively homogenous phenomenon in so far as it referred to a belief system that was shaped by two dominant traditions identified as Calvinism and evangelicalism.[106] By maintaining that individual citizens had the right to disobey the government in matters of Christian conscience, Calvinistic conceptions of the relationship between church and state provided the basis for the radical political philosophy of Northern Ireland evangelicalism.[107] It has thus been argued that the Calvinist radical political tradition, on which Northern Ireland Protestantism draws, inclines towards activism rather than quietism.[108]

For many Northern Ireland evangelicals Protestantism denoted a certain theological conviction which distinguished "biblical Christianity" from the perceived departures from biblical doctrines, manifested primarily—it was claimed—in the Catholic Church. "True Protestantism," declared Ian Paisley,

> is Bible Christianity, the Christianity of the Bible. Protestantism is Christianity, the Christianity of Christ. Protestantism is

105. Wilson, "Biblical Roots of Apocalyptic," 57.

106. Ganiel, "Religious Dissent and Reconciliation," 379–86; Alwyn Thompson, *Fields of Vision*; Bruce, *God Save Ulster!*.

107. The historical origins of these developments are traced in detail in volume 2 of Skinner, *Foundations of Modern Political Thought*.

108. Ganiel, "Religious Dissent," 381.

Christianity, the Christianity of the Apostles. Protestantism is Christianity, the Christianity of the Early Church. Protestantism is nothing less and nothing more than that Holy Religion revealed supernaturally to mankind in the pages of the Inspired Word and centered and circumscribed in the glorious adorable Person of the Incarnate Word, our Lord Jesus Christ.[109]

For some Northern Ireland evangelicals Protestantism was synonymous with "Biblical faith," as evinced rhetorically by Paisley's frequent use of the term, "Bible Protestantism" to identify his professed faith convictions. One Northern Ireland evangelical writing to the *Larne Guardian* expressed this notion of an inherent link between Protestantism and biblical truth with the unequivocal statement that, "The Protestant God is the God of the Bible."[110] Thus, notwithstanding the focus on the political dimensions of Protestantism, which characterizes many of the scholarly accounts of the Troubles, it is important to understand that Northern Ireland Protestantism was not merely a radical political ideology but also a basic theological conviction, the essence of which was constituted by the classic doctrines of Reformed theology such as *sola fide* and *sola scriptura*. The first question for the Northern Ireland evangelical was not "how can I preserve my national identity?" Rather the central question resembled more the anguished cry of the Philippian jailer in the book of Acts: "what must I do to be saved?" (Acts 16:30). In regard to controversial moral and spiritual issues the basic question, which evangelicals purported to ask themselves, was, "what saith the Scripture?" (Rom 4:3).

Another major influence on the historical development of Northern Ireland evangelicalism was the theology of John Calvin, or more accurately, the version of his thought elaborated by his more radical followers, most notably John Knox and Christopher Goodman.[111] Calvin is perhaps best known for his vigorous exposition and defence of predestination and providence[112] and the distinction between the "elect" and the "reprobate."[113] Despite the acknowledgement of the influence

109. Paisley, "Are We to Lose Our Protestant Heritage Forever."

110. Letter published in *The Larne Guardian* (6 October, 1988), 10 (signed by "True Christian").

111. Skinner, *Foundations*, 225f. and *passim*.

112. Helm, "Calvin," 341–48.

113. The twenty-first chapter of Book Three of the definitive 1559 edition of Calvin's *Institutes* has the title, "Of the Eternal Election, by which God has Predestinated Some to Salvation, and Others to Destruction."

of what one scholar called "rigid Calvinism"[114] on some expressions of Northern Ireland evangelicalism,[115] scholarly neglect of the vital trans-formative impact of religious convictions has led to a distorted account of the role of religion in the conflict which must first be illustrated and then redressed.

Limitations

Before engaging in a full critique of the existing scholarly approaches to religion and apocalyptic in Northern Ireland, it is necessary to be clear about the potential limits of this study. Despite its ambitious scope, this book jettisons the notion that any investigation concerning the inter-pretation and reception of texts into host cultures and the complex re-lationships between texts and contexts can aspire to the methodological precision of an exact science. Thus in order to dispel false expectations, it must be understood that this book is neither a sociological account of how ideas affect general social behavior nor a quantitative survey of the "influence" of apocalyptic eschatological ideas in Northern Ireland society during the Troubles. Neither shall this study be drawn into facile speculation about the alleged affinity of cataclysmic apocalyptic proph-ecies to certain types of psychological disposition. The focus of this study is more manageable, more edifying and in the end, I hope, more interesting. The paramount preoccupation of this study is with ideas and how these ideas were expressed in texts and in turn how these texts were interpreted by evangelicals. By focusing on use of apocalyptic-eschatological language within particular cultures of Northern Ireland evangelicalism this book identifies a particular intellectual milieu which stretches across denominations.

Notwithstanding its specific focus, this study draws on a wide array of primary material which emerged from evangelical communities in Northern Ireland. This diversity is reflected in the substantial number of evangelicals, some better known than others, whose texts are cited in what follows. Such are the numbers of evangelicals mentioned that it seemed tedious and potentially distracting to include detailed biograph-

114. Crookshank, *History of Methodism in* Ireland, II:7.

115. See Wright, "Protestant Ideology and Politics," 213–80; MacIver, "Militant Protestant Political Ideology"; Southern, "The Democratic Unionist Party," 125–49; and Hempton and Hill, *Evangelical Protestantism,* 14–15.

ical information for each individual cited. Brief biographical sketches have nevertheless been given in the case of certain lesser-known evangelicals whose texts are cited at regular points throughout the study. The omission of extensive biographical details is also consistent with the general theoretical approach of the whole project which is less focused on individual authors and is instead much more concerned with locating texts within semantic fields of particular discourses.

Another point that must be made in connection with the potential limitations of this work is the fact that male voices predominate throughout this examination of apocalyptic-eschatological language. Within Northern Ireland evangelicalism during the Troubles there appears to have been very few published female evangelical statements of an apocalyptic-eschatological nature.[116] Without wishing to speculate at length as to why this should have be the case, it seems plausible to suppose that the apparent silence of the female voice could indicate that female interpreters might have been uncomfortable with the biblical texts of apocalyptic eschatology.[117] Such reticence might in turn be attributable to the alleged misogynistic overtones of the classic biblical apocalyptic texts, in particular the book of Revelation. Tina Pippin denounces this text as "misogynist male fantasy of the end of time" and condemns the "sexual murder" of the Babylonian Whore in Revelation 18. After drawing attention to the alleged homoerotic undertones of the 144,000 chaste male figures of Revelation 7 and the purported degrading portrayal of women throughout the book, she concludes that the vision of Revelation is one of "misogyny and exclusion by a powerful, wrathful deity. In the Apocalypse, the Kingdom of God is the kingdom of perversity."[118] Whatever the justification of these claims or the broader explanation for the absence of a distinctive female discourse of apocalyptic eschatology within Northern Ireland evangelicalism, it is evident that the issue of gender in apocalyptic-eschatological texts is a highly complex and controversial problem of end-times hermeneutics. Whilst it is not necessary to attempt to account for these difficulties, it is nev-

116. This is not to say that women played a merely passive role in the Troubles. Fran Porter has conclusively demonstrated important ways in which women contributed to the faith and politics of Northern Ireland during the Troubles. See Porter, *Changing Women, Changing Worlds*.

117. Some reasons for this unease are given in Carpenter, *Imperial Bibles Domestic Bodies*, 127–48.

118. Pippin, *Apocalyptic Bodies*, 121–25.

ertheless important to be aware of the gender dichotomy that pervaded the apocalyptic-eschatological discourses of evangelical communities in Northern Ireland.

Although this book shall not pretend to have pronounced the final word on any of these issues, it is hoped that the findings uncovered in the following pages will succeed in bringing the scholarly contributions to the understanding of the Troubles into a mutually-enriching conversation with some of the leading ideas in contemporary millennial studies. Many of the conclusions arising from this research are original and could be of great potential interest to academics and non-specialists alike whose interests relate to other contexts and cultures which today find themselves confronting the same kinds of questions as those addressed in the present study.

1

Religion and Apocalyptic
in Northern Ireland

Introduction to Chapter 1

It has been claimed that the scholarly effort to explain the relationship between religion and conflict in Northern Ireland is in danger of becoming "research saturated."[1] Despite the profusion of articles and monographs, however, genuinely new ideas and original insights into the underlying dynamics of religious convictions in Northern Ireland have been rare. The problem is partly attributable to the dominance of social science approaches, many of which are predicated on the dubious methodological premise that religious convictions and the language in which they assumed textual form can be understood through a proper grasp of the social contexts out of which they purportedly arose. Moreover, despite the considerable academic interest, there remain crucial aspects of the question concerning the role of religion in the Troubles that have not been adequately examined. The apocalyptic-eschatological dimension of the conflict is a notable example of a prominent theme that has not received a level of scholarly interest commensurate with its significance. The aim of the first part of this chapter is to survey some of the main contours of the scholarship in relation to religion and apocalyptic in Northern Ireland and to offer a constructive criticism towards the development of a new approach. The final part of the chapter will consider how this book advances scholarship in millennial studies by offering an

1. Higgins, "Great Expectations," 10.

original approach that departs from both the traditional deprivation thesis as well as more recent revisionist attempts to understand millennial phenomena in culture.

The Study of Religion in the Northern Ireland Troubles: Review and Critique of Existing Scholarship

The role of religion has been a point of great controversy in the historiography of the Northern Ireland Troubles. For many years one of the paramount objectives of historians, social scientists, and even psychologists[2] of the Troubles has been to explain "the significant part which religious belief [was] playing in stimulating conflict and hostility between Protestant and Roman Catholic in Northern Ireland."[3] Some have maintained that the influence of religion was nearly always deleterious and contributed to the exacerbation of sectarian hostility.[4] Others have acknowledged that while religious thought could be misused to serve violent ends, its influence was, on balance, benevolent.[5] Still others have taken the intermediate view that religion was a neutral force and could be used ideologically either to advance the cause of peace or to aggravate existing sectarian antagonism.[6]

Although this question is not the main focus of this study, it does form a constant backdrop to our efforts to understand the characteristics of Northern Ireland evangelicalism. It is thus hoped that the findings of this research will offer a new perspective on the "religion question" by focusing attention away from sociological phenomena and upon the apocalyptic-eschatological substance of the religious convictions of evangelicals.

The Protestant-Catholic dichotomy of religious belief and national affiliation has been widely accepted as an axiom of Northern Ireland society by a wide range of social scientists and historians of the Troubles.[7]

2. O'Donnell, *Northern Ireland Stereotypes*.

3. Hickey, *Religion and the Northern Ireland Problem*, 57.

4. Bruce, *God Save Ulster!*, 246.

5. Gallagher and Worrall, *Christians in Ulster*.

6. Ruane and Todd, *The Dynamics of Conflict*; Ganiel, *Evangelicalism and Conflict*.

7. Examples include: Boal, Murray and Poole, "Belfast: the Urban Encapsulation of a National Conflict"; Brewer, "Sectarianism and Racism," 252–64; Juergensmeyer, *Terror in the Mind of God*, 36–43.

Richard Rose, writing at the beginning of the Troubles, even went so far as to describe Northern Ireland as a "bi-confessional" society.[8] Some scholars have sought to downplay the significance of religion as a factor in the conflict and tend to relegate its importance to its role as an ethnic or national label. Others have maintained that religious forces underpin the political context. In 1984, John Hickey argued that in Northern Ireland "[i]t is more a question of religion inspiring politics than of politics making use of religion. It is a situation more akin to the first half of seventeenth-century England than to the last quarter of twentieth century Britain."[9]

To his credit, Hickey challenged the prevailing sociological accounts of religion in Northern Ireland as "a by-product of the social environment"[10] by suggesting that in Northern Ireland "doctrine can, in fact, account for sociological reality."[11] Despite these perceptive insights, Hickey's analysis is deficient in that it lacks a theoretical basis for the claim that doctrine can be constitutive of social reality.[12]

Throughout the 1980s and early 1990s academic commentators continued to maintain that religion was at the forefront of the Northern Ireland conflict. In 1986 the sociologist Steve Bruce wrote a sociological analysis of the politics and religion of Ian Paisley.[13] After an illuminating analysis of the coalescence between the politics and theology of Paisley and his followers, Bruce came to the conclusion that the "Northern Ireland conflict is a religious conflict."[14] Although other theories were put forward, including the notion that the conflict was a colonial dispute[15]

---

8. Rose, *Governing Without Consensus*, 248.

9. Hickey, *Religion and the Northern Ireland Problem*, 67.

10. Ibid., 59.

11. Ibid., 63.

12. In this respect, Lindbeck's original approach to the relationship between language, culture and doctrine (in his *Nature of Doctrine*) provides a useful and potentially path-breaking perspective. Lindbeck draws on Wittgenstein's performative conception of language in order to demonstrate the extent to which doctrine is derived from an underlying linguistic substrate.

13. Bruce, *God Save Ulster!*

14. Ibid., 249. In his book, *Paisley: Religion and Politics*, despite the refutations of recent critics of his thesis, Bruce maintains that religion was "deeply implicated in the Troubles" and reiterates his earlier insistence that the "Northern Ireland conflict is a religious conflict" (246).

15. MacDonald, *Children of Wrath*.

or a matter of social and economic inequality,[16] the most comprehensive rejection of Bruce's thesis came from John McGarry and Brendan O'Leary in 1995.[17] Recognizing that none of these accounts were able to penetrate "to the heart of divisions in Northern Ireland, as they all simplify, exaggerate and generalize their preferred causal explanation,"[18] Joseph Ruane and Jennifer Todd proposed the notion of a "system of relationships" of difference, dominance and division, which reinforce one another.[19] Religion was regarded as one factor in a plurality of dynamics which animated sectarian conflict in Northern Ireland. Gradually, the notion that religion had any significant role to play in the conflict in its own right was dismissed by many researchers of the Troubles. By 1999, leading scholars had established that the relative insignificance of religious factors was now a matter of "academic consensus."[20]

It may well be the case that the debate regarding whether or not the conflict was "about religion" has been a continual distraction away from the most promising lines of inquiry into the history and culture of Northern Ireland in the twentieth century. The problem with the debate lies not only in the critical assumptions of scholars whose own convictions inevitably lead towards a partisan portrayal of the role of religion in the conflict,[21] but also in the terminological confusion which has arisen, not least in regard to the meaning of the word "religion." Commentators on the Troubles have expressed their uncertainty about where to draw the boundaries between politics and religion in the culture of Northern Ireland Protestants. "Within Unionism," observes Duncan Morrow, "there is clearly an enormous blurring of the doctrinal and the ideological and thus of the border between the religious and the political."[22] The Anglican archbishop, Robin Eames, eager to separate ideologically

16. Smith and Chambers, *Inequality in Northern Ireland.*

17. McGarry and O'Leary, *Explaining Northern Ireland.*

18. Mitchell, *Religion, Identity and Politics*, 3.

19 Ruane and Todd, *The Dynamics of Conflict.*

20. McAllister and Hayes, "Ethnonationalism," 30–48. As recently as 2005, Mitchell has maintained that, "Something of an academic consensus now hangs around the idea that conflict is essentially ethnonational, and that other factors reinforce rather than constitute the ethnic division"; Mitchell, *Religion, Identity and Politics*, 1–2.

21. A good example is Brewer and Higgins, *Anti-Catholicism*, which is characterized throughout by misrepresentations and simplifications of the evangelical positions with which they disagree.

22. Morrow, "Suffering for Righteousness' Sake?" 57.

loaded conceptions of "Protestant" religion from the theological essence of the faith professed by Protestant believers, argued that "part of the difficulty in identifying a religious factor stems from the hijacking of a so-called pan-Protestant religious ethic by those whose interest is entirely tribal and party-political."[23] Eames makes a good case, which points to a basic weakness in the otherwise useful contributions of Steve Bruce to the debate: namely that his sociological apparatus, although elaborate and buttressed by rigorous empirical analysis, lacks the discriminatory capacity necessary to distinguish between "Protestantism" as a convenient focus of patriotic loyalty and "Protestantism" as a matter of theological (not to mention apocalyptic-eschatological) conviction impinging on the sphere of what Paul Tillich called "ultimate concern."[24]

The confusion regarding the definition of religion has been replicated in other scholarly contributions to the debate. According to McGarry and O'Leary, the conflict is a struggle over ethno-national identity, not religion. The confidence with which they repudiate the notion that religion ever had a primary role in the conflict is matched only by the persistence of their lack of engagement with the actual theological convictions underlying religious belief. They can thus renounce any attempt to explain the conflict in terms of "religion" without ever adequately defining what they mean by this term and without examining the theological substance of the convictions underlying the religious beliefs of Northern Ireland evangelicals. For instance, in one section purportedly addressing the "religion question," the discussion is dominated by sociological phenomena such as endogamy, residential and educational segregation, church attendance and community relations rather than the substance of the theological convictions of either Catholics or Protestants. They conclude that the main role of "religion" in the conflict consisted in its capacity to function as "the key ethnic marker, facilitating the residential, marital and educational segregation which helps reproduce the two ethnic/national communities."[25] Again, therefore, the importance of religious convictions is accorded significance only insofar as they are related to sociological phenomena or to

---

23. Eames, "The Religious Factor," 126.

24. Tillich, *Systematic Theology*, I:11–14. Whyte similarly points out some of the problems with Bruce's conception of "religion." See Whyte, *Interpreting Northern Ireland*, 109.

25. McGarry and O'Leary, *Explaining Northern Ireland*, 212.

the national question. All of these shortcomings taken together thus give the impression that the value of their work is gravely compromised.

In a more recent contribution to the debate Claire Mitchell offers a useful discussion of the political significance of a belief in the immanence of the "end times" among Northern Ireland evangelicals. Building on the insights of previous studies which had recognized that many evangelicals regarded the "struggle as one between Christ and Antichrist,"[26] she acknowledges the significant notion that, "some Protestants read the political situation through the lens of Revelation." Mitchell argues that the "end-times theological convictions" of those who interpret the conflict in this way "can lead to political inflexibility." Mitchell's research has also helpfully uncovered some of the ways in which such beliefs coincided with significant political events such as the Good Friday Agreement, which for some evangelicals was a foreshadowing of the events described in prophetic oracles of the Scriptures.[27]

Notwithstanding these useful insights, many studies of apocalyptic belief in Northern Ireland evangelicalism do not emphasize sufficiently the fact that for many evangelicals, religious convictions were not primarily ethnic boundary markers or reservoirs of cultural practices; rather they were held as vital and ultimate matters of faith upon which rested the integrity of the gospel to which they pledged their uttermost allegiance. For the likes of Paisley, this was the gospel of which they should not be ashamed for it was to them "the power of God unto salvation" (Rom 1:16). Paisley's own definition of religion is unequivocal: "to me religion is that form of belief, worship and obedience to the one and only true God as revealed in the Bible and founded by our Lord Jesus Christ."[28] Despite Paisley's well-known and often vociferously articulated unionist convictions, there is no word here of national identity in his definition of religion, even as a subsidiary aspect of religious belief. For him, as for many other evangelicals, religion was a matter of "belief, worship and obedience" upon which rested the eternal fate of his soul and the souls of those to whom it was his duty to preach the Gospel. Thus, as the large display imposing itself above Paisley's pulpit in Martyrs' Memorial puts it, "Woe unto me if I preach not the gospel" (1 Cor 9:16).

26. Whyte, *Interpreting Northern Ireland*, 110.

27. Mitchell, *Religion, Identity and Politics*, 126–27.

28. *New Protestant Telegraph* (17 December, 1988), 3.

Religion was not merely a matter of momentary maintenance of national identity or the preservation of cultural integrity; it was the difference between spending eternity either in the glorious light and joy of heaven or in the place where "the worm dieth not and the fire is not quenched" (Mark 9:44, 46, 48). The focus on one's eternal destiny projected such religious convictions into the sphere of apocalyptic eschatology, which for evangelicals presented a vivid depiction of the spiritual fate not only of their individual souls but of the entire cosmos which was regulated by the eternal decrees of divine dominion. The role of religious factors in the Troubles could be better understood if scholars were to exhibit a greater willingness to understand the conflict from the perspective of the evangelical protagonists.

A major problem that has beset much of the scholarly analysis of the "religious question" in the Troubles has thus been a lack of empathy and serious engagement with the attitudes, values, and religious convictions of the people under investigation. It used to be standard practice for scholars to attribute the Troubles to the "backwardness" of the people of Northern Ireland, particularly in regard to the religious beliefs of evangelical Protestant "bigots."[29] As Arthur Aughey pointed out, the popular perception of Northern Ireland as a culturally and religiously atavistic backwater of Western society created the perception that unionism represented little more than a parochial ideology asserting "the self-justification of an exclusive sect of bigots whose guardians of the faith delight in whipping up their demented enthusiasms."[30] Apocalyptic eschatology in particular was seen as a baneful remnant of the "atavistic" mentality, unworthy of an enlightened and civilized era into which Northern Ireland was purported to have passed.[31] In this regard Ian Paisley has been execrated as the arch-bigot and has been depicted as a "dull and conceited man" whose mind was steeped in "primitive Calvinism."[32] More seriously he has been called "firebrand preacher" and accused of

29. Elliott, "Religion and Identity," 174.

30. Aughey, *Under Siege*, 5.

31. The notion of apocalypticism as a backward influence in the Troubles is replicated in Walker's authoritative history of the Ulster Unionist Party, which refers to the "lingering factor of apocalyptic ethnic hallucinations induced by Orangeism" as one of the factors which prevented the modernisation of unionism and which contributed to the political ruin of David Trimble; Walker, A History of the Ulster Unionist Party, 271. See also O'Dowd, "The Great Reversal," 269.

32. Marrinan, *Paisley*, 207–10.

using "religious ideas and images in legitimising the use of violence."[33] Recently it has been claimed that Paisley's obdurate anti-Catholic convictions put him at variance with the Reformation tradition of Luther, Calvin, and Knox in which he claims to stand as a present-day representative.[34] Some historians have claimed that Protestant anti-Catholic beliefs, such as Paisley's, are "unjustified" and that Protestants should therefore "come to terms with themselves."[35]

Such assertions betray a lack of understanding of the underlying convictions of Northern Ireland evangelicalism. To denounce Paisley's beliefs as irresponsible expressions of ignorant bigotry and irrationalism is antithetical to the researcher's first task,[36] which is to understand on the terms of those whose motivations they are examining. Historians should consider the motivations of Northern Ireland evangelicals on their own terms by understanding, for instance, that if Paisley was persuaded that the Pope *was* indeed the Antichrist, then it would be positively irrational *not* to denounce him in the strongest terms and turn all of his endeavors to curtailing his supposed diabolical authority. Research into the religious dynamics of the Troubles must engage sympathetically with the substance of the theological convictions of evangelicalism. The only way to attempt a comprehensive examination of the "religious question" in Northern Ireland is by taking seriously the apocalyptic-eschatological convictions that underpinned much of the political and religious rhetoric of those involved in the conflict. The aim should not be to discredit or ridicule these convictions but to understand them.

In contrast to other approaches, which treat religion as "a surrogate expression of ethnic or national identity,"[37] this study will attempt a more theologically nuanced conception of religion. Evangelical Protestantism will be regarded as a religious phenomenon that has theological significance in its own terms. In other words, the definition of evangelicalism is not confined to its use as "an easily available means of recognition."[38] The tendency to relegate the significance of religious convictions to the level of national identity and ethnicity is symptomatic of the dominance of

33. Juergensmeyer, *Terror*, 38.

34. Cooke, *Persecuting Zeal*, 47.

35. Irvine, *Northern Ireland*, 222.

36. Skinner, *Visions of Politics*, I:38.

37. Wiles, "What Christians Believe," 595.

38. Bell, *The Protestants of Ulster*, quoted in Aughey, *Under Siege*, 4.

the social sciences in the existing literature on Irish apocalyptic themes. In his introduction to an edited collection of essays on Irish millennialism, Crawford Gribben observes that "Irish apocalyptic scholarship has been dominated by sociological rather than historical or theological methodologies."[39] What Gribben said of Irish apocalyptic scholarship in general can be applied *a fortiori* to the existing literature on apocalyptic themes in the Troubles. The lack of an adequate theological methodology in particular has worked to the detriment of gaining a real grasp of both the apocalyptic convictions themselves as well as the motivations of those who held to them. It is to be regretted that much of the scholarship on the Troubles tends not to focus on the semantic richness and intensity of apocalyptic-eschatological language except in relation to the national question or to another area of scholarly concern. Gribben notes that,

> Irish historical writing has been debilitated by a general reluctance to engage with the influence of religious ideas, allowing their significance only when placed in the context of the national question, and those writers who do discuss aspects of Irish millennialism tend to do so only to illuminate some aspect of wider scholarly concern.[40]

Seeking to redress this unbalance in the existing scholarship, the present study takes seriously the apocalyptic-eschatological aspect of the Northern Ireland Troubles as an issue worthy of study in its own right.

The dominance of the social sciences has led to a tendency to reduce such beliefs in Northern Ireland to typological straitjackets which do not reflect the diversity and complexity of apocalyptic eschatological convictions. Many have overlooked or misunderstood the meanings given to theological terms as they were used in their primary contexts. The thesis developed by John D. Brewer and Gareth Higgins' study of anti-Catholicism is compromised by the authors" apparent neglect of the theological convictions that underpin the anti-Catholic sentiment of some expressions of Northern Ireland evangelicalism. At the outset of their book Higgins and Brewer make it clear that their aim is "not to give both sides of the story" but to "challenge the Protestant com-

---

39. Gribben, "Antichrist in Ireland," 3. For a useful summary of the intellectual history of Irish apocalypticism from James Ussher to Ian Paisley, see ibid., 5–20.

40. Gribben, "Antichrist in Ireland," 3.

munity about anti-Catholicism."[41] The result is a study that reads more like a polemical tract than a sympathetic and dispassionate theological reflection or sociological analysis. Although the book rightly argues that anti-Catholicism is not a monolithic phenomenon, the thesis is weakened by the omission of any reference to how the strands that are identified ("covenantal," "secular," "pharisaic," and "passive") interact with and draw from one another. Moreover, this dubious fourfold typology would not be recognized by the people to whom they purportedly refer, which leads to an approach which is at best inaccurate and at worst patronising. Furthermore, the labelling of strands of apolitical anti-Catholicism as "pharisaic" sounds too much like the stereotyping techniques supposedly employed in anti-Catholic rhetoric itself for such labels to possess any serious scholarly validity. Through their use of such pejoratives, Higgins and Brewer perform the same kind of negative typecasting techniques which they criticize in their fundamentalist opponents.[42]

A critical reading of many of the sociological approaches to the Troubles that have been produced in recent years seems to corroborate the notion that an elaborate conceptual apparatus often proves to be more of an obstacle than an asset to gaining a proper understanding of the issue under investigation. In addition, the excessive focus on particular aspects of non-mainstream evangelical beliefs, such as the notions of the Antichrist, the Great Tribulation, and Mystery Babylon, leads to an unbalanced presentation of the substance and role of apocalyptic eschatology in Northern Ireland. In many studies, apocalyptic eschatology and anti-Catholicism are treated as practically synonymous. The value of Steve Bruce's work is attenuated by the assumption that apocalyptic thought invariably gives rise to anti-Catholic sentiment. "What is important for understanding Free Presbyterians," he maintains, "is the role that Roman Catholicism is supposed to play in the approach to the end-times." Bruce continues to argue that, "Elements of Revelation and the books of Daniel and Isaiah are taken to prophesy the rise of an "Antichrist" who will not only dominate the Church but who will also be a major political force in the 'tribulation.'"[43] Although Bruce's assessment is accurate in relation to some expressions of evangelicalism, his analysis

41. Brewer and Higgins, *Anti-Catholicism*, viii.

42. For a critique of this book see Bruce, "The Sociology of Anti-Catholicism," 205–14; and Williams, "Anti-Catholicism: A Theological Consideration," 227–33.

43. Bruce, *Paisley: Religion, Politics*, 49.

lacks the discriminatory apparatus necessary to recognize the diversity and occasional inconsistency of apocalyptic thought in Northern Ireland. For example, he assumes that according to premillennial interpretations of the end times "it is the office of the papacy that usurps the place of Christ in the Church,"[44] whereas proponents of this outlook in Northern Ireland have been less than consistent in their identification of the Pope as the Antichrist. Admittedly, this was the perspective of some of the most outspoken fundamentalists such as Ian Paisley and Alan Campbell, but these figures by no means held the monopoly of premillennial opinion in Northern Ireland. In his consideration of Northern Ireland evangelicalism, therefore, Bruce's account seems to overlook the complexity and paradox of opinion not only among Northern Ireland evangelicals as a whole; he also underestimates the diversity of opinion even within the Free Presbyterian Church of Ulster to which his analysis of "Northern Ireland evangelicalism" is largely confined. For instance, the prominent premillennial Free Presbyterian Church of Ulster minister, Ivan Foster, wrote a commentary on Revelation in which he maintains, despite his consistent forthright excoriation of the Catholic Church, that he does "not believe that the pope or popes or even the system of Romanism is the Beast, the Antichrist."[45] Bruce's misunderstanding, which arises out of his use of "Paisleyism" and "Northern Ireland evangelicalism" as synonymous terms, is one example of the failure of scholars, particularly from the social sciences, to fully understand the theological nuances of apocalyptic eschatology.[46]

Apocalyptic Rhetoric and Political Violence in Northern Ireland

Another point of controversy in the scholarship has been the question of whether apocalyptic eschatology manifested itself politically

44. Ibid.

45. Foster, *Shadow of the Antichrist*, 154; cf. Gribben, "Protestant Millennialism," 54.

46. This narrow focus, which posits a direct correlation between apocalyptic eschatology and anti-Catholicism, is replicated in other studies. For example, Gareth Higgins' doctoral thesis entitled "Great Expectations: the myth of Anti-Christ in Northern Ireland," which considers the diverse ways in which the myth of the Antichrist has been interpreted by evangelicals, is weak in theological reflection. Moreover, the work relies too heavily on the unconvincing typology, which he and John Brewer developed in the aforementioned earlier study of anti-Catholicism in Northern Ireland. See Higgins, "Great Expectations," 170–71.

in Northern Ireland during the Troubles. Historians disagree about whether apocalyptic language engendered political quietism or whether, on the contrary, such discourses provided a provocation to become politically involved.[47] Myrtle Hill maintains that "in the second half of the twentieth century . . . millennialism took a reactionary, rather than revolutionary form, among Protestants" in Northern Ireland.[48] Hill's notion of a reactive form of apocalyptic belief among Northern Ireland evangelicals in the late twentieth century is to some extent supported by other scholars. Crawford Gribben sets out to describe and account for the endurance of the apocalyptic worldview which has been identified with Protestantism in Northern Ireland.[49] Gribben posits a reciprocal relationship between the apocalyptic mindset and political violence:

> Throughout the Troubles, the political violence perpetrated by Protestants has often been linked to this kind of prophetic hostility. After all, apocalyptic thinking typifies the sectarianism that has fuelled the Ulster crisis, and, as in many other contexts, has been widely associated with political violence.[50]

These findings point to the diversity of apocalyptic eschatology in Northern Ireland, which has not been appreciated sufficiently by previous scholarly treatments. The widespread and long-standing acceptance of the notion that there existed an inherent affinity between apocalyptic eschatology and anti-Catholicism has given rise to many unexamined and unwarranted claims. Examples include a work on the purported potential for the application of the methods and principles of Liberation Theology to Northern Ireland, which contends that eschatology never made a positive contribution to peacemaking efforts in the Troubles but, on the contrary, exacerbated existing sectarian enmity.[51] Despite the widespread use of rhetoric drawn from the vocabulary of apocalyptic eschatology and the "prophetic hostility"[52] that such language has engen-

---

47. In the case of Paisley, it might be expected that his Calvinistic convictions regarding God's sovereign control over all spheres of life would lead to a quietistic acceptance or resignation in regard to political affairs. In order to understand why his Calvinistic convictions led him to the opposite conviction, see Paisley's exposition of Romans 9 in his *Epistle to the Romans*, 141–48.

48. Ibid., 49.

49. Gribben, "Protestant Millennialism," 51–63.

50. Ibid., 53.

51. Gibson, "Gustavo Gutierrez and Northern Ireland," 259.

52. Gribben, "Protestant Millennialism," 53.

dered, the argument that eschatology never inspired constructive social engagement is a claim that cannot be upheld. It has been asserted that the myth that "the pursuit of civil righteousness is advanced by violent means" has provided an ideological justification for the acts of violence committed by loyalist paramilitaries.[53] This study thus goes against the grain of much of the recent scholarship in millennial studies, which has sought to establish indubitable connections between millenarian or apocalyptic thinking and destructive revolutionary violence.[54]

Taking account of the diversity of eschatological convictions in Northern Ireland, Gribben suggests that amillennialists are more likely than their premillennial or postmillennial counterparts to identify the pope as the Antichrist.[55] In contrast to trends in scholarship which emphasize the inseparability of politics and religion in Northern Ireland evangelical worldviews and the Calvinist imperative for political activism,[56] Gribben contends that "Pietism continues to exercise a strong influence on Irish Protestantism."[57] Apocalyptic-eschatological language does not necessarily correspond to pietism as the case of Paisley demonstrates. Groups that make extensive use of apocalyptic-eschatological texts can be inspired by such language either to political engagement or to pietistic withdrawal from worldly affairs. Social scientists have argued that whichever course is taken depends upon a variety of mutually-reinforcing factors, including the internal beliefs of a particular group as

53. Ibid., 53. This notion has been analyzed and critiqued from a theological perspective by the prominent theologian Wink who coined the phrase "The Myth of Redemptive Violence." See Wink, *The Powers that Be*, 42–56.

54. Walliss, *Apocalyptic Trajectories*, 11.

55. This issue raises an interesting point of comparison between American and Northern Ireland evangelicalism. Whereas premillennialism in America has generally rejected the identification of the papacy as the incarnation of the Antichrist, certain expressions of Northern Ireland premillennialism have retained this conviction. Even in Northern Ireland, however, not all adherents of premillennialism identify the pope as the Antichrist, as the case of Ivan Foster demonstrates. Despite this difference, there are clear points of both doctrinal and cultural overlap between American and Northern Ireland evangelicalism. Many of these similarities are described in detail in Livingstone and Wells, *Ulster-American Religion*.

56. Gladys Ganiel, "Politics of Religious Dissent"; Brewer and Higgins, *Anti-Catholicism*, 137.

57. Gribben, "Protestant Millennialism," 55; see also, Bruce, *Edge of the Union*, 35. In an insightful article on the political convictions of the gospel hall tradition in Northern Ireland, Neil Southern examines the diversity of political approaches that exist within evangelical-fundamentalist cultures in Northern Ireland; Southern, "Strong Religion and Political Viewpoints," 433–49.

well as the wider cultural context in which the group is situated.[58] It has thus been said with much truth that millennial thinking "may manifest optimism or pessimism, activism or escapism, elation or disillusionment, or some combination of all of these."[59] The history of the Troubles testifies to the truth of this statement regarding the diversity of cultural and political manifestations to which apocalyptic-eschatological thinking has given rise. Evangelicals in the Troubles exhibited a wide variety of attitudes towards political engagement, ranging from pietism to activism.[60]

Notwithstanding the misunderstandings concerning the nature and role of apocalyptic eschatology in the Troubles, there are many commendable recent scholarly works that have greatly advanced our understanding of the historical origins and nature of evangelicalism in Northern Ireland. Patrick Mitchel's study of evangelicalism and Protestant national identity asks important questions about the cultural and theological dynamics which shaped evangelical identity in Northern Ireland and seeks to assess how evangelicals responded to the turbulent events of the Troubles.[61] He rightly points out that Steve Bruce's "focus on the fundamentalist end of the evangelical spectrum has tended to mask a real diversity of evangelical expression within Northern Ireland."[62] Mitchel identifies four expressions of evangelicalism in Northern Ireland—Orangeism, Paisleyism, the Presbyterian Church in Ireland, and the Evangelical Contribution on Northern Ireland (ECONI)—and discusses each in turn in an analysis which clearly identifies the author's sympathies with the latter expression. His primary focus is "the intersection between evangelicalism and nationalism," which, he admits, leads

---

58. Kaplan, "Absolute Rescue," 128–63.

59. Smylie, "A New Heaven and New Earth," 157.

60. Scholars have been unable to establish unanimity on the point of which stance is prevalent among Northern Ireland evangelicals. Hill (*Time of the End*) and Ganiel ("Politics of Religious Dissent") argue that activism has been prevalent, whereas Gribben ("Protestant Millennialism," 55) makes a strong case for the primacy of pietism. Commenting in more general terms on the diversity of the political implications of millennial belief, Gordon McCutchan contends that, "Millennialism has again and again proven to be a generator of revolution. To the saint's self-reliant freedom from external institutions millennialism adds a vastly expanded self-confidence born of religious and historical certainty." See McCutchan, "Irony of Evangelical History," 318.

61. Mitchel, *Evangelicalism and National Identity*, 3.

62. Ibid., 3–4.

him to omit other aspects integral to evangelical belief and practice, not least apocalyptic eschatology.[63] Another work that has made an important contribution to our understanding of the origins and historical development of Northern Ireland evangelicalism is David Hempton and Myrtle Hill's *Evangelical Protestantism in Ulster Society, 1740–1890* (1992).[64] Despite their avowed aim of producing a "regional study" Hempton and Hill place a great deal of stress on the historical parallels of Northern Ireland evangelicalism and emphasize that the awakening of the 1740s was reflected in similar phenomena in Europe and North America at that time. Hill and Hempton observe that, "The biblical interpretation of political events . . . expressed in the general linking of contemporary social upheaval with the unfolding of a divine plan for mankind, invested all aspects of life with a compelling urgency."[65] Significantly, the authors find that during this period, "the epidemic of prophetical speculation . . . far from being the preoccupation of an esoteric minority, attracted men of surprisingly cultivated tastes and high social standing."[66] This remark can be read as a direct riposte to the "deprivation thesis," which occupied much of the attention of scholars since the important work by Max Weber and Ernst Troeltsch and later by Marxist historians and critics.[67] By introducing the notion of an active text to millennial studies, this work builds upon recent scholarship which has cast doubt on the viability of the "deprivation thesis" as a means of explaining the prevalence of apocalyptic language in general empirical terms of sociological causation.

A New Approach to Millennial Studies: Alternatives to the "Deprivation Thesis"

In terms of method, this book presents an explicit challenge to some of the prevailing trends in millennial studies in the past forty years. Many previous scholarly attempts in history and the social sciences to account for the prevalence of apocalyptic-eschatological language in specific social contexts have set out on the basis of an unexamined assumption:

63. Ibid., 8, 9.
64. Hempton and Hill, *Evangelical Protestantism*.
65. Ibid., 28.
66. Ibid., 95.
67. Shantz, "Millennialism and Apocalypticism," 25–28.

that such language strikes its deepest roots in the allegedly fertile soil of social, economic, or political hardship or oppression. This notion was once the basic theoretical foundation of scholarly investigation of apocalypticism, spanning almost every discipline across the arts, humanities and social sciences.[68] Much of what follows will attempt to cast doubt on the long-cherished assumption that apocalyptic eschatology necessarily thrives in turbulent periods of upheaval among people who either are or who feel themselves[69] to be downtrodden or marginalized.[70] One of the regrettable consequences of this preconception both in the historiography of the Troubles and in the broader field of millennial studies has been a tendency to assume that the language of apocalyptic eschatology was essentially a reactive phenomenon.

Recent tendencies in millennial studies have rightly evinced a growing disposition to question explanations of apocalyptic phenomena that attempt to invoke the "deprivation thesis," which asserted, as the 1908 Hasting's *Encyclopaedia of Religion and Ethics* put it, that such millennial ideas as the Antichrist legend are to be found "only among the lower classes of the Christian community, among sects, eccentric individuals and fanatics."[71] There is a well-established tendency among sociologists as well as biblical scholars to assume that apocalyptic eschatology invariably gains its widest following among the disenfranchised and marginalized. The "deprivation thesis" which asserts that, "stress and social upheaval are leading reasons why apocalyptic ideas flourish and increase in any particular time period" became a commonplace of early sociological treatments of apocalyptic phenomena, notes Richard Kyle.[72] For many years the "deprivation thesis" received widespread acceptance

68. In the field of biblical studies, sustained attempts to find sociological explanations for apocalyptic texts began with the publication in 1959 of Plöger's *Theokratie und Eschatologie*. An early exponent of this approach was Max Weber; see Weber, *Sociology of Religion*, 106.

69. Collins remarks that "the crucial element is not so much whether one is actually oppressed as whether one feels oppressed"; see Collins, *Crisis and Catharsis*, 84.

70. For a comprehensive bibliographical account of the history of the "deprivation thesis" up to the early 1990s, see Daniels, *Millennialism: An International Bibliography*. For a more recent, succinct account, see Shantz, "Millennialism and Apocalypticism," 18–43.

71. Bousset, quoted in Lawrence, *Apocalypse*, 37–38.

72. Kyle, *Last Days*.

among many scholars, particularly those with Marxist leanings.[73] The relationship between instances of material privation or political oppression and the emergence of apocalyptic language was posited as a matter of cause and effect.

The "deprivation thesis" has also influenced biblical studies and theological approaches to the study of apocalypticism. In his authoritative study of the origins of early Jewish apocalyptic eschatology, Paul Hanson asserted that, sociologically, groups exhibiting apocalyptic beliefs are often in a position of "powerlessness and disenfranchisement *vis-a-vis* the controlling powers."[74] "Deprivation" undertones can also be discerned in an influential treatise on eschatology by Jürgen Moltmann[75] and in some works of Liberation Theology.[76] It is important for scholars in millennial studies to distinguish between the dubious "deprivationist" assumption that apocalyptic-eschatological discourses are an invariable function of contexts of social hardship and the perfectly legitimate notion that such texts' sympathies "lie entirely with the persecuted and marginal elements in society."[77] Despite the recent discrediting of the "deprivation thesis," there remains, in the opinion of one scholar, "widespread agreement" on the point that "a direct correlation exists between the desperate situation of the author and his group and the embracement of the apocalyptic-eschatological perspective."[78]

Nevertheless, recent scholars in history, biblical studies, and literary theory have cast serious doubt on the reliability of the "deprivation thesis." "Apocalypticism," claims L. L. Grabbe, "does not necessarily arise in times of crisis, nor is it always the product of the oppressed, the marginalised and the powerless."[79] Stephen Cook reached a similar conclusion based on his reading of Zechariah 1–8, a text written by the

73. Thompson argued that millennial movements were outward manifestations of an underlying "chiliasm of despair" among the labouring classes; see Thompson, *Making of the English Working Class*, 411; cf. Eric Hobsbawm, *Primitive Rebels*, 57.

74. Hanson, *Dawn of Apocalyptic*, 251.

75. Moltmann, *Das Kommen Gottes*, 171.

76. For example, see Richard, *Apocalypse*, 3.

77. Hays, *Moral Vision of the New Testament*, 181. Schüssler-Fiorenza takes this idea even further by suggesting that apocalyptic-eschatological texts "can be read rightly only by those who are actively struggling against injustice"; Schüssler-Fiorenza, *Revelation*, 183.

78. Sim, *Apocalyptic Eschatology*, 63.

79. Grabbe, "Social Setting," 30.

ruling theocratic authorities in post-exilic Judah, which he cited as proof that "an apocalyptic worldview need not be a fringe phenomenon."[80] Writing in 1995, Cook maintained that the notion that apocalypticism would invariably appeal to groups which felt themselves to be alienated and dispossessed was "inadequate to account for the phenomenon of millennialism."[81]

Using the notion of a gradual drift away from the "deprivation thesis," Douglas Shantz has helpfully classified the scholarship of millennialism and apocalypticism according to "three generations." Building on the gains of the first (pre-1970) and second (1970s and 1980s) generations, the third generation (post-1990) of scholarship, explains Shantz, has been careful not to succumb to "the ongoing tendency towards reductionism and the citation of the deprivation theory as a means to millennial understanding."[82] Thanks to the scholarly efforts of these revisionist approaches, there is now a widespread recognition that "apocalypticism and millennialism arise in a wide variety of social contexts and encompass a broad range of emphases and perspectives."[83]

One significant work that emphasizes the notion of millennialism as a cross-cultural phenomenon is the *Oxford Handbook of Millennialism* (2011), edited by Catherine Wessinger. It is clear from the opening pages that Wessinger's definition of millennialism extends beyond Christian exegesis of Revelation 20:1–10 and includes a broad range of utopian movements from a variety of religious traditions and cultural contexts. Although it is undoubtedly the case, as Wessinger suggests, that Christian

---

80. Cook, *Prophecy and Apocalypticism*, 153. It should be noted for the sake of balance that Collins questions Cook's conclusions. Collins points out that since Judah was a marginal province on the edge of the Persian empire, Zechariah was nevertheless a marginal text even though it emerged from Judah's ruling elite; Collins, "Eschatological Dynamics," 77. This confusion may be attributed to the neglect of an important distinction raised by Landes between what he calls "hierarchical millennialism" and "demotic millennialism"; see Landes, *Heaven on Earth*, 22–27.

81. Cook lists ten specific instances which have brought into question the credibility of the "deprivation thesis" as a reliable model of contextual explanation; Cook, *Prophecy and Apocalypticism*, 35–40.

82. Shantz, "Millennialism and Apocalypticism," 33.

83. Ibid., 43. Although many have rejected the "deprivation thesis" others have sought to reclaim the thesis by revising it in the light of criticism and redeeming it as a model that can still be applied profitably to the study of millennial phenomena. Collins, in *Crisis and Catharsis*, introduces the notion of "relative deprivation," which posits the idea that even if the first century Christians were not subject to persecution, the *perception* that they were contributed to the unique appeal of the book of Revelation among early Christian communities.

assumptions expressed in the terms pre- and post-millennial "are found in non-Christian millennial movements,"[84] it does not follow that the reified categories of "catastrophic" and "progressive" millennialism,[85] adopted by Wessinger from the Christian terms pre- and postmillennial, offer the most apposite models for understanding the millennial beliefs of these non-Christian movements. The danger is that such importation of Christian categories of millennial beliefs to analyze the worldviews of a Hindu or Islamic apocalyptic sect will lead to a reduction of the complex nature of the beliefs of these unique interpretive communities to an alien system of classification. This danger is especially present in the case of scholars who might lack Wessinger's and Landes' deep and nuanced understanding of the cultural diversity of millennial beliefs. The argument has also been persuasively made that these categories are not even particularly helpful for understanding Christian millennial belief, particularly in the case of interpretive communities that predate the use of the terms, pre- and postmillennialism.[86] Nevertheless, despite these potential shortcomings, the *Handbook of Millennialism* offers a sustained interdisciplinary analysis of some of the most important expressions of millennial belief in the world today. Significantly, moreover, in terms of millennial studies, the work marks a definitive break from the "deprivation thesis" that once dominated the millennial scholarship.

Another work that signals an equally decisive and important break with the "deprivation thesis" and draws on an equally broad range of scholarship is Richard Landes' comprehensive assessment of millennial belief, *Heaven on Earth: The Varieties of Millennial Experience* (2011). Along with Wessinger's *Oxford Handbook on Millennialism*, Landes' study, which is the fruit of several decades of notable scholarly examination of the origin and nature of millennial belief, looks set to become one of the defining works in millennial studies for a generation. Landes offers a definitive statement on millennial studies which focuses on the perspectivism and diversity of millennial belief, noting that "one person's

84. Wessinger, "Millennialism in Cross-Cultural Perspective," 5.

85. A similar distinction is present in Landes' conception of "cataclysmic" vs. "transformative" millennial visions; Landes, *Heaven on Earth*, 31–33.

86. According to the *Oxford English Dictionary*, the term "premillennial" first appeared in 1846, "postmillennial" in 1851. For a lucid critique of the usefulness of these terms in the context of the puritan confessions, see Gribben, "Eschatology of the Puritan Confessions," 51–78.

messiah is another one's antichrist."[87] Notwithstanding this emphasis on the diversity of millennialism as a cross-cultural phenomenon, Landes seeks to posit a series of what he calls "laws of apocalyptic dynamics" through which millennial belief and action can purportedly be characterized and explained according to empirical principles of scientific analysis.

Landes and Wessinger have made an important contribution to millennial studies by taking seriously the appeal and influence of apocalypticism as a major factor in world history as well as in individual motivation. It can thus be hoped that their efforts will provide a new stimulus to rigorous academic inquiry into the origins, nature and outcomes of millennial belief by recognizing that millennialism is much more than a passing fad determined by random numbers or arbitrary historical events and developments. Rather millennial belief is symptomatic of the perennial cultural and linguistic structures of human consciousness that give rise to apocalyptic visions as collective means to overcome what Wessinger calls "the unpleasant limitations of the human condition."[88]

Given the systematic refutations of the "deprivation thesis" offered by Wessinger and Landes and a host of other recent scholars, this study is thus not the first to challenge the notion that apocalyptic-eschatological belief can be explained primarily by understanding the social conditions out of which millennial visions purportedly arise. This study is nevertheless the first, full-length systematic rebuttal of this thesis in relation to evangelical communities in the Northern Ireland context. This work draws on some of the most promising path-breaking endeavors of those who have gone before and arrived at conclusions that have undermined the plausibility of the contextual explanations for discursive phenomena. Nevertheless, whilst the insights contained in many of the works, including those cited above, are thought-provoking, energetic, and vigorously articulated, many of them are based largely on inference and polemic. A common shortcoming is the deficiency of a substantial body of evidence to support their theoretical conjectures. This study aims to supply this deficiency by focusing on the case of the Northern Ireland Troubles and summoning a wide variety of textual support for its claims without compromising on the theoretical rigor and consistency of the overall argument.

87. Landes, *Heaven on Earth*, 15.
88. Wessinger, *Oxford Handbook of Millennialism*, 5.

Another major problem with even the third generation scholarship, including the contributions particularly of Wessinger but also of Landes, is that despite its criticism of moribund sociological notions of deprivation and contextual causation, its exponents continue to operate within the theoretical frameworks bequeathed to them by the first generation. For instance, social or psychological phenomena are still accorded primacy in their critiques, even though they arrive at different conclusions. Even Stephen Cook, who has been one of the chief critical interrogators of the "deprivation thesis" in recent years, remains committed to sociological models of explanation for apocalyptic phenomena, even though his findings are at variance to reductive accounts of the origins of apocalyptic-eschatological discourses. Cook's commitment to the sociological emphasis on contextual origins is apparent in his stated aim "to provide alternative sociological understandings of the development of Israelite apocalypticism."[89] Such sociological approaches are unable to achieve a proper understanding of millennial phenomena they purport to elucidate because they take for granted the underlying linguistic and conceptual assumptions that underpin apocalyptic belief.

The method developed in the following examination of Northern Ireland apocalyptic eschatology signals a departure even from the third generation scholarship by arguing that the very terms of the argument need to be overhauled if we are properly to grasp the meaning and significance of millennial discourses. Therefore, while my interrogation of the "deprivation thesis" has been informed by the critiques of the second and third generation scholars, this study represents a much more fundamental challenge to *both* the "deprivation thesis" *and* the more recent revisionist theories by changing the terms of the debate in such a way as to emphasize the complexity of the relation between text and context in the explanation of apocalyptic-eschatological phenomena.

Although there have been some movements in the "third generation" away from the "deprivation thesis" in the broader field of apocalyptic and millennial studies, these developments are not apparent in the scholarly discussions of the Northern Ireland Troubles. In this scholarly arena, the tacit assumptions of the "deprivation thesis" continue to inform much of the debate. Gareth Higgins' analysis alludes to the notion that apocalyptic fervor in Northern Ireland reached its greatest intensity and achieved widespread acceptance during times of social or political

89. Cook, *Prophecy and Apocalypticism*, v.

crisis. Betraying his commitment to sociological theories of causation, he concludes that "apocalyptic speculation appears to be strengthened when certain conditions prevail in society."[90] This assumption underpins many scholarly works not only of Irish millennialism but also of more general accounts of the role of religion in the Troubles.[91] Claire Mitchell claims that during "times of communal difficulty or crisis, the role of religion in the symbolic construction of community [could] be more intense."[92] The same theoretical principle informs Myrtle Hill's analysis of millennial beliefs in Northern Ireland.[93] She contends that, "social and political disruption and a feeling of vulnerability seem to characterise those periods when intellectual theological interpretation and popular fears merge in a reading of contemporary events as part of a more universal confrontation between good and evil."[94] According to Hill, Paisley's fundamentalist convictions made him a man "for whom the dramatic discourse of millennial ideology [was] particularly well-suited."[95] Although there is much to commend in her study, it remains the case, as Crawford Gribben has noted, that these conclusions remain "largely untested by the brevity of Hill's pamphlet."[96] It is thus necessary to provide a more detailed and nuanced account of the ways in which apocalyptic-eschatological language functioned during the Troubles by taking into account the polyvalence and complexity of contextual causation.

Consonant with the notion of apocalyptic eschatology itself, which postulates a period of destructive upheaval preceding a positive period of constructive resolution and consummation, the aim of this book is not merely to criticize and cast down but to provide viable methodological alternatives with which to consider the interpretation of apocalyptic-eschatological discourses. I will argue that in Northern Ireland during the Troubles apocalyptic eschatology was most fundamentally a linguistic phenomenon, possessing its own system of rules governing its use in

90. Higgins, "Great Expectations," 139.

91. Examples include O'Farrell, "Millennialism, Messianism and Utopianism," 45–68; and Brown, "The Church of Ireland," 49–64.

92. Mitchell, "Behind the Ethnic Marker," 15.

93. Hill, *Time of the End*.

94. Ibid., 4.

95. Ibid., 51.

96. Gribben, "Antichrist in Ireland," 5.

the evangelical cultures in which it was prevalent. This study is therefore a literary theoretical analysis of ideas, which, whilst taking cognizance of contextual and cultural influences in the processes of text production, is most basically concerned with the biblical apocalyptic-eschatological texts themselves. Underlying this approach is a methodological argument which will exemplify an alternative way of understanding apocalyptic-eschatological language which moves beyond notions of sociological contextual explanation and which does justice to the complexity of the question regarding the extent to which language interacts with several layers of social context.

Despite the considerable advances made in recent years and the pioneering scholarly contributions of those authors listed above, it remains the case that "a detailed history of Irish protestant millennialism has still to be produced."[97] By bringing strands of Irish evangelical apocalyptic-eschatological rhetoric into dialogue with some of the most promising lines of inquiry in millennial studies, the aim of this study is to advance an original and consistent argument that will go some way towards filling this significant scholarly lacuna. This work will also exemplify a sympathetic yet critical method, which despite being theoretically-engaged will remain empirically-grounded. At the level of methodology, therefore, this book sets out a viable approach to the study of apocalyptic eschatology that will be of service to other scholarly pursuits in the broader area of millennial studies. The elucidation and justification of the methodological principles of this new approach will be the focus of the first part of the following chapter.

97. Gribben, "Antichrist in Ireland," 2.

2

Texts, Contexts, and Cultures

Introduction to Chapter 2

The aim of this chapter is to provide the theoretical grounds for my main hypotheses. The first part will set out the theoretical basis for the notion of the text as an active agent in the interpretive process. The second part also focuses on theory and deals with the conceptual structure of the argument, based on a methodical examination of texts, contexts, and cultures. After introducing general theoretical considerations to these three concepts, this chapter will then elucidate their application and relevance to the case of Northern Ireland evangelicalism during the Troubles. These descriptions shall be complemented by several examples of apocalyptic-eschatological discourse from a relatively broad spectrum of evangelical conviction in Northern Ireland. Although based largely on the primary sources, chapter 2 will also be deeply engaged in the leading literary theoretical approaches to the study of the relationship between texts and readers. This chapter draws insights from New Historicist and post-structural approaches to critical theory. Both of these perspectives open up promising lines of inquiry into the semantic negotiations and discursive power plays involved in the reception of apocalyptic-eschatological language into evangelical cultures.

The Study of Texts

In the present moment of academic time, the interpretation of texts has become the paramount issue underpinning much of the debate in the social sciences, literary criticism, theology, and philosophy. Anthony Thiselton remarks that "the most radical question of all in hermeneutics concerns the nature of texts, because the decision to adopt given interpretive goals depends not simply on the needs of the modern reading community but also, more fundamentally, on the nature of the particular text which is to be understood."[1] The Latin root of the English word "text" is the verb *textere,* which means to weave, as in the weaving of fabric.[2] Corresponding to the notion of text as a textile which is woven and enmeshed in other fabrics, theologians, philosophers, and literary theorists have established a certain degree of unanimity on the point that the world is constituted by a system of inter-related signs and that it belongs to the human condition to be involved in an unceasing hermeneutical process of interpreting the world through these interrelated signs. Thus Paul Ricoeur and Hans-Georg Gadamer have argued that the hermeneutical task lies at the heart of what it means to be human. If Ricoeur and Gadamer are correct to say that our "way of being-in-the-world is irreducibly hermeneutical,"[3] it follows that to be human is to live in a world of signs that are expressed in "texts" out of which arise systems or networks of meaning,[4] which corresponds to the notion of "our nature as the symbol-using animal."[5]

In the broadest sense, texts are the linguistic mechanisms or signs through which human experience is expressed and embodied.[6] When signs are recognized in common by many people, each of whom comes to a shared understanding of the meaning of particular texts, a distinctive culture begins to emerge.[7] Culture is an important, even inescap-

1. Thiselton, *New Horizons in Hermeneutics*, 49.

2. A text is "a fabric, woven (Latin *textere/textus*) from many threads." See Blumenthal, *Facing the Abusing God*, 60.

3. Stiver, "Theological Method," 16.

4. Stiver, *Theology After Ricoeur*, 50.

5. Burke, "Theology and Logology," 153.

6. Berrio, *Theory of the Literary Text*, 94.

7. Lévi-Strauss, *Structural Anthropology,* 62–63. Whilst emphasizing the variability of the semantic content of signs, Levi-Strauss argued that underlying such variation were certain universal laws which are deeply ingrained in collective human consciousness. This principle enabled him to uncover the structural correspondence between language and social relations, which he demonstrated using empirical data collected from his observations of "primitive" social orders, as he does in his magisterial, *Tristes Tropiques*.

able, factor in hermeneutics for, as philosophers such as Heidegger and Gadamer have insisted, all interpretation is derived from a "hermeneutic pre-understanding."[8] This idea corresponds to the notion that there is invariably an "implicit fore-structure that guides all interpretation in advance upon which all interpretation draws."[9] Culture is important because through its practices and underlying assumptions, it provides the discursive frameworks within which such pre-understandings are encoded. From the perspective of hermeneutics, cultures can thus be seen as semiotic systems arising out of shared knowledge and values based on common interpretations of texts.[10] As comprehensive vectors of meaning in which signs are inscribed, "texts" comprise all manner of expressions of human creative effort.[11] In the context of Northern Ireland evangelicalism, such expressions include books, pamphlets, sermons, broadcasts, songs, ballads, and hymns as well as non-verbal cultural artefacts such as artistic representations, icons, murals and logos, and cultural practices.

In our attempts to find an alternative to the contextualizing tendencies of contemporary sociological analysis which has largely prevailed in the secondary literature on the Troubles, the most promising lines of inquiry are opened up by literary theory. Twentieth-century literary criticism problematized the notion of the text.[12] According to Jacques Derrida, a text can no longer be thought of as "a finished corpus of writing, some content enclosed in a book or its margins," but must instead be understood to constitute "a differential network, a fabric of traces referring endlessly to something other than itself."[13] Thus, according to this broad conception of the text as a network through which meaning is constituted in a rhetoric of categorical difference, a text may be said to comprise the "basic unit of investigation" in the study of human interactions.[14] Most importantly for our purposes, Derrida presents an original way of understanding the relationship between text and context. Developing a theory of language as interrelated signs whose relation-

8. Thiselton, "Bible and Today's Readers," 441.

9. Caputo, *Weakness of God*, 113.

10. Ward, *Cultural Transformation*, 5.

11. Gadamer, *Gesammelte Werke*, viii, 350.

12. Birch, *Language, Literature, and Critical Practice*, 10–11.

13. Derrida, "Living On," 84.

14. Schreiter, *Constructing Local Theologies*, 55.

ship is constituted by virtue of their difference from each other, Derrida contends that, "every sign, linguistic or non-linguistic, spoken or written ... can break with every given context, and engender new contexts."[15] Furthermore, Derrida has shown that the notion of "context" is attended by an inherent instability which proselytizes every attempt to ascribe to it the last word in hermeneutical analysis.[16] Derrida regards context not as a stable entity or as the ultimate hermeneutical key that will somehow unlock the meaning of a text but as "a collectivity of presences organizing the moment of ... inscription" of a written sign.[17] Since there is no single presence that could be said to constitute the sole stabilizing context, the meaning of the text is always "indecidable."[18]

These insights correspond to the notion of "iterability," which posits a theory of linguistic signs as being inherently repeatable in ways which are unrelated to the initial intentions in which they were originally inscribed.[19] As one of Derrida's commentators put it, this theory maintains that "language simply cannot be tied down to a single speaker, intention, or context. ... A piece of language that could only be used once would not be language."[20] Iterability thus means that "meaning cannot be merely context-bound."[21] Derrida's problematization of context is connected to his suspicion of any attempt to reduce texts to logocentric principles through the invocation of a supposed extra-linguistic axiom which purports to elucidate the "true" meaning of the text with any degree of finality or closure.[22] Extending this suspicion to our own subject, the use of apocalyptic eschatological language, we must be careful not to reduce this language and its embodiment in texts to principles of supposedly objective interpretation purportedly supplied by social contexts. We should aim, instead, to locate "moment[s] of alterity within a

---

15. Derrida, *Margins of Philosophy*, 320.

16. See ibid., 310, in which Derrida states that "context is never absolutely determinable[,] ... its determination is never certain or saturated." See also Derrida, "Living On," 78, 84.

17. Derrida, "Signature Event Context," 182.

18. Silverman, *Textualities*, 80–82.

19. Vanhoozer, *Meaning in This Text*, 78.

20. Ibid., 78.

21. Hobson, *Jacques Derrida*, 98.

22. Reynolds and Roffe, *Understanding Derrida*, 91.

text" by identifying "a domain of textuality irreducible to logocentric conceptuality."[23]

The text is therefore in the world but not of the world. Taking cognisance of Derrida's problematization of "context," historians and literary critics have developed a new understanding of what Louis Montrose calls the "dialectic between the text and the world."[24] The subtlety of the dialectic consists in the notion that although the production and interpretation of texts is indeed shaped by the social context, the relationship is not a simple one of cause and effect. Montrose's dialectic construes the text as something active and thus involved in itself in the formation of the social conventions through which it is interpreted.[25] Moreover, Derrida further problematizes the role of context in text production and interpretation through his implicit claim that contexts ought not to be considered as fixed sociological axioms but as transient linguistically-constituted matrices of discourse.[26]

The relation between text and context constitutes the basic issue not only of hermeneutics but also of all scholarly inquiry in the arts and humanities.[27] My argument is not confined to local concerns about Northern Ireland evangelicalism, but exemplifies an innovative approach to the reading of literary texts which seeks to understand the complexity and intricacy of the relationship between text and context concerning the interpretation of apocalyptic-eschatological language. This study thus presents an explicit critique of certain social scientific approaches, which, in their zeal to establish dialogical affinity between texts and the contexts out of which they are said to have emerged, have overlooked the ambiguity and polyvalence of this extremely intricate relationship. The text informs the context as much as *vice-versa*. This work departs from existing studies by presenting a new method which aims to move beyond simplistic theories of contextual causation towards a more integrated understanding of the texts, contexts and cultures of Northern Ireland evangelicalism. Although this does not quite amount

23. Critchley, *Ethics of* Deconstruction, 28.

24. Montrose, *Purpose of Playing*, 2.

25. It is important to keep in mind that Derrida himself, as already noted, did not dismiss the role of context. He merely wished to emphasize its polyvalent, transient, and indeterminable nature; Derrida, "Living On," 81.

26. Derrida, *Limited Inc*, 9.

27. Thiselton, *New Horizons in Hermeneutics*, 49.

to a full displacement of texts from their social milieu, it does constitute a move away from an almost exclusive focus on the world "*behind* the text" towards the world "*of* the text" as well as the world "*beyond* the text," to borrow the terms of Paul Ricoeur.[28]

If contextualists were to object to these claims with the contention that all texts can be historicized, I would rejoin by affirming with the New Historicists that it is equally the case that history can also be textualized according to the underlying structures of the discourse in which all historical thinking is constituted.[29] Historians and biblical scholars have been accustomed to establishing cause and effect relationships between texts and their contexts, sometimes forgetting that a context, in common with a text, can be deconstructed; that is, it can be liberated to yield multiple, possibly infinite meanings based on the experience and aspirations of the interpreter. The preoccupation with establishing causal relationships between texts and contexts by subordinating the latter to the former also conveniently sidesteps the complicating factor of the different levels of semantic negotiations between the reader and author that invariably accompany the act of reading. This study does not attempt to establish the absolute predominance or antecedence of either texts or contexts in the process of interpretation. Nevertheless, given that many of the scholarly studies of Irish apocalypticism have tended to offer contextual readings of apocalyptic beliefs,[30] the balance of this argument is tilted slightly in favor of textuality over and against contextuality.

This inclination towards textuality is grounded in the notion that historical contexts are created by linguistically-constituted systems of signification just as much as language itself is constituted by historical contexts.[31] As George Steiner, the "veritable priest of reading,"[32] put it, "Language happens in time but also, very largely, creates the time in

28. Ricoeur, *Time and Narrative*, II:5–6; Stiver, *Theology After Ricoeur*, 63–66. Elsewhere Ricoeur refers to the text as a mode of discourse which functions as a "projection of a world"; Ricoeur, *From Text to Action*, 76.

29. This notion is articulated with considerably acuity by Montrose in his article, "New Historicisms," 392–418.

30. See, for instance, Gribben, "Antichrist in Ireland," 1–30.

31. This is one way of interpreting Montrose's concept of the "dialectic between the text and the world"; Montrose, *Purpose of Playing*, 2.

32. Scott and Sharp, quoted in Vanhoozer, *Meaning in This Text*, 198.

which it happens."[33] Language is thus neither a labelling-system which we use to ascribe appellations to things nor even an unavoidable aspect of human social interaction; rather, language is better conceived as "a communal phenomenon that shapes the subjectivities of individuals rather than being primarily a manifestation of those subjectivities."[34] This assertion also recalls the notion of Heidegger's later philosophy of language as "the abode of Being."[35] Intellectual developments in anthropology and literary theory have also affirmed that historical consciousness is itself bound by certain pre-existing linguistic conventions,[36] which constitute the textuality that "inhabits everything we think, and do, and hope for."[37]

The notion of textuality as a universal enveloping mechanism whose presence underlies every facet of human history and experience is at least one way of understanding Derrida's famous dictum—"*il n'y a rien hors du texte*" (there is nothing outside the text).[38] This idea converges with the corresponding notion of the "inability of language to represent anything outside its own boundaries."[39] Thus, out of the "linguistic turn," which has defined much of twentieth-century philosophy and literary criticism,[40] has arisen the notion that language itself is con-

33. Steiner, *After Babel*, 144.

34. Lindbeck, *Nature of Doctrine*, 33.

35. Heidegger uses the term *"Aufenthalt des Daseins"* (abode of being) in *Kant und das Problem der Metaphysik*, 258. For further explications of this notion in his later thought (in English translation), see Heidegger, *What Is Called Thinking?*, 245ff.; see also Heidegger, *Poetry Language Thought*, 189–210. A similar conception of the "ontology of language" is elaborated from an explicitly theological perspective by Balthasar in his *Ganze im Fragment*.

36. Lévi-Strauss, *Structural Anthropology*, 62–63 and *passim*.

37. Caputo, *Radical Hermeneutics*, 6.

38. Derrida, *Of Grammatology*, 158, 163. A further definition is given by Vanhoozer who interprets this claim as meaning that "all language and all thought, every word and every concept is part of a worldwide web of signifiers[;] . . . there is no knowledge that is not mediated by some signifying system or other." Vanhoozer, *Meaning in This Text?*, 111.

39. Jay, "Should Intellectual History Take a Linguistic Turn?" 89.

40. The linguistic turn involved a "radical questioning of language's capacity—or indeed its need—to refer to extra-linguistic reality"; Fodor, *Christian Hermeneutics*, 147. The central contention of the thinkers behind the linguistic turn was, in the words of Katz, that "certain philosophical problems can be represented correctly as questions about the nature of language" and that these problems "can be solved on the basis of theoretical constructions that appear in linguistic theory"; Katz, "Philosophical

stitutive of contextual reality. Far from merely describing, reflecting or corresponding to a pre-existing world that exists "out there," language is in fact ontologically anterior to the social context it creates and fashions according to its own internal logic of signification (i.e., its "grammar").[41] In other words, as one theologian put it, "language is internally related to the world rather than externally related to it."[42] Language is thus endowed with a "world-constituting character."[43] Referring to the notion of the "linguisticality of existence" (*Sprachlichkeit der Existenz*) and the concept of "language events" (*Sprachereignisse*), theologians and literary theorists affirm that language possesses ontological as well as descriptive or mimetic attributes.[44] Theorists such as Gadamer and Dilthey extend-

---

Relevance of Linguistic Theory," 101. Rorty defines the "linguistic turn" as "the view that philosophical problems are problems which may be solved (or dissolved) either by reforming language, or by understanding more about the language we presently use"; Rorty, *Linguistic Turn*, 3.

41. The fact that the ancient Greeks used the expression *onoma*, meaning "name" to signify what contemporary English speakers recognize as "word" indicates, according to Gadamer, that their thinking was characterized by "the inner unity of word and object" (*die innige Einheit von Wort und Sache*). See Gadamer, *Gesammelte Werke*, I:409. Thus Greek philosophy began with the assumption that words are only names of things; that is, that they do not constitute or even represent reality themselves. The notion that language is itself constitutive of reality was one of the principal theoretical insights of Ferdinand de Saussure in his *Course in General Linguistics*. The ideas expounded in Saussure's *Course* (first published in French as *Cours de linguistique générale* by his students Charles Bally and Albert Sechehaye in 1916) became either the basis or point of departure for all subsequent scientific study of language and is still credited by many as the founding text of what became known as "structuralism." The philosophical implications of the notion of language as constitutive of reality were scrupulously interrogated and expanded by Martin Heidegger who conceived of *Dasein* as "a living thing whose Being is essentially determined by the potentiality for discourse" (*Being and Time*, 47); cf. Heidegger, *Vom Wesen der Sprache*, 156. See also, Ernst Fuchs, *Hermeneutik*, 69. Heidegger also recognized that "words and language are not wrappings in which things are packed for the commerce of those who write and speak. It is in words and language that things first come into being and are." See Heidegger, *Introduction to Metaphysics*, 13.

42. Kallenberg, *Ethics as Grammar*, 116.

43. Ibid., 218. On his way to this conclusion, Kallenberg considers the theories of meaning formulated by Ludwig Wittgenstein who contended in his *Philosophical Investigations* that meaning is determined not by the limits of the language in general (as he had argued in his earlier *Tractatus*) but by the particular discursive worlds which we inhabit.

44. Detweiler and Robbins, "From New Criticism to Poststructuralism," 241.

ed this notion to the study of culture positing a notion of "linguisticality as the foundation of the human sciences."[45]

This idea corresponds to structuralist approaches which posited the notion of language as a differential network of interconnected meaning—"a system of signs defined by their differences alone."[46] Since the relationship between the signifier (*signifiant*) and the signified (*signifié*) was of an entirely arbitrary nature and the meaning of signs was thus constituted by mutual determinations arising from their differential variations,[47] there was no necessary correspondence between language and a supposed extra-linguistic reality.[48] There thus arose a conception of language as constitutive of reality.[49] Language creates reality not through its correspondence to supposedly pre-existing things or objects but through the principles inherent in its own mechanisms of signification. As one philosopher, paraphrasing Gadamer, put it, "language does not simply reflect the structure of being; rather it is in language that our experience originates and constantly changes. . . . Our whole experience of the world-in-itself unfolds in language."[50]

Thus the concept of the "linguisticality of existence"[51] is presupposed by the notion of the self-referential nature of language and entails an implicit break with the "myth of language as a mirror of reality."[52] This notion is in turn predicated upon an ontological presupposition that the world is experienced through language and that the linguistic worlds which we inhabit are the only worlds there are. In other words, there is no world "behind" the text and thus no transcendent reference point, whether it be the Hegelian Absolute Idea, the Marxist dialectic,

---

45. The meaning and implications of the notion of "*Sprachlichkeit als Grundlage der Geisteswissenschaften*" are discussed at length in Annika Krüger, *Verstehen als Geschehen*, 135–56.

46. Ricoeur, *The Conflict of Interpretations*, 250.

47. Fodor, *Christian Hermeneutics*, 127.

48. Said, *Beginnings: Intention and Method*, 38.

49. Taylor thus refers to "the artificiality of the distinction between social reality and the language of description of that social reality," pointing out that, the fact that "language is constitutive of the reality, is essential to its being the kind of reality it is." See Taylor, *Philosophy and the Human Sciences*, 34.

50. Horn, *Gadamer and Wittgenstein*, 61.

51. This term is borrowed from the German, "*Sprachlichkeit der Existenz*." See for example, Pilnei, *Wie ensteht christlicher Glaube?*, 153.

52. Rorty, "Nineteenth-Century Idealism," 152.

the omnipresent Will, the Oedipus complex, or any other supposedly extra-linguistic metaphysical concept.[53]

As well as its parallels with certain intellectual currents associated loosely with "poststructuralism,"[54] many readers may perceive methodological affinities between this approach and that exemplified by some expressions of New Historicism.[55] There is an undeniable kinship here in so far as my method is characterized, like New Historicist approaches, by its "privileging of textuality, language and representation as the basis for historical analysis."[56] The aims of this study are also consonant with New Historicism in so far as I shall endeavor to provide a methodological basis for an insightful exploration of the relationship between literature and history,[57] which has been identified as one of the most beneficial applications of the New Historicist method.[58] As historians have already begun to realize, the challenge posed by such hermeneutically-engaged linguistic approaches to the study of the relationship between texts and contexts has the potential to overturn "traditional literary and historical modes of interpretation by undermining materialist theories of experience and the ideas of causality and agency inherent in them."[59]

53. Fiddes, *Promised End*, 33.

54. Poststructuralism is well defined by Raval as a thoroughgoing repudiation of the notion of texts as "structures of determinate meaning accessible by objective critical procedures"; see Raval, *Art of Failure*, 119.

55. This approach is characterized by an overriding interest in what Montrose calls "the historicity of texts and the textuality of histories." See Montrose, *Purpose of Playing*, 5.

56. Brannigan, *New Historicism*, 9.

57. One of the broader consequences to have resulted from these developments has been the dissolution of traditional boundaries between "literary" and "historical" texts, which Skinner credits partly to the influence of Derrida. See Skinner, *Reason and Rhetoric*, 14. Similarly Collingwood sought to ascertain the difference between literature and history and concluded that the only difference that occurred to him was that historians in contrast to novelists or poets *aspire* to be true; Collingwood, *Idea of History*, 246.

58. Ibid., 11. "New Historicist" approaches are also characterized by an emphasis on the production of power and an overriding emphasis on the role of culture in mediating these power relationships. For this reason Graham Ward remarks that "New Historicist" approaches constitute "a marriage between Foucault and . . . Clifford Geertz." See Ward, *Theology and Contemporary Critical Theory*, 66.

59. Spiegel, "History, Historicism," 60.

Apocalyptic-Eschatological Texts in Northern Ireland Evangelicalism

The case of apocalyptic-eschatological language in Northern Ireland during the Troubles, I will argue, offers an exemplary manifestation of these general methodological observations. In common with other contexts in which such language was prevalent, there were in Northern Ireland certain underlying "discursive practices," which endowed particular statements with semantic consequence and in some instances polemical efficacy.[60] Alluding to the importance of these conventions, Montrose avers that, "In any actual situation of signification, the theoretical indeterminacy of the signifying process is delimited by the historical specificity of discursive practices, by the operative constraints and resources of the reading formation within which that signification takes place."[61] Although these "discursive practices" are embedded in the social and material conditions, it is also the case that they are in turn generative of these conditions. The intricacy of this dialectic helps us to understand the complexity of the relation between text and context in terms of how language functions in culture.

This dialectical approach can be applied to our study through its potential to surmount the social and political dualistic categories that often manifested themselves in the Northern Ireland context. These categories included: "Unionist" and "Nationalist," "Protestant," and "Catholic," "evangelical," and "liberal," and "premillennial," and "amillennial." Instead of treating these phenomena as sociological "givens" (as do too many of the scholarly discussions of Northern Ireland),[62] this examination of apocalyptic-eschatological language in Northern Ireland follows the critical orientation of recent developments in cultural studies that sees these alleged "timeless axioms" as arising from different types of discourse. As such they can be explained by their enmeshment in the discursive matrixes that are negotiated by power relations, which regulate what passes as a true account of the situation.[63]

---

60. This is how I interpret the notion of "congruity," as formulated by Roman Jakobson and Morris Halle in their important book, *Fundamentals of Language*, 76.

61. Montrose, *Purpose of Playing*, 7.

62. See, for example, Bruce, *Paisley: Religion and Politics*, 48.

63. Foucault, "Afterword," 216–26.

Apocalyptic eschatological language during the Troubles was often suffused with ideological insinuation. Such language could become aligned with the political aspirations of particular evangelical groups, whose apocalyptic-eschatological worldviews became formative of their convictions.[64] As such, apocalyptic eschatology was vulnerable to being conscripted into the service of an ideology, according to the pre-convictions and objectives of those by whom it was so used.[65] The universal scope and metaphorical quality of apocalyptic-eschatological language further augments the polarization of the hermeneutical appropriation of such texts. Even the most cursory glance at the history of the political interpretations of biblical apocalyptic-eschatological texts will reveal that the images and concepts of apocalyptic eschatology can be summoned to the defence of the political status quo just as readily as they can be called to instigate the overthrow of the powers that be.[66] A proper investigation should be able to account for these different appropriations of common texts not merely in terms of contextual variations but as a result of a complex causal nexus consisting of a multiplicity of textual, contextual and convictional aspects.

As well as retaining a dynamic dialectical conception of the relationship between texts and contexts, millennial studies must also acquire a more subtle and nuanced conceptual vocabulary with which to investigate and scrutinize apocalyptic discourse. The most important words in the millennial studies researcher's vocabulary are not "pre-," "post-," and "a-millennial" but "text," "context," and "culture." In order to avoid confusion it is necessary to explain the meaning of these concepts in relation to the Northern Ireland Troubles and then to explore their potential significance for future investigations in millennial studies.

---

64. This insight is at the heart of the theology of McClendon in his trilogy of systematic theology: *Ethics, Doctrine* and *Witness*. This idea is exemplified methodologically and expressed persuasively throughout Parushev, "Walking in the Dawn of the Light."

65. Such abuses in other contexts have been identified and criticized by scholars working in millennial studies; see Northcott's incisive critique of the use of apocalyptic-eschatology to justify American imperialism in his *Angel Directs the Storm*. The danger of such exploitation in theological discourse in general has been ascertained and discussed at length by Moltmann in his *Crucified God*, 231–322.

66. For examples of apocalyptic-eschatological language being made to serve the interests of the ruling powers, see Northcott, *Angel Directs the Storm*, 75. A historical example of apocalyptic eschatology being used for insurrectionary purposes is the Münster Rebellion of 1534–35; see Arthur, *The Tailor King*.

The conception of a "text" as a site of "convergence of various and potentially contradictory cultural discourses"[67] opens up new perspectives on the broader hermeneutical question of how evangelicals interpret formative texts, pre-eminently the Bible. This was the fundamental "text" for evangelicals in Northern Ireland, as it was and remains for other evangelicals in different contexts.[68] The term, "the Word of God" was used widely by evangelicals from across the denominational spectrum to describe the Bible, especially among those most inclined to perceive the Troubles from an apocalyptic-eschatological perspective. Believing that "holy men of God spake as they were moved by the Holy Ghost" (2 Pet 1:21), evangelicals asserted that "the real Author of Scripture is the Holy Spirit."[69] The Bible, maintained Lurgan Baptist pastor, Denis Lyle, is "the sacred Word from God. It is inspired, it is practical and it is profitable."[70] Ian Paisley made the point somewhat more magniloquently, "The Bible is the Book, the only Book, the unique volume. Other publications are merely books and should always be placed in that category. [The Bible is] . . . the Word of God[,] . . . the revelation of God embalmed in human language."[71]

Maintaining the fundamentalist evangelical conviction that the Bible "alone holds the key to the Christian understanding of history,"[72] it appears that for Paisley the Bible was the *only* text necessary for theological reflection. When he composed his *Exposition of the Epistle to the Romans* during his incarceration in H. M. Prison, Crumlin Road, Paisley revealed that his only references were "my father's Bible—a large Newberry edition, the Englishman's Greek New Testament and Young's Analytical concordance."[73]

The widespread privileging of the Bible to the point of positively excluding all other texts raises significant interpretive and moral questions posed at the beginning of this chapter. For instance, if evangelicals do indeed make a claim for the exceptionality or exclusivity of the Bible,

---

67. Montrose, *Purpose of Playing,* xii.

68. As noted earlier, Bebbington included biblicism as one of four general defining characteristics of evangelicalism.

69. Hanko, "The Sufficiency of Scripture," 1.

70. Lyle, *Countdown to Apocalypse,* 14.

71. Paisley, in *Revivalist* (July, 1977), 2.

72. Reid, "The Problem of the Christian Interpretation," 99.

73. Paisley, *Romans,* 11.

their approach would fall under the poststructuralist critique of appealing illegitimately to an omnipotent, authoritative text, which certain interpreters claim is the "meta-text." Such a notion of meta-textuality thus becomes the paradigmatic exemplar of an authoritative textuality, which sets the hermeneutical rules that govern the interpretation of all other texts. The evangelical appeal to a single, definitive text thus seems to be at variance to the poststructuralist critique of the notion of a single text or context that provides an omnipotent hermeneutical perspective.[74]

The exclusivity of the biblical texts is manifested in the reverential terms employed by evangelicals to signify their allegiance to these writings. For instance, evangelicals from a variety of denominations evinced a profound veneration towards the authority of the Scriptures, which were signified by the lofty appellation, "Word of God." The long tradition of such veneration was manifested in the history and tradition of the Orange orders.[75] One Orange hymn referred to the Bible as "the beacon of hope," which Orangemen would never give up "for all the powers of darkness, the Devil and the Pope."[76] Evangelicals continually reiterated their purported conviction that the Bible, as the unique revelation of God, ought to be the final authority on all matters of faith and practice. Baptist pastor Kenneth Humphries contended that the Bible was "unique among all literature. Though penned by many writers from varied cultures over a span of 15 centuries, it is the masterpiece of a single author, the Creator of the universe."[77] Such elevated conceptions of the Bible were not confined to Ian Paisley or to evangelical Baptist pastors. The paramilitary organization, the Ulster Volunteer Force, claimed to hold a high view of Scripture, which, in their official publications, they referred to as "the inspired Word of God," which was to be preferred to "the uninspired ravings of Marx, Lenin or Connolly."[78] Similarly non-fundamentalist expressions of evangelicalism in Northern Ireland, such as ECONI, evinced a particular veneration for the Bible. In the post-Bel-

74. Acknowledgement to Dr Sam Slote of Trinity College Dublin for this insight.

75. Mitchel, *Religion, Identity and Politics*, 49.

76. "Protestant Hymn." In *Illustrated Orange Song Book*, 18.

77. Humphries, *Battleground of Truth*.

78. *Combat* 2 (April, 1975), 3. This article was written by Billy Mitchell of the UVF Brigade Staff who wrote under the pseudonym, "Richard Cameron." Bruce notes that Mitchell used the pseudonym in order to "signify his attachment to the Scottish covenanting tradition." See Bruce, "Fundamentalism and Political Violence," 400.

fast Agreement (1998) context, David Porter of ECONI maintained that "the Bible remains for us the Word of God, the final authority on matters of faith and practice."[79] Thus although there existed a broad consensus on the authority and inspiration of the biblical texts across the spectrum of Northern Ireland evangelicalism, these groups nevertheless read the texts through a different hermeneutical lens. The fact that such divergent interpretations of the Bible could arise despite a common belief in the divine inspiration of the biblical texts as "the Word of God" indicates the key role of hermeneutics in understanding and accounting for these differences.

Hermeneutical issues pertain not merely to the interpretation of the biblical texts but also to their selection. Although a central tenet of evangelical biblical interpretation was that, "*all* Scripture is given by the inspiration of God, and is profitable for doctrine, for reproof, for correction, for instruction in righteousness" (2 Tim 3:16, emphasis added), there were certain texts which had a particular resonance among certain expressions Northern Ireland evangelicalism. Such texts included those parts of the Bible which contain apocalyptic-eschatological material, most notably the book of Revelation,[80] particularly among groups on the fundamentalist end of the evangelical spectrum.[81]

79. *lion & lamb* (Winter, 1998), 3.

80. It needs also to be acknowledged that biblical scholars have uncovered a variety of early Jewish apocalyptic texts dating from about BC 250 to AD 100 (which are known collectively as the Pseudepigrapha). In many of these texts such figures as Abraham, Moses, and Joshua are identified much more explicitly within an apocalyptic-eschatological framework than is the case in the conventional, canonical Jewish and Christian Scriptures. Since there is virtually no evidence that these apocryphal texts ever influenced Northern Ireland evangelicals during the Troubles, however, it seems reasonable to assume that, despite their apocalyptic-eschatological content, they are not relevant to the present inquiry. It is also important to be aware of the variety of English language Bible translations which were used by Northern Ireland evangelicals during the Troubles. In Northern Ireland the question concerning the translation of the Bible into the English language has provoked a lively and at times vehement debate. My use of the 1611 Authorised Version (or King James Bible) should not be construed as a decision to side with the traditionalists or even as a personal preference but as a recognition of its grandeur and historicity which ensured that this translation retained a particular appeal for many evangelicals in Northern Ireland during the Troubles. The King James was also the translation favored by those Northern Ireland evangelicals who most emphasized the apocalyptic-eschatological teachings of the Scriptures, and so my use of it in this study could rightly be seen as a reflection of my desire to engage with this thought on the terms of these evangelicals themselves.

81. Brewer claims that evangelicals in Northern Ireland exhibit "a preference for

In contrast to the pseudepigrahical texts of the inter-testamental period, the apocalyptic-eschatological portions of the biblical canon, particularly the book of Revelation, were read widely by evangelicals in Northern Ireland. As well as being "the most radical and the most popular text of biblical eschatology,"[82] Revelation was a significant text in the cultures of Northern Ireland evangelicalism during the Troubles. Biblical scholars have emphasized the uniqueness of Revelation among the other books of the New Testament. The distinctiveness of Revelation is recognized by theologians and philosophers[83] to consist in a variety of stylistic and formal attributes, most notably its imaginative and arresting images and symbols, which German scholarship has called "*die prophetische Bildsprache der Apokalypse*" (the prophetic picture-language of the Apocalypse).[84] German theology has also maintained the uniqueness of Revelation as "the only book in the New Testament which has history as its theme."[85] Revelation has thus been construed as a text which sets forth "a metanarrative of universal history."[86] As well as being unusual "in the sheer prolific extent of its visual imagery,"[87] Revelation, as the "Christian conclusion to the prophetic tradition of Israel"[88] and "the most Semitic of all New Testament books,"[89] is also distinguished by its copious allusions to the prophecies of the Hebrew Bible, providing "a glittering array of anti-types to Old Testament texts."[90] It has even been noted that more than half of the verses in Revelation can be traced directly to the Hebrew

Old Testament covenantal theology and New Testament apocalyptic passages." See Robin and Strath, eds., *Homelands*, 284. Old Testament scholarship has examined the close relationship between covenant and eschatology, arguing that each implies and involves the other. See Clements, *Prophecy and Covenant*, 108–9, and *passim*.

82. Keller, *Apocalypse Now and Then*, ix.

83. Derrida recognizes the significance of Revelation as the text "which dominates the whole of Western apocalyptic." See Derrida, "On an Apocalyptic Tone," 50.

84. Langenberg, *Prophetische Bildsprache*. Räpple refers to this distinguishing characteristic of Revelation as "the provocative imagery" of the Apocalypse. See Räpple, *Metaphor of the City*, xiii.

85. Schlier, "Zum Verständnis der Geschichte," 265.

86. Gribben, *Puritan Millennium*, 235.

87. Bauckham, *Theology of the Book of Revelation*, 9.

88. Cohn, *Cosmos, Chaos*, 213.

89. Siew, *War between the Two Beasts*, 10.

90. Fiddes, *Promised End*, 18.

Bible.[91] Ferrei Jenkins claims that, "Revelation is the most thoroughly Jewish in its language and imagery of any New Testament book. This book speaks not the language of Paul, but of the Old Testament prophets Isaiah, Ezekiel, and Daniel."[92]

The prophets listed by Jenkins in this quotation, with the likely exception of Daniel,[93] were active in Israel from the eighth to the sixth centuries before Christ, which, scholars have argued, witnessed the highpoint of the prophetic consciousness of the ancient Israelites.[94] This period also witnessed the prophecies of Amos, Hosea, and Jeremiah. Seeking to account for the development of early Judeo-Christian conceptions of apocalypse, Paul Hanson put forward an original but not infallible argument. In contrast to the prevailing opinion of scholarship at the time, Hanson argued that the development of Jewish apocalyptic eschatology, from which the language of Revelation was derived, was not (*pace* Hans-Dieter Betz and Martin Buber)[95] an invention of second-century visionaries under Egyptian or Persian influences[96] but was deeply embedded in the prophetic tradition from the times of the earliest prophecies of the Hebrew Bible. Thus despite his allegiance (albeit not an uncritical one) to the "deprivation thesis," there is nevertheless an important theoretical point of coalescence between my approach and that of Hanson's, in so far as he is led to the conclusion that the apocalyptic-eschatological language of the Hebrew prophets arose not solely as a contextual response to contemporary events but out of an awakening of a prophetic consciousness derived from an ancient textual tradition.[97]

Although the world of Jewish apocalyptic eschatology may seem to be far removed from twentieth-century evangelicalism in Northern Ireland, one of the recurring motifs of Northern Ireland evangelical interpretations of apocalyptic-eschatological texts was the identification

91. Holtz, "Sprache als Metapher," 11.

92. Jenkins, *Old Testament in the Book of Revelation*, 22.

93. According to Hammer, there seems to be something of a scholarly consensus on the point that the book of Daniel was produced during the second century BC; see Hammer, *Book of Daniel*, 3.

94. Wheeler Robinson, *Christian Experience*, 142.

95. Buber, *Kampf um Israel*.

96. Kippenberg, "Die Geschichte der Mittelpersischen Apokalyptischen Traditionen," 49–80.

97. Hanson, *Dawn of Apocalyptic*, 282, 402, and *passim*.

of the fate of ancient Israel and that of contemporary "Ulster." In some instances the implications of this identification were carried through to posit the notion that a direct biological genealogical continuity between the ancient Israelites and contemporary British people. "We Ulster people," claimed Alan Campbell, one of the most outspoken British-Israelite evangelicals in Northern Ireland, "are . . . the literal flesh and blood seed and descendants of the patriarchs Abraham, Isaac and Jacob[,] . . . we are the seed of Israel . . . of the ten tribes."[98] In other instances the identification was used metaphorically in order to provide a prophetic perspective from which to interpret the self-perception of many evangelicals in Northern Ireland as an embattled minority of God's people in the midst of hostile powers. The conviction that the apocalyptic-eschatological biblical texts, such as Revelation, applied directly to them in their predicaments also endowed these texts with considerable influence and significance. The theologian Ian Boxall, in his commentary on John's Apocalypse, notes that for many Christians, "Revelation is a gift for God's people of the last days, not a historical relic of a bygone age. In short, it is a text about the eschatological future which threatens at any time to break into the present, and therefore calls for an urgent response on the part of its readers."[99]

This approach can be perceived in certain Northern Ireland evangelical interpretations of apocalyptic-eschatological texts, such as Revelation 16, which, according to Ivan Foster, presents "a resume of the events that will mark the end of the age."[100] It will be shown that this was how many evangelicals in Northern Ireland during the Troubles interpreted apocalyptic-eschatological texts, above all that "enigmatic book"[101]—the book of Revelation.

Consider the imagery and symbolism which characterize the book of Revelation: four terrifying horsemen bringing death and destruction in their wake (6:2–8), anguished scenes of people crying out to the rocks to crush them to death (6:16); torrents of blood flooding the earth (16:4); hordes of demonic locusts rising out of a dark abyss and smiting earth's anguished inhabitants (9:2–10); a ferocious dragon, the sweep of whose tail sets one third of the stars in the firmament careening off

98. Campbell, "The Anglo-Irish Agreement."

99. Boxall, *Revelation*, 106.

100. Foster, *Antichrist*, 156.

101. *Frontiers* (Winter, 1999), 22.

their course (12:3–4); a prostitute dressed in scarlet and purple riding a beast with seven heads and ten horns and carrying a cup containing all manner of filth and grime (17:3–4); carnivorous birds gorging themselves on the flesh of slain warriors (19:21); lakes of unquenchable fire into which people and demons are cast together (19:20; 20:10, 14–15; 21:8)—all these fearful and, sometimes, violent images express the terror that is typically evoked from reading the book of Revelation.[102] The violent imagery and the alleged vicious pleasure that the author takes in the contemplation of the violent downfall of the powerful provoked Nietzsche into characterizing Revelation as "the most rabid outburst of vindictiveness in all recorded history."[103]

Yet these depictions of disaster, desolation, and condemnation are set alongside the following images of restoration, compassion, and consummation: a slain lamb whose sacrifice has redeemed the world from sin (5:6) and who leads God's people to "living fountains of waters" (7:17); new heavens and a new earth (21:1); a magnificent "New Jerusalem" descending from the clouds (21:2); life-giving rivers of healing waters and a tree of life whose leaves have the power to heal nations (22:2); gates of pearls and walls of precious stones (21:18–21); a redeemed community whose incandescent countenances reflect the radiance of the heavenly city (22:4–5); and a compassionate God who comes to dwell in the midst of his people (21:3) and who wipes the tear-stained faces of the countless myriad of those who are invited to participate in the life of the New Jerusalem (7:17; 21:4), to experience the eternal joy of God's presence and to reign with him "forever and ever" (22:5).

The recurrent juxtaposition of horror and healing, disaster and delight, fury and forgiveness, helplessness and hope that characterize apocalyptic-eschatological writings, corresponds with the variations in the interpretive responses evoked from Northern Ireland evangelical readings of texts such as Revelation. While some saw in Revelation a transformative manifesto for social justice to be realized in the "here-

102. Such passages have often led critics to oppose or reject the book. Pippin complains that "the Apocalypse is full of terror and torture. I resist this ancient text, as I resist contemporary contexts of horror." See Pippin, Apocalyptic Bodies, 121, 125. A counter-argument to Pippin's protest can be found in Barr, Reality of Apocalypse, 256–59; and by Räpple, Metaphor of the City, 23–24.

103. Nietzsche, quoted in Hays, Moral Vision of the New Testament, 169. For a Nietzschean reading of the Apocalypse which sees the text as a perverse manifestation of a frustrated will to power, see Lawrence, Apocalypse.

and-now," others perceived only an exhortation to remain faithful in the midst of apparent perpetual degradation and apostasy. Their vocation was to "shine like stars in the midst of a crooked and perverse generation" (Phil 2:15). Believing that "the whole world lieth in wickedness" (1 John 5:19), many denied the efficacy of human endeavors to ameliorate social ills through social activism or political engagement on the ground that such efforts would prove ineffectual against the ineluctable onslaught of the satanic figure of Antichrist in the last days. Furthermore, these endeavors would distract evangelicals from the apparent priority of saving souls from the wrath to come.[104] Since the biblical texts supposedly prophesied a process of interminable decline in the state of the world until the second coming, many evangelicals believed that their energies should be invested exclusively in conversion activities. Any attempt to bring renewal or change to the social order, so it seemed, would be a futile gesture, akin to polishing the brass on a sinking ship.[105]

Thus in some instances apocalyptic-eschatological texts served as a conduit for political apathy among Northern Ireland evangelicals.[106] Hopes were directed not towards worldly transformation through social activism but a cataclysmic and forceful imposition of the divine will through supernatural intervention. At times despair over the Troubles reached such levels that it became commonplace among many Northern Ireland evangelicals to believe that the situation was "so serious that only prayer, repentance and Divine intervention can save us."[107] Such deliverance had an apocalyptic dimension which was drawn from the major themes of the book of Revelation, including the beast (Rev 13), mystery Babylon (Rev 17 and 18) and the messianic warrior on the white horse (Rev 19). As Alan Campbell put it: "Just as William of Orange . . . delivered God's people . . . by the overthrow of priestcraft, popery and tyrannized power, so in like manner He who is great David's greater Son is coming again to cut short the days of tribulation, to save His own elect people and destroy Mystery Babylon."[108]

104. See, for example, *Irish Baptist* (March, 1991), 10–11; *Protestant Telegraph* 10 (28 May, 1966), 10.

105. Gribben, *Writing the Rapture*, 6. Gribben attributes this image to the American evangelist, D. L. Moody (1837–99).

106. Gribben, "Protestant Millennialism," 55.

107. Campbell, *For What Should Ulster Pray?*, 4.

108. Campbell, *Let the Orange Banner Speak*, 30.

Although not every evangelical church would have agreed with these particular interpretations, Northern Ireland evangelicals generally shared an often uncritical assumption that the images and symbols of biblical apocalyptic-eschatological texts were somehow not limited to the specific circumstances in which they were originally created. These texts were assumed to possess the capacity to break out of the original context and to become hermeneutically re-appropriated to their own contexts. Evangelicals interpreted apocalyptic-eschatological texts in this way in order to provide a transcendent perspective on the contemporary events and thus to yield a supposedly prophetic insight on an apparent deeper significance of the developments taking place in the world around them. For instance, in the case of the Scarlet Woman of Revelation 17 and 18, Northern Ireland evangelicals, despite their differences, tended to attribute her identity to contemporary manifestations of social or ecclesial depravity.[109]

The notion that the book of Revelation has been a significant influence in the formation of evangelical identity in Northern Ireland is established by the ubiquitous allusions to passages of the Apocalypse in the texts produced by leading evangelicals from a variety of denominations. Some evangelicals even went so far as to assert the primacy of Revelation as a book of "special significance" among the other books of the canon.[110] In contrast to those who found its imagery and symbolism to be "obscure," the Free Presbyterian minister, Ivan Foster, discovered in Revelation "much that was eminently practical."[111] Concluding his commentary, Foster maintained that Revelation "stands in eminence above other Scripture, since it is the closing word of the canon of Holy Scripture."[112]

---

109. The next chapter will include examples of such identifications.

110. Foster, *Shadow of the Antichrist*, 7. At the other end of the evangelical spectrum in Northern Ireland, the Baptist pastor David McMillan deemed Revelation to be important enough to merit selection as the subject of his MPhil thesis, which is an intriguing work that provides a rare example of an evangelical writing from personal experience to argue for an alternative to the supposedly facile sensationalism of speculative futurist approaches which often dominated evangelical interpretations of biblical apocalyptic-eschatology in Northern Ireland. McMillan thus wrote of the pressing need to "retrieve the Apocalypse from the grip of the extremes of futuristic speculation or moribund literary criticism"; McMillan "The Role of the Seven Beatitudes," 167.

111. Foster, *Shadow of the Antichrist*, 5, 12.

112. Ibid., 230.

Ian Paisley's preference for apocalyptic-eschatological texts was demonstrated by his frequent use of passages from Revelation in sermons in order to expound other biblical texts. A notable example was in 1967 when Paisley preached on the stories of the patriarchs in the book of Genesis. A journalist from the socialist republican paper, the *Irish Democrat*, who witnessed the sermon offered the following observations,

> The lesson was taken from the Book of Genesis. . . . From Genesis to Revelations [*sic*] he wandered freely, but it was clear when he reached the latter book he was on his most familiar and sympathetic ground. The Apocalypse has always provided food for prophets and for this modern prophet of anti-Catholicism [Paisley] it proves rich indeed. To him the central figure of the Apocalypse, the Great Beast or Babylon, is none other than the Roman Catholic Church itself, and he interprets the modern Ecumenical Movement as the extension of the rule of the Great Beast over all the tribes of earth that is foretold in the Apocalypse for the latter days of the world.[113]

If we can credit the accuracy of this journalist, this observation affords an illuminating insight into how Paisley interpreted even non-apocalyptic texts such as Genesis from an over-arching prophetic framework offered by the book of Revelation, which also determined Paisley's hostile attitude towards the Catholic Church.

Other Northern Ireland evangelicals similarly commented on the apocalyptic-eschatological themes of Revelation in order to expound other biblical texts. In a theological commentary on the minor prophet, Haggai, the Baptist pastor, Sam Gordon, interprets the text of Haggai 2:9 ("'and in this place I will grant peace', declares the Lord Almighty") as a prophecy concerning the second coming of Christ—a meaning not immediately apparent in the original text. Commenting on this text, Gordon writes that "the prophet was doubtless again looking down over the centuries to the moment when in a later Temple, the Messiah will speak peace to all who seek him."[114] The adoption of apocalyptic-eschatological themes in order to expound such books as Haggai, is indicative of the use of apocalyptic-eschatological texts such as Revelation as a framework with which to interpret other biblical texts. In other words,

---

113. The journalist's article was republished in the *Protestant Telegraph* (4 February, 1967), 5.

114. Gordon, *Moving On With God*, 95.

apocalyptic-eschatological biblical passages became at once both texts to read and contextual paradigms through which to read other texts.

My claim is that evangelicals used an apocalyptic-eschatological contextual paradigm not only to interpret other (apocalyptic and non-apocalyptic) biblical texts but also other non-verbal "texts" such as the decisive events in the political, social and cultural history of the Troubles. Thus, when speaking of the notion of a "text" we must not confine ourselves to the analysis of literary or biblical texts.[115] The kind of rules that govern the production of texts correspond to the discursive practices of human rituals and institutions. As Clifford Geertz has pointed out, a symbol, a ritual, or an event, like a written text, can be made to yield a multiplicity of meanings and significance.[116] The privileging of apocalyptic-eschatological material as the hermeneutical key to unlock the meaning of the other biblical texts likewise invites criticism from poststructuralist hermeneutics, which repudiate any such interpretive bias which elevates one type of genre to the status of a paradigm for the interpretation of other portions of the text.

The ubiquitous use of apocalyptic-eschatological texts such as Revelation as an interpretive paradigm with which to interpret non-apocalyptic "texts" was a tendency that extended beyond the Free Presbyterian Church of Ulster. Texts produced by the Irish Baptists likewise affirmed the significance of Revelation. The lukewarmness of the Laodicean church in Revelation 3:16, remarked one evangelical Baptist, "mirrors so accurately the materialistic values that predominate in our thinking today." The book of Revelation, he continued, is "more relevant than tomorrow's newspapers."[117]

Although the book of Revelation was the pre-eminent text of Northern Ireland evangelical apocalyptic eschatology, there were other apocalyptic-eschatological biblical texts that became prominent in

115. On this point see Ricoeur, *Hermeneutics and the Human Sciences*, 197–221. Commenting on Ricoeur, Rowan Williams notes that he widens the notion of textual interpretation to include "all systems of significant human action, capable of interpretation through present responses of significant action." See Williams, *Wrestling with Angels*, 97.

116. This conviction was expounded through an intriguing analysis of the rituals and ceremonies associated with Balinese cockfights in Geertz, *Interpretation of Cultures*, 412–53.

117. *Irish Baptist* (March, 1985), 3. Similarly Alan Campbell referred to the "Laodicean church age in which we live"; Campbell, *Light from Nahum*, 4.

Northern Ireland evangelical cultures during the Troubles. Many evangelicals, disavowing the distinction that theologians since Marcion of Sinope (c. 85–c. 160) have posited between "the vengeful tribal god of the early Old Testament and the God who is revealed as self-giving Love through Jesus Christ,"[118] insisted that the Hebrew Bible was just as much the "Word of God" as the writings of Matthew, Mark, Luke, John, and Paul. As one evangelical writing for the *Larne Guardian* put it in a letter entitled, "Old Testament Cannot be Dismissed": "the Old Testament, no less than the New is the inspired word of God."[119]

Biblical apocalyptic eschatology is not restricted to the book of Revelation or to the New Testament. In the 1960s German scholarship began systematically to demonstrate that the Yahwistic theology of covenant and promise found in the Hebrew Bible[120] was heavily impregnated with the language of apocalyptic eschatology.[121] In recent years biblical scholars have done much to uncover the ways in which the apocalyptic-eschatological vision of Revelation was influenced by the writings of the Hebrew Bible prophets such as Jeremiah,[122] Ezekiel,[123] Isaiah,[124] Daniel,[125] and Zechariah.[126] The great extent to which the author of Revelation

---

118. Thatcher, *Savage Text*, 59.

119. *Larne Guardian* (6 October, 1988), 10.

120. The use the term "Hebrew Bible" rather than "Old Testament" follows a scholarly convention which criticizes the latter term on account of its being an arbitrary Christian designation. I use the former term in the knowledge that not all of what is called the "Hebrew Bible" was written in Hebrew; some books and passages were written in Aramaic (e.g., Ezra 4:8—6:18; 7:12–26; Jer 10:11; Dan 2:4—7:28). For an up-to-date discussion of the conventions surrounding the uses of these terms, see Routledge, *Old Testament Theology*, 18–22.

121. Preuss, *Jahwehglaube und Zukunftserwartung*; Mueller, *Urspruenge und Strukturen*. An important forerunner to these works was Gressmann, *Ursprung der israelitisch-jüdischen Eschatologie*. The third volume of Bloch's *Principle of Hope* (1236–41) also contains an illuminating treatment of the apocalyptic dimension of Moses' teaching.

122. Mounce, *Book of Revelation*, 209, 287, 306–11.

123. Vanhoye, "L'utilisation du livre d'Ezéchiel," 436–76; Ruiz, *Ezekiel in the Apocalypse*.

124. Fekkes, *Isaiah and Prophetic Traditions*.

125. Beale, *Use of Daniel in Jewish Apocalyptic Literature*.

126. Jauhiainen, *Use of Zechariah in Revelation*.

borrows from these biblical authors highlights the conceptual interrelation among the texts of apocalyptic eschatology.[127]

Despite these overlaps, however, there are few biblical scholars today who would contend that the biblical texts constitute a complete and unitary conception of apocalyptic eschatology. There are disparities even within the Gospel accounts. Whereas for Matthew, Mark, and Luke, apocalyptic eschatology appears as a temporal category or as a process which unfolds in the course of history, eschatological themes in John's Gospel take on quite a different form of expression. Biblical scholarship has noted that the Johannine eschatology "brings its own peculiar set of problems."[128] As Joseph Ratzinger explains, apocalyptic eschatology is understood by the author of the Fourth Gospel to be a category of existence (*eine Existenzkategorie*), which deals with the question of "authenticity" (*Eigentlichkeit*).[129] John presents a vision of eschatology in which judgment and salvation are conceived not as episodes yet to occur at some indeterminate point within historical time but rather as either present realities or as events which have already taken place (cf. John 3:18; 5:25; 12:31).[130] Thus apocalyptic eschatology ceases to be, as Paul Tillich put it, "an imaginative matter about an indefinitely far (or near) catastrophe in time and space and becomes an expression of our standing in every moment in face of the eternal, though in a particular mode of time."[131] Whilst the specific details of the differences and similarities between the diverse biblical texts may be left to biblical scholars, any

127. Bauckham also helpfully identifies important points of similarity between Revelation and the extracanonical Jewish apocalypses; see Bauckham, *Climax of Prophecy*, 38–91.

128. Hayes, *Visions of a Future*, 59; see also Kysar, *John, the Maverick Gospel*, 99–112.

129. Ratzinger, *Eschatologie*, 42. This perspective is commonly associated with Bultmann and his *Gospel of John*. This thesis was advanced by Dodd's controversial notion of "realized eschatology," which asserted that, "'The eschaton has moved from the future to the present, from the sphere of expectation into that of realised experience'"; see Dodd, *Parables of the Kingdom*, 50. Balthasar attributes the lack of any sustained reference to John's Gospel in the *Theology of Hope* to Moltmann's opposition to realized eschatology; Balthasar, *Theo-Drama*, V:169.

130. Despite this emphasis on the present reality of the eschaton, John does retain a notion of a future eschatological consummation in the "last day" (John 5:28–29; 6:39–40; 44, 54).

131. Tillich, *Systematic Theology*, III:395. Notwithstanding these influential arguments, commentators generally agree that the eschatology of John's Gospel does not relinquish the future entirely; see Macquarrie, *Principles of Christian Theology*, 355; Barrett, *Gospel according to St. John*, 179.

serious literary-theoretical inquiry into the use of apocalyptic eschatology by evangelicals during the Troubles must at least recognize both the extent of the interrelation as well as the disparities that exist between the biblical apocalyptic-eschatological texts.

Like the book of Revelation, many of the prophecies contained in the Hebrew Bible exhibit a recurrent juxtaposition of hope and fear, tribulation and consolation. Northern Ireland evangelicals understood well that several of the themes and characters of Revelation find their parallels both in the prophecies of the Hebrew Bible and other passages from the New Testament. As the Baptist pastor Sam Gordon put it, "Whatever the New Testament writers understood about the day of the Lord, they gleaned their info [*sic*] from the Old Testament prophets."[132] Similarly the Anglican evangelical, Ron Elsdon, recognized that "Revelation is steeped in references to the Old Testament."[133] Many Northern Ireland evangelicals sought to piece together various biblical passages from the New Testament and the Hebrew Bible in order to develop a coherent account of the predicted end-times events. These accounts focused especially on certain salient apocalyptic themes, including prophecies concerning the Antichrist, the Great Tribulation, the Day of the Lord, the Final Judgment and the life in the hereafter.

The Antichrist was a seemingly omnipresent figure of Northern Ireland apocalyptic eschatology during the Troubles.[134] He was invoked in a variety of contexts using an equally variegated selection of biblical texts. The most commonly-cited text in relation to the Antichrist among evangelicals in this period was the text of 2 Thessalonians 2:2–7, which because of its saliency, is worth quoting at length:

> The day of Christ is at hand. Let no man deceive you by any means: for that day shall not come, except there come a falling away first, and that man of sin be revealed, the son of perdition; who opposeth and exalteth himself above all that is called God, or that is worshipped; so that he as God sitteth in the temple of God, shewing himself that he is God . . . For the mystery of iniquity doth already work.

Patrick Mitchel rightly observes that evangelical allusions to the "mystery of iniquity" and the "powerful delusion" have often served to com-

132. Gordon, *Hope and Glory*, 181.

133. Elsdon, *The Lamb Wins*, 35.

134. Gribben, "Protestant Millennialism," 51.

pound evangelical anxiety that the Catholic Church planned to destroy the constitution of "Protestant Ulster."[135] This text was read in conjunction with an array of biblical passages. Commenting on the text of the "idle shepherd" of Zechariah 11, the British-Israelite Pentecostal pastor, Alan Campbell, preached that,

> Throughout the Scriptures we are warned by the prophets and by the apostles against false shepherds. Paul called him the man of sin. John in his letters called him Antichrist. Daniel called him a little horn. John the Revelator called him the beast and Zechariah here calls him the idle shepherd.[136]

Thus the "man of sin" of 2 Thessalonians was regarded widely as the same individual depicted alike in 1 John 2:18, Daniel 7:8 and 8:9, Zechariah 11:17, and Revelation 13.[137] At the end of Zechariah's prophecy the combined armies of Antichrist lay siege to Jerusalem but are annihilated in a great wave of apocalyptic ferment. God intervenes to smite the armies with a "terrible disease," which causes the flesh of soldiers to rot away and their tongues and eyes to rot in their sockets (Zech 14:12). This depiction of God's people defeating their foes against overwhelming odds through the supernatural intervention of God in a final apocalyptic conflagration was an image which resonated powerfully with the fears and hopes of many evangelicals in Northern Ireland during the Troubles.

Contextualization and Crisis

The fact that these biblical apocalyptic-eschatological texts possessed a distinctive resonance among Northern Ireland evangelicals who identified their own plight with the context of the besieged Israelites of the Old Testament reminds us of the need to give appropriate attention to the importance of context as a shaping factor in evangelical interpretations of such texts. Scholars from a wide range of disciplinary perspectives have become increasingly interested in the notion of contextualization as a means towards gaining a more comprehensive understanding of the

135. Mitchel, *Evangelicalism*, 155.

136. Campbell, "Zechariah's Antichrist Prophecy."

137. In October 2009, the claim that the Antichrist of John's epistles was the same as the man of sin depicted in 2 Thessalonians 2 was still being made and published on Northern Ireland evangelical websites. The website of the Evangelical Protestant Society affirmed that, "We believe the Man of Sin to be the Antichrist."

meaning and significance of their primary texts. As a result of the linguistic theories developed by Wittgenstein and expounded by Anglophone analytical philosophers, it is widely acknowledged that communicative acts are grounded in grammars of meaning, which constitute "systems of rules for pairing semantic and phonetic interpretations,"[138] which are rooted in the circumstances of the formation of speech acts.[139] Context has thus been identified as an indispensible factor in explaining the meaning of communicative action.[140] It is now widely acknowledged that important insights concerning the meaning of a text can be gained through the "historical reconstruction of the life-world within which the language [of the text] acquires its proper currency."[141] The notion that theological ideas are birthed in contexts of crisis arising out of a sense of alienation and disillusionment is at least as old as Hegel and Marx. Marx was the first major thinker to contend with thoroughness and systematic analysis the great extent to which social consciousness is determined by social being.[142] In the field of biblical studies, the significance of context has been acknowledged widely for several decades. Biblical scholars have learned from leading philosophers of language by recognizing "the centrality of the literary and historical context, that is, the linguistic and extra-linguistic dimension, to the whole issue of meaning. . . . [T]he semantic analysis of a concept involves not only syntax, but also the historical-cultural background behind the statement."[143]

Contextual approaches thus look beyond the formal unity of the text under investigation and focus on the cultural context in which certain texts were interpreted and in which they acquired a particular semantic currency based on the historical experience of the interpreters.[144] By focusing on the dynamics of social change and how such transitions have affected particular groups, the historical-contextual model endeav-

138. Chomsky, "Symposium on Innate Ideas," 123.

139. Wittgenstein, *Zettel*, §67.

140. Vanhoozer, *Meaning in This Text*, 250.

141. Thiselton, *New Horizons*, 561. These notions have been extended by certain theologians to the extent that it has been claimed that all theology is an inherently contextual enterprise. See Bevans, *Models of Contextual Theology*, 3, 8 and *passim*.

142. In reality Marx's conception of the relationship between ideas and the social conditions out of which they arise is much more complicated than many crude summaries of Marx's thought often suggest, as Rigby notes in his *Marxism and History*, 281.

143. Osbourne, *Hermeneutical Cycle*, 83.

144. Jeanrond, *Text and Interpretation*, 6.

ors to elucidate the often complex interaction between hermeneutical reception and the material conditions of text production in order to identify instances of continuity and discontinuity in the way in which a particular group has interpreted basic texts.

Although contextual considerations cannot be disregarded in this study, the correlation between the Troubles and the crisis theology of Northern Ireland evangelicalism was by no means a simple relationship of cause and effect. In their zeal to establish the contextual origins of discourse, previous scholarly engagement with evangelicalism in Northern Ireland has neglected to consider that apocalyptic-eschatological language itself, as an interpretive paradigm through which to read "texts," also took on contextual attributes. Thus, despite the considerable advances made by contextual approaches to our understanding of the social conditions in which such language flourishes, we must not forget that apocalyptic-eschatological texts are not merely words arising from certain contexts; they are living and active vectors of meaning, produced ultimately not by contexts or traditions but by individuals whose reasons for invoking these texts are grounded in a complex matrix of motivations pertaining to their existential, communal and anastatic convictions.[145] As dynamic repositories of semantic substance, texts can in themselves be said to constitute a context or a framework of interpretation. This context during the Troubles was one of crisis. However, rather than simply being used in response to specific instances of crisis, apocalyptic-eschatological language became active in determining evangelical perceptions of the crisis.

The concept of crisis is also pertinent to our inquiry into the function of apocalyptic-eschatological language in Northern Ireland during the Troubles. As a corollary to the main thesis concerning the complex relationship between text and context, another important point is that rather than being a response to a particular instance of crisis, the apocalyptic-eschatological language of the Bible for evangelicals informed how they understood their context crisis. In other words, evangelicals were able to interpret the Troubles as a decisive time of crisis because they perceived in some of the leading events and developments of the time the fulfilment of ancient prophecy which was articulated accord-

145. See McClendon, *Ethics,* chapters 1 and 2. In volume two of his systematic theological trilogy McClendon defines such convictions as the "enduring, basic beliefs that typify cultures"; McClendon, *Doctrine,* 54.

ing to the concepts and symbolism of apocalyptic eschatology, which is the biblical language of crisis. The kind of crisis with which the evangelicals believed themselves to be confronted was thus conditioned by their interpretation of the Bible, in particular apocalyptic-eschatological prophecies concerning the "end-times." The biblical texts thus became formative of the contexts against which evangelicals interpreted the events of the Troubles.

Philosophers have elucidated some of the main elements of "crisis" both as a category of existential dislocation and as a kind of social disruption. At the heart of a crisis is a breakdown of epistemological norms through their exposure to new circumstances to which they no longer correspond. Epistemological crises, argues Alasdair MacIntyre, arise when an individual "comes to recognize the possibility of systematically different possibilities of interpretation, of the existence of alternative and rival schemata which yield mutually incompatible accounts of what is going on around him."[146] Emphasizing continuity, MacIntyre insists that an epistemological crisis is resolved "only by the construction of a new narrative which enables the agent to understand both how he or she could have held his or her original beliefs and how he or she could have been so drastically misled by them."[147] The resolution of an epistemological crisis, therefore, always awaits the emergence of an alternative narrative that can give a perspective on the shortcomings of the previous narrative and that also yields new insights and proposals for how to progress.

Since these moments of epistemological dislocation can yield such insights, the notion of crisis, despite its connotations of chaos, discontinuity and disorder, must not be considered solely or even primarily under its baneful aspects. Arthur Liebert made the sage comment that "a time without a crisis is a dead time as a man without a crisis is a dead man."[148] Thomas Kuhn insisted that "crises are a necessary precondition for the emergence of novel theories."[149] What Liebert said about human existence and Kuhn maintained about crises in intellectual paradigms can be said a fortiori when applied to narrative conceptions of faith as understood from the apocalyptic-eschatological perspective of an

146. MacIntyre, "Epistemological Crises," 139.

147. Ibid., 140.

148. Liebert, quoted in *Bambach, Heidegger*, 39.

149. Kuhn, *Structure of Scientific Revolutions*, 77.

evangelical community, such as those in Northern Ireland during the Troubles. After crisis comes the period of consummation and hope and the period of crisis was seen as an indispensible prerequisite to its realization.

At first it may appear that the kind of theology that emerged from the Troubles and which derived considerable inspiration from apocalyptic-eschatological biblical texts was a product of the volatile context of crisis which engulfed Northern Ireland in this period. It may be claimed that evangelical pastors and theologians produced a kind of apocalyptic theology which reflected the crisis of the time. As Alister McGrath claims, "The theologian, in common with every other inhabitant of the flux of history, finds himself or herself within a tradition—an inherited complex of symbols, values and pre-understandings which fixes a world-view and functions as a framework for communication, in which the past obstinately impresses itself upon the present."[150] This statement applies to present-day literary theorists and theologians just as much as it does to those who are the subject of their investigations. Nevertheless the truth of this statement and the lucidity with which it is expressed should not blind us to the importance of the texts themselves as factors which were formative of the apocalyptic-eschatological convictions of Northern Ireland evangelicals, which in turn affected how these people responded to their context. Moreover, many evangelicals in Northern Ireland would have had little immediate experience of the Troubles. For some of them, their experience was shaped by the apocalyptic-eschatological texts and by commentators, pastors and politicians who drew on these texts. This exposure to the language of apocalyptic eschatology gave them a vocabulary with which to express their hopes and fears. In other words, their experience of the Troubles was shaped by the biblical texts. Thus in order to understand the formative influence of apocalyptic-eschatological texts on the evangelical cultures of Northern Ireland it is necessary first to consider the context of the Northern Ireland Troubles in relation to the salient biblical apocalyptic-eschatological texts identified above.

In 1981 as part of the "Day of Action" campaign to galvanise resistance to the perceived existential threat posed by Republicans to the constitutional status of Northern Ireland, Ian Paisley and his followers published a poster which declared in large, bold print that, "The Crisis of

150. McGrath, *Genesis of Doctrine*, 81.

our Generation is Now Upon Us."[151] Such attitudes were not confined to Paisley and the Free Presbyterian Church. Evangelicals across the whole denominational spectrum identified the Northern Ireland Troubles as a period of unprecedented crisis, which was perceived as a contemporary fulfilment of what had been prophesied particularly in the apocalyptic-eschatological biblical writings. Commenting on the violence and bloodshed of Bloody Sunday and the murderous reprisals and counter-reprisals which followed, the Presbyterian Church in Ireland referred to "the disregard for law and order" in Northern Ireland and maintained that, "This orgy of lawlessness is . . . the natural outcome of deep-rooted tendencies in our thinking which have affected alike our religion and our law. It is a breakdown in the moral character of our people."[152]

The sense of crisis was reflected in the official publications of leading evangelical churches and para-church organizations such as the Orange Order. A 1982 issue of the Orange Standard alluded to the "lawlessness and prevalence of evil practices" and lamented that, "spiritual life has disappeared, and as chapels have closed, bingo halls, social clubs and strip clubs have mushroomed."[153] Eleven years later, the same magazine maintained its lament over the "lawlessness and a sadistic violence" with which Northern Ireland had apparently been overrun.[154] The evangelical churches were equally conscious of the context of crisis in which they lived. The Portadown Baptist pastor, Denis Lyle, bewailed the "moral corruption, spiritual apostasy, widespread lawlessness" and the "blatant promiscuity" which had become "the order of the day."[155] In August 1970, the front page of the Protestant Telegraph led with an article which asserted that Northern Ireland was in "a perilous state; law and order has [sic] broken down and the "no-go" lands remain unpoliced."[156] Likewise, the editorial of a 1988 edition of the *New Protestant Telegraph* drew attention to the multifaceted nature of the continuing crisis of the Troubles:

151. "Day of Action" poster, published in *Protestant Telegraph* (21 November, 1981), 3.

152. Committee on National and International Problems, *Christians in a Situation of Conflict*, 189.

153. *Orange Standard* (March, 1982), 1.

154. *Orange Standard* (April, 1993), 6.

155. Lyle, *Countdown*, 30.

156. *Protestant Telegraph* 29 (August, 1970), 1.

> The dark shadow of lawlessness and the darkest shadow of all,
> the shadow of terrorist killings lie across our Province. We have
> a Prime Minister who has sold us. We have a Government which
> has destroyed us. We have a Parliament which has betrayed us.
> We have Security Forces which are not permitted to defend us.
> We have Churches which have misled us.[157]

Regardless of what we may make of these remarks, they do go beyond the crude proof-texting methods which often characterized the analysis of current affairs in evangelical publications during the Troubles. Although not explicitly derived from any specific biblical text, the language is redolent of biblical themes of lawlessness. In this connection, the "dark shadow of lawlessness" may well be a conscious allusion to the "man of sin" of 2 Thessalonians 2:7 but the phrase is used in such a way as to appeal to a broader base of political supporters beyond the fundamentalist core of Northern Ireland evangelicalism.[158]

"Few books could be more relevant to our present situation than the Revelation given to John toward the close of the 1st Century," wrote one of the contributors to the Irish Baptist magazine in 1978. "It is a message of boundless hope," he continued, "given to a persecuted church, which was struggling to spread its wings in the midst of a hostile and changing world."[159] By supplying an apocalyptic-eschatological perspective on the tragic and often violent events of the Troubles, passages from Revelation, 2 Thessalonians and other biblical apocalyptic-eschatological prophecies concerning end times events and personages were regarded by Northern Ireland evangelicals as timely texts for a contemporary crisis.

Such passages offer a perspective on the important issue of the considerable influence of Revelation on Northern Ireland evangelicals. Many discerned what were to their minds certain unambiguous parallels between their own plight as a besieged Christian remnant amid the prevailing apostasy associated with the Troubles and the plight of the early Christian church amid the terror of Roman imperial tyranny, as described throughout the book of Revelation.[160] As Terence McCaughey

---

157. *New Protestant Telegraph* (September, 1988), 2.

158. The *New International Version* translates this phrase as "the secret power of lawlessness."

159. *Irish Baptist* (December, 1978), 15.

160. The imperial first-century context of Revelation is examined in depth in Kraybill, *Imperial Cult and Commerce*.

has argued, the perception of living in an "historical cul-de-sac," which engendered a pessimistic assessment of their plight, often exacerbated the fear that evangelicals were living in the end times.[161] This was the experience of many Northern Ireland evangelicals during the Troubles. Referring to Jesus' letters to the angels of the seven churches in the second and third chapters of the Revelation, one evangelical observer noted that, "The background to these letters may be the ancient world of the Roman Empire, and some of the names given to the problems may be unfamiliar, but a closer look shows an astonishing similarity to our own situation."[162] Even the interpretations of leading Northern Ireland evangelicals, which were ostensibly general theological commentaries on biblical passages, were full of references to the crisis of the Northern Ireland Troubles. The crisis of the Troubles lurks conspicuously behind Ivan Foster's commentary on the book of Revelation, which contains references to the "terror stricken land" of "Ulster"[163] as well as the alleged villainy of contemporary political leaders such as Gerry Adams and Martin McGuinness, all of which were perceived as manifestations of the great tribulation outlined in Revelation 6–19.[164]

Despite such evident references to the context of crisis, much of the theological reflection on apocalyptic eschatology by Northern Ireland evangelicals was not so much a response to specific events as it was a pre-determined framework through which these events were interpreted. Historians of Ireland have uncovered pervasive strands of millennial discourse which were deeply woven into the fabric of Irish history. These studies imply that apocalyptic language was not a product of specific instances of political crises but functioned as a set framework through which to interpret the apparent prophetic significance of prevailing social events and trends. For instance, this scholarship has done much to uncover the substance and influence of millennial discourses in eighteenth- and nineteenth-century Ireland. Challenging the prevailing opinion established by such scholars as Patrick O'Farrell[165] and Terence Brown[166] that Ireland in the nineteenth century witnessed very little mil-

161. McCaughey, *Memory and Redemption*, 44.
162. *Irish Baptist* (September, 1984), 4 (emphasis added).
163. Foster, *Shadow*, 13.
164. Ibid., 95.
165. O'Farrell, "Millennialism, Messianism and Utopianism," 45–68.
166. Brown, "The Church of Ireland," 49–64.

lennial ferment, Irene Whelan contends that "the prophecies of Pastorini, which coincided with the ascendancy of Captain Rock, contained many of the ingredients of a well-developed millenarian tradition."[167] Other historians have uncovered the influence of millenarian belief in the shaping of crucial events in Irish history, such as the Rebellion of the United Irishmen in 1798.[168] Recent studies have demonstrated the widespread influence of apocalypticism on Irish culture during the tenth and eleventh centuries when apocryphal apocalyptic Latin texts were widely translated into Irish.[169] According to one historian these texts "inspired a rich development of texts in the native language."[170] It has also been discovered that apocalyptic eschatology was a decisive influence on early Irish art, particularly in the iconography of the high crosses from the period between c. 600 and 800 AD, which were replete with images possessing distinctly apocalyptic and eschatological overtones.[171]

The lack of a perceptible increase in apocalyptic-eschatological speculation in many evangelical publications during times of particular unrest is one indication of the relative insignificance of the immediate context to apocalyptic-eschatological speculation. Rather, the general context of crisis, in all its multifaceted aspects was interpreted through an apocalyptic-eschatological paradigm and articulated by a discourse derived more from the biblical texts than by the immediate social context. In other words, this was a case not of context acting upon the interpretation of apocalyptic-eschatological texts but of these texts providing the conceptual framework with which to interpret the context of the crisis. This difference, although subtle, is vital to a proper understanding of how apocalyptic language functioned in Northern Ireland during the Troubles and thus is essential to gaining a proper grasp of evangelical perceptions of the conflict as a whole.

It is clear that evangelicals from across the denominational spectrum, along with the majority of the population of Northern Ireland as a whole, were conscious of living in the midst of crisis. "There is no

167. Whelan, *Bible War in Ireland*, 143.

168. McBride, *Scripture Politics*, 195–201; Hempton and Hill, *Evangelical Protestantism*, 27–30; Hill, *Time of the End*, 17–31.

169. Ryan, "Fixing the Eschatological Scales," 184–95; Heist, *Fifteen Signs of Doomsday*.

170. McGinn, *Apocalypse Theory*, 69.

171. Veelenturf, "Visions of the End," 144–73.

doubt that we are living in momentous times," noted one evangelical contributor to the *New Protestant Telegraph*.[172] Even several years after the Good Friday Agreement and the ceasefires of the main Loyalist and Republican paramilitary groups, evangelicals still used the language of crisis, which if not explicitly apocalyptic or eschatological, nevertheless evoked a sense of urgency which resonated with the notion of apocalyptic discontinuity, crisis, and confusion. Writing for the *lion & lamb* in 2006 one evangelical commentator took a broad perspective on Northern Ireland culture and concluded that, "We are in the middle of a major cultural revolution. . . . The old world of knowledge, power structures, beliefs, etc. and, significantly for us, the metanarrative of religion, has been deconstructed of its former meaning and authority."[173]

Although we cannot discount the role of context in explaining the phenomenon of Northern Ireland apocalyptic eschatology, we must recognize that the texts of apocalyptic eschatology were active agents in the processes of their interpretation and were thus to a great extent formative of the historical milieu out of which they emerged. However, contextual factors cannot be discounted in explaining why such texts acquired particular resonance during certain periods.

The Cultures of Northern Ireland Evangelicalism

Any attempt to conceptualize the complex relationship between texts and contexts will invariably raise the question of the role played by the host culture in the hermeneutical process. Like texts and contexts, culture is a polyvalent concept irreducible to sociological typologies. Family customs, political debates, religious rituals, scientific beliefs and practices, literature and the arts—all of these and innumerable other human activities fall within the capacious orbit of "culture." One way of thinking about culture is to consider it as the interpretive space in which "texts, images, artefacts, and ideas are moved, disguised, translated, transformed, adapted, and reimagined" in a perpetual creative process.[174] In the same way that I have maintained that apocalyptic-eschatological language, by providing a worldview with which to perceive the Troubles, began to take on contextual attributes in its own right, so have anthro-

172. *New Protestant Telegraph* (March, 1991), 5.

173. *lion & lamb* (Spring, 2006), 6.

174. Greenblat, *Cultural Mobility*, 4.

pologists made similar claims with respect to culture. The roles of culture and context, it is claimed, are related to such an extent that culture in itself constitutes a context.[175] Moreover, the reciprocal relationship between cultures and texts is established by Robert Schreiter, who avers that one way to think about culture is to consider it as "the total sum of . . . texts shared by a given people."[176] Considered alongside the notion of a text as "a single sign or series of signs, bearing a message,"[177] this idea supports Peter Burke's definition of culture as "a system of shared meanings, attitudes, and values, and the symbolic forms . . . in which they are expressed or embodied."[178]

Whilst the indivisibility of culture and context may be maintained on formal grounds, it is helpful to make a distinction for heuristic purposes. Whereas the contextual question seeks to account for how external influences affected text production, the culture question focuses on the embodiment of ideas into host groups. According to the "cultural semiotic" approach developed by Clifford Geertz, a culture is constituted as a miscegenation of various systems of meaning established by traditions and practices through which people are able to form shared convictions in terms of their collective participation in these common conventions.[179] Culture is conceived as "a vast communication network, whereby both verbal and nonverbal messages are circulated along elaborate, interconnected pathways, which, together, create systems of meaning."[180]

The notion that a widespread academic interest in apocalyptic eschatology is a symptom of a broader crisis in culture is a thesis that has already been demonstrated in other contexts, such as that of Edwardian England.[181] The question concerning the viability of apocalyptic-eschatological discourse in our context, however, was not primarily a matter of academic disputation among contending factions representing different intellectual perspectives. In Northern Ireland during the Troubles, we are dealing on the contrary with a multi-layered clash of

175. Geertz, *Interpretation of Cultures*, 14.

176. Schreiter, *Local Theologies*, 55.

177. Ibid., 54.

178. Burke, *Popular Culture*, ix.

179. Geertz, *Interpretation of Cultures*, 10; see also Ward, *Theology and Contemporary Critical Theory*, 67.

180. Schreiter, *Local Theologies*, 49.

181. Chapman, *Coming Crisis*.

diverse convictions, many of which were manifestations of an underlying apocalyptic-eschatological worldview. Many of the cultures in which these convictions were embodied cannot be reduced to the categories of "evangelical" and "liberal"; still less is it possible to divide the cultures of Northern Ireland into "Protestant" and "Catholic." The diversity of cultures is seen in the fact that apocalyptic-eschatological language became an acceptable and even respectable medium of expression among many Northern Ireland evangelicals during the Troubles; for others it remained an embarrassment or a dangerous field of discourse vulnerable to ideological abuse.[182] Although such language was always at the disposal of evangelicals to use in a variety of contexts, the experience of the crisis of the Troubles changed how people responded to its use.

This study is not the first to have discovered that the "culture of Northern Ireland evangelicalism" is particularly difficult to characterize. Indeed, the term itself is rather misleading, since it implies a uniformity and homogeneity that does not reflect the diversity of competing moral and doctrinal visions expressed by the various groups in Northern Ireland that identified themselves as "evangelicals." Moreover, an accurate account of the relation between apocalyptic eschatology and evangelicalism during the Troubles must recognize that the evangelical cultures of Northern Ireland did not constitute a homogeneous unit of pure theological conviction but, rather, an inchoate conglomeration of diverse, highly-nuanced, and occasionally contradictory religious, cultural, and political worldviews. Evangelicals affiliated themselves to a wide variety of organizations. The differences were not merely organizational but were based on a combination of political, social, and doctrinal issues.

Despite the heterogeneity of evangelical cultures, historians and sociologists have attempted to categorise Northern Ireland evangelicalism according to certain basic analyzable classifications. Patrick Mitchel has focused on Orangeism, Paisleyism, the Presbyterian Church of Northern Ireland, and the Evangelical Contribution on Northern Ireland, which he uses as case studies of different emphases within the evangelical tradi-

---

182. This danger was identified in the Northern Ireland Baptist David McMillan's thesis on the book of Revelation which sought to deconstruct the commonplace notion that Revelation is an apocalyptic text. Instead, McMillan argues, the text is primarily a pastoral epistle in form, structure and intention which contains apocalyptic imagery only as a means to support the pastoral exhortations contained in the text. See McMillan, "Seven Beatitudes," 62 and *passim*.

tion in order to elucidate the relationship between religion and identity.[183] Gladys Ganiel has similarly posited a distinction between "mediating evangelicals," "traditional evangelicals," and "post-evangelicals."[184] Since Mitchel's focus is upon the intersection between evangelical belief and nationalistic ideology and Ganiel's analysis is concerned with evangelical attitudes to conflict resolution, these typologies cannot be transferred uncritically to an investigation of the very different issue of evangelical interpretations of apocalyptic eschatology. For our purposes, rather than focusing on denominational disparities among the patchwork of Northern Ireland evangelical cultures, a more appropriate division to make is one which penetrates to the heart of the theological convictions common to evangelicals across the denominational spectrum and to consider these core beliefs in relation to apocalyptic eschatology. In this regard the various cultures of Northern Ireland evangelicalism may be said to correspond in varying degrees to the notions of hope, fear, and semantic dualism, each the subject of the succeeding chapters.

Although all these three aspects reasserted themselves continually and indiscriminately across the whole spectrum of evangelical cultures, it is the case that each of these emphases corresponded to an identifiable pattern within particular cultural expressions of Northern Ireland evangelicalism. The explanation for the extent to which one aspect was emphasized over another within particular evangelical subcultures consists in a variety of internal and external discursive historical factors. The elucidation of these factors provides a new perspective from which to formulate proper conceptualizations of the ways in which texts and contexts interact. In relation to apocalyptic language one way of considering this relationship is through a close analysis of the basic existential categories of fear and hope and how they were articulated in evangelical discourses.

---

183. Mitchel, *Evangelicalism and National Identity.*
184. Ganiel, *Evangelicalism and Conflict.*

3

Apocalyptic Fear

"In the last days perilous times shall come"

Introduction to Chapter 3

The Antichrist, the Man of Sin, the Whore of Babylon, the Great Apostasy, apocalyptic lawlessness, and the Great Tribulation—these are subjects that might seem more at home in a prayer meeting in a fundamentalist evangelical church in East Belfast than on the national airwaves of the BBC. In any case, these apocalyptic topics are certainly not the themes which one would normally associate with Radio 4's *Desert Island Discs.* Yet in one broadcast in the summer of 1988, these were precisely the issues that dominated the discussion on Radio 4's flagship program.[1] Whereas most guests would choose classic numbers by such composers as Mozart and Chopin or songs by popular singers and modern bands, the songs chosen by the guest that morning to take on the imaginary desert island included a hymn with the portentous title, "When the Trumpet Shall Sound."

Sue Lawley's desert island castaway on that occasion was Ian R. K. Paisley. During the dialogue Paisley alluded to his perception of "the dark clouds of lawlessness" which had originally persuaded him that God had called him to take an active political role.[2] Reporting on Paisley's interview a few weeks after its first broadcast, even the columnists of the

---

1. The programme was first broadcast on 7 August 1988.
2. *Ballymena Times* (31 August, 1988), 19.

Ballymena News perceived the incongruity of such beliefs in the context of the national broadcast, admitting that Paisley spoke about issues that were "not usual for *Desert Island Discs*."[3] Yet these subjects were at the heart of the worldview not only of Paisley but also of thousands of evangelicals throughout Northern Ireland during the Troubles. They are also apparent in lesser-known publications throughout the Troubles. Eight years before Paisley's Radio 4 broadcast, an article appeared in the official newspaper of the Orange Order, the *Orange Standard,* in which the author shared with his readers his "prophetic" insight into the Troubles, which he had purportedly derived from reading the prophets of the Hebrew Bible:

> The troubles we are suffering bear great importance in themselves and yet it is only a part of a chain of events being masterminded throughout the world. We are on the verge of the last great thrust of Satanic power against God and his people. . . . How do we know this? If we turn to Ezekiel chapter 38 and 39 we see God's plan unfolding.[4]

The ways in which such appropriations of biblical apocalyptic-eschatological texts demonstrate a new way of understanding the relationship between these texts and the social context will be the main focus of this chapter. Many evangelicals were convinced that the biblical apocalyptic-eschatological texts, such as Ezekiel 38 and 39 among others identified in the previous chapter, constituted "a resume of the events that will mark the end of the age."[5] An important part of these end-times speculations was the "great tribulation," which, it was feared, would be accompanied by growing signs of moral decadence and spiritual apostasy. There is clear evidence to demonstrate that evangelicals interpreted the Troubles through their reading of the biblical texts, which were read as symbolic or even literal descriptions of their actual experience of the conflict.

Chapter 3 thus deals with the various ways in which apocalyptic language shaped the fears of certain expressions of Northern Ireland evangelicalism. Such language, it will be shown, gave imaginative shape to the deepest fears of many evangelicals regarding the rise of the Antichrist, Mystery Babylon, and the one-world Religion of the Beast.

---

3. *Ballymena Times* (24 August, 1988), 24.

4. *Orange Standard* (March, 1980), 5.

5. Foster, *Antichrist,* 156.

Substantiating the theoretical arguments advanced in the previous chapter, the argument throughout shall be that certain biblical texts played a decisive role in the processes of signification within the discourses of certain expressions of Northern Ireland evangelicalism which contributed to the hermeneutical re-appropriation of apocalyptic-eschatological signs into which such fears were encoded. After a consideration of some of the salient developments of each manifestation of apocalyptic eschatology in Northern Ireland, the focus will return to the contention that apocalyptic eschatological language was not so much a response to a crisis as it was a means through which the events of the crisis were conceptualized according to the semantic norms stipulated by the biblical texts through which these events were interpreted.

Ecumenism, the Harlot Church, and the Religion of the Beast

In Revelation 17, John uses vivid language to depict an image he received in a vision:

> And the woman was arrayed in purple and scarlet colour, and decked with gold and precious stones and pearls, having a golden cup in her hand full of abominations and filthiness of her fornication: And upon her forehead was a name written, MYSTERY, BABYLON THE GREAT, THE MOTHER OF HARLOTS AND ABOMINATIONS OF THE EARTH. And I saw the woman drunken with the blood of the saints, and with the blood of the martyrs of Jesus: and when I saw her, I wondered with great admiration. (Rev 17:4–6)

For many Northern Ireland evangelicals, the object of innermost fear was the Catholic Church, often identified with this mysterious woman of John's vision. An evangelical publication described the above passage from Revelation 17 as a text which "draws the picture by God Himself of the Roman Catholic apostasy and the great Church of the Antichrist."[6] The conviction that the Pope was Antichrist[7]—a view described by Gareth Higgins as an "eschatological myth" which is "invoked as the *piece de resistance* of anti-Catholicism"[8]—was a pervasive motif of much

6. *Revivalist* (May, 1982), 3.

7. The Antichrist referred to "a demonic-human adversary of Christ who will appear before the second advent as the last oppressor and persecutor of Christians"; Cox, *In These Last Days*, 42.

8. Higgins, "Great Expectations," 208, 210.

evangelical anti-Catholic rhetoric during the Troubles.[9] Many, including Ian Paisley, shared the conviction of Alan Campbell that "Anti-Christ refers not to one man who shall appear at the end of this age but to the entire dynasty of Popes right up to and including the present Pope, John Paul II."[10] The notions that "the Papal head of the Romish Church blasphemously takes the place of the Father, Son and the Holy Ghost" and that "the principle of the Papacy is a Satanic parody of the Christocentric principle in the Kingdom of God" are typical of the kind of allegations against the Catholic Church made by fundamentalists within Northern Ireland evangelicalism.[11] "Perhaps Roman Catholics might ask why we refer to their Church as the system of the Beast," wrote one evangelical correspondent in a letter to the *Belfast Telegraph*. "The answer," the writer continued "lies primarily in the bearing their Church's doctrines hold in relation to those explicitly set forth in the Word of God . . . . [T]he Roman Church's doctrines oppose those of God's Word, being demonstrably the machinations of men throughout the ages, many sincere but sincerely wrong, the rest just plainly devious."[12]

9. Bruce, *Paisley: Religion and Politics*, 45, 49, 78, 185; Bernard McGinn, *Anti-christ:*, 252; Tonge, *Northern Ireland: Conflict and Change*, 101.

10. Campbell, *Anti-Christ Revealed*. The belief that the biblical Antichrist was the system of the Papacy was prevalent among the magisterial reformers; see Firth, *Apocalyptic Tradition*, 35.

11. *New Protestant Telegraph* (September, 1988), 7; Paisley, *St. Bartholomew*, 130–31. It is also important to bear in mind that while there were many vocal exponents of the notion of the papal Antichrist, there were others who rejected this idea and maintained that the biblical antichrist was a particular individual invested with great political power who would become manifest at the end of time and whose rise to power would inaugurate the "Great Tribulation" which would culminate in a final assault of the allied "Gentile" nations against the Jews in Israel at a place called Armageddon. These beliefs bear the mark of premillennial dispensationalism which originated in Ireland in the early decades of the nineteenth century but which struck its deepest root in American evangelical culture, particularly under the influence of the *Scofield Reference Bible* [1909]. One such Northern Ireland evangelical exponent of these views was the Baptist pastor, Kenneth Humphries, who said thus of the battle of Armageddon: "This particular place will, in a day to come be a literal mount of slaughter where the most amazing conflict in our earthly history will take place. It is the very place where the Antichrist will gather the armies of the world together for the sole purpose of wiping Israel off the face of the map." In contrast to the notion of the papal Antichrist, advocates of the premillennial interpretation maintained that Antichrist had not yet been made manifest and that when he was, he would be a figure of great political power. See Humphries, *Battleground of Truth*.

12. "Scriptural Significance of 666," *Belfast Telegraph* (January 13, 1997).

Despite the detailed attention that sociologists have paid to the anti-Catholic disposition of sections of Northern Ireland evangelicalism, some scholarly contributions tend to neglect the vital apocalyptic-eschatological wellspring out of which much anti-Catholic sentiment arose.[13] As already intimated, anti-Catholicism during the Troubles cannot be understood outside of its apocalyptic-eschatological context. At issue is the question of why the Catholic Church was execrated to such a great extent by certain expressions of evangelicalism throughout Irish history in general and during the Troubles in particular. The Catholic Church was mistrusted not merely because it was perceived as a threat to civil liberties or national self-determination, but also because many regarded it as the embodiment of the spirit of the Antichrist. The Catholic Church was thus branded as the "Harlot Church" whose alleged endorsement of the Republican murder of Protestants ranked her alongside the mysterious figure of Revelation 17, described by John as the wicked Whore of Babylon who had become "drunk with the blood of the saints and with the blood of the martyrs of Jesus."[14] In 1970, Paisley sent a letter to the Queen in which he associated the Catholic Church with the "Great Whore" described in the book of Revelation.[15] A commentary on Revelation 17 in an article published in the *New Protestant Telegraph* in June, 1989, posited an explicit identification between the Catholic Church and the Babylonian Harlot of this passage. "The Church of Rome," claimed the author, "has been drunk with the blood of the Protestants." The further allegation that the Catholic Church "has slain millions through the centuries" was adduced as proof of the identification of the Church as the bloodthirsty harlot of Revelation 17.[16] During the Troubles, Northern Ireland evangelicals produced full-length tracts in defence of the notion that the Catholic Church was the Scarlet Woman of the Apocalypse.[17] According to one evangelical, the

---

13. An exception to this general tendency is MacIver, "Ian Paisley and the Reformed Tradition," 359–78. Even this article, however, does not penetrate into the substance of the apocalyptic-eschatological convictions which underpinned much of the anti-Catholic sentiment in Northern Ireland.

14. *New Protestant Telegraph* (24 June, 1989), 8.

15. Brewer and Higgins, *Anti-Catholicism,* 139.

16. *New Protestant Telegraph* (24 June, 1989).

17. Campbell, *Scarlet Woman of the Apocalypse.*

Papacy had slaughtered fifty million people.[18] Thus the identification of the Catholic Church as the "latter-day Babylon" was a typical and consistent feature of certain fundamentalist expressions of Northern Ireland evangelicalism throughout the Troubles.[19]

The best-known and most vociferous—but by no means the most militant—critic of the Catholic Church during the Troubles was Ian Paisley. For Paisley and his American patron and collaborator, Bob Jones Snr., the Catholic Church was the latter-day representative of "ecclesiastical tyranny" and the "mother of cruelty."[20] This Church, argued Jones in a foreword to Paisley's 1972 book on the Massacre of St. Bartholomew, is "the Harlot Church stained with the blood of the saints . . . the enemy of freedom and the servant of Antichrist."[21] In August 1976, Paisley's magazine, *Revivalist,* contained the text of the Statement of Faith of the World Congress of Fundamentalists in which the Catholic Church was not merely denounced as a sub-Christian organization but condemned as a Satanic church under the direct control of diabolical principalities and powers. The statement declared unequivocally that, "the Church of Rome is Satanic in origin and objective."[22]

In the European Parliament building in Strasbourg in 1988, as the Pope stood up to address the delegates, Paisley heckled the Pontiff with the declamation, "I denounce you as Antichrist!" While most mainstream, "secular" newspapers at the time condemned Paisley's "puerile outburst"[23] as a "cheap publicity stunt,"[24] they failed to notice that behind Paisley's own epithets—"synagogue of Satan,"[25] "apostate body,"[26] "the spawn, the offspring of . . . the Devil"[27]—lay a real fear of the Roman Catholic Church and the ecumenical World Council of Churches

---

18. Campbell, *Great Tribulation,* 26.

19. *Protestant Telegraph* (10 June, 1967).

20. Jones' fundamentalist rhetoric is analyzed extensively in Lewis, *Romancing the Difference,* 107–9 and 113 for a consideration of Jones' anti-Catholic rhetoric.

21. Jones "Foreword" to Paisley, *Massacre of St. Bartholomew,* x.

22. *Revivalist* (August, 1976), 12.

23. *Today* (12 October, 1988). *Today* was a UK tabloid that was in print between 1986 and 1995.

24. *Irish News* (12 October, 1988).

25. Paisley, *Roman Catholic Priests,* 13.

26. Paisley, *Antichrist: An Exposition,* 6.

27. Ibid., 58.

through which it was believed the Beast (or "Antichrist"), with the spiritual assistance of the False Prophet of Revelation 13:11–18, would establish a unified, yet apostate, universal church.[28] For anti-Catholic evangelicals the Catholic Church was not only "the source of all of Ireland's evils, woes, divisions and bloodshed"[29] but also the herald and harbinger of the one-world church of Antichrist. Ivan Foster articulated this fear by implicating the Roman Catholic Church and the ecumenical movement explicitly as the main agents behind the attempt to establish a satanically-inspired religion of the Beast:

> Antichrist will be very much indeed in the promotion of the false ideals of the whore of Babylon, which is today seen in embryo in the ecumenical union being sought between Rome so-called Protestant churches and various other heathen religions. This will develop until there will be only one religious system recognized by men . . . that of the Harlot of Babylon.[30]

The presence of such an apostate church representing an all-encompassing one-world-religion was perceived by many as the precondition for the arrival of the Antichrist. This supreme representative of evil would then take control of the counterfeit, apostate church and unleash his terror against the latter-day faithful Christian remnant who had not succumbed to the deception of the false religion of the Beast. Even the popular press acknowledged this concern among some sections of the population. The *Belfast Telegraph* reported that, "What is given in other Scriptures is that world government is inevitable and that a religious-political figure will arise called the Anti-Christ, aping God. . . . It is not hard to imagine a world figure rising to take over unified states across the world."[31]

In this connection Ian Boxall notes that many evangelicals, particularly those adhering to premillennialist interpretations of the end times, have "tended to dismiss the Ecumenical Movement as a syncretistic endeavour inspired by Antichrist."[32] There is abundant evidence from the texts of various expressions of Northern Ireland evangelical-

28. This conviction was also at the heart of the teaching of American premillennial dispensationalism, according to Carpenter's *Revive Us Again*, 39, 49, 89, 145, 249.

29. Campbell, "A United Ireland—What Saith the Scriptures?"

30. Foster, *Antichrist*, 139.

31. *Belfast Telegraph* (14 July, 1997).

32. Boxall, *Revelation*, 114.

ism to support this statement. Indeed, such was the fear of a syncretistic one-world-system at the end of time that every attempt to establish
inter-faith dialogue was interpreted by many evangelicals as a maleficent
prognostication of the establishment of the prophesied united apostate
religion which would accompany the fearsome events associated with
the apocalyptic conflagration at the end of time. Thus, the establishment
of the World Congress of Faiths—founded in 1963, which sought to
establish a forum for dialogue between Buddhists, Catholics, Quakers,
Hindus, Muslims, Sikhs, and Jews—was denounced by some Northern
Ireland evangelicals as "a typical instance of the Roman Anti-Christ re-
vealing itself."[33] A 1967 edition of the *Protestant Telegraph* condemned
the World Congress of Faiths which, it insisted, "is intent on fostering
'belief' of one sort or another. Then, in the very last days when men's
hearts will fail them for fear . . . the Roman Anti-Christ will succour
and conquer them with lying wonders."[34] As this quotation makes clear,
the evangelical author believed that the Catholic Church was the main
driving force behind the efforts to prepare the way for Antichrist. In
the same way that John the Baptist had made straight the paths for
Christ at his first coming (Mark 1:3), so was the Harlot Church paving
the way for Antichrist to rule the world. Other expressions of Northern
Ireland evangelicalism similarly lamented this apparent "move towards
syncretism" and "the building of a World Faith, which would embrace
Islam and the heathen religions of the Far East."[35] These views, which we
find to prevail throughout the evangelical texts of the late 1960s, were
still widespread in the lead up to the Good Friday Agreement of 1998.
The 1997 issue of the Northern Ireland evangelical publication, *Battle
Standard,* contained an article which commented on the link between
the ecumenical movement, the perceived emergence of Catholic hegemony and the rise of Antichrist,

> The whole current of . . . ecumenism is set towards the ultimate
> union of all Christians in one world church (probably under
> the leadership of the Pope). . . . The attempt to come to terms
> with non-Christian religions so as to achieve a world religion is

33. *Protestant Telegraph* (27 May 1967), 9.

34. Ibid.

35. Campbell, *Great Tribulation,* 16. This booklet is based on a series of lectures
given by Campbell in locations throughout Northern Ireland in 1984.

no remote ambition with some. If so, it would pave the way for Antichrist with a vengeance.[36]

This conviction echoed the fear which Paisley had articulated in 1971 when he warned that the aim of the Ecumenical Movement is the creation of "a Super One World Church."[37]

This fear persisted throughout the Troubles. Similar language was used to address a variety of political and religious developments. In 1975 in the context of the expansion of the allegedly Catholic-controlled European Union, Paisley lamented that,

> we are moving into a time of religious persecution, when these nations of Europe are going to insist on one church; one church for Europe and that church will be the Roman Catholic Church. The apostate churches that are in our land, in the World Council of Churches, do you know what they are doing? They are helping to build the kingdom of the Anti-christ. They are part of this great apostasy.[38]

Thus the assertion made by Worrall and Gallagher that "ecumenical endeavour to increase understanding between the Churches comes under suspicion because a political sell-out is feared" must be treated with caution.[39] For many evangelicals the ecumenical danger was perceived not so much as a political hazard to the constitutional status of Northern Ireland as an apocalyptic threat to the eschatological fate of "Protestant Ulster." It was also assumed that when he came, Antichrist would devote considerable attention to the destruction of Northern Ireland as one of his first priorities,[40] owing to the province's alleged status as "the last bastion of Bible Protestantism in Europe."[41] "Ulster" was thus perceived as being particularly vulnerable to an end times attack by Antichrist. Another noteworthy observation in regard to the above quotation is that

36. *Battle Standard* 1/1 (October, 1997), 2.

37. *Protestant Telegraph* (10 April, 1971), 5.

38. Paisley, *Revivalist* (June, 1975), 14–15. In this article Paisley referred to the Common Market as "the kingdom of the Anti-christ." Interestingly, Paisley wrote this article before he became an MEP. There is no evidence that Paisley's views on the EU changed after he became an MEP in 1979. Even as late as 2010, Paisley continued to condemn the Catholic Church.

39. Gallagher and Worrall, *Christians in Ulster, 1968–1980*, 191.

40. Campbell, *For God and Ulster*, 25.

41. Paisley, quoted in O'Malley, *Uncivil Wars*, 178.

although the context and the focus of the threat had changed from the World Congress of Faiths in 1963 to the World Council of Churches and the European Union in 1975, the language of the apocalyptic critique remained essentially unchanged. The European Union represented the same kind of threat posed by ecumenical movement, namely that it would be used by the Papacy to extend its diabolical influence over world affairs. The European Union was thus denounced as "the kingdom of the Anti-christ."[42] An article in a 1967 edition of the *Protestant Telegraph* even alleged that the Common Market was being established exactly according to the supposed prophetic blueprint contained in Zechariah 5 and 6.[43]

The apocalyptic eschatological language of biblical passages such as Zechariah and Revelation were thus the hermeneutical framework through which evangelicals interpreted contemporary events. A booklet published in 1985 by Ronald Cooke, an American supporter of Ian Paisley with apparent links to Bob Jones University, gives us an insight into how this interpretive framework might be applied by evangelicals, such as those from Northern Ireland who read Cooke's text. Expounding and defending Paisley's interpretation of the Pope as the Antichrist and the Catholic Church as the wicked Harlot of the Apocalypse, Cooke declared that, "the biblical exegete, whatever else he sees in Revelation 17 and 18, sees an evil ecclesiastical conglomerate dominating the end time" and insisted that Paisley's interpretation of this passage is "not a bigoted one but a biblical one."[44] Complaining that, "Modern man is almost blinded to the possibility of the World Council of Churches and/or the Papacy being connected to the Harlot Religion and Mystery Babylon the Great," Cooke maintained that the threat of the Catholic Church consisted in its vulnerability to an ecumenical takeover by the Antichrist. This dark satanic figure, Cooke speculated, would likely turn out to be the Pope.[45] "The ecumenical movement is made to order for one person (Antichrist) to assume the leadership of an apostate super 'church,'" warned Cooke, who added that, "this person could well be the Pope of Rome."[46] The author further observes that "Paisley identifies the

---

42. *Revivalist* (June, 1975), 14–15.

43. *Protestant Telegraph* (10 June, 1967), 6.

44. Cooke, *Paisley and Mystery Babylon*, 3.

45. Ibid., 43.

46. Ibid., 29.

Papacy with the Mother of Harlots because he believes that it is consistent with the true exegesis of Revelation 17 and 18."[47] It thus seems that for some Northern Ireland evangelicals such as Paisley, a "plain reading" of Revelation would yield the "true" interpretation (i.e., that the Pope was the Antichrist) to anyone who had the spiritual insight to discern the signs of the times.

Anxiety among Northern Ireland evangelicals concerning the possibility of the establishment of a One World Religion by a Papal Antichrist was a permanent feature in the apocalyptic backdrop to the Troubles. Resistance to the Ecumenical Movement, specifically the World Council of Churches as the supposed harbinger of Antichrist, was not restricted to the Free Presbyterian Church or to the fringe of extreme-conservative Northern Ireland evangelicalism. In the early 1970s a vigorous debate ensued within the Presbyterian Church in Ireland over the issue of whether they should remain as a member of the World Council of Churches. In 1972 the PCI published a paper, which admitted that "'There is a sharp division of opinion in our Church concerning membership in the W.C.C. There are some who are determined, if they can, to take us out of the Council and there are some equally determined, if they can, to keep us in it."[48]

Those who campaigned to remain in membership appealed to Gospel texts such as John 17:21–23, arguing that "the summons to unity is a matter of central rather than peripheral concern to the Church."[49] In 1975 the moderate Presbyterian minister, John Barkley, added his voice to the debate, arguing in favor of membership on the grounds that, "Our heritage in Irish Presbyterianism is one of seeking co-operation and unity with our fellow-Christians. It is not one of separation."[50] On the other side of the debate, the opposition to membership often manifested a sense of apocalyptic eschatological fear. Some resisted the WCC on conventional, non-apocalyptic grounds by invoking the allegedly biblical mandate of Christian separatism by dichotomizing the concepts of truth and unity.[51] Other objectors, however, based their op-

---

47. Ibid., 45.

48. Presbyterian Church in Ireland (hereafter PCI), *Our Membership in the World Council of Churches*, 3.

49. Ibid., 23.

50. Barkley, *Irish Presbyterianism*, 9.

51. An example is that given in the first page of the January 1998 edition of the

position to the WCC on the apocalyptic ground that the ecumenical movement would probably turn out to be the Apostate Church of the one-world-religion allegedly prophesied in the Scriptures. This church, it was supposed, would be taken over by Antichrist, thus inaugurating the Great Tribulation and its apocalyptic culmination. The report took these concerns seriously and sought to articulate the fears of many who believed that, "The WCC moves slowly but inexorably towards one all-embracing Church—one in control and organization."[52] Those within the Presbyterian Church who sought separation from the WCC organized themselves into the CCW (Campaign for Complete Withdrawal).[53] This intriguing play on initials is yet a further indication of the extent to which the debate revolved around language games and the utilization of the power of words in political action. The Campaign published a document which argued for withdrawal on the grounds that the World Council was "a corruption of or a counterfeit Christianity."[54]

Certain elements within the Presbyterian Church, particularly those with close links to the Orange orders, exhibited a certain distrust towards the Catholic Church on the grounds that the church was in reality a mass-organized apostasy,[55] albeit without the same kind of explicit emphasis on the possible apocalyptic-eschatological implications of the Catholic Church's status as an apostate body (such as its co-option by the Antichrist and the False Prophet). In July 1966 the Baptist Norman Porter addressed the Loyal Orange Lodge at the Presbyterian Assembly Hall in Belfast maintaining that, "the Church of Rome is that evil system portrayed in the Scriptures from which we must forever keep apart." In anticipation of the imminent apocalyptic conflagration in Northern

---

Battle Standard in which it is maintained that, "the true believer in God's Word can never sacrifice truth upon the altar of union." The Orange Order put forward a similar case, arguing that, "Unity in truth is the essential thing. There can be no unity where truth is interpreted differently . . . while a unity of the Reformed Churches is possible that which includes Roman Catholicism has no prospects of success." See, *Orange Standard* (November, 1990), 6.

52. PCI, *World Council of Churches*, 7.

53. This organization was also called the "Campaign for Concerted Witness to Reformed Truth" and was chaired by the Rev. W. Fleming and Rev. R. Dickinson. The latter, as well as being a Presbyterian minister and a member of the Orange Order, was also the Campaign's Secretary.

54. Campaign for Complete Withdrawal, *The World Council of Churches*, 1.

55. Porter, *Ecumenism . . . Romanism*, 4.

Ireland he warned that "the final battle with our ancient foe still lies before us."[56]

Conservative expressions of the Pentecostal churches in Northern Ireland also identified the Catholic Church as the supreme nemesis of "biblical Christianity" in the end times. The voluminous tracts written by the anti-Catholic Pentecostal preacher, Alan Campbell, exhibit an unyielding and intractable antipathy towards the Catholic Church. In these texts the apocalyptic-eschatological language of his anti-Catholic assertions is unmistakable. Although Campbell perceived the global dimensions of the alleged international Catholic conspiracy to expurgate biblical Christianity from the world, many of his remarks address the situation in Northern Ireland directly. "The New World Order," he speculated, "with its concept of a One World Government, Economy and Religion seeks the final destruction of little Ulster."[57] At the centre of this purported diabolical conspiracy was the Catholic Church, in alliance with other "heathen factions" such as Communism.[58]

The basic fear of the Catholic Church as the latter-day harbinger of the prophesied and much-feared ecumenical, apostate church which could be easily co-opted by the Antichrist remained a constant feature of evangelicalism in Northern Ireland during the Troubles. This fear, as we have demonstrated, was rooted in a certain apocalyptic-eschatological understanding of biblical prophecy. The January/February 1978 edition of the evangelical *Ulster Bulwark* contained an article in which the author expressed the fear of many Northern Ireland evangelicals that there would soon come a one-world-religion under the dominion of the Antichrist. Quoting from Revelation 12:11, he averred that, "We are now living at the 'end time' very near to the Lord's Return. But before He comes there will be a last desperate attempt by Satan to wipe out the Church of Christ. . . . In that process all the powers of evil will be drawn together for the final attack."[59]

The author further claimed that, "the wicked [are] becoming more wicked and joining their forces to create a Wicked World System with

56. Porter, quoted in Garland, "Ulster Volunteer Force," 136.

57. Campbell, *For God and Ulster*, 25.

58. The resemblance of the red Communist flag to the color of the garments worn by the Babylonian Whore of Revelation was not lost on Northern Ireland evangelicals. See *Protestant Telegraph* (10 June, 1967), 7.

59. *Ulster Bulwark* (January/February, 1978), 4.

wickedness permeating every facet of society and life." Behind these deplorable developments lay the malevolent machinations of a comprehensive Catholic conspiracy, the wickedness and depravity of which, it was assumed, would continue to escalate until the final eschatological battle. In 1982 when Galtieri's Junta invaded the Falkland Islands, Paisley's *Revivalist* called attention to the allegedly crooked Catholic credentials of the autocratic Argentine regime. Thus, the *Revivalist* invoked the image of the Scarlet Woman of the Apocalypse through which to ascertain the deeper significance of the Argentine assault, holding the Catholic Church ultimately responsible for this act of aggression which was part of an alleged global conspiracy aimed at the extirpation of "biblical Christianity" in the last days.[60]

One of the basic tenets of some expressions of Northern Ireland apocalyptic eschatology was that the conspiracy would continue to deepen and that the forces of darkness would exercise more and more dominion until the final eschatological battle. This passage taken from the *Ulster Bulwark* which insists that as the end times drew to a close, the powers of evil would escalate at the expense of the gospel is typical of the sentiment of many contemporaneous pessimistic speculations: "Confusion and error will increase. Error will abound. Truth and falsehood will be treated as equal. The false priests of Rome will have more authority [than] those who seek to proclaim the gospel."[61] Again the Catholic Church was identified as the preeminent harbinger of the latter-day apostasy. The notion of a continual Rome-led march into the degradation of end-times wickedness was not limited to fundamentalist or Paisleyite expressions of Northern Ireland evangelicalism. The Orange orders likewise expressed their concerns regarding the alleged baneful influence of the Catholic Church as Northern Ireland moved further into the last days. Although the apocalyptic-eschatological aspect of the social critique is less conspicuous than in the evangelical fundamentalist texts, the influence of such thinking is apparent nonetheless.

The opposition to any kind of accord with the Catholic Church— which one finds to prevail throughout a variety of Orange texts ranging

60. *Revivalist* (May, 1982).

61. *Ulster Bulwark* (March/April, 1989), 5.

from ballads,[62] newspaper articles,[63] and booklets[64]—was not usually infused with the same level of apocalyptic-eschatological urgency that is common in the texts to have originated from other expressions of Northern Ireland evangelicalism.[65] The Orange orders consistently denounced the Catholic Church as "the determined foe of Protestant Ulster" rather than as the "whore of Babylon" or the handmaid of the Antichrist, as was typical of Paisleyite fundamentalist evangelicalism. Nevertheless, the apocalyptic-eschatological aspect of the anti-Catholic critique was not entirely absent even from the texts of the Orange orders. Pamphlets and booklets denouncing the Catholic Church received favorable reviews in the Orange press.[66] The most prominent example is the booklet written by Clifford Smyth entitled, *Rome—our Enemy* (1974). Smyth was an Orangeman and later a prominent figure in Unionist politics as well as a member of the Free Presbyterian Church. Although the brunt of the critique is directed against traditional Catholic doctrine and practice, such as the Mass and the Confession, the appraisal is informed throughout by an underlying apocalyptic-eschatological objection to the claims of the Catholic Church. This Church, claimed Smyth, was not merely a sponsor or Republican terror, but an underlying malignant spiritual presence in the Troubles and an agent of Antichrist and the "spiritual hosts of wickedness."[67] Baptist texts also allude to the underlying dynamic forces of an apocalyptic-eschatological struggle between the angels of light and the spiritual hosts of darkness. "Behind the scenes," affirmed one writer for the *Irish Baptist* in 1978, "there is a conflict between the powers of light and the forces of darkness, and that ultimately the battle in this universe is between Christ and Satan."[68] In a letter to the *Belfast Telegraph* in 1997, a Methodist minister likewise made connections between the violent factions in the Troubles and the

62. Many of these are collected in a songbook published in 1987 by The Ulster Society, entitled, *The Orange Lark*.

63. *Orange Standard* (October, 1979), 6.

64. Smyth, *Rome—Our Enemy*.

65. Interestingly the Orange order even referred to itself as an "ecumenical movement," albeit in a more restricted sense as a Protestant organization that has "brought together men of different [Protestant] denominations in a brotherhood." See *Orange Standard* (November, 1990).

66. *Orange Standard* (December 1974/January 1975), 3.

67. Smith, *Rome*, 78.

68. *Irish Baptist* 101 (December, 1978), 15.

underlying eschatological battle between the kingdom of Christ and the satanic powers of darkness.[69]

The Troubles as a Sign of the Apostasy of the End Times

One of the destructive consequences of this end-times conflict between the dark forces of apostasy and the light of the gospel, according to certain evangelicals, was a decline in the spiritual and moral condition of Northern Ireland caused mainly by the Catholic Church, "the system of moral apostasy."[70] "Northern Ireland may have a good Christian heritage," observed the premillennial Portadown Baptist pastor, Kenneth Humphries, "but sadly much of the good foundation is no longer with us, it is slowly being eroded away day after day."[71] This view was typical of pessimistic premillennial projections of the end times of which Humphries was a leading exponent. Adherents to premillennialism, as Richard Bube notes, tend to "look forward to nothing more than continued degradation of the world and disintegration of human society until Christ returns to establish justice and righteousness by His power."[72] In the context of the Northern Ireland Troubles in which the signs of such disintegration were seen in the violence, chaos and the breakdown of law and order of this period, this idea found ready acceptance among a significant proportion of the evangelical community.

Many evangelicals blamed the Catholic Church for the perceived spiritual enervation and concomitant moral decline of Northern Ireland. The expression of grief for the passing of a bygone era of revival on account of alleged Catholic and ecumenical harlotry recurs like a leitmotif throughout the Orange and evangelical fundamentalist press of the late 1970s and 1980s. Taking Revelation 18:23 ("for by thy sorceries were all the nations deceived") as its leading text, an article in the *Protestant Telegraph* in 1970 lamented that in "these last days . . . we are witnessing a Satanic invasion of the mind, a conquest of conscience that establishes a bridgehead in the already sadly depleted spiritual life of the

---

69. *Belfast Telegraph* (5 July, 1997), 13.

70. Foster, *Antichrist*, 186.

71. Humphries, *Battleground of Truth*.

72. Bube, "Optimism and Pessimism," 215–29; cf. Wessinger, *Handbook of Millennialism*, 5.

nation."[73] The *Orange Standard* regularly contained expressions of regret over the "lawlessness and prevalence of evil practices"[74] in Northern Ireland which had contributed to the Protestant community becoming a "broken and disunited people." An article in the September 1988 edition of the *Orange Standard* contained similar sentiments of lamentation: "Today the Ulster Protestant culture has become a shadow of what it was. Moral problems, complacency, along with the fever of ecumenism with Rome have divided and demoralised many Protestants."[75] Similarly Clifford Smyth bewailed the supposed moral and spiritual heights from which Northern Ireland was alleged to have fallen. Bemoaning the fact that "the Bible is reviled and Romanism has revived," Smyth observed that, "many have grown weary; there has been a falling away from the faith; false teaching and false christs have ushered in a generation of complacent and godless sinners who care nothing for the truth."[76] Here is another example of how the language of biblical apocalyptic eschatology was appropriated to provide a perspective on the Northern Ireland Troubles. This single sentence contains a plethora of allusions to biblical apocalyptic-eschatological material. In Luke's Gospel, Jesus is recorded as having warned his disciples of a coming period of unparalleled fear and terror, which would be accompanied by frightful signs that would leave "men's hearts failing them for fear, and for looking after those things which are coming on the earth: for the powers of heaven shall be shaken" (Luke 21:26); Matthew's Jesus similarly warned of false christs, declaring that "many shall come in my name, saying, I am Christ; and shall deceive many" (Matt 24:5); likewise Paul warned in his second epistle to Timothy that in the end times there would come "men of corrupt minds, reprobate concerning the faith" who would "resist the truth" (2 Tim 3:8). Interpreting these texts, evangelicals wove together their different perspectives on the end times into a contemporary narrative through which to make sense of their own lived experience of crisis.

An article from the May 1975 issue of the *Orange Standard* contains yet another vivid image which made effective use of apocalyptic-eschatological imagery in order to convey the alleged spiritual truth underlying the battle against the Catholic Church. The article invokes

73. *Orange Standard* (March, 1981), 1.

74. *Orange Standard* (March, 1980), 5.

75. *Orange Standard* (September, 1988), 8.

76. Smyth, *Rome*, 83.

the apocalyptic-eschatological parable of the wheat and tares which grow together in the same turf as an evocative metaphor for the struggle between Protestants and Catholics: "wheat and tares grow together in the same field. The virile Christian witness of Ulster was always in train with a pseudo-religion which was to spawn the callous criminal and depraved revolutionary by whom we have suffered so much."[77] This parable refers to the coming of the Son of Man who will bring judgment to the earth by throwing the wicked tares ("Catholics") into the fire and preserving the worthy wheat ("Protestants"). The attempt of the evangelical writer to establish semantic concurrence between the wicked tares and the enemies of "Ulster" was an example of an adroit and creative application of apocalyptic-eschatological rhetoric to the contemporary circumstances of Northern Ireland evangelicalism. Not only would the agricultural allusions of this parable have been particularly pertinent to the many readers of the *Orange Standard* from rural or farming backgrounds, but also the interpretive strategy employed in this instance distinguished itself from the usual literalism of many fundamentalist evangelical attempts to read their culture and the "signs of the times" in light of the apocalyptic-eschatological texts. Instead of resorting to crude identifications between contemporary figures and biblical apocalyptic-eschatological symbols, the writer invited readers to enter imaginatively into the narrative and thereby to discern for themselves the fusion of the horizon of the text and that of their contemporary experience.

This interpretation is also noteworthy because it offers a commentary upon an interpretation already offered within the text itself. Notwithstanding the evangelical appeals to the "Word of God" which was to be the "final authority," such interpretations reveal that evangelicals were not content to leave the interpretation offered by Jesus in the text, but instead felt obliged to offer a further reading of their society in light of their interpretation on the biblical text. This is recognized by perceiving that the text from Matthew 13 quoted above contains not only the parable but also Christ's interpretation of it: "The enemy that sowed them is the devil; the harvest is the end of the world; and the reapers are the angels." Thus the reading offered by the Orange evangelical contributor cited above, which expanded on these categories, can be seen as an "interpretation of an interpretation." Furthermore, if evangelical preachers reading this article had decided to use this text as the

77. *Orange Standard* (May, 1975), 8.

basis for their coming sermon, the text would have undergone a further process of interpretation not only on the part of the preachers but also by their congregations.

Although these notions are purely speculative, their very possibility exemplifies some of the theoretical insights outlined above by underlining the conception of a text both as "a communicative act and the object of subsequent interpretive acts."[78] The interpretation of apocalyptic-eschatological texts, such as the Parable of the Sower, and their continual reinterpretation is thus an illustrative example of a general hermeneutical process in which "meaning deploys itself by transcending its contexts, and by uniting those contexts often in new and unpredictable ways."[79] The notion of the text becoming involved in ceaseless processes of interpretation and reinterpretation thus corresponds to the notion of the inescapable endlessness of hermeneutical processes and the inherent iterability of texts, which invariably transcend the circumstances and any authorial intentions which might have governed the moment of their initial inscription.

Despite the vigor with which the Orange press attacked the Catholic Church, it is important to remember that the fear of the end-times apostasy, although largely attributed to the alleged malevolent influence of "Romanism," purportedly extended beyond the Catholic Church and encompassed a whole range of social and political developments such as the rise of Communism and humanism. The Grand Master of the Orange Lodge from 1971 to 1996, speaking at the height of the Troubles in 1974, perceived what he called, "a mistaken belief . . . that the drift from faith was a 'Romeward trend.'" Instead he suggested that the apostasy could be attributed to a "pagan Protestantism or a humanistic or Communistic stand." He further warned of "the growing peril . . . of growing ungodliness" posed by these threats.[80] Furthermore there were many Northern Ireland evangelicals who rejected the identification of the Pope as the Antichrist as the root cause of the alleged great apostasy. In conscious refutation of the Pope-as-Antichrist thesis, the Northern Ireland Conservative politician, author, and onetime President of the Evangelical Alliance, Fred Catherwood, made a case early on in the Troubles that,

78. Vanhoozer, *Meaning in This Text*, 368.
79. Kelly, *Language, World and God*, 79.
80. *Orange Standard* (June, 1974), 9.

> Anti-Christ is not confined to one church at one time. The spirit
> of anti-Christ is alive in many churches at many times. One per-
> son may personify the spirit at one time and another at another;
> there may be someone nearer the end who personifies it espe-
> cially, but it cannot be identified with the head of one church at
> one time or at all times.[81]

Even some of the most anti-Catholic communities of Northern Ireland evangelicalism admitted that Rome was not alone in its apparent crusade against Protestantism. Paisleyite publications expanded the orbit of those whom they considered to be their latter-day spiritual adversaries. Thus "the Modernists, the Ecumenists, the New Evangelicals, the Neo-Pentecostalists [and] the Communists" were lumped together with "the Romanists" as "enemies of the cross of Christ" (Phil 3:18).[82]

There can be little doubt that for many Northern Ireland evangelicals the manifestations of the end-times apostasy during the Troubles were tangible and ubiquitous. The forces of darkness were gathering themselves together and preparing for their final onslaught against "little Ulster."[83] On this point there was unanimity among several expressions of evangelicalism ranging from Baptists,[84] Pentecostals,[85] Free Presbyterians,[86] Anglicans,[87] Methodists,[88] and the Orange orders.[89] Many feared with the concerned author of an article which appeared in the May 1982 edition of the *Revivalist* that, "This is a dark day, but darker days are ahead of us."[90] Attempting to view the Troubles from an apocalyptic-eschatological perspective, one writer for the *Irish Baptist* expressed the views of many evangelicals from across the denomina-

81. Catherwood, *Christian Duty in Ulster Today*, 18.

82. *Revivalist* (August, 1976), 1.

83. Campbell, *For God and Ulster*, 25.

84. *Irish Baptist* 93 (July, 1971), 4.

85. McConnell, *A Light on a Hill*, 106.

86. *Revivalist* (July, 1977), 1.

87. Writing for the *Belfast Telegraph* (19 July, 1997), Anglican clergyman, Houston Kelvey, remarked: "The theory is that our streets will not get better. In fact, they may get worse. Television, multi-national global business, the whole rearrangement of modern life have left many people without a sense of morality."

88. See Methodist minister Edward McDaid's comments in the letter section in the *Belfast Telegraph* (5 July, 1997).

89. *Orange Standard* (April, 1993); *Ulster Bulwark* (January/February, 1978).

90. *Revivalist* (May, 1982), 9.

tional spectrum when he claimed that, "the Christian who views the world from the perspective of the Throne of God is aware of the fact that the forces of darkness will gather momentum as we move toward the close of the age."[91] The time leading up to the point of the expected supernatural intervention of God at the end of history would be characterized by an "ongoing and intensifying tribulation and apostasy," predicted the Reformed Presbyterian minister, Frederick Leahy.[92] Many evangelicals equated these dark forces with their political and religious enemies, such as the IRA and the Catholic Church. For others the threat was posed not merely by the religious forces of "hell-inspired Romanism" or "apostate Anglicanism"[93] but also non-religious organizations such as the BBC which some alleged to be conspiring in a plot to destroy Northern Ireland evangelicalism in the end times. The January 1967 edition of the *Protestant Telegraph* reported an evangelical protest against the "diabolical blasphemy" of a recently-broadcast BBC programme which denied the virginity of Mary and which portrayed Christ as her illegitimate son. Ian Paisley, who led the protest and addressed 1,000 people outside Broadcasting House in Belfast, expressed his dismay in the following lament, which interpreted the programme as further proof that the biblical prophecies concerning end times apostasy were now being fulfilled:

> I never thought I would live to see the day, in this city, when the BBC would so blatantly insult the Saviour, and so diabolically cast a sneer upon the virginity of the Lord's mother and upon the sinlessness of God's well-beloved Son. . . . But, of course we are living in days of apostasy, in days of darkness when damnable doctrines are being preached, and the BBC has become one of the most notorious agencies for the damnable doctrines of the devil.[94]

91. *Irish Baptist* 101 (December, 1978), 18.

92. Leahy, *Victory of the Lamb*, 97.

93. *Protestant Telegraph* (3 October, 1981), 4.

94. *Protestant Telegraph* (7 January, 1967), 3. In the following edition, several readers send letters in support of Paisley's protest. Some of the respondents gave English and Scottish addresses which indicate that the *Protestant Telegraph* enjoyed a readership that extended beyond the borders of Northern Ireland. The editors continued to complain in their 21 November 1970 issue that, "the B.B.C. is biased and discriminates against true Christians."

Whilst some threats, such as that of "blasphemous" BBC productions were perceived as originating from outside of the church, others originated within the church through the dissemination of "damnable heresies" (2 Pet 2:1) and the "doctrine of devils" (1 Tim 4:1). Such was Satan's cunning and malice in the end times that he always launched simultaneous attacks from within and outside the church. Thus such movements as the Charismatic Renewal, which emerged after 1960, were branded by some evangelicals as the latest manifestation of the satanic conspiracy against "biblical Christianity" and the deception through the performance of "lying wonders" which would accompany Antichrist and the false prophet in the end times.[95] "The spirit of the Charismatic Renewal," claimed the *Protestant Telegraph*, "is the spirit of Antichrist," and another diabolical device for the advancement of the Catholic Church's "great deception to further union with Rome in the great apostasy [sic] of this generation."[96] By 1989 the Free Presbyterian Church alleged that the apostasy instigated by the ecumenical movement had infiltrated the evangelical churches in Northern Ireland to such an extent that it felt compelled to issue its "statement from the General Presbytery":

> It is with deep regret that we see such churches as Christian Brethren, the Baptist Union of Scotland and the Salvation Army among the already ecumenically-hardened Churches of our nation. Because of this sad departure from the Word of God and the deception on the part of ecumenical clergy, we must, before God, raise our voice in protest against this further attempt to extinguish the light of the gospel truth in this our beloved nation.[97]

The tenor of this statement, despite its undertones of lament, is somewhat resigned. It is as though those who drafted the statement were able to acknowledge with a certain degree of equanimity the prevailing apostasy of the churches, since this was clearly the Great Apostasy predicted in ancient holy writ which was now being fulfilled.

Thus every apparent indication of ecclesial or social decline was accompanied by a presentiment of apprehension and thus subjected to a searching evangelical critique which often possessed evocative apocalyptic-eschatological undertones in order to add conviction to the censure of purportedly deleterious social developments. Regarding homosexual

95. *Protestant Telegraph* (27 May, 1967), 9.

96. *Protestant Telegraph* (21 November, 1981), 4.

97. The statement was published in the *New Protestant Telegraph* (15 April, 1989), 1.

activity as "the vilest act and most debasing thing imaginable,"[98] some fundamentalists responded with vehement opposition to the attempts made to liberalize the laws concerning homosexuality in Northern Ireland. The proposed changes in the legal status of homosexuality were developments that provoked a heated response from Paisley and other fundamentalist evangelicals. As well as regarding the proposed amendments to the law as a sign of a world in the last throes of the Great Apostasy, many evangelical churches articulated their protests using the language of apocalyptic eschatology, such as "crisis" and "social breakdown" and "lawlessness" to describe the advance of what many called "sodomy." This was a clear allusion to the infamous scene depicted in Genesis 19:1–29, in which God destroys the cities of Sodom and Gomorrah with fire and brimstone allegedly on account of the inhabitants' sin of homosexuality.

The ubiquitous use of the word, "sodomy," is significant to our discussion of the use of apocalyptic-eschatological language, for in the New Testament Jesus links the story of Sodom and Gomorrah to the terrible judgment upon sin which will accompany the final judgment. Speaking of the city of Capernaum which rejected his message, Jesus declared that, "it shall be more tolerable for the land of Sodom in the day of judgment, than for thee" (Matt 11:24). As the proposed "sodomy Laws" were advanced by the British government so as to apply to Northern Ireland, the *Irish Baptist* reported that the increase in gay activism was a clear "symptom of moral decay which is gaining a deep-seated hold on the country."[99] The following year the Baptist Union of Ireland published a report to the Secretary of State for Northern Ireland, entitled, "Comments on the Proposal for a Draft Homosexual Offences Order 1978." In this report the Union warned that, "To give free rein to it [homosexual practices] . . . is in our view a recipe for the disintegration and destruction of society."[100] Almost exactly the same kind of language was employed at this time in the *Ulster Bulwark* in response to these changes in the law. The editors warned that, "If these laws become a reality the whole moral fabric of our society will be in danger of collapsing" and further claimed that the government's attempt to force changes to the legal status of homosexuality amounted to an act

98. Paisley, *Romans*, 27.

99. *Irish Baptist* 100 (December, 1977), 6–7.

100. *Irish Baptist* 101 (November, 1978), 28.

of "moral terrorism."[101] Once the acts had been passed, the *Bulwark* protested that Northern Ireland had since become "a land polluted with carnality and wickedness."[102] Some of the literature produced by the Ulster Unionist Party several years later in the mid-1990s likewise lamented these developments: "Parliament has voted to lower the age of consent to eighteen years for homosexuals, thus marking another milestone in this Kingdom's slide into the midden of moral filth and decay."[103] Although this quotation contains no direct allusion to apocalyptic-eschatological language, the critique can be located in the same semantic field as some of the more explicitly theological critiques of these developments. Thus the writer may be regarded in this instance as having drawn on a dominant apocalyptic-eschatological trope of social criticism even if he was not in fact conscious of having done so. Nevertheless, the writer may indeed have been fully aware of the apocalyptic-eschatological undertones of his condemnation of homosexuality for he concludes his caustic critique with a compelling comment, which invokes the eschatological motif of justice and judgment upon sin: "We also recognise something which the sodomites, among others, do not, and that is, we will all have to face the Judge of all the earth one day."[104] As late as 2001 Northern Ireland evangelicals continued to use the same kind of rhetoric to lament these allegedly deplorable social trends: "Today we see legislation increasingly influenced by prevailing humanistic philosophies. Homosexual 'rights' are being acknowledged and radical feminist demands met in a growing number of countries."[105] In this instance the author, F. S. Leahy, linked these developments to the apocalyptic-eschatological biblical teachings concerning the "Great Tribulation," which he said was to characterize "the whole period between Christ's two comings and will reach climactic proportions before Christ returns."[106]

According to many evangelicals, the spiritual deterioration of Northern Ireland went hand in hand with moral decline. Furthermore, these lamentable phenomena, many alleged, could be traced back to

101. *Ulster Bulwark* (January/February 1978), 10.

102. *Ulster Bulwark* (January/February 1979), 2.

103. *Ulster Review* (March, 1994), 14–15. The *Ulster Review* was the journal of the Ulster Young Unionist Council.

104. Ibid., 15.

105. Leahy, *Victory of the Lamb*, 88.

106. Ibid.

a common source: the Catholic Church. Throughout the 1980s the evangelical press linked the apparent rise of homosexual activity to the increase in reported instances of sexual abuse committed by Catholic priests. As well as arguing generally that Catholicism has "a tendency to cultivate a certain moral blindness,"[107] it was also alleged that up to 50 percent of Catholic priests were homosexuals.[108] The Orange orders likewise often lamented the process of social degeneration and the proliferation of apocalyptic lawlessness, which many regarded as inexorable. The *Orange Standard* in 1982 complained that, "we in Northern Ireland in common with the rest of the United Kingdom have seen our land become the 20th century Sodom and Gomorrah."[109] The Orangeman, Clifford Smyth—who, ironically, outed himself as a transvestite in a series of articles in the *Belfast Telegraph* in 2005[110]—in 1974 bewailed the alleged breakdown of Northern Ireland society and the concomitant signs of ruin which he said were "all facets of a spiritual malaise which would drag us into the pit."[111] The note of social lament is also to be heard in the texts of Reformed evangelicalism. As late as November 2003 the Presbyterian magazine, *The Christian Irishman,* contained an article which lamented the apparent moral decline of Northern Ireland which manifested itself in blasphemy and godlessness: "In modern developed societies the rejection of God is manifest. Ours is an age of unbelief. God is now effectively abolished from public discourse. His name is rarely mentioned except in blasphemy."[112]

Evangelicals believed that they were living in apocalyptic times in which society was disintegrating all around them. It seemed that the time of the "Great Tribulation" had come.

107. *New Protestant Telegraph* (14 October, 1990), 2.

108. *New Protestant Telegraph* (28 January, 1989), 1.

109. *Orange Standard* (November, 1982), 5.

110. *Belfast Telegraph* (20–21 July, 2005).

111. Smyth, *Rome* (1974), 84. This phrase also appears in one of Smith's election pamphlets from 1974, entitled, "Vote for the Right Man: Clifford Smyth, Official Unionist."

112. *Christian Irishman* (November, 2003), 11.

The Proliferation of "damnable heresies" during the Troubles

Other signs that were interpreted by some Northern Ireland evangelicals as an end-times satanic assault against the true church of "biblical Christianity" included the broader developments in theological scholarship in this period, many of which did not go unnoticed by Northern Ireland evangelicals. The turbulent events which marked the start of the Troubles coincided with a radical "shaking of the foundations" of theological scholarship,[113] which to some extent corresponded with the prevailing social upheaval of the late 1960s and 1970s. Sociologists have already uncovered the extent of the crisis of the churches in Britain during the 1960s. Callum Brown traces the decline to a single year, arguing that, "suddenly in 1963, something very profound ruptured the character of the nation and its people, sending organized Christianity on a downward spiral to the margins of social significance."[114] Theological commentators have noted that this was "an era of confusion in which many people were searching for new answers" and that no previous era in human history "had witnessed such rapid secularisation combined with new, intense hopes for humanity."[115] This was a time of unparalleled secularization, political protest, and the mobilisation of social movements campaigning for individual freedoms, civil rights, and armament reduction. Northern Ireland was by no means detached from the cultural and political ferment of the 1960s and 1970s. Neither was the world of theological scholarship. In an attempt to meet the new challenges posed by the crisis, many theologians attempted to recast Christian faith in terms understandable to the emerging culture. Appealing to Dietrich Bonhoeffer's claim that Christianity had to reimagine itself in a world which had now "come of age,"[116] theologians began to proclaim the "death of God," to ask questions such as "does God lie at the center of Christian faith and proclamation?"[117] and to address what they felt was "the isolation of faith from the concrete and present reality of human existence."[118] Drawing on Hegel and Nietzsche, many theologians de-

---

113. Gilkey, *Naming the Whirlwind*, 9.

114. Brown, *Death of Christian Britain*, 1.

115. Grenz and Olson, *20th-Century Theology*, 170.

116. Selby in de Grunchy, ed., *Cambridge Companion to Dietrich Bonhoeffer*, 226–45.

117. Altizer, *Gospel of Christian Atheism*.

118. Ibid., 2.

parted from classical theism and preached instead what they called a "Gospel of Christian Atheism." Included in the reforming program was a radical overhaul of traditional conceptions of apocalyptic eschatology, which was recast as a mythological representation of an alleged innate existential yearning for transcendence, rather than as a literal description of actual historical events.[119] Alongside but independent of these radical deviations from classical theism was the publication of alternative Bible translations to the standard King James Version of 1611. These included the *Good News Bible*,[120] the *New International Version*[121] and most notably the controversial *New English Bible* in 1961 (New Testament) and 1970 (Old Testament and Apocrypha).[122]

The inclusion of these developments in our present inquiry is justified by the fact that there is evidence from the primary sources that Northern Ireland evangelicals themselves showed an interest in them. Many fundamentalist evangelicals perceived in their emergence the fulfilment of biblical prophecies concerning the dissemination of "damnable heresies" (2 Pet 2:1), which were believed to characterize the last days. Some evangelicals were so repulsed by these ideas that they concluded that these apparent profane deviations from "biblical truth" must have been the work of a malevolent spirit of the end times. Perhaps even Satan himself, knowing that "he hath but a short time" (Rev 12:12), was at work in their propagation. This view was held particularly by fundamentalist evangelicals who interpreted these drastic departures from traditional theism as manifestations of the spirit of Antichrist whose teachings and false doctrines were to become increasingly prevalent in the last days. It is highly feasible to assume that Paisley had these developments in mind, particularly Bultmann's endeavors to purge the Christian faith of its mythological vestiges, when he exclaimed:

119. The most significant theologian associated with these endeavors was Rudolf Bultmann. The English translations of his two most significant works, *Theologie des Neuen Testaments* and *Das Evangelium des Johannes*, appeared in 1970 and 1971 respectively.

120. First published as the New Testament under the title, *Good News for Modern Man*. The translation of the Old Testament was finished in 1976 and both testaments were published under the title, *Good News Bible: The Bible in Today's English*.

121. First published as the New Testament only in 1973 and then as the Old and New Testaments in a single volume in 1978.

122. Paisley condemned these modern versions as translations inspired by the Antichrist. See *Protestant Telegraph* (17 February, 1973), 3.

> This assault on the doctrine of the Virgin Birth is, however, but one phase of a great battle to evacuate the supernatural from Christianity and to reduce it to the plane of natural religion. These naturalists in religion are out to destroy supernatural Christianity. They go through the Bible and tell us there is no supernatural revelation there; they go through the Birth of Christ and tell us there is no supernatural incarnation there; they go through the Person of Christ and tell us there is no supernatural deity there.[123]

Another example is the reception of the controversial book consisting of seven essays edited by John Hick, entitled *The Myth of God Incarnate*, and published in 1977. In this book Hick and the other contributors sought to downplay the uniqueness of Christ. Hick's theological convictions led him to the belief that a more comprehensive conception of God could facilitate dialogue between adherents of different faiths. The articles in the book proceed from the premise that Jesus was "a man approved by God (Acts 2:21) for a special role within the divine purpose and that the later conception of him as God incarnate . . . is a mythological or poetic way of expressing his significance for us."[124] Such assertions provoked outrage among some Northern Ireland evangelicals who perceived in such "blasphemy" the latest manifestation of ecumenical syncretism that was to pave the way for the Antichrist to assume control of the church. The front page of the July 1977 edition of the *Revivalist* contained a scathing review of Hick's book, which it rather predictably denounced as "a blasphemous attack on the Deity of our Lord Jesus Christ." For the editors and readers of the *Revivalist*, Hick's book was adduced as a certain proof that the end times were now at hand. "The book itself," protested the irate reviewer, "stands as a monument to the truth of the Prophetic Word that in the last days men shall deny, "the only Lord God and our Lord Jesus Christ" (Jude 4). Speaking of what it called "this dark age of apostasy," the *Revivalist* invoked 1 Timothy 4:1 and declared that Hick and his "apostate" Anglican collaborators were teaching the "doctrine of devils," which, it was alleged, were to become more widespread as the end times approached their apocalyptic denouement.[125]

123. Paisley, *Christian Foundations*, 16. The year that Paisley published these remarks, 1971, was also the year of the publication of the English translation of Bultmann's controversial *Gospel of John*.

124. Hick, ed., *Myth of God Incarnate*, iv.

125. *Revivalist* (July, 1977), 1.

In a booklet devoted specifically to the refutation of Hick's thesis, Ian Paisley made an explicit link between the heretical tendencies of recent theological scholarship, such as those represented by Hick, and the end times apostasy forecast in biblical prophecy:

> as the Age of grace climaxes to its conclusion and the great worldwide apostasy foretold by the Spirit of God in prophecy is unfolded there shall come attack after attack upon the true Gospel by the presentation of a counterfeit gospel, and an attack upon the true work of the Holy Spirit by the operation of a counterfeit work of a satanic spirit.[126]

Paisley also responded fervently to the proliferation of alternative Bible translations which appeared during this period. The modern translations were condemned by Paisley and many other Northern Ireland evangelicals on account of their perceived accommodation to the liberalizing trends of the age. Paisley's denunciations of alternative translations as manifestations of the spirit of the Antichrist in the end times were stated clearly and unambiguously.[127]

The Stability and Continuity of Apocalyptic-Eschatological Language during the Troubles

Many of the expressions of apocalyptic-eschatological fear cited above can be elucidated through an examination of the underlying linguistic conventions at play in their use and propagation in the cultures of Northern Ireland evangelicals. In these instances the apocalyptic-eschatological language employed by evangelicals was involved in shaping the worldviews of evangelical readers. Apocalyptic eschatology became an interpretive paradigm which was used to provide an overarching perspective on a wide variety of events, each of which was read in terms of apocalyptic categories and symbols derived from ancient texts. It remains to be demonstrated that apocalyptic-eschatological discourse was no mere response to particular instances of crisis but, on the contrary,

---

126. Paisley, *Myth of God Incarnate Reviewed and Refuted*, 23.

127. Bruce, *History of the Bible*, 247. Paisley's attacks on modern Bible translations predates the Troubles by several years. Bruce noted that Paisley's "blunderbuss attack . . . misfired . . . by suggesting that the inclusion of the Apocrypha in a Protestant Bible was an innovation," pointing out that the deuterocanonical books had been included by the Geneva and King James translators as "a matter of course."

provided the vocabulary and conceptual framework with which the crisis itself was articulated and interpreted.

When we compare apocalyptic-eschatological discourses between different periods in the Troubles, we are struck by their semantic and formal resemblance. Apocalyptic-eschatological language seems not to have evolved but to have remained fairly constant throughout the conflict and to have functioned relatively independently of the events and circumstances associated with the Troubles. The lack of reference to the immediate context of a particular political crisis makes it very difficult to contextualize the apocalyptic-eschatological rhetoric of Northern Ireland evangelicals during this period.

One way of demonstrating the problems of contextualizing apocalyptic-eschatological utterances is to consider why so many Northern Ireland evangelicals considered the Pope to be the Antichrist and why the articulation of this conviction remained so constant throughout the Troubles. The association of the Bishop of Rome with the Antichrist or "man of sin" of 2 Thessalonians 2 was a significant undercurrent of the end-times convictions of the leading sixteenth-century reformers, most notably Martin Luther.[128] The Pope-as-Antichrist thesis antedated the Troubles by several centuries and it acquired particular prominence during certain periods in the history of Irish Protestantism, including the Northern Ireland Troubles. Although the apocalyptic language used to condemn the Pope as Antichrist remained fairly constant even up to the time of the Northern Ireland Troubles, the historical context was an important factor in determining how evangelical interpreters used this language for particular political and religious purposes. Therefore, although context was important in determining how the language was used or why such language assumed prominence at a particular time, the apocalyptic-eschatological language of evangelicals was not merely a reflection or response to particular historical contexts. As historians have pointed out, apocalyptic eschatological debate has been at the center of the history of Irish theological controversy since the Reformation and

128. Meyer, "Das Papstum bei Luther," 306–28; Asendorf, *Eschatologie bei Luther,* 173–87. The notion that the Pope was the fulfilment of certain biblical prophecies concerning the Antichrist is at least as old as the thirteenth century. See Wainwright, *Mysterious Apocalypse,* 57–61. In his *Inferno,* Dante, although falling short of an explicit identification, nevertheless censured the power abuses of the popes of his day, including Boniface VIII, who is placed by the poet in the circle of hell reserved for those guilty of simony; Dante, *Inferno,* Canto XIX, 100–101.

has made a decisive contribution to the shaping of Irish Protestantism.[129] From the early seventeenth century until the time of the Troubles, the Pope-as-Antichrist thesis was a significant force in the discourse of Irish Protestantism. The link between the head of the Catholic Church and the mysterious iniquitous apocalyptic figure of 2 Thessalonians 2 was first codified in the *Irish Articles* of 1615, which as Crawford Gribben observes, was "the first European confession of faith to formally identify the Antichrist as the Pope."[130] Alan Ford has helpfully highlighted the anti-Catholic bias of the *Irish Articles* by comparing them to the *Thirty-Nine Articles* of 1562, which regulated the belief and practice of the English Church. "For the most part," he explains, "the English anti-Catholic articles were included verbatim, but strengthened by the addition of further material."[131] An example of such "further material" was Article 80 of the *Articles*, which posited unequivocally that the Pope was "that man of sin, foretold in the Scriptures."[132] Although this identification does not appear in the *Thirty-Nine Articles*, it was retained by the Reformed Churches and later enshrined in the Westminster Confession of 1647.[133] This codification of Reformed doctrine remained foundational to evangelical beliefs in Northern Ireland well into the twentieth century, even though there were many, notably moderate voices within the Presbyterian Church in Ireland, which challenged the necessity of

129. Ford, *Theology, History and Politics*, 76–84. Ford refers to apocalyptic as the "underlying theme" of Protestant theological polemics against various alleged abuses of the Catholic Church. Apocalyptic anti-Catholic rhetoric was a constant feature of the theological debates in Cromwellian Ireland; see Gribben, *God's Irishmen*. Referring to a later period, McBride has helpfully uncovered the extent to which the worldviews of some of the leading figures of the Rebellion of the United Irishmen in 1798 were derived from apocalyptic-eschatological biblical texts; see McBride, *Scripture Politics*, 195–201.

130. Gribben, *God's Irishmen*, 8.

131. Ford, *Theology, History and Politics*, 93.

132. The full quotation from Article 80 reads thus: "The Bishop of Rome is so far from being the supreme head of the universal church of Christ that his works and doctrine do plainly discover him to be that 'man of sin' foretold in the Holy Scriptures, 'whom the Lord shall consume with the spirit of his mouth, and abolish with the brightness of his coming.'"

133. Chapter XXV of the Westminster Confession identifies the Pope as "that antichrist, that man of sin, and son of perdition that exalteth himself against Christ, and all that is called God."

the inclusion of this divisive contention of the papal Antichrist in the canonical formulation of the Church's belief.[134]

The apocalyptic ferment which characterized the history of post-Reformation Irish theological controversy bequeathed to twentieth-century Northern Ireland evangelicalism a field of discourse charged with profound apocalyptic undertones. The distinctive discursive legacy, cultivated from a long tradition of theological polemics in Irish history, created the conditions which facilitated the notion among evangelicals that contemporary events were infused with apocalyptic significance. Thus if we wish to understand the context of apocalyptic-eschatological rhetoric in Northern Ireland during the Troubles, we have recourse not to the immediate events of the Troubles but to the broader discursive context of Irish apocalypticism which facilitated the development of an idiomatic vocabulary which found expression in a variety of verbal and non-verbal textual forms in the period between 1967 and 2007. The events of the Troubles were interpreted by numerous evangelicals in relation to where they fitted with what one evangelical publication referred to as "the great unveiling of the prophetic calendar of God."[135] As historians have already observed, "massacre stories from 1641, the siege of Derry, the Famine, disestablishment, and the persecution of Protestants after the institution of the Free State have each been retold as elements of a larger apocalyptic narrative."[136] The framework and texture of this narrative originated in the ancient apocalyptic-eschatological biblical texts, especially the book of Revelation. This text, when read in conjunction with the other biblical apocalyptic-eschatological material, became the vantage point from which evangelicals could perceive their suffering from the eternal perspective of God's ultimate purpose, which for evangelicals was suffused with eschatological hope.

The "apocalyptic narrative" bestowed an element of perceived continuity between the historical experience of the evangelicals in "ages past" and the evangelicals who lived through the Troubles.[137] Since

134. At a lecture delivered at the Public Closing of the Presbyterian College, Belfast on 26th May, 1967, Presbyterian John Barkley asserted that, "subscription to the Westminster "Confession of Faith" in Irish Presbyterianism does not involve acceptance of the statement that the pope is "that antichrist, that man of sin and son of perdition." See Barkley, *Antichrist*, 12.

135. *New Protestant Telegraph* (March, 1991), 5.

136. Gribben, "Protestant Millennialism," 52.

137. This phrase is derived from hymn "O God our Help in Ages Past." Although

apocalyptic-eschatological language had a trans-generational quality, it became possible for one generation of contemporary evangelicals to feel as though the wrongs perpetrated by their enemies in a previous age, even extending back many centuries, constituted just as much an injustice to them in their age. The discursive legacy of anti-Catholic theological hermeneutics thus created the narrative framework through which evangelicals in the Troubles could regard the Catholic-orchestrated massacres of the planters in 1641 and the Siege of Derry in 1689[138] as acts of injustice that retained a compelling contemporary relevance because they were interpreted in the scheme of continuity established by the overarching apocalyptic struggle which transcended generations and historical contexts. An extract from an article written against the ecumenical movement in a 1990 issue of the *New Protestant Telegraph* captures this sentiment succinctly: "Our Bible is against unity with the Roman Antichrist for such is what the Bible and the Homilies of the Church of England declare the Pope to be. . . . Our history is against such

---

composed by the English theologian, logician and hymn writer, Isaac Watts in 1719, this hymn became widely popular among Northern Ireland evangelicals. Watt's hymn, explained one evangelical writing for the *Orange Standard*, became "'Ulster's National Anthem' and [has been] used worldwide in times of national remembrance and emergency . . . the finest hymn in the English language"; *Orange Standard* (April, 1984), 6. As well as being sung regularly throughout churches in Northern Ireland, the words of the hymn were often quoted on the covers or in the articles of evangelical publications. See *New Protestant Telegraph* (25 February, 1989), 6. When Northern Ireland evangelicals sang with passion the words of the hymn, "O God our help in ages past, our hope for years to come," they were not merely indulging in religious triumphalism, but were expressing their identity through their sense of continuity with those who had been similarly faithful to God in "ages past." The reference to "our help in ages past" is significant. "Ages past" implies ages in the distant past, long preceding the lifetime of those who were alive to be able to sing these words. Could it be that this line appealed to Northern Ireland evangelicals specifically because it linked them to their predecessors through the continuity established by the overarching apocalyptic narrative? If so, the "our" in the line "our help in ages past" is a clear expression of commonality between contemporary evangelicals and their spiritual forebears from previous centuries. The significance of this particular hymn to Northern Ireland evangelicals has been recognized by many scholarly contributions towards the understanding of the Troubles, including Mitchell, *Religion, Identity and Politics*, 40; McIntosh, *Force of Culture*, 50; Bryan, *Orange Parades*, 12; Bruce, *Paisley: Religion and Politics*, 124.

138. This event in particular has been recognized by the historiography to have been one of the turning points in Irish history: Bardon, *History of Ulster*, 158; Dawe and Foster, eds., *Poet's Place*, 262.

unity because the struggles to escape Rome's persecutions of Protestants cannot be forgotten."[139]

The continuity was established by the apocalyptic narrative out of which arose the conviction that the evangelicals during the Troubles were involved in the same apocalyptic-eschatological struggle as their spiritual forefathers. As John Brewer points out, "Ulster's contest is the recurring conflict between good and evil, truth and error, which are age-old battles."[140] The Bible, from which Northern Ireland evangelicals claimed to derive their worldview, makes it clear that the Christian's warfare is not against "flesh and blood" but against the "rulers of the darkness of this world, against spiritual wickedness in high places" (Eph 6:12).[141] Since, unlike flesh and blood, these powers were seen to be spiritual, they transcended time. Although Northern Ireland evangelicals during the Troubles were aware that they were not fighting the same flesh and blood enemies as those who resisted the Siege of Derry in 1689, some were nevertheless convinced that they were engaged in battle against the same spiritual powers. While the particular historical manifestations of Antichrist had changed, the basic underlying spiritual essence of the "enemy" remained identical.[142]

Thus, A. Y. Collins' notion that apocalyptic-eschatological biblical texts such as Revelation should be read as "a poetic interpretation of human experience in which ancient patterns of conflict are used to illuminate the deeper significance of currently experienced conflict"[143] could be applied with equal precision to the use of apocalyptic-eschatological language in Northern Ireland during the Troubles. Perceiving the "deeper significance" of their "currently experienced conflict," many evangelicals believed themselves to be engaged in a fight not against par-

139. *New Protestant Telegraph* (October, 1990), 4. The reference to the "Homilies of the Church of England" in this quotation is peculiar and apparently inexplicable, especially considering that the Church of England, in contrast to the Church of Ireland, never formally codified the notion of the Pope as Antichrist in any of its official statements.

140. Brewer, "Contesting Ulster," 285.

141. The New International Version accentuates the other-worldliness even more than the King James Version by translating ἐντοῖςἐπουρανίοις as "in the heavenly realms."

142. A similar point is made by Gribben in relation to the millennial discourses of the seventeenth-century Puritans, whose various theological and political enemies became "subsumed into the same eschatological personality—they were all the soldiers of Antichrist." See Gribben, *Puritan Millennium*, 181.

143. Collins, *Combat Myth*, 3.

ticular individuals who could be historicized according to a particular social context; this was an apocalyptic struggle against a spiritual enemy, whose underlying identity, however much it might adjust its outward manifestation according to different periods of history, remained fundamentally the same in spiritual essence. Crucially, moreover, since the evangelicals during the Troubles and their spiritual forefathers from the time of the Plantation and onwards all read essentially the same texts, they thus can be said to have occupied a common "semiosphere" through which to interpret the meaning of prevailing trends and events.[144]

A close analysis of the apocalyptic-eschatological rhetoric of Northern Ireland evangelicals reveals the extent to which these attitudes prevailed among some evangelical cultures during the Troubles. In 1975 Paisley denounced the IRA as "devotees of that godless monster which has drenched Ireland with blood for many generations—the godless monster of a United Ireland."[145] It is notable that the real enemy which Paisley identifies in this passage is not the individual IRA terrorist but the alleged animating evil power of the "godless monster" which lay behind particular acts of terrorism. Moreover, the "godless monster" is a metaphor reminiscent of the various evil beasts which appear in apocalyptic texts such as Daniel and Revelation. His use of the word, "devotees" suggests that he believed the IRA terrorists were hapless pawns of the "real" underlying enemy, "the godless monster," which was not only spiritual but also explicitly apocalyptic in nature and intention. Thus it can be shown that apocalyptic-eschatological texts provided evangelicals with the vocabulary and the worldview through which they could frame a conception of their enemy. The transcendent nature of the apocalyptic-eschatological language reflected the quality of timelessness of the perceived enemy, who was invariably identified with one of the characters depicted in the biblical texts pertaining to the end times, such as the Beast, the man of sin or the Scarlet Woman.[146] Even movements and or-

144. The term "semiosphere" is borrowed from Pyman, "Prism of the Orthodox Semisphere," 103–15.

145. Paisley, *A Call to the Protestants of Ulster*, 1.

146. Alternative identifications of the Scarlet Woman of the Apocalypse, which might have challenged the hegemony of the "Pope-as-Antichrist," were rarely made by Northern Ireland evangelicals. In my extensive research of magazines, sermon transcripts and newspaper articles, I found only one alternative interpretation, which consisted in the identification of the Scarlet Woman as the symbolic representation of unbridled consumerism. An article from *Frontiers* invoked the Babylonian Whore in

ganizations which, superficially, appeared to have very little in common were perceived to be animated by a common apocalyptic-eschatological malevolent power. For instance, two apparently unrelated phenomena such as the Charismatic Renewal ("the spirit of Antichrist")[147] and the European Union ("the kingdom of the Antichrist")[148] were "read" as texts of a common narrative and were branded with the same terms derived from apocalyptic eschatology.

Since the perceived underlying enemy, the Antichrist, was always the same, regardless of the particular manifestations he assumed in particular historical contexts, Northern Ireland evangelicals could effectively reproduce the same kind of language to address a variety of situations. These, as we have already demonstrated, included threatening events and developments within the church including the upsurge of ecumenical activism, the emergence of worldwide inter-faith bodies, the proliferation of the charismatic movement, the perceived widespread apostasy of formerly "Bible-believing" churches and the dissemination of "blasphemous" literature by leading theologians, such as John Hick's syncretism and Altizer and Hamilton's theology of the death of God. Alongside these apparent threats within the church appeared the social and cultural perils of the European Union, changes in the legal status of homosexuality and the alleged associated disintegration of society as well as "profane" television broadcasts that cast doubt on the virgin conception of Christ. Each of these events and processes was textualized in so far as each became a text which was infused with meaning and significance according to the apocalyptic-eschatological narrative.[149]

One of the most conspicuous instances of the process through which apocalyptic eschatology transforms events into texts is to be seen in the ways in which evangelicals understood the words of ancient texts to be literal descriptions of the events that were taking place before their eyes. In one notable article purporting to uncover the apocalyptic-eschatological significance of the expansion of the European Union, an

a critique of consumerism by identifying her as the "prostitute of materialism" whose wares "sound uncomfortably similar to what we buy from Lunn's, Next, Habitat, Body Shop, Sainsbury's deli counter and Bavarian garages." See *Frontiers* (Winter, 1999), 22. See also Elsdon, *The Lamb Wins*, 30, which identified Babylon with the system of "decadent capitalism."

147. *Protestant Telegraph* (21 November, 1981), 4.

148. *Revivalist* (June, 1975), 15.

149. Robbins and Palmer, eds., *Millennium*, 5.

evangelical author substituted the archaic terms of biblical language for modern equivalents relating to contemporary affairs. Thus the word "ephah" (the ancient measuring unit applied to the weighing of dry produce) contained in Zechariah's prophecy was replaced by "big business." Similarly the "woman" depicted in Zechariah 5 as the embodiment of wickedness was interpreted as a direct reference to contemporary apostate Roman Catholicism. So when Zechariah wrote, "And he cast it [the woman] into the midst of the ephah" (Zech 5:8), the evangelical author averred that what Zechariah really meant was, "And he cast the Roman Catholic Church in[to] the midst of Big Business."[150] Such interpretations of biblical texts, which attempted to expose the alleged nefarious plotting of the Catholic Church by interpreting current events in the light of biblical apocalyptic-eschatological passages, were an enduring feature of Northern Ireland evangelical hermeneutics during the "Troubles." The reconfiguration of the ancient biblical writings thus created the conditions whereby an event could be transformed into a text by virtue of its perceived role in contributing to the procession of the overarching apocalyptic-eschatological narrative.[151]

This chapter has elucidated the diverse evangelical uses of apocalyptic-eschatological language in relation to the notion of fear which pervaded evangelical discourses during the Troubles. The analysis of the various texts quoted above has thus illuminated the hermeneutical processes through which written texts become constitutive of perceptions of contextual reality. In particular this chapter has explained how the ancient texts of biblical prophecy can contribute to the process through which events become textualized. The apocalyptic-eschatological narrative conferred meaning and order upon otherwise contingent and unconnected events. In the semantic field of apocalyptic eschatology, every seemingly incidental event becomes suffused with purpose and intentionality. Richard Landes identifies this as a condition of "semiotic arousal" in which "everything has meaning, patterns." Landes remarks that in such a condition "the smallest incident can have immense importance and open the way to an entirely new vision of the world, one in which forces unseen by other mortals operate."[152] Adapting Landes' insights to the purposes of this study, we may say that in a condition of

---

150. *Protestant Telegraph* (10 June, 1967), 6.

151. Pannenberg, "Hermeneutics and Universal History," 113.

152. Landes, "Millenarianism and the Dynamics of Apocalyptic Time," 4.

"semiotic arousal," events are transformed into texts. Apocalyptic eschatology, by imparting a quality of narrative cohesion to apparently discon-
nected events, transforms these events and renders them conformable
to the interpretive norms derived from the "prophetic calendar" supposedly laid out in the texts of apocalyptic eschatology. The notion that
apocalyptic-eschatological language could impart such a narrative cohesion brings us to one of the cornerstone conceptions of evangelical hope
in Northern Ireland during the Troubles. Accordingly, whilst pursuing
the analysis of the subtle dialectic of textuality and contextuality, the
next chapter will consider the issue from the perspective of hope.

4

Apocalyptic Hope

"And I saw a new heaven and a new earth"

Introduction to Chapter 4

"Hope," according to Richard Landes, "is the key to understanding the apocalyptic mind-set."[1] Acknowledging the ways in which apocalyptic eschatology can transfigure notions of chaos and crisis into an overarching narrative of directionality, purpose and hope, it is important to consider how apocalyptic-eschatological language shaped the deepest aspirations of evangelicals in Northern Ireland. Just as pervasive as Antichrist, the Whore of Babylon, the False Prophet, and the Great Tribulation in Northern Ireland evangelical discourses were the symbolic representations of apocalyptic-eschatological hope such as the messianic Lamb of God, the New Jerusalem and the new heavens and new earth. Thus the same evangelical who could speak in dire tones of the "great abyss of the damned" and the "furnace of everlasting fire"[2] could also exclaim bombastically his hope of an anticipated apocalyptic-eschatological consummation with the same rhetorical grandiloquence:

1. Landes, "The Fear of an Apocalyptic Year 1000," 245. Wessinger makes a similar point in her introduction to the Oxford Handbook of Millennialism, when she defines millennialism as "the audacious human hope that in the imminent future there will be a transition—either catastrophic or progressive—to a collective salvation." See Wessinger, "Millennialism in Cross-Cultural Perspective," 3.

2. Paisley, *Mr Lostman*, 9.

> What a thrill when we sit down with Christ in His throne even
> as He also overcame and is sat [*sic*] down with His Father in His
> throne! What eternal majesty! What undiminishable glory! What
> infinite bliss![3]

Similarly one Northern Ireland evangelical could lament that, "Our age
is marked by deepening gloom and despair," and yet in the same breath
could speak exultantly of "the glorious appearing of our great God and
Saviour, Jesus Christ, which will result in the final defeat of all His enemies, and the establishment of new heavens and a new earth in which
righteousness will be triumphant."[4] Other evangelicals expressed their
hope in resurrection and eternal life in the terms bequeathed to them
by the biblical texts of apocalyptic eschatology. One text thus refers to
the "resurrection body" of Philippians 3, which "shall be incorruptible."
The same text expands on this hope, noting that, "Not only will we be
free from the effects of sin—sickness and death and the grave, but it will
never again be possible . . . that sin and death return."[5] Such conceptualizations of apocalyptic-eschatological hope were widespread in the
discourses of evangelicalism in Northern Ireland during the Troubles.

Hope and Crisis in Northern Ireland Evangelicalism

One striking peculiarity of Northern Ireland evangelical apocalyptic-
eschatological discourses was thus the way in which they created a rich
and diverse semantic habitat in which the most fearful expressions of
anxiety and dread could coexist with the most radical declarations of
hope and messianic expectation. In the strange world of apocalyptic-eschatological discourse, hope and fear are indeed opposites; but they are
opposites which, as in the case of convexity and concavity or centrifugal
and centripetal forces, are ironically predicated on each other. In other
words, it would be impossible to conceive of one without the other. This
might offer a clue as to why no other comparable field of discourse is so
replete with such striking and paradoxical consociations and contrasts
between hope and despair. This distinctive quality of apocalyptic-eschatological discourse is a reflection of the semantic content of the biblical
texts themselves in which, as already noted, are characterized above all

3. Paisley, *Romans*, 132.
4. *Irish Baptist* 100 (March, 1977), 3.
5. *Covenant Reformed News*, vol. 8, no. 13, 1.

by radically contrasting symbolism and logic-defying juxtapositions of hope and fear.

At first glance, the New Testament seems to depict the end times as a period of untold adversity that will multiply until the final apocalyptic conflagration, which will usher in the reign of Christ. Several times the New Testament appears to associate the approach of the end times as a period marked by the proliferation of heresy, sin and social and moral degradation (2 Tim 3:1–5; 2 Pet 2:1–3, 9–22; Jude 8–16). Yet alongside this apparently bleak depiction of historical development, the biblical narrative as a whole also testifies to history as a creative force culminating in the emergence of a messianic kingdom alluded to by the prophets.[6]

The hope in this messianic kingdom, together with the other imaginative hopes of Northern Ireland evangelicals, such as these quoted above, were textual projections. As George Steiner remarks, since imagination is inconceivable without language, imaginative projections are invariably linguistic projections.[7] In the case of Northern Ireland evangelicals, not only were these projections derived from biblical texts, they also involved a creative interpretation of these texts. Evangelicals sought to imagine how the perceived message of biblical apocalyptic-eschatological texts addressed them in terms of their historical experience. For many evangelicals, particularly those associated with ECONI, this process of embodying apocalyptic-eschatological hope invariably implied an element of involvement in the political efforts to resolve the Troubles. In such instances the textuality of anastatic convictions can thus be said to have become constitutive of the political outlook of Northern Ireland evangelicals. Far from being invoked in response to political events, such texts were employed proactively not only to interpret the meaning of particular events but also to determine the political conduct of evangelicals in a context of conflict. This chapter is accordingly directed towards illustrating the ways in which Northern Ireland evangelicals interpreted the Troubles in light of the hermeneutic of hope which they derived from their readings of apocalyptic-eschatological texts.

It would be difficult to overstress the magnitude of teleological notions of apocalyptic-eschatological consummation in Christian dis-

---

6. See, for example, Isa 2:1–4; 11:1–2; 18:3–7; 19:18–24; 25:1–8; 42:1–4; 45:12–25; 60–66; Jer 12:14–17; Ezek 16; 39:21–29; 47:22–23; Dan 2:35; 7:14,27; Joel 3:4; Amos 9:8–15; Zech 8:3, 20–23; 9:9–10; 14:9–21; Mal 1:11.

7. Steiner, *After Babel*, 145.

courses of hope. Wolfhart Pannenberg makes the point lucidly in the following observation:

> The future of God's kingdom for those whose coming Christians pray in the words of Jesus (Matt. 6:10) is the epitome of Christian hope. All else that is related to it, including the resurrection of the dead and the last judgement, is a consequence of God's own coming to consummate his rule over his creation.[8]

Biblical texts, which allude to "the restitution [ἀποκατάστασις] of all things" (Acts 3:21) and depict utopian scenes of lions lying down with lambs, provided the building blocks out of which evangelicals constructed a distinctive hermeneutic of hope. Evangelicals used such texts to interpret their present experience according to their deepest apocalyptic-eschatological aspirations relating to the vanquishing of death and the inauguration of the new creation. Northern Ireland evangelical magazines and booklets published during the Troubles are permeated throughout by such apocalyptic-eschatological motifs. Even the titles of such magazines themselves indicate the central place of apocalyptic-eschatology in the worldviews of Northern Ireland evangelicals. One evangelical organization, ECONI, for instance, named its official publication, *lion & lamb*, after the evocative depiction of the messianic redemption of the natural world.[9] Hope was a vital and indispensible constitutive element of the worldviews of evangelicals in Northern Ireland. This was as true of fundamentalist evangelicalism, such as that of Paisley, as it was of the most moderate evangelical groups such as ECONI. As one evangelical, writing in the *Christian Irishman*, put it, "Hope is one of the chief psychological and spiritual needs of mankind. Just as lungs need oxygen, so the human spirit needs hope."[10] By focusing on such statements as these, this chapter will illustrate the pervasiveness of apocalyptic-eschatological conceptualizations of hope in the discourses of Northern Ireland evangelicalism.

Since the focus was upon the articulation of fear among evangelical communities in Northern Ireland, chapter 3 invariably dealt more with those fundamentalist expressions of Northern Ireland evangelicalism. In these interpretive communities the discourses of apocalyptic-

8. Pannenberg, *Systematic Theology*, III:527.

9. The October 1994 issue of the *lion & lamb* (page 2) states explicitly that the inspiration for the title was the depiction of the messianic lamb in Revelation 5.

10. *Christian Irishman* (January, 1984), 15.

eschatological fear were more prevalent than in more moderate groups of evangelicals among whom such fears were not emphazised to the same extent. Thus, in order to rectify the imbalance, this chapter will demonstrate that in the Northern Ireland Troubles there were many evangelicals whose religion was "one of reconciliation and compassion," and who regarded their task as one of "seeking to express this faith by pursuing political reconciliation."[11]

The previous chapter demonstrated that evangelicals in Northern Ireland applied apocalyptic-eschatological language almost indiscriminately to a variety of social and religious events and developments about which they entertained profound fears and misgivings based on their reading of biblical texts. Their fears were thus made to correspond to the grave depictions of end-times tribulation predicted in these texts. These depictions constituted a series of set expectations, which were largely resistant to permutation and impervious to contextual influences. This chapter argues that the same interpretive tendencies were manifested just as conspicuously at the opposite pole of apocalyptic eschatology, which expressed hope in the second coming of Christ and the promise of deliverance, redemption, resurrection and eternal life. Although this chapter considers the opposite end of the existential spectrum of apocalyptic-eschatological conviction, its basic argument has in common with the argument of the previous chapter the fundamental claim that apocalyptic-eschatological language, far from being a response to particular instances of social or political upheaval, was itself formative of the social context which it shaped according to its own dynamics of signification.

There can be no doubt that many of the biblical apocalyptic-eschatological texts predict a very bleak future for humanity. Speaking of the unendurable suffering of humanity in the end times, John writes that "in those days shall men seek death, and shall not find it; and shall desire to die, and death shall flee from them" (Rev 9:6). As well as depicting people being scorched by the sun, smitten by deadly locusts, afflicted by plagues and boils and finally thrown into fiery pits of eternal torment, apocalyptic-eschatological texts also describe the unimaginable suffering of those whose eyes will rot in their sockets and whose flesh will decompose instantaneously in a moment of great apocalyptic con-

11. MacIver, "Clash of Symbols," 372.

flagration (Zech 14:12).[12] Notwithstanding the response of fear and foreboding which these lugubrious depictions of apocalyptic doom were apt to elicit from their readers, it remained the case that for evangelicals the apocalyptic-eschatological vision was ultimately one of hope.[13] "Apocalypse," notes Catherine Keller, "transforms the object of fear into the site of hope."[14]

Yet this potential has not been recognized consistently in scholarly investigations of apocalyptic phenomena. "To be sure," remarks Dereck Daschke, "scholars have long noted the pathology in apocalypticism and millennialism but have missed the "healthy" resolution that counterbalances it."[15] This general statement could also be applied to the scholarly contributions towards the understanding of the Troubles. On the rare occasions where a writer mentions the role of apocalyptic eschatology in relation to evangelical identity in Northern Ireland, the phenomenon, as already mentioned and enumerated with examples in the Introduction, is apparently universally represented in terms of its baneful effects as an alleged leading factor in the exacerbation of sectarian hostility.[16] The unfortunate consequence of this tendency has been that the more tranquil yet no less pervasive and vigorous notes of hope have not been heard amid the noise, smoke and commotion of fear-inducing, belligerent Doomsday-orientated apocalyptic-eschatological discourses such as those cited in the previous chapter.

Apocalyptic-eschatological discourse in the Northern Ireland Troubles must not be understood merely as providing the ideological substrate of divisive sectarian rhetoric. In its positive application, such discourse supplied the conceptual vocabulary for a genuine theology of hope and reconciliation. In evangelical discourses prominent notes of apocalyptic-eschatological hope can be discerned even within the notion of crisis. The time of the Troubles was indeed a period of crisis but in the evangelical imagination this was a crisis that was mitigated and

12. The American premillennial dispensationalist Hal Lindsey interprets this text from Zechariah's prophecy as a prediction that God will employ nuclear weapons to punish his opponents. See Lindsey, *Late Great Planet Earth*, 163–64.

13. A clear example of this perspective in the context of Northern Ireland evangelicalism is an article entitled, "The Present Crisis and the Throne of God," which was published in the *Irish Baptist* (December, 1978), 15–18.

14. Keller, *Apocalypse Now*, 6.

15. Daschke, *City of Ruins*, 20.

16. See, for instance, Gibson, "Gustavo Gutierrez and Northern Ireland," 259.

punctuated throughout by hope. Although the period of the Troubles is considered by popular opinion and by academic consensus as a time of unprecedented crisis, the notion of "crisis" *per se* should not lead us to reject the possibility of discerning vigorous tones of hope amid the discursive cacophony of Northern Ireland apocalyptic eschatology. Apocalyptic-eschatological language can even transfigure seemingly hopeless notions such as "crisis." Under such discursive conditions, crisis and opportunity become two sides of a common hope. As noted in chapter 2, many Christian accounts of apocalyptic eschatology posit the notion that crisis is the prerequisite of hope, for hope has in common with crisis that "it begins in terror and utter disorientation in the face of the collapse of all that is familiar and well known."[17] As Jürgen Moltmann puts it, "Whoever talks only of "crisis" without recognizing these opportunities is talking out of fear and without hope."[18] Theologians, philosophers and literary critics thus recognize that crises can overturn traditional assumptions and can thereby become fertile ground for creative original insights and imaginative exploration of new possibilities.[19]

There thus exists a certain dialectical tension between hope and fear, which in the case of apocalyptic-eschatological discourse is mediated through the notion of crisis. This tension has been recognized by scholars representing a variety of disciplinary perspectives. Alluding to the reception of the book of Revelation in seventeenth-century England, the historian, William Lamont, observes that interpretations of Revelation oscillated between "the pessimistic belief in an imminent doomsday, and the optimistic expectation of an earthly paradise."[20] Theologians have also recognized that in order to avoid becoming a purely negative position, apocalyptic-eschatology requires "an imminent eschatological intervention of God in history."[21] The sense of living in the end times and the perception that the predictions contained in biblical apocalyptic-eschatological texts were coming to fulfilment could provoke a variety of responses.[22] Even among those who lived in fear of imminent apostasy, however, there remained the unshakeable and "lively hope" (1 Pet 1:3)

17. Alison, *End Times*, 161.

18. Moltmann, *Kirche in der Kraft des Geistes*, 11, 64–66.

19. MacIntyre, "Epistemological Crises," 140.

20. Lamont, "Richard Baxter," 70.

21. Faragau, "New Purchase on Larger Meanings," 18.

22. Randall, *What a Friend We Have in Jesus*, 165.

in their divine deliverance and eschatological rewards once the time of trial had subsided.

It is small wonder, therefore, that widely divergent interpretive responses to apocalyptic-eschatological texts arose in Northern Ireland during the Troubles. The biblical apocalyptic-eschatological material itself evinces a creative, often perplexing, dialectic between hope and fear, reality and potentiality, and transcendence and immanence. "The book of Revelation addresses a crisis in which the believing community is torn between hope and reality," observes Paul Hanson.[23] The rhetoric of Northern Ireland evangelicals likewise reflected the tension between hope and despair, light and darkness which is intrinsic to apocalyptic-eschatological rhetoric. Although there were many who were persuaded that "the years between now and the millennium will constitute an escalation of despair for the mass of people,"[24] evangelicals did not allow themselves to be overcome by apocalyptic negativity. No matter how desperate their plight, evangelicals always retained their trust in the "Book of Truth,"[25] which told of their "blessed hope" (Titus 2:13). After the time of trial they would receive eschatological rewards, the like of which the "eye hath not seen, nor ear heard" (1 Cor 2:9). Perhaps in conscious allusion to this text from 1 Corinthians, Ivan Foster remarked that, "The delights of God's glory are beyond our reckoning."[26] Similarly a Baptist evangelical invoked this text to emphasize the hidden mysteries of death and eternal life. He drew attention to the inability of human language to encapsulate the true weight of eschatological glory that was to be experienced by those invited to the eschatological feast of the lamb: "Heaven is no castle in the air! . . . It is a bright reality, surpassing in glory all the glowing attempts of man to depict it[;] . . . our capacity at present is too limited to comprehend what Heaven is like."[27] These readings of the biblical texts remind us that for Northern Ireland evangelicals the interpretation of apocalyptic-eschatological texts was not merely a matter of philosophical semantics but of real engagement with what one

23. Hanson, *Visionaries*, 11.

24. *Frontiers* (Spring, 1997), 3.

25. *New Protestant Telegraph* (September, 1988), 2.

26. Foster, *Antichrist*, 228.

27. Henderson, *Irish Baptist* (August, 1976), 6.

evangelical referred to as "the great eternal issues"[28] concerning the ultimate destiny of human souls and the spiritual fate of the cosmos.

Since the hopes of many evangelical Protestants were constituted by such apocalyptic-eschatological visions, it is simply not the case, as some social scientists have claimed, that during the Troubles, "The aspirations of Protestants [were] largely restricted to the maintenance of their position and cultural autonomy within Ulster."[29] This was certainly not true of those "Protestants" whose aspirations were directed towards the "eternal glory" (2 Tim 2:10), which supposedly awaited them in heaven. Their ultimate hope was not national or cultural autonomy but "new heavens and a new earth, wherein dwelleth righteousness" (2 Pet 3:13) and "A holy, heavenly city, a city housing the glory of the Almighty."[30]

Northern Ireland Baptists expressed their hope in "a future far more glorious than we can ever imagine," and reaffirmed this conviction in spite of inauspicious social or political circumstances with the assurance that "not all the powers of wicked men can keep this from coming."[31] Paisley continually reaffirmed his assurance that even during the intensification of the apocalyptic struggle in which he believed himself to be engaged, divine providence would ensure that he would remain like the apostle Paul, "troubled on every side, yet not distressed . . . perplexed, but not in despair . . . cast down, but not destroyed" (2 Cor 4:8–9). "The Lord is blessing us," Paisley declared in 1972,[32] "and amidst the darkness and apostasy, thank God, is the Light that shineth more and more unto the perfect day."[33] Twelve years later, preaching on a passage from Revelation 17, Paisley continued to encourage and warn his congregation with the same message of comfort and exhortation: "Yes, there will be darkness, but I can tell you, there is going to be a great deal of light in the last day[,] . . . we are going to see great days of blessing as well as great days of battle and great days of darkness."[34] Interpreting their experience in the light of apocalyptic-eschatological texts, many

28. *Belfast Telegraph* (3 August, 1996), 5.

29. Bruce, Taylor and Wallis, "Ethnicity and Evangelicalism," 301.

30. Foster, *Antichrist,* 223.

31. Clarke, *Irish Baptist* (September, 1969), 4.

32. 1972 is identified by social scientists and historians as the bloodiest year of the Troubles.

33. Paisley, *The Ulster Problem,* 10.

34. Paisley, "The Woman Rides the Beast," 8.

evangelicals endured their perceived hardship with a degree of equanimity. Paisley could thus affirm, as he did at the start of the Troubles that, "The darkest days in Church history were always the brightest days for the Church of Jesus Christ."[35] In the same way that the author of 2 Corinthians exhorted the congregation with the encouragement that "our light affliction, which is but for a moment, worketh for us a far more exceeding and eternal weight of glory" (2 Cor 4:17), so were Northern Ireland evangelicals during the Troubles consoled by the message of hope that lies at the heart of the biblical apocalyptic-eschatological texts.

The apocalyptic-eschatological hermeneutic of hope enabled evangelicals to interpret the apparent proliferation of violence and evil as a necessary prelude to a much-awaited final judgment. This eschatological judgment would seal their ultimate vindication. After the time of trial, which would be shortened "for the elect's sake" (Matt 24:22), there would come a day of eschatological reckoning in which "the Son of man shall come in his glory, and all the holy angels with him" (Matt 25:31). On this day justice would be established, evil would be punished and the faithful remnant that withstood the time of trial would be rewarded—"he that shall endure unto the end, the same shall be saved" (Matt 24:13).[36] Thus regardless of how ominous or inauspicious the circumstances associated with the experience of the "Great Tribulation," Northern Ireland evangelicals, as Alan Campbell put it, could always "see light at the end of life's dark tunnel."[37]

Such positive affirmations offer new insights into the hope of Northern Ireland evangelicals during the Troubles, particularly the ways in which hope was negotiated through the interpretation of apocalyptic-eschatological texts. "We forget or ignore, at our peril," insisted one Northern Ireland evangelical, "just how incredible is the whole business of believing in a second coming."[38] Although this remark was directed originally towards the encouragement and exhortation of an intended audience of evangelical readers, the caution is equally pertinent to aca-

35. Paisley, *Fundamentalism vs. Apostasy*, 1.

36. The notion of apocalypse as a decisive event culminating in the vindication of the righteous and the punishment of the wicked is a common theme in millennial studies. See, for example, *Charles, Eschatology; Collins, Apocalyptic Imagination; Klaus Koch, Apocalyptic Literature*.

37. Campbell, *Great Tribulation*, 41.

38. *Frontiers* (Spring, 1997), 2.

demics today wishing to understand the basic theological convictions of evangelical cultures in Northern Ireland.

For evangelicals across Northern Ireland the second coming of Christ was at the heart not only of their apocalyptic-eschatological expectations but also of their innermost existential convictions. Most of the scholarly discussions of Northern Ireland evangelicalism overlook or misconstrue the vital impact of the anastatic convictions on evangelical faith communities and thereby misunderstand the underlying dynamics of the evangelical worldview which they profess to elucidate. Since the notion of hope has been almost entirely disregarded in the scholarly discussions of the Troubles, it is necessary to illustrate the diverse ways in which apocalyptic-eschatological hope was expressed in Northern Ireland evangelicalism.

Apocalyptic Hope and the Sovereignty of God

The notion of the second coming of Christ was connected to a fundamental belief in the sovereignty of God.[39] One of the cornerstones of evangelical conceptions of hope was the belief that God, as an omniscient Being, was able to direct all earthly events towards the fulfilment of a predetermined sovereign plan.[40] This conviction led evangelicals to apocalyptic-eschatological speculations regarding how this sovereign God would intervene on their behalf in the affairs of the world. The apocalyptic-eschatological hope in a final consummation and the inauguration of a golden era of eternal glory was part and parcel of the teleological conception of history and the concomitant notion of a sovereign God. Among many evangelical groups, the conviction of a sovereign God was thus allied to the hope that Christ would one day return to

39. Classic Reformed evangelical expressions of the link between divine sovereignty and the *parousia* can be found in Committee on National and International Problems, *The Church's comment on Political Affairs*, 8.

40. This connection between the sovereignty of God and apocalyptic-eschatological hope has been a recurring theme of evangelical conceptions of the end times, particularly in the Reformed tradition. A link between divine sovereignty and apocalyptic-eschatological worldviews is made by the Reformed theologian D. A. Carson in his *Divine Sovereignty and Human Responsibility*. The link is also explored in standard commentaries on the book of Revelation. See, for example, Caird, *Commentary on the Revelation*, 72; Lohse, *Offenbarung des Johannes*, 41. The link is to some extent implied by the biblical texts themselves, as for example Revelation 19:6, which contains the ringing declaration, "Alleluia: for the Lord God omnipotent reigneth."

the earth in power in a decisive act of supernatural intervention which would lead to the irrevocable establishment of his kingdom rule.

At the heart of these hopes of several evangelicals during the Troubles was thus a vigorous conception of divine sovereignty. God was perceived, in the words of the *Ulster Bulwark*, as "the controller of the universe."[41] In his capacity as sovereign Lord, it was supposed by evangelicals that God would intervene supernaturally in order to destroy sin, death and Satan and establish the kingdom of God on earth. In the discourses of Northern Ireland evangelicalism, the issue of divine sovereignty was inextricably linked to the issue of apocalyptic-eschatological expectations about how God would intervene on behalf of his people to achieve his ultimate purposes. The primary texts produced by a wide range of Northern Ireland evangelicals are replete with allusions to the sovereignty of God, many of which are tied to an explicitly apocalyptic-eschatological conception of history and providence. For instance in 1981 when 142 Democratic Unionist Party councillors were elected in the local government elections, the victory was regarded by evangelical editors of the *Protestant Telegraph* as having been won "under God" with this particular instance of electoral success being attributed to an auspicious dispensation of divine providence.[42]

The doctrine of divine sovereignty, however, was not dependent upon particular events such as favorable election results in order to establish its veracity in the mind of Northern Ireland evangelicals. The conviction, as one evangelical put it, that "the Lord is Sovereign in every situation"[43] was an unvarying feature of many evangelical professions of belief. The fact that this belief also appears to be particularly prevalent among Presbyterian and Free Presbyterian evangelicals indicates the enduring influence of Reformed expressions of evangelical belief and practice. It was the doctrine of divine sovereignty, according to one evangelical Presbyterian publication, "perhaps more than any other that gives to Presbyterians the stiff upper lip in the days when troubles assail

41. *Ulster Bulwark* 19 (May/June, 1989). Interestingly the exact same expression appeared twenty-two years earlier in the *Protestant Telegraph*, which referred to God as "Controller of the Universe." See the *Protestant Telegraph* (10 June, 1967), 6.

42. This was how the result was reported in the *Protestant Telegraph* (6 June, 1981), 5.

43. Lyle, *Countdown*, 53.

them."[44] The central place of the doctrine of sovereignty was continually reiterated by the Presbyterian Church in Ireland. "The primary aim of the Scriptures," according to one of its official statements, "is to bear witness to the sovereign rule of God over all human life and to acknowledge that rule revealed and established in Jesus Christ."[45] According to the Northern Ireland Reformed Presbyterian minister, F. S. Leahy, everything was under the "sovereign control" of God who was working out his purposes in accordance with "the good pleasure of his will" (Eph 1:5).[46] Reformed evangelicals affirmed the sovereignty of God in the midst of crisis engendered by the threat of man-made apocalyptic scenarios, such as the prospect of nuclear conflagration. "The ultimate key to the world's history," according to one evangelical Presbyterian writing in the *Christian Irishman*, "is held, not in the hands of men with nuclear weapons, but in the nail-pierced hands of the Prince of peace."[47]

Evangelicals of other denominational affinities likewise predicated their hope on notions of divine sovereignty, which, according to one interpretation, referred to "God's controlling, directing, and using all things for His own purposes."[48] The Covenant Reformed Fellowship based in Ballymena regarded God's sovereignty as an axiomatic aspect of Christian faith that constituted "the fundamental truth upon which rests all doctrine."[49] Paisley's own views on divine sovereignty and providence were expressed with typical unequivocality: "Nothing is left to chance. God sees what is going to happen, because He planned it so. His foreknowledge rests on His foreordination. How otherwise would the Scripture be true? 'Who worketh all things after the counsel of His own will' (Eph 1:11)."[50]

The notion of a God in absolute control over all world events recurs like a leitmotif throughout Alan Campbell's anti-Catholic tracts. Political events, he claimed, are part of "the overall plan of Almighty

44. *Christian Irishman* (January, 1973), 9.

45. Committee on National and International Problems, *The Church's comment on Political Affairs*, 8.

46. Leahy, *The Victory of the Lamb*, 1.

47. *Christian Irishman* (September, 1973), 4.

48. *Covenant Reformed Fellowship News*, vol. 1, no. 14, 1.

49. *Covenant Reformed Fellowship News*, vol. 1, no. 1, 1.

50. Paisley, *An Exposition*, 138.

God who knows the end from the beginning"[51] and whose purposes are guaranteed by the inexorability of his "sovereign will."[52] Although his main concern was always Northern Ireland, or "Ulster," Campbell was writing in this instance about the French Revolution. He wrote his commentary on this decisive episode in European history from an apocalyptic perspective which considered such momentous events in terms of their prophetic significance. Campbell employed the same method in his commentary on the massacre of 1641, in which similar language is found to prevail.[53]

Even those such as Alan Campbell and Ian Paisley, whose militantly-held convictions placed them towards the fundamentalist fringe of Northern Ireland evangelicalism, were to some extent able to establish parity with more moderate evangelicals, including those affiliated with ECONI, on the issue of divine sovereignty. Making an explicit link between divine sovereignty and the Christian conception of hope ECONI likewise affirmed that, "the Christian message is a message of hope. We know that *God is in control of this world* and is working his purposes out in Christ."[54] Baptist texts from the Troubles also abounded with affirmations of hope based on an underlying conviction that in the midst of the apparent chaos and contingency of their historical experience, God was working with purposeful intent to realize his sovereign plan for the world. For "the Christian living in times of crisis," the apocalyptic vision of God enthroned in the heavens, remarked one Baptist evangelical, is "a scene of indestructible hope, for we are shown that God is in *absolute control* of the universe."[55]

The hope in the second coming provided continual consolation for evangelicals in the Troubles. "The doctrine of our Lord's return," maintained Baptist pastor, Denis Lyle, "comforts our hearts in the midst of scorn and grief."[56] Similarly, Ivan Foster, in his commentary on Revelation, was adamant that John's Apocalypse was written for the "comfort and blessing" of the reader and that "nothing can advance these

51. Campbell, *The French Revolution*, 4.

52. Campbell, *Light from Nahum*, 14.

53. Campbell, *Remember 1641*.

54. ECONI, *Dreams and Visions* (Belfast: ECONI, 2003), 91 (emphasis added).

55. *Irish Baptist* 101 (December, 1978), 15 (emphasis added).

56. Lyle, *Countdown*, 43.

like a clear understanding of the sovereignty of God and the irresistible nature of his will and purpose."[57] The *Christian Irishman* likewise contained an article which articulated a similar apocalyptic-eschatological conception of Christian hope based on divine sovereignty:

> Christian hope has a firm basis. It is founded upon the belief that God is in control of His universe. This earth and we human beings have a special part in His plans . . . at long last we shall see and experience the final fulfilment of all the wonderful promises of God.[58]

Similarly the editorial of the December 1976 issue of the *Irish Baptist* contained the following expression of hope derived from a confidence in God's sovereignty and its definitive manifestation in the anticipated second coming:

> let us not forget that He has said that He will come again. The fulfilment of this promise is now the Blessed Hope of the Church. . . . Our world is in a sad state. Evil abounds, and it seems to become more intense and more extensive day by day. It is understandable that a spirit of pessimism is spreading amongst all classes of the community. Many see little hope of salvaging our civilisation. But here is ground for optimism. Christ is to come again, and because we believe that we look for a new earth in which dwelleth righteousness (2 Peter 3:13).[59]

These texts manifest a certain cautious confidence that even amid experiences of great suffering, a beneficent divine providence was at work which ensured that "all things work together for good to them that love God, to them that are called according to his purpose" (Rom 8:28).

In many cases the doctrine of divine sovereignty also presupposed the notion of a God who intervenes on behalf of his people. The Presbyterian evangelical magazine, *Frontiers,* expressed faith in "a purposeful God *who is involved in his world.* . . . Therein lies the solid foundation for genuine hope."[60] Many expressions of apocalyptic-eschatological hope were predicated on the assumption that prophecy and divine sovereignty were inextricably linked. "All prophecy finds its

---

57. Foster, *Antichrist,* 172.

58. *Christian Irishman* (February, 2001), 5.

59. *Irish Baptist* 99 (December, 1976), 2.

60 *Frontiers* (Spring, 1996), 19 (emphasis added).

final application and fulfilment in the . . . sovereignty of the Lord Jesus," insisted Baptist pastor, Denis Lyle.[61] Conceptions of divine sovereignty were thus inseparable from the concomitant notion of the fulfilment of what Ivan Foster referred to as the *"great vision of God's redemptive purposes in Christ."*[62] Similarly David MacMillan, a Baptist pastor and a leader of ECONI, using exactly the same terminology, interpreted Revelation 20 as an eschatological vision in which, "Justice is done for the followers of the Lamb who maintained in the face of persecution, and even died for, this *great vision of God's redemptive purposes in Christ*, which Satan ever sought to thwart and destroy. All is recreated and evil is forever contained."[63]

Any consideration of the notion of such a "great vision" or an ultimate divine purpose working itself out through the course of history leads naturally to a consideration of the ultimate culmination of this purpose. The doctrinal essence of this conviction is consistent with our earlier definition of apocalyptic eschatology as the belief which hopes for the establishment of a new and better world order brought about by divine intervention.

Central to the apocalyptic-eschatological worldview is "the belief that God has fixed the course of history."[64] History thus proceeds according to an overarching purpose or divine plan through which those "with ears to hear" could discern and thereby overcome immediate experiences of present hardship. The potential for this conviction to engender apocalyptic-eschatological hope was recognized by Northern Ireland evangelicals. The onetime Principal of the Irish Baptist College, David Kingdon, made a clear link between apocalyptic eschatological hope and the notion that life was infused with meaning and purpose:

> Life is not an endless series of cycles . . . this abnormal state of affairs which we call life is not going to last forever, for the Lord Jesus Christ is going to return to judge all men, and to do away with sin and death finally and completely. When He returns He will make all things new—He will bring in "a new heaven and a new earth, wherein dwelleth righteousness."[65]

61. Lyle, *Countdown*, 24.
62. Foster, *Antichrist*, 148 (emphasis added).
63. McMillan, "Seven Beatitudes," 148 (emphasis added).
64. Sim, *Apocalyptic Eschatology*, 41.
65. *Irish Baptist* 93 (July, 1971), 7.

For those whose thinking was orientated around apocalyptic-eschatological texts and who imbibed the notion that history was proceeding according to a fixed divine plan, all events, as they occurred, were perceived in the light of how they corresponded to a supposedly predetermined apocalyptic blueprint. As such, evangelical interpretations of events were often characterized by a hermeneutical re-appropriation aimed at achieving the required consonance between such events and their apocalyptic-eschatological expectations.[66] The instances in which this interpretive principle manifested itself could be adduced as further illustrations of the semiotic theory that the relation between texts and contexts is basically dialectical in so far as contexts can be understood as a confluence of particular texts. For many evangelicals in the Troubles, the meaning of their social context of crisis was shaped by pre-established paradigms derived from biblical texts.

Appended to general conceptions of divine sovereignty and the belief that all events corresponded to a fixed plan was a conviction that God had ordained a process leading to an ultimate eschatological consummation.[67] Since God controlled the course of all world events, history was understood as possessing "an irreversible direction toward a future goal."[68] For Northern Ireland evangelicals the nature and circumstances leading to this consummation were derived from interpretations of biblical apocalyptic-eschatological texts. Thus the notion of an ultimate, divinely-ordained trans-historical narrative of directionality and purpose and its concomitant notion of a sovereign God who directs this process inevitably raises issues connected with apocalyptic eschatology. Apocalyptic-eschatological notions of hope and a resolute belief in the sovereignty of God can thus be construed as distinct yet reciprocal themes which permeated Northern Ireland evangelical cultures during the Troubles. According to Stephen O'Leary, the narrative of crisis and

66. Kermode, in *Sense of an Ending*, 9, identifies such re-appropriation as one of the main tenets of apocalyptic hermeneutics.

67. This conviction was vigorously expressed by Augustine who remarked that the eschatological awareness of the lineality of the historical process, leading to a glorious consummation, offered the hope of escaping the "false circuitous routes" of historical contingency; *City of God* XII.14, 488. The eschatological conception of history as a process culminating in a utopian consummation, from Augustine to Marx, has been at the heart of many philosophical attempts to reflect on the meaning and significance of historical development. This notion is even to be found in Plato's *Statesman*, 273c.

68. Löwith, *Meaning in History*, 54.

divine sovereignty at the heart of apocalyptic rhetoric possesses a vigorous appeal in the sense that it inculcates in readers' minds the persuasion that, "their lives do have a meaning and purpose in the face of apparently meaningless suffering and evil."[69] This further demonstrates the notion that the biblical apocalyptic-eschatological texts created systems of meaning through which evangelicals interpreted their experience of crisis during the Troubles.

Two Visions of Apocalyptic Hope in Northern Ireland Evangelicalism

The precise ways in which evangelicals conceived of the nature, timing and significance of apocalyptic-eschatological hope was the crucial distinction which permeates the various approaches to apocalyptic eschatology in Northern Ireland. If we follow Michel Foucault in conceiving of discourse as "a linguistic unity or group of statements which constitutes and delimits a specific area of concern, governed by its own rules of formation with its own modes of distinguishing truth from falsity,"[70] it is possible to distinguish two primary discourses in the Northern Ireland evangelical conceptions of apocalyptic-eschatological hope which emerge from the texts. Maintaining with Derrida the notion that texts themselves can reveal to us ideas and phenomena that cannot be reduced to concepts,[71] I shall refrain from the temptation to attach a label or to ascribe a typology to these discourses. The differences between the two discourses revolved around the different semantic fields created out of the negotiations of apocalyptic-eschatological hope, which were distinguished from each other by the divergent systems of meaning inherent within the kind of apocalyptic-eschatological language employed.

These different systems of meaning were generated by fundamentally conflicting conceptions of apocalyptic eschatology. The first was characterized by a steadfast hope in a sudden and cataclysmic intervention of God who would violently do away with "the wicked and perverse generation" (Phil 2:15) and "deliver [them] from this present evil world, according to the will of God and our Father" (Gal 1:4). Positing a notion of God as a *Deus ex machina*, the hope expressed by such discourses was

69. O'Leary, *Arguing the Apocalypse*, 42.

70. Weeks, "Foucault for Historians," 111.

71. Derrida, *Of Grammatology*, 56–57; Derrida, 'Signature, Event, Context,' 180–82.

characterized by an expectation of "a rescue, and a violent rescue, carried out by an authority who comes down from on high to sort things out."[72] Expecting a sudden and violent end in which God would act decisively with "a mighty hand and an outstretched arm" to "remake the world in a huge firestorm of destruction,"[73] this discourse generally inculcated an ethic of perseverance until the end rather than of participation with God in working for social justice in accordance with a transformative eschatological vision of the present. These discourses demonstrate the ways in which "millennial pessimism about the perfectibility of the existing world is crossed by a supreme optimism."[74] Like the second kind of discourse, the first always kept in view a vision of what one evangelical called "our great hope for the future."[75]

The second type had in common with the first notions of an interventionist God but conceived of the nature and purpose of such intervention in distinct and contrasting ways. Contrary to the notion of a definitive violent ending, these discourses emphasized human instrumentality in apocalyptic-eschatological processes through participation with God towards the gradual realization of a predetermined eschatological aspiration. Such hopes were based on a vision of the "kingdom of God," which as a result of the resurrection was already accessible to believers in a proleptic sense. With certain qualifications,[76] this distinction could be said to correspond to O'Leary's distinction between what he calls "tragic" and "comic" types of apocalyptic rhetoric. Denying the efficacy of human endeavors to achieve social transformation, "tragic apocalyptic argument," O'Leary explains, "does not gain its urgency from any attempt to influence the outcome of events; rather, it seeks to orient its hearers into a proper alignment toward cosmic forces locked in a titanic struggle with a predetermined outcome."[77] By contrast, the

72. Alison, *End Times*, 162.

73. Strozier, *Apocalypse*, 2.

74. Tuveson, "Millenarian Structure of the *Communist Manifesto*," 327.

75. *Frontiers* (Spring, 1996), 2.

76. One of the main qualifications is that O'Leary's "tragic" type of apocalyptic rhetoric usually involved an element of date-setting in which the time of the second coming of Christ was often predicted with considerable exactness. By contrast, date-setting was not a prevalent feature of apocalyptic-eschatological discourses in Northern Ireland, even among those evangelicals whose militantly-held convictions placed them towards the fundamentalist end of the spectrum.

77. O'Leary, *Arguing the Apocalypse*, 88.

comic type of discourse downplayed divine determinism and sought to inculcate an ethic of human participation in the endeavors to build the New Jerusalem indefinitely until the unknown and unspecified time of Christ's return. According to those whose convictions were formed by this discourse of apocalyptic-eschatological hope, the kingdom of God was not merely a future event to be awaited with faithful forbearance, but a living reality that was bursting forth in their midst.[78]

These differences should not lead us to the conclusion that the first discourse was devoid of hope. Even among those evangelicals who entertained the most pessimistic impressions of the supposed prevalent lawlessness in society and the intensification of the struggle against the forces of the Antichrist in the end times, there remained an unassailable core of hope in the ultimate triumph of good over evil. In spite of the "great calamities which [were] approaching this world," there remained "a light shining in the midst of darkness," which assured them of their ultimate victory.[79] However, since their interpretations of apocalyptic-eschatological texts led some evangelicals to assume that the forces of darkness and apostasy would continue to escalate until the end of the world and the inauguration of an eternal order, the kind of result hoped for could be brought about only by a decisive supernatural intervention of God. "Knowing that he has a short time,[80] Satan will counter-attack with boundless fury, directing his spleen against the church until the second coming of Christ," warned F. S. Leahy.[81] Thus since the vehemence of the satanic offensive against the true church was set to intensify as the end-times events took their course, it could only be hoped that God would intervene with mighty works of power to save his faithful rem-

78. These convictions correspond very closely to the central tenets of a movement within the church known as "Dominion Theology." This was an activist renewal movement which was committed to the gradual transformation of every sphere of social and political life into conformity with God's intention and will. According to Roger Olson, such activist commitments were at the heart of the theological convictions of the New England Puritans. See Olson, *Story of Christian Theology*, 503. For a discussion of the relevance of Dominion theology in connection with the end times, see Benware, *Understanding End Times Prophecy* (chapter 8).

79. Paisley, *The Woman Rides the Beast*, 3.

80. A reference to Revelation 12:12: "Woe to the inhabiters of the earth and of the sea! for the devil is come down unto you, having great wrath, because he knoweth that he hath but a short time."

81. Leahy, *Victory of the Lamb*, 85.

nant who had endured the onslaught of the Antichrist.[82] Such hope thus posited a strict discontinuity between the present age of sin and death, which would be eradicated, and the future order of righteousness and life, which would take its place.

What do their interpretations of apocalyptic-eschatological texts reveal about how Northern Ireland evangelicals inhabiting this world of discourse conceived of this future order? Among those who professed a hope in a violent rupture at the end of time which would inaugurate a new order of divinely-imposed righteousness, there was a recurrent focus on particular texts of the Hebrew Bible, particularly the books of the law. The hoped-for world would be one in which God would compel obedience to his statutes, which would be honoured and obeyed by all. Such was the alleged wickedness and fallen state of humankind that such a state of affairs could be imposed only by force:

> It is an absolute surety that the time is near at hand when God will establish His Law throughout all the earth. . . . All over our Anglo-Saxon lands, our people cry out for law and order, as they witness the rise of crime, and banditry, terrorism and immorality, the breakdown of society and the economy. We are witnessing the death throes of an old order out of harmony with God's Law and the birth pangs of a new order of the ages that will be in conformity to His Law.[83]

The hope was that "at the end of life's dark tunnel . . . our King, the Lord Jesus will arise and return to cut short the days and to establish His righteous government upon the earth."[84] Expressing similar hopes, an evangelical contributor writing in the *Orange Standard* remarked similarly that, "the outcome of Armageddon will see the establishment of Gods [*sic*] Kingdom on earth based on the laws, statutes and judgements as laid down in Leviticus and Deuteronomy by Jehovah."[85] Such hopes corresponded with the apocalyptic-eschatological convictions of their exponents. Drawing explicit parallels with the Hebrew Bible, some evangelical communities identified themselves with the ancient Israelites as an embattled but faithful remnant people, struggling to

---

82. As Morrow points out, "Persecution and suffering for the sake of righteousness have long been central leitmotivs in Northern Irish politics"; Morrow, "'Suffering for Righteousness' Sake?'," 56.

83. Campbell, *Why We Believe*, 14.

84. Campbell, *Great Tribulation*, 41.

85. *Orange Standard* (March, 1980), 5.

stave off the assaults of the Antichrist until Jesus returned to vindicate his suffering people and reward their faithfulness.[86] In these kinds of discourse, militaristic imagery was widely deployed. "The battle motif that recurs throughout the Bible comes powerfully to the fore in the book of Revelation," claimed F. S. Leahy.[87] In some instances evangelical interpretations of salient historical events were made to correspond with the bellicose, warlike imagery of apocalyptic-eschatological texts. An official pamphlet of the Orange Order epitomizes such an attempt to establish this kind of correspondence: "In Revelation 6:2 and 19:11 we read of another white horse and a rider going 'forth conquering and to conquer.' This is Christ, the Word of God. Just as William served under God on that fateful day and won a tremendous victory so should we today."[88] The connection the author makes in this instance between the depiction in Revelation 19 of the messianic figure on the white horse and King William of Orange is illustrative of the ways in which the apocalyptic imagination and interpretation of apocalyptic-eschatological texts can influence perceptions of salient past events. Historians have found evidence that William rode not a white horse but a brown horse during the Battle of the Boyne.[89] Thus the iconic representation of William riding a white horse of victory, which is displayed on the frontispiece of the pamphlet from which the above quotation was taken, has more to do with retrospective apocalyptic projections onto historical events than with accurate representation of historical facts and demonstrates how apocalyptic-eschatological texts can often function as distorting lenses on the history of a community.[90]

These discourses found public expression in a variety of outlets and it would be impossible to identify an unbroken consistency in the apoc-

86. For instances of such identifications see *Ulster Protestant* (November, 1973), 4, in which a correspondent, after quoting from the apocalyptic-eschatological passages of Matthew 24 and 2 Timothy 3, remarked that "God's children in Ulster are experiencing the truth of these words. Like Israel today, their enemies are at their gates." See also the article, "Back to the Bible an Ulster Priority," *Orange Standard* (September, 1988), 11, which included references to a sermon by Nelson McCausland who preached on the sixth chapter of the book of Jeremiah and claimed that "there are many parallels between the state of Israel in the time of Jeremiah and the state of our land today."

87. Foster, *Antichrist*, 114.

88. Smyth, *Message of the Banners*, 16.

89. Harris, *Revolution*, 305.

90. Akenson, *God's Peoples*, 139–40.

alyptic-eschatological interpretations of any single Northern Ireland evangelical publications. For instance, the above citations of articles from the *Orange Order* may lead us to assume that the paper presented a consistent premillennial perspective on the end times which emphasized the saving of souls over social justice. Yet this same paper also contained articles which contradicted this emphasis. In an entry from the May 1975 issue we read that, "Any man or mission which is striving for the advancement of the Kingdom of God in our society deserves the practical help and prayerful encouragement of everyone who knows the Lord and has experienced the joy of His salvation."[91]

In apparent contradiction to premillennial teachings about the imminent end of the world, the *Irish Baptist* evinced an unambiguous concern for the well-being of the environment: "One hall mark of a Christian should be a concern for the well-being of other people springing from an active social conscience. He should therefore be actively opposed to pollution of any kind."[92]

The ambiguity manifests itself even in publications associated with more fundamentalist expressions of Northern Ireland evangelicalism, such as the *New Protestant Telegraph*. For all its emphasis on saving souls and its purported anticipation of a violent rupture at the end of the world and the consequent futility of campaigning to save the environment, the *New Protestant Telegraph* expressed similar concerns about the greenhouse effect[93] and pollution in the Irish Sea.[94] This Paisleyite "premillennial" publication even urged the government to combat the pollution caused by refrigerators and leaded petroleum[95] and sought to persuade its readers of the need to recycle their waste.[96] These examples of ambiguity and apparent contradiction remind us not to make simplistic categorizations which would reduce particular publications to a single apocalyptic-eschatological perspective, for instance, by labelling their theology "pre-," "post-" or "a-millennial."

Some evangelicals thus regarded themselves as an embattled remnant community of faithful Christians in a wicked and sinful world.

91. *Orange Standard* (May, 1975), 8.
92. *Irish Baptist* 93 (August, 1971), 14.
93. *New Protestant Telegraph* (28 January, 1989), 6.
94. *New Protestant Telegraph* (September, 1988), 8.
95. Ibid., 7.
96. *New Protestant Telegraph* (15 April, 1989), 8.

Their hope was set not on social transformation but on a decisive, super-natural—and even violent—act of deliverance. When we turn from this perspective to the apocalyptic-eschatological hope of those evangelical communities which inhabited the second type of discourse, we encounter a significant change in outlook. In the interpretations of apocalyptic texts among these communities we are confronted with the emergence of a transformative eschatology which draws on apocalyptic-eschatological texts in order to formulate a vision of hope through which to transfigure the present. The potential for apocalyptic-eschatological texts to expand horizons of hope by allowing the boundless realms of imaginative transcendence to break into the temporal world of concrete existence has been recognized by several literary critics and theologians representing a wide variety of hermeneutical perspectives. According to one literary theorist, apocalyptic texts embody the innate human longing for "total presence" and "the all-inclusive transformation of reality" by releasing "the imagination from concrete reality."[97] Theologians have likewise acclaimed such insights. Most notably, Paul Fiddes develops the imaginative potential of apocalyptic-eschatological texts in order to pursue new lines of theological enquiry.[98]

The Development of a Transformative Apocalyptic-Eschatological Hope in Northern Ireland Evangelicalism during the Troubles

Among those who have been at the forefront of the endeavors to develop a transformative theology of hope has been Jürgen Moltmann. His *Theologie der Hoffnung*, first published in 1964, sought to salvage the atheistic dialectic utopianism of Ernst Bloch[99] through a biblical reintegration of Bloch's central tenets developed in *Das Prinzip Hoffnung* (1954–59). Moltmann's biblical appropriation of Bloch's ideas resulted in an explicitly theological formulation of the thesis that eschatology is concerned not only with the "end times," but is radically implicated in present struggles for social justice. Developing the then radical notion

97. Beardsley, *Literary Criticism*, 53, 57.

98. Fiddes (in *Promised End*) builds on the achievements of his earlier *Freedom and Limit* in order to chart the literary and theological terrain of eschatology and open up new horizons of inquiry in theology and literary criticism.

99. Moltmann, *Im Gespräch mit Ernst Bloch*.

that theology *is* eschatology, Moltmann's thinking was rooted in the insight that Christians, confronted with an eschatological vision of God's future reign of justice and peace, "not only wait for it [the kingdom of God], but also look for it, love it, and strive for it." He continues, "The eschatological will lead to decisions that are live options in the present. The decision for the goal determines the means that lead to the goal."[100]

Critical of Schweitzer and Barth for their alleged unexamined adherence to the supposedly static ontological categories of leading strands of classical Greek philosophy, Moltmann insisted that "the language of Christian eschatology is not that of the Greek logos but of *promise*." Developing a notion of Christian eschatology as the language of promise (*Verheißung*), Moltmann claimed that "the truth of God is not in the *logos* of the epiphany of the eternal present,"[101] but in the promise of the coming kingdom of God which breaks into the present *from* the future.[102] From the premise of a transformative eschatology, Moltmann developed the argument that, "The social revolution of overturning unjust conditions is the immanent obverse side of the transcendental hope of the resurrection."[103] Reversing the notion that apocalyptic-eschatological discourse is concerned with endings, Moltmann claims that such language is most fundamentally connected to the notion of new beginnings:

> Christian expectation of the future has nothing whatsoever to do with the end, whether it be the end of this life, the end of history, or the end of the world. Christian expectation is about the beginning: the beginning of true life, the beginning of God's kingdom, and the beginning of the new creation of all things into their enduring form.[104]

Moltmann's thinking in this instance owes much to Karl Barth who had taught that eschatology was not about the end of the world but about the relationship between historical time and divine timelessness.[105]

Arguing against the positivist notion that human thought and action are generated by prior empirical conditions, Moltmann acclaims

100. Moltmann, quoted in Bracken, *World without End*, 46; 131.

101. Moltmann, *Theologie der Hoffnung*, 34.

102. Thistelton, *The Hermeneutics of Doctrine*, 544–45.

103. Moltmann, quoted in Schmithals, *Apocalyptic Movement*, 228.

104. Moltmann, *In the End—the Beginning*, x.

105. Barth, *Church Dogmatics* I.1, 530f. For a detailed account of Barth's conception of hope see also McDowell, *Hope in Barth's Eschatology*.

Ernst Bloch's insight that human beings are motivated primarily by hope and potentiality. Proceeding from the governing hypothesis that the essential reality of God is to be located in the future, Moltmann maintained his conviction that Christian faith is essentially "forward looking and forward moving, and therefore also revolutionising and transforming the present,"[106] Moltmann developed a transformative conception of eschatology in which "the goad of the future stabs inexorably into the flesh of every unfulfilled present."[107] Rather than hoping for supernatural deliverance through a decisive act of divine power, the apocalyptic-eschatological vision sought to transform the world by aligning human action along the eschatological contours of the vision of the realization of social justice. "Because Christians know that they have the rights of citizenship in the coming kingdom," urges Moltmann, "they will do what is best in the kingdom of the world in which they live, and will contribute their ideas about justice and freedom to their political community."[108] This vision thus implied a conception of apocalyptic eschatology as a social critique which is, as Wolfgang Pannenberg puts it, "at the heart of a Christian realism in appraising the conditions of human existence in the present world."[109]

It was these approaches to the interpretation of apocalyptic-eschatological texts that prompted several evangelicals in Northern Ireland to consider the potential for such texts to be used to overcome conventional sectarian distinctions, particularly between "Protestant" and "Catholic," and thereby to support peace-building and reconciliation initiatives. Moltmann contends that out of the anticipation for the coming of the peaceable kingdom of God, there "arises the hope for the expectation of the transformation of this whole world into the kingdom of God."[110] As well as opening the way for scholars to "think eschatologically about culture, the arts, music, and literature,"[111] the imaginative vision of Moltmann's transformative eschatology, properly conceived, furnishes

---

106. Moltmann, *Theology of Hope*, 16.

107. Ibid., 21.

108. Moltmann, quoted in Volf and Katerberg, *Future of Hope*, 22.

109. Pannenberg, "Constructive and Critical Functions," 124.

110. Moltmann, *Das Kommen Gottes*, 17.

111. Griesinger, "Shape of Things to Come," 206–7.

important conceptual resources for the struggle to realize justice and peace on the earth.[112]

The notion of conforming present human conditions to the justice and righteousness that is characteristic of God's coming reign on earth is apparent to the extent that one might reasonably speculate whether Moltmann's direct influence lay behind the expressions of evangelical groups during the Troubles.[113] Consider, for instance, the passages from articles in Northern Ireland evangelical publications in the mid to late 1990s, many of which read like paraphrases of extracts from Moltmann's *Theology of Hope*, especially his notion that eschatology teaches humanity to act "in the light of the promised future that is to come."[114] Concluding his thesis, Moltmann maintains that for Christians, as a result of their hope for the future, which is founded in the promises of God:

> The horizon of expectation within which a Christian doctrine of conduct must be developed is the eschatological horizon of the expectation of the kingdom of God, of his righteousness and his peace with a new creation, of his freedom and his humanity for all men . . . this present world becomes . . . open for loving, ministering self-expenditure in the interests of a humanising of conditions and in the interests of the realisation of justice in the light of the coming justice of God.[115]

This statement can be compared with extracts from an article which appeared in a 1998 publication of *Frontiers*: "Aspirations to peace in a stable political framework must be set in the context of the eschatological framework of Scripture . . . a true eschatology must address the

---

112. Hart, "Imagination for the Kingdom of God?" 54.

113. During informal conversations, some of the former leaders of ECONI confirmed to me that they had read Moltmann and that his works, particularly his *Theology of Hope*, had been influential in the formation of ECONI's approach to how they interpreted the peace process in the light of their faith and political commitments. One may also discern the influence of the Mennonite theologian John Howard Yoder on the Northern Ireland peace process. In one of his early essays, "Peace without Eschatology," Yoder argued that any lasting and theologically viable peace settlement must be seen within an eschatological framework and in light of the anticipated peaceable kingdom of God. See Yoder, *The Royal Priesthood*, 143–67. Yoder's influence was best described as indirect as it issued primarily through the contributions of one of his protégées, Stanley Hauerwas, who was personally involved in the peace process in the late 1990s.

114. Moltmann, *Theology of Hope*, 22.

115. Ibid., 334–38.

contemporary situation."[116] The following comment from a 1998 edition of the *lion & lamb* invites an even more explicit comparison with Moltmann's assertions:

> The vision of new heavens and new earth tells us not only what God will bring, but what God loves and desires; and if we learn from eschatology what God loves and desires, we may accept the limitations of the present, but we shall strive to make the present as far as possible an anticipation of the future.[117]

The same themes, reminiscent of Moltmann's *Theology of Hope*, are alluded to in the following quotation taken from a different issue of the *lion & lamb*: "To worship God is to belong to a new humanity whose homeland is not of this world . . . to follow him is to declare a new allegiance to Jesus as Lord and to engage in a struggle against all that is in conflict with the kingdom."[118]

These texts represent a conscious attempt on the part of Northern Ireland evangelicals not merely to ascertain the supposed deeper meaning of their experience of the political crisis. They were also used interpreted so as to elucidate their assumed present responsibilities in relation to the crisis in the light of an apocalyptic-eschatological vision of the future. Similarly, in his PhD thesis on the potential application of Liberation Theology to the Northern Ireland context, the Northern Ireland evangelical Andrew Gibson (who contributed regularly to the *lion & lamb*) invoked Jürgen Moltmann's *Theology of Hope* in making the following case:

> If God is in all of history and will finally bring all things to his perfect conclusion, the reality of the eschatological Kingdom of God reaches back in time to influence the life of the world in the present. . . . The ultimate victory of God and the ultimate resolution of all things powers human hope and gives direction to human social and political endeavour.[119]

The life and actions of the church were thus, as Moltmann put it, "to correspond to the peace of God in this world of conflict (1 Corinthians

116. *Frontiers* (Summer, 1998), 26.

117. *lion & lamb* (Autumn, 1998), 6.

118. *lion & lamb* (Spring, 2000), 5.

119. Gibson, "Gustavo Gutierrez and Northern Ireland," 260. Gibson's bibliography includes several works of Moltmann.

7:15) and enact this peace in advance (Ephesian 4:3) because the faith community lives from the peace of God through the reign of Christ (Romans 5:1)."[120] Northern Ireland evangelicals deployed a hermeneutic of hope in order to yield transformative interpretations of apocalyptic eschatological texts. These texts were read so as to generate a vision of the world as it could be, which prompted evangelicals to perceive their political duties in light of their expectations of apocalyptic-eschatological fulfilment.

For evangelicals whose thinking was constituted by this kind of discourse, the apocalyptic-eschatological vision of the future was not merely something to be awaited passively as one might have expected a sudden divine dispensation given from on high; rather the vision, which was derived from the texts of apocalyptic eschatology, constituted a mandate for decisive action in order to ensure that the anticipated and hoped-for fulfilment would come to pass. In contrast to discourses of catastrophic apocalyptic intervention which hoped for the annihilation of the world and the subsequent establishment of a new order of imposed righteousness, the second discourse of hope accentuated the temporal dimensions of apocalyptic-eschatological consummation, maintaining that the world would not be obliterated but redeemed. Present action was thus invested with eschatological significance. As Paul Tillich put it, "since eternal life is participation in the divine life, every finite happening is significant for God."[121] Human efforts to achieve peace, reconciliation, and social justice were thus seen as acts of "proleptic cooperation with God in the eschatological transformation of the world into the new creation."[122] These convictions were derived from a particular interpretation of biblical prophecy. As one contributor to *Frontiers* put it, "The Bible encourages us to the cautious hope that this earth will be the scene of perfect justice, peace and reconciliation; we do not hope for a purely other-worldly heaven."[123] Although some fundamentalists rejected such hopes for social justice or the transformation of world into an eschatological new creation as a manifestation of "a religion that minds earthly things,"[124] this was not true of all fundamentalist

120. Moltmann, *Kirche in der Kraft*, 318.
121. Tillich, *Systematic Theology*, III.398.
122. Althouse, *Spirit of the Last Days*, 73.
123. *lion & lamb* (Autumn, 1998), 5.
124. *Covenant Reformed News*, vol. 8, no. 8, 1.

evangelicals. For instance, Paisley shared the hope for a new creation. Commenting on Romans 8, he declared that, "The liberty of the glory of the sons of God . . . will be shared by all creation."[125] The vision of a redeemed creation, moreover, was constitutive of the convictions of Northern Ireland evangelicals and as such supervened on their political activities and worldviews. For many evangelicals the "vision of hope" derived from biblical apocalyptic-eschatological texts was the operating paradigm which not only defined the conceptual limits of their political and social engagement but also opened up new imaginative possibilities through the transformational application of these texts.

The first and most obvious aspect of the vision to be understood is that it was constituted primarily by the biblical apocalyptic-eschatological texts. Sometimes the articulation of the vision in the various texts of Northern Ireland evangelicals draws explicitly from these texts. This is the case in one ECONI peace-building booklet which stated that "the Bible's vision is of humanity united in worship and praise" and used apocalyptic texts such as Revelation 7:9–10 in order to support such claims.[126] In other cases the influence of biblical apocalyptic-eschatological texts was implicit, such as in the numerous evangelical texts which expressed indistinct hopes for "the coming of the kingdom of God in our midst."[127] The imminence of this kingdom recurs like a motif throughout Northern Ireland evangelical discourses of apocalyptic-eschatological hope. One text published by ECONI is particularly illustrative of this notion of the kingdom of God as a present reality:

> The kingdom of God promises a radically different future for all who enter it. Christian hope demands that we are open to God's future which is *already at work in our present circumstances.* However, in our fearful desire for certainty and control we can resist the incredible newness of God's future and the surprising ways of the kingdom which are deeply subversive of the ways of the world.[128]

In contrast to the first discourse of hope, the second posited a conception of the kingdom of God not as something to be imposed forcibly by divine decree once God had done away with a world purportedly lost to

125. Paisley, *Romans*, 133.
126. ECONI, *Thinking Biblically, Building Peace*, 128.
127. *lion & lamb* (Spring, 2000), 7.
128. ECONI, *Dreams and Visions*, 88 (emphasis added).

sin, the flesh and the devil. Rather the kingdom of God was regarded as an exemplary prototype of an eschatologically-constituted "new creation of all things" (*die Neuschöpfung aller Dinge*)[129] which Christians could experience proleptically by belonging to the faith community. Building the kingdom of God "on earth as it is in heaven" was thus elevated to the level of an eschatological imperative. ECONI recognized the political implications of this prototype of the redeemed humanity, as is clear in the statement that, "Belonging to this coming kingdom compels us . . . to work for justice and peace in a fallen world."[130] Interestingly, this kind of language preserved the pessimistic assessment which characterizes the first discourse ("fallen world") but retained a conception of the kingdom of God as the sphere of transformative regeneration of contemporary society that was present and active in the world. All of ECONI's activities were directed towards the fulfilment of what it called the "Christian vision of what society should be."[131] Acknowledging the reality of sin in a "fallen world," ECONI did not abandon hope in transforming society and devote itself solely to saving souls, as some other evangelical groups in Northern Ireland did, most notably the Brethren.[132] Rather, following the publication of their booklet, *For God and His Glory Alone*, in 1988 members of ECONI launched an energetic campaign, which included organizing conferences to discuss evangelical perspectives on the conflict. Keeping in mind their overriding goal to establish "the Kingdom of God and the Lordship of Christ in Northern Ireland,"[133] ECONI also established links with the press and were often consulted by major media corporations to offer an evangelical perspective on the current affairs of Northern Ireland. In addition, ECONI facilitated encounters between political representatives from nationalist and unionist communities and evangelical churches throughout Northern Ireland. As already demonstrated in this chapter, ECONI emphasized the openness, transcendence and inclusivity of the biblical apocalyptic-eschatological texts in order to facilitate dialogue among different Christian groups during the Troubles. More traditional evangelicals, however, tended to read the same texts

---

129. Moltmann, *Theologie der Hoffnung*, 28.

130. *lion & lamb* (Autumn, 2006), 5.

131. *lion & lamb* (Autumn, 1995), 3.

132. Southern, "Strong Religion and Political Viewpoints."

133. *lion & lamb* (Autumn, 1995), 3.

more as exhortations to remain faithful in the midst of apostasy than to work for social justice.

The transformative applications of the apocalyptic-eschatological vision of hope extended to endeavors to build relationships among the various churches of Northern Ireland. Although the previous chapter considered the ways in which apocalyptic-eschatological texts such as Revelation 17 and 2 Thessalonians 2 were invoked to execrate the Catholic Church and to deprecate ecumenical initiatives, there were also instances of Northern Ireland evangelicals using apocalyptic-eschatological texts to promote ecumenical dialogue. Whereas many of the texts quoted in chapter 3 sought to inculcate fear and suspicion of the ecumenical movement by unfavorable comparisons of the Pope with the Antichrist and the Catholic Church with the one-world-religion of the Beast, there were other evangelicals who used apocalyptic-eschatological language in order to encourage ecumenical endeavors. Such attempts were often based on the apocalyptic-eschatological vision of the diversity of the various peoples who are summoned to be part of the redeemed humanity. Taking its cue from the text of Revelation 7, one evangelical text argued in favor of ecumenical dialogue on the basis of an apocalyptic-eschatological vision of hope: "We look forward to the day . . . when there will be that "great multitude that no one can count, form every tribe, people and language, standing before the throne and in front of the lamb" (Rev 7:9).[134] Expressions of affirmation of the universal apocalyptic hope were used to promote a vision of social inclusion with the aim of negating the dichotomizing influence of the sectarian mentality, which posited a strict division between "Protestant" and "Catholic." The Presbyterian minister, John Dunlop, contended that, "We could do with more of our life marked by agility; more affirmation of joy beyond sorrow; more celebration of apocalyptic extravagance using the doxologies sung by choirs composed of millions from all over the earth (Revelation 5:11–13)." Using quotations from the book of Revelation, he suggested that such celebration of "apocalyptic extravagance" could be used to inculcate "a mental attitude which is . . . capable of accommodating diversity."[135] In Northern Ireland where issues of identity and nationality ("Protestant" and "Catholic," "Irish" and "British," "Unionist" and "Nationalist") had produced such a considerable degree of conflict and

134. ECONI, *Evangelicals and Catholics*, 10.

135. Dunlop, *A Precarious Belonging*, 81, 91.

sectarian enmity, the apocalyptic-eschatological vision of a redeemed community, diverse yet united in a common purpose of worship and praise provided a particularly poignant visualization of hope. This apocalyptic-eschatological vision, as one document put it: "anticipates the full expression of place and identity—the covenanted people of God in the new heavens and the new earth—where belonging and identity are not destroyed but are expressed in their God-given and God-honouring fullness."[136]

Among those evangelicals who conceived of apocalyptic-eschatological language as a means with which to provide "an alternative picture painted of the potentialities and possibilities inherent in God's future,"[137] one of the leading symbols of hope was this image of the "new heavens and a new earth" (Isa 65–66; 2 Pet 3:13; Rev 21:1).

The notion of a heavenly city as the object and destination of apocalyptic-eschatological hope was at the heart not only of Northern Ireland evangelicalism but also of the ancient Israelites of the Hebrew Bible. In contrast to the wicked city of Babylon, the object of fear and revulsion,[138] Jerusalem, the focus of hope and veneration, was depicted as the "city of God" and the "holy habitation of the Most High" (Ps 46:4) as well as a sanctuary where God's people were destined to live in safety (Isa 54:11–12; 61:3, 10; 65:13–22). The eschatological city of the New Jerusalem, in particular, served as an evocative metaphor of apocalyptic-eschatological hope and as such constituted the conceptual point at which "the goals of hope in our lives, and what we ourselves expect of life, fuse with God's promises for a new creation of all things."[139] This vision of a new creation was reinforced by a recurrent emphasis on the immediacy and immanence of "the kingdom of God," which when read in conjunction with the texts of biblical prophecy, was invested with apocalyptic-eschatological connotations.

136. Thompson, *Fields of Vision*, 127.

137. Hart, "Imagination for the Kingdom of God," 54.

138. In the Hebrew Bible, wicked cities were commonly depicted as harlots (Isa 1:21; 23:16–17; Jer 2:20–31; 13:27; Nah 3:4).

139. Moltmann, *Spirit of Life*, 155.

Toward a Hermeneutic of Hope: Fusing the Hope of the Text with the Historical Experience of the Reader

The transformative readings of apocalyptic-eschatological texts through which Northern Ireland evangelicals interpreted their society thus offer a searching insight into the deeper hermeneutical questions raised in chapter 2. The notion of evangelical readers interpreting ancient texts in such a way as to create horizons of hope out of their present circumstances can be brought into creative critical dialogue with influential accounts of interpretation in contemporary literary theory, such as those of Gadamer and Ricoeur. Gadamer rejects the conventional approach of having to choose whether the text is shaped by its interpretation or whether an interpretation is shaped by the text. He contends instead that texts reveal their meaning only through the imaginative participation of the reader in the act of interpretation. Interpretation for Gadamer is a two-way process in which the text determines the interpretative horizon of the reader just as much as the interpreter shapes the meaning of the text.[140] Following Heidegger,[141] Gadamer observes that readers approach texts pre-soaked in prejudices and habits of seeing the world which he calls their "horizon."[142] The text too has a horizon for it is loaded with assumptions and presuppositions which have been involved in its production, organizing its "moment of initial inscription."[143] Gadamer locates "understanding" at the point of the interpretive fusion between the horizon of the reader and the horizon of the text.[144]

140. Gadamer, *Gesammelte Werke*, I:305–12.

141. To a greater extent than Ricoeur, Gadamer's hermeneutics is grounded firmly in ontology. The ontological roots of Gadamer's thinking on the constitution of "horizons" can be traced back to Heidegger's conception of "the elemental historicity of Dasein" (*die elementare Geschichtigkeit des Daseins*); cf. Heidegger, *Being and Time*, 41. Gadamer follows Heidegger in expanding the circumference of the hermeneutical circle beyond exegetical concerns to embrace the notion of understanding in general. Understanding (*das Verstehen*) was conceived not merely as a cognitive operation resulting in knowledge of facts but as something inherent to human being-in-the-world. Understanding was thus as much concerned with ontology as with epistemology; cf. Heidegger, *Being and Time*, 184.

142. Gadamer conceives of a horizon as "the range of vision that includes everything that can be seen from a particular vantage point." See Gadamer, *Truth and Method*, 301–5.

143. Johnson, *System and Writing*, 52.

144. Gadamer writes, "*understanding is always the fusion of these horizons suppos-*

Extending Gadamer's notion of interpretive fusion, Paul Ricoeur likewise employs a notion of participation in seeking to formulate a conception of the relationship between the text and its readers in the production of meaning. Ricoeur seems to concur with Derrida's notion of "iterability" when he acclaims the insight that the meaning of the text is not to be equated with the intentions of the author. Ricoeur affirms that "the text's career escapes the finite horizon lived by its author. What the text means now matters more than what the author meant when he wrote it."[145] Thus, as Kevin Vanhoozer remarks, commenting on Ricoeur's hermeneutics, "The autonomy of the text is the condition of its "surplus" of meaning; that is, of its re-ascending its original situation and having something to say to readers in the present."[146] Gadamer himself substantiates the notion that the meaning of texts always surpasses the author's intention:

> To understand . . . does not mean primarily to reason one's way back into the past, but to have a present involvement in what is said. . . . What is fixed in writing has detached itself from the contingency of its origin and its author and made itself free for new relationships.[147]

Both Gadamer's notion of a creative participation of readers in the text leading to the fusion of horizons and Ricoeur's argument that a text is capable of transcending its initial referent underscore the notion that these texts were living and active vectors of signification. As such they were capable of generating new meanings rather than being mere responses to a context of crisis. Ricoeur pursues these insights to a consideration of the effect of the text on the reader: "If the reference of the text is the project of a world, then it is not the reader who primarily projects himself. The reader rather is enlarged in his capacity for self-projection by receiving a new mode of being from the text itself."[148]

---

edly existing by themselves. . . . In a tradition this process of fusion is continually going on, for the old and new are always combining into something of living value, without either being explicitly foregrounded from the other." See Gadamer, *Truth and Method,* 306.

145. Ricoeur, *Interpretation Theory,* 30.

146. Vanhoozer, *Meaning in This Text,* 107.

147. Gadamer, *Truth and Method,* 391, 395.

148. Ricoeur, *Interpretation Theory,* 94.

The notion of an active text implicit in Gadamer and Ricoeur corresponds to Catherine Keller's notion of a "hermeneutic of relation" in which the relationship between the text and the reader evinces "an uncontrollable and irreducible mutuality."[149] Crucially to our discussion of apocalyptic-eschatological language, the "hermeneutic of relation" also allows the text to be read as the domain not of empirical actuality but of imaginative potentiality. Texts do correspond to the world, Ricoeur concedes, but the relationship is not one of empirical, subject-object referentiality but of an eschatological awareness on the part of the reader in whom the text awakens what Ricoeur, drawing on Kierkegaard, calls a "passion for the possible."[150] Although texts cannot be said to represent the fixed totality of the empirical reality of the world to which they refer, they do nevertheless refer to the real world of the possible, which for Ricoeur, following Aristotle, is just as *real* as the world of present actuality. Ricoeur refers to "the disclosure of a possible way of looking at things, which is the genuine referential power of the text."[151] Thus texts are not merely conduits for the human mind's apprehension of given empirical reality but function also as harbingers of the future, which, "through imagination and symbolism," open up "new levels of awareness."[152] By "outlining a new way of being in the world," texts contribute to the "enlarging of our horizon of existence."[153]

In seeking to fuse these insights with "New Historicist" conceptions of the "dialectic between the text and the world," we can contend that in the case of apocalyptic-eschatological texts, this dialectic consists in the imaginative space created by texts for engagement on the part of the interpreter who through the encounter with the text is presented

149. Keller, "Eyeing the Apocalypse," 255. There are obvious theoretical parallels between this notion of the mutuality of the hermeneutical interaction between the reader and the text and the insights of quantum theory which has discovered that "the description of the observed depends on the determination of a frame of reference or a universe of discourse" and that the separation between the observer and the observed is not a necessary axiom of scientific method but a "metatheoretical choice." See Castell and Ischebeck, *Time, Quantum and Information*, 205.

150. Ricoeur, "Freedom in the Light of Hope," 407, 411; Fiddes, *Promised End*, 45–47. According to Vanhoozer, this "passion for the possible" constitutes the "driving force behind Ricoeur's whole philosophical enterprise"; Vanhoozer, *Biblical Narrative*, 6.

151. Ricoeur, *Interpretation Theory*, 92.

152. Macquarrie, *In Search of Humanity*, 105.

153. Ricoeur, *Interpretation Theory*, 37, 88.

with a new vision of seeing the world. These imaginative visions in turn become formative of subsequent interpretations of texts in a process that leads to the envelopment of the horizon of the text and that of the world into a yet greater horizon.[154] As Montrose himself put it:

> Representations of the world in written discourse participate in the construction of the world: They are engaged in shaping the modalities of social reality and in accommodating their writers, performers, readers, and audiences to multiple and shifting positions within the world that they themselves both constitute and inhabit.[155]

This way of conceiving the "New Historicist" dialectic of the textuality of history and the historicity of texts in light of a hermeneutics of imagination and hope is consistent with Ricoeur's conception of texts not as empirical descriptions of the world as it is but as imaginative explorations of the world as it could be.[156] Ricoeur's notion can be applied with particular truth to the biblical apocalyptic-eschatological texts which are particularly suited to imaginative interpretations that open up to the reader new worlds of discourse. Drawing on Ricoeur's notion of the "surplus of meaning," Paul Fiddes remarks that "human existence is orientated forwards in a passion to be, and this is the true basis of hope."[157] This orientation of human existence which "projects itself" into an open future consisting of boundless possibilities[158] finds its definitive expression in apocalyptic-eschatological texts, which present a vision of the future as the sphere—to use the phraseology of Ernst Bloch's dialectical utopianism—of "not-yet realized possibilities" (*noch nicht verwirklichte Möglichkeiten*).[159]

154. Horn, *Gadamer and Wittgenstein*, 59.

155. Montrose, *Purpose of Playing*, 2–3.

156. Ricoeur acknowledges his debt to Moltmann when he remarks that "I have been very much taken with—I should say, won over by—the eschatological interpretation that Jürgen Moltmann gives to the Christian kerygma in his work *The Theology of Hope*"; Ricoeur, "Freedom," 404.

157. Fiddes, *Promised End*, 40.

158. This conception of human existence owes much to Martin Heidegger's conception of *Dasein* as being irreducibly constituted by temporality and thus embracing possibility just as much as actuality; Heidegger, *Being and Time*, 183–90. Ricoeur credits Heidegger with these insights in volume three of his *Time and Narrative*, III:253–58.

159. Bloch, *Das Prinzip Hoffnung*, V:727.

The interpretations of apocalyptic texts by Northern Ireland evangelicals, such as those quoted above, exemplify many of the theoretical principles discussed here. The dialectic between the text and the world manifested itself in the "passion for the possible" which was exhibited in several evangelical interpretations of apocalyptic-eschatological texts. Indeed, in these instances the biblical apocalyptic-eschatological texts may be said to have undergone what Ricoeur calls "the refiguration process through which the reader contributes to a text's meaning through his or her active questioning and response."[160] This view presupposes that a text is a hermeneutical space of semantic potentiality and that this potential cannot be realized until a reader awakens the latent possibilities inherent in the text. As Werner Jeanrond remarks, "Unread texts remain no more than pure possibilities."[161] Jeanrond is correct as far as he goes, but it is also important to bear in mind that the encounter of the reader and the text is not an interaction of an active subject interpreting a passive object but a meeting of two active agents, interacting together on a common level of textuality.

In some ways the reader is constituted by textuality just as much as the text which he or she is interpreting. As Roland Barthes, casting himself in the role of interpreter, says, "I am not an innocent subject, anterior to the text. . . . This me which approaches a text is itself already a plurality of other texts."[162] This notion is predicated on the concept of an active reader who participates in the creation of meaning not by imposing his or her presuppositions onto the text but by interacting with the text in a relation of (as Barthes would have it) "playful" reciprocity.[163] Since the readers' presuppositions, which are brought to bear on the interpretation of apocalyptic-eschatological texts, are themselves constituted by texts, it can be averred that the fusion of the readers' horizon and the horizon of the interpreted text is at its most basic level a consociation which takes place at the level of textuality. Thus rather than being a "passive recipient of a message," a reader is, on the contrary, "actively engaged in a process of reading transactions and responses."[164] This

160. Ricoeur, quoted in Detweiler and Robbins, "Twentieth-Century Hermeneutics," 270.

161. Jeanrond, *Text and Interpretation*, 73.

162. Barthes, quoted in Vanhoozer, *Meaning in This Text*, 78.

163. Champagne, *Literary History*, 84.

164. Thistelton, *New Horizons*, 50.

does not, however, amount to an unqualified endorsement of "reader-response theories"[165] which assert that the meaning of a text "depends entirely on the process of symbolisation that takes place in the mind of the reader";[166] for if this process, as we have claimed, is constituted, in common with the interpreted text itself, by textuality, it follows that any interpretive fusion between the readers' horizon and that of the "processes of symbolisation" takes place just as much in the text itself as in the "mind of the reader." Nevertheless, in so far as the relationship between the text and interpreter is a relationship constituted by textuality, we can begin to formulate a conception of interpretation which substantiates the general semiotic theory concerning the ways in which texts become formative of social reality. This remains the case even if we concede that "texts come to life only when people become involved in them" and that it is impossible to grasp a text's meaning "without due regard to this personal involvement of people in the production and reception of texts."[167] This conclusion is self-evident if we grant, as I have argued, that the two active agents in the hermeneutical process (i.e., the reader and the text) are both constituted in textual terms.

These insights can be applied to the use of apocalyptic-eschatological language by Northern Ireland evangelicals in their formulations of hope. One of the ways in which readers become co-creative of meaning is through processes of forming imaginative consociations between the world of their historical experience and the world of the text. Such correlations are possible only because of the interpretive equivalence between these two realms which consists in their common basis in textuality. Although this principle could be applied in theoretical terms to all texts, they are particularly pertinent to apocalyptic-eschatological texts. Among the collective totality of possible human discourses, apocalyptic eschatology possesses an unusual capacity to be interpreted in such a way as to yield affectual associations between the two worlds of the readers' historical experience and the world of the object text.

Such interpretive approaches can be illustrated by examples taken from instances of evangelical interpretations of apocalyptic-eschatolog-

---

165. Thiselton defines these approaches as theories which "call attention to the *active role of communities of readers* in constructing what counts for them as 'what the text means.'" See Thiselton, *Thiselton on Hermeneutics*, 489.

166. Tompkins, *Reader-Response Criticism*, xvi.

167. Jeanrond, *Theological Hermeneutics*, 78.

ical texts during the Troubles. Commenting on Revelation 21:25 ("And the gates of it [the heavenly city] shall not be shut at all by day"), Ron Elsdon, a Church of Ireland evangelical commentator, related Revelation's vision of peace and security to the aspirations of Christians in Northern Ireland for similar security in the midst of terror campaigns and sectarian murder: "To Christians living in Northern Ireland, living for so long with security gates at the entrances to their towns and cities, verse 25 [of Revelation 21] is a particularly poignant detail."[168] This comment is a fitting example of how the meaning of an apocalyptic-eschatological text was created neither *ex nihilo* nor from the social context but from the reader's imaginative engagement with the text which opened up new horizons of hope based on the textually-derived anastatic expectations of the interpreter. The apocalyptic-eschatological image of a heavenly city whose open gates signify peace, welcome, hospitality and security, is contrasted with the historical experience of the interpreter's sense of vulnerability and insecurity associated with the continual terrorist threats and the corresponding need for security checks and closed gates.

Such texts exemplified a dynamic relationship between the interpretation of an apocalyptic-eschatological text and the historical experience of the interpreter through which a particular meaning emerges. Similarly, when another evangelical writer expressed his hopeful anticipation of "the time when the fullness of God's redemptive work in Jesus Christ will be realised" and that "this is our hope and it is made credible when Christians live in the present reality of what we believe is to come,"[169] he was likewise participating in a hermeneutical process which interpreted the biblical text as the means through which to conceive of a world of textual possibilities that could be realized by living in the hope of the apocalyptic-eschatological vision.

Salvation, Resurrection, and Eternal Life

From the perspective of evangelicals, the universal vision of apocalyptic-eschatological consummation entailed decisive consequences not merely for the redemption of the cosmos but also for the salvation of individual souls. In some ways death, as the definitive and unavoidable cessation of human life, could be regarded as the point at which apocalyptic es-

168. Elsdon, *Lamb Wins*, 39.
169. *lion & lamb* (Spring, 1999), 17.

chatological discourses can be brought into dialogue with existential conceptions of crisis and the anxiety of the radical negation implied by the ontological "shock of non-being" at the prospect of non-existence.[170] Death signals the point at which the focus of apocalyptic eschatology shifts from speculation concerning the general spiritual destiny of the universe and moves towards a personal crisis of an existential nature. Apocalyptic eschatology thus addresses both issues of personal salvation and social and cosmic transformation.[171] In evangelical settings, apocalyptic eschatology invariably addresses the issue of the hope for eternal life, and by extension, also has something to say about the meaning and significance of death. Apocalyptic eschatology in the Northern Ireland evangelical conceptions of hope was no exception.

One of the most striking and recurring characteristics of Northern Ireland apocalyptic-eschatological language was its frequent juxtaposition of soteriology and eschatology.[172] Since the issue of death provides a site of correlation between existential and apocalyptic-eschatological discourses, the question now arises of how the issue of death has been considered from existential perspectives. Such perspectives can then be applied to specific Northern Ireland evangelical interpretations of such texts dealing with death and resurrection in an apocalyptic-eschatological context. Existential readings of death can be invoked to inform our discussion of how evangelicals used apocalyptic-eschatological texts in their attempts to overcome the "last enemy" (1 Cor 15:26). In the thought of Martin Heidegger the note of hope, although severely muted, was considered in terms of existential categories of resolve in the face of death and authentic modes of being. For Heidegger the basic issue confronting human existence (*Dasein*) was the fact of its own non-being (i.e., its death). For Heidegger death as an "impending event" was not

170. Tillich, *Systematic Theology*, I:207. The link between apocalyptic eschatological and existential modes of thinking has been identified and utilized by leading philosophers and theologians. According to Nikolai Berdyaev, apocalyptic eschatology, in announcing the end of history thereby proclaims "the victory of existential time over historical time, of creative subjectivity over objectivisation, of personality over the universal-common, of existential society over objectivised society"; Berdyaev, *Slavery and Freedom*, 265.

171. Gowan, *Eschatology in the Old Testament*, 122.

172. Gribben has also identified such juxtapositions in the conversion narratives of Puritan millenarianism during the English Civil War. See Gribben, *Puritan Millennium*, 189.

merely an occasion at the end of life but a constant existential presence that permeated the inner ontological depths of human existence. Death was thus "*something that stands before us, something impending.*"[173] Since the fact of non-existence cannot be "outstripped" the only way to confront death is by maintaining an attitude of "anticipatory resoluteness" towards the fact of non-being.[174] Thus Heidegger contends that "the authentic self is the becoming self" which is aware of its temporality and organizes itself around the master concern of death.[175] In contrast to Sartre, for whom death was the ultimate proof of the absurdity of existence, something which "removes all meaning from life,"[176] Heidegger contended that only the fact of death is capable of organizing life around this master concern in such a way as to bestow meaning and beauty on human life: "Once one has grasped the finitude of one's existence, it snatches one back from the endless multiplicity of possibilities which offer themselves as closest to one . . . and brings *Dasein* into the simplicity of its fate."[177] By taking control of its fate and organizing itself around the impending state of its non-being, *Dasein* exerts a "superior power" over death which gives rise to an "*impassioned freedom towards death*"[178] from which emerges a truly authentic existence which is characterized by an "unshakeable joy" tempered by "sober anxiety."[179]

The basic problem with Heidegger's account, from an evangelical point of view, is that by locating the resources of hope solely within human existence and thereby not allowing scope for the intervention of God to act decisively to defeat and surmount death, his account appears to engender hopelessness.[180] If the highest conception of authentic being

173. Heidegger, *Being and Time*, 294.

174. Ibid., 295, 308.

175. Ibid., 348.

176. Sartre, *Being and Nothingness*, 539. The full quotation reads, "Thus death is never that which gives life its meanings; it is, on the contrary, that which on principle removes all meaning from life. If we must die, then our life has no meaning because its problems receive no solution and because the very meaning of the problems remains undetermined."

177. Heidegger, quoted in Moltmann, *Theology of Hope*, 256.

178. Heidegger, *Being and Time*, 311.

179. Ibid., 358, 436.

180. Theologians, including Karl Rahner and Jürgen Moltmann have criticized what they see as the hopelessness engendered by Heidegger's account by arguing that true hope requires that life rather than death should have the final word in the human

towards which human existence can aspire is its awareness of the master concern of death, then the vision of human life set forth becomes little more than the living presence of impending death.[181] The scant references to hope to be found in *Being and Time* restrict its utility to lightening the load of being rather than supplying being with the resources to surmount its annihilation.[182] Heidegger, after all, acknowledges the "certainty" of death which still ultimately triumphs over human life by "lay[ing] claim" to it.[183] Although Heidegger has been attacked for postulating an apocalyptic hermeneutic,[184] his perspective was largely devoid of any conception of apocalyptic eschatology, especially as a means of overcoming the master concern of death.[185] For Heidegger death was something not to be surmounted, still less conquered, but confronted with resolution and accepted with authentic recognition of its impending presence on *Dasein*.

By contrast, the conquest of death—portrayed in one biblical text as the retraction of "the sting of death" (1 Corinthians 15:56)—was at the heart of Christian conceptions of apocalyptic eschatology, as Northern Irish evangelicals were well aware. Professing faith in "the God of the living" (Mark 12:27), Christian teaching has been inherently inclined to-

---

story; see Sheehan, *Karl Rahner*, 310. It may be said in Heidegger's defence that he never intended to give an account of hope, but a sober reflection on the tragedy and paradox of human existence, in which case his ultimately forlorn diagnosis, although inadequate for evangelicals, would be justified on its own account. Heidegger would have almost certainly classified apocalyptic-eschatological visions of escaping death through supernatural activity as another manifestation of "inauthentic Being-towards-death" (*Being and Time*, 308).

181. Alves, *Theology of Human Hope*, 135.

182. Heidegger, *Being and Time*, 395–96.

183. Ibid., 299.

184. According to Sacchi, Heidegger's ontology is apocalyptic in the sense that his thought "depends on an epiphany of Sein that *reveals* it to thought itself" and takes "its principles from . . . revelation." This charge leads Sacchi to the conclusion that Heidegger was no "true philosopher" for "he did not grasp the fundamental differences that exist between genuine philosophising and mere thinking, between a lover of the truth of things and a passionate adorer of the thought immanent to a thinking subject's consciousness"; Sacchi, *Apocalypse of Being*, 4, 141.

185. Heidegger's *Being and Time* offers only a cursory reference to hope but even here the redemptive potential of hope is severely restricted, allowing only for the possibility to lighten the burden of being. See Heidegger, *Being and Time*, 395–96. The word, "*Hoffnung*" (hope), appears only six times in the whole of the original text of *Sein und Zeit*.

wards the affirmation of life.[186] Whilst accepting the self-evident fact that "it is appointed unto men once to die" (Heb 9:27), evangelicals' hopes were constituted by the vision set out in apocalyptic-eschatological biblical texts such as that proclaimed by Isaiah who spoke of a day when God would "swallow up death in victory . . . and it shall be said in that day, Lo, this is our God; and we have waited for him, and he will save us: this is the Lord; we have waited for him, we will be glad and rejoice in his salvation" (Isa 25:8).[187] Corresponding to this hope was a firm conviction in the resurrection of Christ as a historical event of cosmic magnitude. "The Christian hope for the future," Moltmann remarks, "comes of observing a specific, unique event—that of the resurrection and appearing of Jesus Christ."[188] Recognizing with leading theologians that "Christianity stands or falls with the reality of the raising of Jesus from the dead by God"[189] and that "the whole thinking of the New Testament is governed by belief in the Resurrection,"[190] Northern Ireland evangelicals insisted that the resurrection was "the focus of all our hopes."[191] According to Pauline eschatology, Christ's resurrection was not merely a unique messianic event that took place at a certain point within historical time but an apocalyptic-eschatological occasion of trans-historical significance and potentially universal salvific efficacy (1 Cor 15).[192] As the prefiguration of the new redeemed humanity, the resurrection signi-

186. As Ratzinger puts it, "Christlicher Glaube ist dem Leben zugewandt. Er glaubt dem Gott der Lebendigen" ("Christian faith is turned towards life. It believes in the God of the living"); Ratzinger, Eschatologie, 89–90.

187. This text which spoke of death being "swallowed up in victory" was at the heart of Paul's conception of the Christian hope of the conquest of death and eternal life. Such appropriations of texts from the Hebrew Bible by later contributors to the New Testament support our general thesis about the importance of the active text in the hermeneutical process.

188. Moltmann, Theology of Hope, 194.

189. Ibid., 165.

190. Cullmann, Immortality of the Soul, 27.

191. "The Covenant Reformed News" vol. 8, no. 12, 1.

192. Schweitzer, Mysticism of Paul, 98. Martyn argues that the cross itself was an apocalyptic event and that the apocalypse is essential to a proper understanding of Paul's of how Paul comprehends the significance of the cross. Commenting on Galatians, Martyn remarks that "the focus of Paul's apocalyptic lies not on Christ's parousia but rather on his death." See Martyn, "Apocalyptic Antinomies," 420–21. From a very different perspective Thomas Altizer comes to the same conclusion regarding the "one absolutely apocalyptic event" of the crucifixion; Altizer, Contemporary Jesus, 199.

fied the final victory over sin and death and was the prelude to cosmic salvation which would culminate in the cosmic redemption symbolized in the eschatological metaphor of the New Jerusalem.[193] In light of the resurrection the new humanity could share in the hope that the "mighty power" which God "wrought in Christ when he raised him from the dead" was also at work among those who believed (Eph 1:19–20).

These hopes were prevalent in the discourses of Northern Ireland apocalyptic eschatology. According to one evangelical interpretation, the resurrection was "the hope-filled triumph of life over injustice and death, acting as a foretaste of our own resurrection."[194] The key texts in the formulations of resurrection hope for many evangelicals were the following passages from 1 Corinthians and Philippians:

> For the trumpet shall sound, and the dead shall be raised incorruptible, and we shall be changed. For this corruption must put on incorruption, and this mortal must put on immortality. (1 Cor 15:52–53)

> Our citizenship is in heaven, from where also we look for the Saviour, the Lord Jesus Christ, Who shall change our lowly body, that it may be fashioned like his glorious body, according to the working by which he is able even to subdue all things unto himself. (Phil 3:20–21)

One evangelical contributor to the *Irish Baptist* in 1969 expressed his hope that the second coming of Christ would inaugurate a mysterious process in which believers shall put on a "spiritual body" which was to be "incorruptible, glorious, powerful—a body not prone to decay, not subject to death, not hindered by feebleness, not limited by natural laws, a body capable of going around God's universe without a spaceship made by man!"[195] In 2004 Irish Baptists continued to profess the same hope:

> The resurrection . . . is the assurance of the ultimate triumph of God in the future . . . Jesus Christ defeated death by rising from

---

193. Notwithstanding the pre-eminence of the resurrection as a unique event of apocalyptic-eschatological magnitude, it is also important to acknowledge, as Hegel did, the apocalyptic significance of the crucifixion a full and pure apocalyptic event. Altizer, commenting on Hegel's *Phenomenology*, regards the crucifixion as a uniquely apocalyptic event: "one shattering all ancient horizons and worlds, and ushering in an absolutely new world." See Altizer, "Apocalypticism and Modern Thinking," 2.

194. Campton and Biggar, *Divided Past*, 10.

195. *Irish Baptist* (September, 1969), 4.

> the dead. This means that in fellowship with him we will be given
> new bodies like his resurrection body. . . . The resurrection [is]
> the pledge of eternal life with Christ and the basis of Christian
> hope.[196]

As the "basis of Christian hope," evangelicals realized the uniqueness
of the resurrection to their theology of hope. "Our hope is in the resurrection of Christ and is . . . unique to Christianity," maintained one
evangelical Presbyterian commentator, who continued:

> Jesus the living saviour, imparts a living hope unto his people.
> . . . Life is surrounded, supported, strengthened and sweetened
> by the Lord Jesus living in us. Hope is also forward looking for
> we not only experience the life of God but we are ensured of a
> life with God.[197]

These expressions of hope in the resurrection of the body and eternal life
with Christ thus remained a constant feature of evangelical expressions
of hope. The affirmations of hope of Northern Ireland evangelicals were
predicated upon the apocalyptic-eschatological biblical texts, which
transcended their social contexts and offered an overall perspective from
which to interpret their experience of crisis in the light of this textually-
constituted hope. The resurrection and the crucifixion were interpreted
as successive stages of a common eschatological event. Thus in the words
of Samuel Carson, one time President of the Irish Baptist Union, the
"cross is . . . at the center of history. . . . Ages past looked forward to it,
these last days are all dated from it."[198] The "amazing cross" was thus seen
as the crucial stage in God's plan to redeem the world and a necessary
prelude to the cosmic redemption inaugurated in the resurrection.

Hope in the Rapture

For some evangelicals, eschatological hope was bound up with their expectation that, immediately prior to the anticipated "Great Tribulation,"
Christ would return to the earth to reclaim his people by snatching
them out of the earth and transporting them to heaven, thereby spar-
ing them of "the wrath to come" (1 Thess 1:10). Belief in the rapture,

196. *Irish Baptist Life* (April, 2004), 11.
197. Kelly, *Bible Study Guide: 1st Peter*, 4.
198. Carson, *The Amazing Cross*, 8.

one of the central tenets of premillennial dispensationalism, was prevalent among many Baptist, Brethren, and Pentecostal evangelicals in Northern Ireland. Denis Lyle spoke of his hope that, "The living will be raptured and both the living and the dead will be reunited around the Coming Bridegroom."[199] Samuel Carson, also an influential Baptist pastor, likewise maintained that, "The hope of the church is the coming of the Lord 'to the air' for His own, commonly called the rapture of the church."[200] Baptist pastor Ian Wilson explained through a sermon delivered to his congregation that the reason why the church was allegedly not alluded to after chapter 4 of the book of Revelation was because "it [had] been removed from earth at the rapture."[201] The doctrine of the secret rapture, however, was by no means a conviction held by the majority of evangelicals during the Troubles. The doctrine found stringent criticism among anti-Catholic evangelical fundamentalists such as Alan Campbell, who devoted a whole booklet to proving "the unscriptural nature of the Secret Rapture doctrine," which he execrated as a "Jesuit fable."[202] This statement again reminds us of the need to avoid premature distinctions among evangelicals in Northern Ireland. Notwithstanding his denunciations of Catholics and "apostate" Protestants, Campbell seems progressive in certain contexts, such as his views on the rapture. In fact, Campbell was in agreement with ECONI in his repudiation of the rapture, even though politically, at least, Campbell and ECONI were at opposite ends of the spectrum. This fact demonstrates that in the Troubles, there was no clear and consistent correlation between theological convictions and political beliefs.

Evangelical statements relating both to the rapture and to the resurrection organize themselves according to the taxonomy which emerged earlier in this chapter. Those evangelicals who professed hope in the rapture generally interpreted the biblical apocalyptic-eschatological texts as literal descriptions of a postponed era of righteousness. This age would be enacted definitively through supernatural intervention at a specific point in the future. Those evangelicals who were sceptical of the rapture, by contrast, tended to read the same texts as expressions of hope derived from the Pauline notion that "the present life of the believer

199. Lyle, *Countdown*, 43.
200. *Irish Baptist* 91 (July, 1969), 6.
201. Wilson, "That Amazing Book."
202. Campbell, *Is the Secret Rapture Scriptural?* 6.

is in part a realised existence of the new creation."[203] This distinction cannot be posited without some qualification, however, as it may seem to conflate Paisleyite fundamentalism with the more moderate expressions of evangelicalism such as ECONI, both of which were largely non-dispensational. Nevertheless, even those fundamentalists who were sceptical of the rapture retained a firm conviction that the world would be saved only after a period of violent upheaval culminating in a direct supernatural intervention of God to create a new heavens and a new earth. This period was believed to be set out in the biblical texts, which were accordingly interpreted as a blueprint of what was to take place at the end of the world. Those evangelicals associated with ECONI, by contrast, tended to interpret apocalyptic-eschatological texts not as literal descriptions of future events but as portrayals of an imaginative vision of immanent hope. These apparent anomalies and qualifications serve to reinforce the point made throughout this study that evangelicalism in the Northern Ireland Troubles was a decidedly idiosyncratic phenomenon characterized by contradiction, internal conflict and incongruity. Nowhere were these inconsistencies more apparent than in the apocalyptic-eschatological hopes of Northern Irish evangelicals.

The Central Place of Apocalyptic Hope in Northern Ireland Evangelicalism

Two fundamental conclusions can be drawn from the findings of this chapter. First, the indiscriminate ways in which Northern Ireland evangelicals applied the hermeneutic of hope to their interpretation of a wide variety of apocalyptic-eschatological texts corresponds to the broader thesis that evangelical readers were bound just as much by pre-existing discursive frameworks of interpretation set by the biblical texts as they were by social contexts. Moreover, these context themselves were generated by the random interplay of discourse within the apocalyptic-eschatological semiosphere inhabited by Northern Ireland evangelicals. Secondly, this chapter has shown that Northern Ireland apocalyptic-eschatological discourses encompassed a wide variety of

---

203. Scroggs, "Eschatological Existence," 125. Theologians now recognize the great extent to which Paul's theology was derived from apocalyptic-eschatological hope. As Beker notes, "It is impossible to conceive of authentic Pauline theology without apocalyptic hope." See Beker, *Triumph of God*, 33.

expressions in which the note of hope was by no means absent. These findings necessitate a revision to previous scholarly accounts which have considered apocalyptic language in the Troubles only under its sectarian or fear-inducing, anti-Catholic aspects. In the light of the theologies of hope developed by Northern Ireland evangelicals from a variety of denominational perspectives, it is no longer possible to associate apocalyptic-eschatological language with the an exclusively pessimistic teleology or as a discursive function of a supposed "combination of historical pessimism and local tragedy that has maintained the zero-sum nature of traditional evangelical politics."[204] Some scholarship has even implied that apocalyptic-eschatological language always exacerbated rather than alleviated the existing sectarian tensions. For example, in his unpublished PhD dissertation on the purported potential for the application of Liberation Theology to the Troubles, Andrew Gibson claims that, "NIE [Northern Ireland Evangelical] eschatology . . . has never led to significant social engagement. If anything, it has led to greater social dislocation as it has supported anti-Catholicism of all shades and thence much violence."[205] The problem here is that the argument is too narrow. The findings of this chapter, which have illustrated some similarities between certain expressions of Northern Ireland evangelicalism and the transformative eschatology of Jürgen Moltmann, entail a reconsideration of the role of apocalyptic eschatology in the Troubles. In particular, this chapter has cast considerable doubt upon the prevailing view that apocalyptic-eschatological discourses were little more than fuel for sectarian ideologies. In the light of these findings, it would be unfeasible to maintain that apocalyptic eschatology in the Troubles was nothing more than a terminological arsenal of hostile epithets that merely exacerbated tensions and bolstered sectarian bigotry and anti-Catholicism.

The above analysis has elucidated several ways in which Northern Ireland evangelicals utilized the eschatological framework of a redeemed humanity to overcome sectarian divisions. Evangelicals actively employed apocalyptic-eschatological language to facilitate reconciliation between hostile national groups and faith communities. The eschatological vision of a redeemed community comprising "every tribe, tongue and nation" and participating in a shared hope enabled evangelicals to celebrate ecumenical initiatives which gave expression to the supposed

204. Gribben, "Protestant Millennialism," 58.
205. Gibson, "Gustavo Gutierrez and Northern Ireland," 259.

call of the churches to be archetypes of unity and reconciliation in the midst of a situation of conflict.

It is true that for some evangelicals, apocalyptic eschatological texts depicting a faithful remnant people warding off the satanic incursions of the Antichrist in the end times added impetus to the conviction in the theological justification of the notion that one was justified in being "busily engaged for God in Holy Warfare."[206] Such beliefs can engender dangerous millennial ideologies among evangelical communities and can find violent outlets. These exclusivist convictions are often predicated on an incontrovertible faith in the justice of one's cause. In relation to evangelicalism and the issue of violence, Christian groups can thus become persuaded that they are the chosen people fighting the battles of the Lord. It thus becomes possible, as Moltmann notes, for such a people genuinely to believe that the violence they perpetrate and wars they fight are justified because they are really "crusades in a divine mission rather than naked power struggles."[207] There were, however, other Northern Ireland evangelicals, by contrast, who perceived what they regarded as a vision of a peaceable kingdom of God and sought to apply its principles in a concerted effort towards achieving reconciliation through a vision of social inclusion. This chapter has demonstrated conclusively that these evangelical applications of the transformative and reconciling capabilities of apocalyptic-eschatological texts must be taken into account alongside the fear-inducing and enemy-making readings of such texts considered in chapter 3.

206. *Battle Standard* 1/1 (October, 1997), 1.
207. *Das Kommen Gottes,* 171.

5

Apocalyptic Dualism

"Because thou art lukewarm,
and neither cold nor hot,
I will spue thee out of my mouth"

Introduction to Chapter 5

The divergent interpretations of the texts of Northern Ireland apocalyptic eschatology and the semantic oscillations between hope and fear
exhibited in evangelical hermeneutics substantiate Montrose's definition
of a text as a site of "convergence of various and potentially contradictory cultural discourses."[1] This chapter examines the nature of these discourses and how apocalyptic-eschatological language was expressed in
the rhetoric of Northern Ireland evangelicalism. More specifically, chapter 5 explores the ways in which apocalyptic-eschatological worldviews
corresponded to the political convictions of evangelical interpretive
communities. The aim is thus to investigate how the political and social
rhetoric emanating from these evangelical communities corresponded
to the semantic fields arising out of the apocalyptic-eschatological texts
we have investigated. Chapter 2 explored some of the hermeneutical
implications of the notion that meaning is hermetically sealed in the
anarchic systems of difference comprising linguistic structures. These
theoretical ventures offered a perspective on the notion that the world

1. Montrose, *Purpose of Playing*, xii.

which we inhabit is defined to a considerable extent by the ways in which we use and interpret language. Accepting this premise, we are led towards a deeper probing into the salient semantic fields that emerged from the evangelical interpretive communities that read the biblical apocalyptic-eschatological texts.

This chapter thus addresses the influence of dualistic interpretations of apocalyptic-eschatological texts on evangelical political and religious rhetoric. What follows can be classified as an inquiry into the origins of the semantic dualism associated with some aspects of Northern Ireland evangelical social and political engagement during the Troubles. This rhetoric can be shown to have been firmly rooted in the texts of biblical apocalyptic eschatology, which were read in such a way as to yield uncompromising convictions among their readers. Since this argument leads to the conclusion, albeit from a different perspective, that the texts of apocalyptic eschatology were active agents in the formation of evangelical worldviews, this chapter reinforces our main argument that apocalyptic-eschatological language, rather than being a response to specific events, was in fact constitutive of evangelical interpretations of these events.

Chapter 5 thus shifts the focus towards the semantic dichotomies which characterized both evangelical interpretations of biblical apocalyptic-eschatological texts and these texts themselves. The analytical objectives of this chapter revert from an elucidation of the existential categories of fear and hope and move towards an exclusive concentration upon the polarized semantic fields as they were expressed in the rhetoric of Northern Ireland evangelicals. The primary quality of such rhetoric will be shown to be the uncompromising expression with which apocalyptic-eschatological utterances were articulated. A variety of examples from Northern Ireland evangelical interpretations of biblical texts will be brought into conversation with a selection of critical approaches in biblical studies and literary theory. The aim throughout will be to demonstrate the extent to which much of the uncompromising rhetoric that emerged from the cultures of Northern Ireland evangelicalism was derived from particular interpretations of certain apocalyptic-eschatological biblical texts.

Absolute Distinctions in Apocalyptic-Eschatological Language

Alongside the existential aspects of fear and hope, one of the most recurrent characteristics of apocalyptic-eschatological discourses in Northern Ireland was their tendency to organize concepts in terms of binary classifications. The notion that societies are built upon such classifications is by no means new to cultural[2] or linguistic studies.[3] In the same way that philosophers have speculated on the ways in which aesthetic[4] and ontological[5] categories organize themselves into dichotomous elements,[6] cultural anthropologists have revealed the extent to which human perceptions of the natural and social worlds are derived from binary distinctions, such as those between right and left, up and down, day and night, male and female, clean and unclean, good and evil, right and wrong, death and life.[7] Since such tendencies have asserted themselves universally among diverse cultures throughout the world, some anthropologists have concluded that bivalence must be "a fundamental property of either the natural world or the human brain."[8]

The tendency to organize concepts into binary classifications is undoubtedly one of the hallmarks of hermeneutical approaches to apocalyptic-eschatological texts.[9] The interpretations of these texts by Northern Ireland evangelicals were no exception. Apocalyptic-

2. Edgar and Sedgwick, *Cultural Theory*, 27–28. Since the work of Alfred Radcliffe-Brown (1881–1955), one of the foundational suppositions of cultural anthropology has been that binary oppositions "structure perception and interpretation of the natural and social world."

3. Jakobson and de Saussure contended that language in its phonetic aspects organizes itself according to binary oppositions. See Jakobson and Saussure, "L'arbitraire du Signe," 599–603.

4. For example, Nietzsche's "Dionysian" and "Apollonian" categories of aesthetic perception.

5. For example, Heidegger's "*Sein*" and "*Nichtsein*" and Sartre's "*Être*" and "*Néant*."

6. For example, Nietzsche posited an aesthetic theory of tragedy which conceived of a creative interplay of two poles: the ecstatic chaos of Dionysian element and the epic harmony of the Apollonian aspect; Nietzsche, *Geburt der Tragödie*.

7. Bull succeeds in bringing these anthropological insights into a creative and insightful dialogue with scholarly discussion about the meaning and significance of the apocalypse; Bull, *Seeing Things Hidden*, 52ff.

8. Bull, *Seeing Things Hidden*, 53–54; Lévi-Strauss, *Elementary Structures*, 136.

9. This hermeneutical trait is almost universally recognized by biblical scholars. See, for instance, Sim, *Apocalyptic Eschatology*, 35–41, 81–87; O'Callaghan, *Christological Assimilation*, 122ff.

eschatological texts added semantic substance to the conviction that the Troubles were ultimately a battle between mutually-contradictory metaphysical entities, "an eternal conflict between good and evil,"[10] in which the stakes were incalculably high; no less than the spiritual destiny of the cosmos was at issue. Evangelicals involved in the conflict, in turn, did not see themselves primarily as people involved in a political struggle over national or cultural identity; rather they saw themselves as "cosmic warriors in the battle with evil."[11] The Troubles was "a manifestation of a greater spiritual conflict . . . a struggle between the forces of good and of evil."[12] Such an understanding of the Troubles was deemed to be necessary in order to grasp what one evangelical called "the spiritual background and dimension to the conflict."[13]

The texts of biblical apocalyptic eschatology depict a world in which the boundaries between good and evil are clearly demarcated and absolute.[14] The blessed community of God's redeemed people is set in contrast to the wicked and hostile world.[15] The clearly demarcated polarization between the wicked world of sin and the blessed community of the redeemed was a single manifestation of the juxtaposition of semantic dualism, which was one of the most distinctive qualities of evangelical interpretations of apocalyptic-eschatological texts during the Troubles. Using the analogy of such texts as the Parable of the Sower which sets the good wheat sown and cultivated by the "Son of Man" in contradistinction to the evil tares planted and raised up by "the devil," many Northern Ireland evangelicals interpreted the conflict in terms of such absolute categories. These interpretive tendencies were particularly evident in the biblical conceptions of good and evil, and the righteous or blessed and the unrighteous or cursed which punctuate the original biblical texts. Above all, as biblical scholars have revealed, the book of Revelation, as the classic text of apocalyptic eschatology, is not merely interspersed with semantic dualism but is also organized around a set of

10. *Protestant Telegraph,* quoted in Whyte, *Interpreting Northern Ireland,* 108.

11. Landes, *Heaven on Earth,* 16.

12. Campbell, "The Anglo-Irish Agreement."

13. Campbell, *Remember 1641,* 24.

14. Husch, *Something Coming,* 191.

15. Hays, *Moral Vision,* 181.

dualistic categories, which constitute the core structure of the apocalyptic narrative.[16]

Among Northern Ireland evangelicals, there was even the suggestion that the biblical apocalyptic-eschatological texts taught that the semantic distance between such dualistic categories as good and evil was not static or constant but would increase continually up until the denouement of the end times. This conviction was based on the apparent biblical teaching that the approach of the end would be marked by the multiplication of vice, heresy and perversity (2 Tim 3:1–5; 2 Pet 2:1–3, 9–22; Jude 8–16) as well as the decline of faith (Luke 18:8), hope (Luke 21:26), and love (Matt 24:12). Writing a commentary on Revelation 12 for the *Ulster Bulwark,* one evangelical expressed his conviction that, "as time draws near to the end the line of demarcation between good and evil becomes more clear."[17] The juxtaposition of metaphysical antinomies gave rise to further interpretations of the Troubles such as that of an Irish Baptist evangelical who asserted that despite the complexities of the conflict and the contending parties involved in the conflict in Northern Ireland, the struggle was ultimately of a spiritual nature, a matter of good versus evil:

> behind the scenes there is a conflict between the powers of light and the forces of darkness, and that ultimately the battle in this universe is between Christ and Satan. . . . Indeed we know in the final analysis there are really only two movements on earth that we must reckon with, the Church and the World, the former made up of the children of God and under the authority of Jesus Christ, the latter made up of unbelievers who are under the sway of the Evil one.[18]

The texts of the parables themselves, particularly those which sought to illustrate spiritual realities by narrative techniques and heuristic devices involving the invocation of earthly images such as wheat and tares, mustard seeds, vineyards and pearls of great price, could be said to be inherently hermeneutically disposed to dualistic interpretations which separated reality into a spiritual "signified" and its corresponding

16. According to Gager, Revelation presented to its readers a series of oppositions in a pattern of "rhythmic oscillation"; Gager, *Kingdom and Community,* 49–57, 64–65.

17. *Ulster Bulwark* (January/February, 1978), 4.

18. *Irish Baptist* 101 (December, 1978), 15.

earthly "signifier."[19] This interpretive tendency is reflected in the text of Revelation itself which depicts a cosmic setting in which human history occurs simultaneously in heaven and on earth (Rev 5:8–12; 6:9–11; 7:9–17; 15:1–3).

The Troubles as an Apocalyptic Struggle between Good and Evil

The Manichean bifurcation of the cosmos into Good and Evil, which was a recurring motif of apocalyptic-eschatological discourses, introduced a new dimension to a host of other, pre-existing dichotomies in Northern Ireland evangelicalism during the Troubles: "Protestant" vs. "Catholic"; "biblical Christianity" vs. "apostate Protestantism"; "Unionist" vs. "Nationalist"; "true Protestants" vs. "everyone else." Under the discursive conditions inculcated by apocalyptic eschatology, such distinctions took on a deeper significance in the eyes of many evangelicals. The dichotomizing repercussions of apocalyptic-eschatological language were played out in the political aspects of the Troubles. The rhetoric of "Not an Inch," "Ulster says No!" and "Never, Never, Never, Never," and other uncompromising slogans, although not inherently apocalyptic or eschatological or even evangelical, will be shown to have their counterpart in an apocalyptic-eschatological worldview, which perceived the Troubles ultimately not as a conflict between Loyalists and Republicans or Protestants and Catholics but as a particular manifestation of a cosmic clash of metaphysical entities of Good and Evil, Light and Darkness and ultimately between Christ, "the Word of God" (Rev 19:13) and "that old serpent, called the Devil, and Satan, which deceiveth the whole world" (Rev 12:9).

As violence erupted in Northern Ireland in the wake of the Civil Rights movement and the subsequent Protestant backlash, evangelical responses were shaped by biblical texts, which were assiduously perused in order to interpret the "signs of the times." In 1967 at the start of the

19. The extent to which eschatology governs the interpretation the Gospel parables, and by extension, the interpretation of the teachings of Christ in general, has been the subject of a lively and extended debate in among biblical scholars. Marcus Borg makes a case for separating Jesus' teachings from their supposed eschatological backdrop. See Borg, "A Temperate Case," 81–102. Responding to Borg, Allison makes the contrary claim that eschatology is indispensible to the correct interpretation of the parables. See, Allison, "A Plea for Thoroughgoing Eschatology," 651–68. Other theologians have since entered the debate. For a summary of recent scholarly debate on this question, see Klyne Snodgrass, Stories with Intent, 477–564.

upsurge in violence, Clifford Smyth sent a letter to the *Ulster Protestant* magazine in which he warned of a "watershed in history, a great spiritual conflict is taking shape."[20] These interpretive tendencies were present in many Northern Ireland evangelical interpretations of the supposed deeper significance of the Troubles.

Other evangelicals likewise perceived the seriousness of the situation in light of the supposed spiritual clash underlying the outbreak of violence. Take for instance, this statement from an article on the front page of the *Protestant Telegraph* in February 1971: "Northern Ireland is now enveloped in *a war with the forces of subversion*; and any further escalation will have disastrous consequences for every citizen."[21] At one level, the "war with the forces of subversion" could simply be interpreted as a reference to the struggle against the IRA and the Republican movement in general. However, the texts of apocalyptic eschatology, which inculcated the notion that, as one evangelical expressed it, "The battle in the world today is a battle between Satan and God,"[22] introduced another way of interpreting this statement. This "war" could also be interpreted in light of apocalyptic-eschatological discourses as an allusion to the mythical battle against the "mystery of iniquity" and the "lawlessness" of Antichrist or the "Man of Sin." Regardless of whether such allusions were part of the author's conscious intentions, they could certainly have been interpreted by many of their evangelical readers in this way. As Steve Bruce remarked in 1994, "There are in Northern Ireland Protestants who see all history as a struggle between the forces of good and evil, God and the Devil, Christ and the Anti-Christ."[23] Gribben likewise makes the apt observation that for many Northern Ireland evangelicals, "The conflict on the streets was the ultimate conflict in microcosm—a local representation of the constant struggle between good and evil, the kingdom of God and the deceptions of Satan."[24] A clear example of this conviction at play in Northern Ireland evangelical interpretations of apocalyptic-eschatological texts is found in Denis Lyle's following assertion in his

---

20. The letter containing this statement is appended in Smyth's anti-Catholic monograph, entitled *Rome—Our Enemy*, 78.

21. *Protestant Telegraph* (13 February, 1971), 4 (emphasis added).

22. *Protestant Telegraph* (19 June, 1976), 7.

23. Bruce, *Edge of the Union*, 22.

24. Gribben, "Protestant Millennialism," 53.

commentary on the contemporary significance of the seven churches in chapters 3 and 4 of Revelation:

> A line has been drawn in the sand. Sides have been taken, and a war has been declared. Hell is officially in session. And the church is under attack. With mounting hostility, the kingdom of Satan is engaging in a full scale war against the church of Jesus Christ. The foul forces of darkness are escalating their campaign against the people of God with an unholy vengeance. Like two weather fronts colliding, a violent storm is brewing across the horizon as never before. . . . Hell is in direct conflict with heaven.[25]

The belief that the cosmos was locked in a spiritual conflict between good and evil was echoed with equal resolution by the Reformed Presbyterian F. S. Leahy, who stated unequivocally that, "Two kingdoms confront each other in mortal combat: the kingdom of Satan and the kingdom of God."[26] In the eyes of many evangelicals, the Troubles were thus a manifestation of an unremitting spiritual conflict, "a war of the forces of light against the forces of darkness."[27]

These textually-constituted apocalyptic-eschatological convictions became so ingrained in the thinking of Northern Ireland evangelicals that they constituted a hermeneutical reference point, a set paradigm against which to interpret social and political events and developments. These were interpreted in terms of how they corresponded to the ultimate battle in the heavenly realms between the "Son of man . . . and all the holy angels" (Matt 25:31) and the "rulers of the darkness of this world . . . [and] spiritual wickedness in high places" (Eph 6:12). Apocalyptic eschatological texts thus generated the notion that "cosmic events are bound up with historical events" and that "the whole cosmic process is linked with what happens to humanity."[28] This conviction is clearly present in the following reading of the conflict by one contributor to the *Irish Baptist* who offered an interpretation of the apocalyptic-eschatological battle underlying every instance of sectarian violence and civil unrest associated with the Troubles and elsewhere throughout the world: "The world-wide eruption of anarchy and violence which we are witnessing

---

25. Lyle, *Good, the Bad and the Lukewarm*, 45, 47.

26. Leahy, *Victory of the Lamb*, 8.

27. Barkun, "Millenarians and Violence," 248.

28. Cullmann, *Salvation in History*, 82.

today is one manifestation of the activities of those principalities and powers, those rulers of the spiritual darkness of this world."[29]

Such interpretations give us insight into the ways in which apocalyptic-eschatological texts create dualistic worldviews in which "the cosmos or supernatural realm is divided into two opposing forces. On one side stands God and the holy angels and on the other stands a host of evil angels who have fallen from grace."[30]

A notable example of the same interpretive tendencies in Northern Ireland evangelicalism is Ivan Foster's commentary on the book of Revelation, which is pervaded throughout by a clear and uncompromising moral and spiritual dualism. Commenting on the Babylonian harlot of Revelation, Foster avers that,

> There have ever been God's truth and the devil's lie operating in the world. There have been the true and the counterfeit, the Christ and the antichrist, the true prophet and the false prophet, the Holy Spirit and the spirit of the antichrist, the gospel and another gospel. . . . We are part of Christ's church . . . or we are part of the false system symbolised here by the Harlot.[31]

These quotations demonstrate how an interpretation of an apocalyptic-eschatological text that posits a series of strict dichotomies between competing entities can engender a corresponding notion of absolute allegiance in which the reader is called upon to declare his or her true loyalties—one is either "good" and belongs to the true Church of Christ or one is "evil," in which case they belong to the false religion of the harlot. These interpretations also exhibit what one biblical scholar calls the "strict dualism on the group human level,"[32] in which the events in "this world" find their apocalyptic-eschatological counterpart in a supposed cosmic conflict in "the world above." Since human history was understood to be taking place simultaneously in heaven and on earth, the conflicts occurring in "this world" and "the world above" were understood as symbolically related yet temporally distinct: "The two worlds were thought to interact; this world depended for its very existence on the other, but by the same token things done in this world could by an

---

29. *Irish Baptist* 94 (March, 1972), 2.

30. Sim, *Apocalyptic Eschatology,* 35; cf. Stemberger, *Geschichte der Jüdischen Literatur,* 28–29.

31. Foster, *Antichrist,* 179–80.

32. Sim, *Apocalyptic Eschatology,* 35.

essentially mysterious mode of operation have effects in and upon the other world."[33]

An apocalyptic-eschatological drama involving an ultimate struggle between Good and Evil was thus being enacted on the world stage in which "the war in *heaven* between the Lord . . . and Satan is played out on *earth* by their respective agents."[34] Thus from the texts of apocalyptic-eschatology a worldview emerges which posits the notion that "the unseen but very real heavenly world determines what will happen on earth and in the affairs of humans."[35] As Sim puts it, "human wickedness is inextricably linked to angelic wickedness. Evil human individuals and institutions work in the service of Satan and his wicked forces."[36]

A typical example of this conviction at work in Northern Ireland evangelical interpretations of the Troubles is found in a letter written to the *Belfast Telegraph* by an evangelical Methodist minister, which contained the following segment:

> As a Christian, I know that those who are not for Christ are against Him. . . . I know that we cannot be on the fence—that as Luke 11[[37]] reminds us there is no middle ground between evil and good, darkness and light, Satan and God. . . . In this context, I believe the work of the IRA and UFF to be Satan-inspired.[38]

The final sentence of this quotation offers a particularly illuminating example of how apocalyptic eschatology was used to undercut social dualisms such as those between Republican organizations like the Irish Republican Army and Loyalist groups like the Ulster Freedom Fighters by subsuming them both into a common apocalyptic-eschatological identity. The evangelical author regarded both organizations not primarily as representatives of divergent political ideologies and aspirations, but as the agents of a common spiritual master—Satan. Thus, in the eyes of this evangelical interpreter, the political differences between the IRA and the UFF were superficial compared to the underlying commonality of destruction, death, and chaos caused by both organizations, which

33. Nineham, *Use and Abuse of the Bible*, 51.

34. Siew, *War Between the Two Beasts*, 3.

35. Grabbe, "Prophetic and Apocalyptic," 117.

36. Sim, *Apocalyptic Eschatology*, 40.

37. The author is presumably alluding to Luke 11:23, in which Jesus is reported as having said, "He that is not with me is against me."

38. *Belfast Telegraph* (5 July, 1997).

thereby, in his view, put them in the same spiritual category as instruments of the devil. The hermeneutical impetus for the transposition of the dichotomy from "Republican" and "Loyalist" to "Satan" and "Christ" was supplied in this instance by a biblical text concerning apocalyptic eschatology.

The Uncompromising Rhetoric of Northern Ireland Evangelicals and Its Basis in Biblical Apocalyptic-Eschatological Texts

The cosmic dualism of biblical apocalyptic eschatology was reflected in other ways in the language used by Northern Ireland evangelicals during the Troubles. From the Pauline conception of sin and grace to the Johannine dialectic of darkness and light, the biblical texts, particularly in the New Testament, pulsate with tension generated by the radical dualism which is multiplied throughout the texts by the creative employment of various imaginative rhetorical strategies. In the apocalyptic-eschatological texts, one of these rhetorical devices was the juxtaposition of antinomies in such as way as to undercut any potential residual notion of semantic ambiguity in the text. Such juxtapositions left the reader in no doubt that he or she was called upon to make a decisive choice between good and evil and that there was no possibility of compromising between these mutually exclusive categories. In the hermeneutics of crisis associated with the Troubles, these interpretive tendencies became common among Northern Ireland evangelicals. "The sense of historical crisis," observes Stephen O'Leary in an admirable rhetorical study of apocalyptic discourse, is intensified in apocalyptic rhetoric "by a binary opposition of good and evil, forming a dialectic with no room for compromise."[39] The relationship between the uncompromising rhetoric of apocalyptic eschatology and the demand of absolute commitment made of the reader is vividly depicted in Christ's warning to the complacent and lukewarm church at Laodicea in Revelation 2:16–19:

> I know thy works, that thou art neither cold nor hot: I would thou wert cold or hot. So then because thou art lukewarm, and neither cold nor hot, I will spue thee out of my mouth . . . be zealous therefore, and repent.

---

39. O'Leary, *Arguing the Apocalypse*, 64.

Not only did some Northern Ireland evangelicals quote examples of uncompromising, apocalyptic language from the text of Revelation; others went further and used such texts as a justification for their own use of extreme language in order to address contemporary issues. On 8 November 1974, one of the leaders of the Orange Order alluding to Christ's warning to the tepid Laodicean church, gave an address in which he urged Orangemen to renounce lukewarmness:

> It is fashionable to tone down religious distinctions in this ecumenical age. Tonight I challenge all of us to a position of Protestant extremism. The Lord not only said "he that is not with me is against me," but also in the Book of Revelation repudiated a lukewarm approach.[40]

The absolute distinctions that seemed to characterize apocalyptic-eschatological language were augmented by a prolific array of binary oppositions created by imaginative and targeted employment of metaphor to achieve specific rhetorical goals. For instance, the clear distinctions between Christ and Antichrist, the powers of good and the hosts of darkness, imply there can be no room for compromise or thought of concession. As Paisley put it, echoing Luke 11:23: "If we are not of Christ we are of Satan."[41]

This kind of approach that insisted on the absolute dichotomy between apocalyptic-eschatological categories was a persistent feature of Northern Ireland evangelical discourses. One obvious example was Ian Paisley, whose militantly fundamentalist theological reading of the Troubles was pregnant with the idiomatic vocabulary of biblical apocalyptic eschatology and a corresponding cosmic-dualistic interpretation of the supposed deeper significance of the conflict. One of his fundamentalist apologists provides a helpful insight into the biblical origins of Paisley's absolutist interpretation of the Troubles:

> The Gospel is a battle cry against all satanically originated falsehood. There is no quarter asked or given in this war. It is a battle the results of which are eternally measured. This is the same battle . . . which has been waged throughout history between false seed

40. *Orange Standard* (December 1974/January 1975), 3.

41. *New Protestant Telegraph* (March, 1991), 4. Interestingly, such rhetoric was echoed years later by George W. Bush after the 11 September terrorist attacks. Bush declared in his State of the Union Address that, "either you are with us or you are with the terrorists." See Northcott, *Angel Directs the Storm*, 167.

and the true seed . . . light and darkness, between truth and error.
. . . To him [Paisley] truth and error are not differing degrees of
the same thing, but they differ radically in kind—not in degree.
. . . Paisley stands apart from the false doctrine of Romanism and
the hell-inspired ecumenical movement.[42]

Such pronouncements substantiate the argument that the sociological
counterpart of apocalyptic-eschatological language is a combative situation between at least two contending parties. This line of thought has
been traced by sociologists whose insights have been informed by their
research into the Troubles. One such example is Mark Juergensmeyer
who remarks that apocalyptic-eschatological schemes can create the
conditions in which "one is confronted with the idea of dichotomous
opposition on an absolute scale. . . . No compromise is deemed possible.
The very existence of the opponent is a threat, and until the enemy is
either crushed or contained, one's own existence cannot be secure."[43]
Another way of making this point from the perspective of critical theory
would be to say that the rhetoric of apocalyptic-eschatology seemed to
stipulate absolute commitment from its readers. Such absolute commitment formed the natural political counterpart to the semantic oppositions that characterize the biblical apocalyptic-eschatological texts.

The absolutist interpretive demands posed by texts such as
Revelation were reinforced through an eclectic array of contrasting
metaphors emerging from the apocalyptic-eschatological imagination.
For instance, the messianic lamb of the Apocalypse, identified as the
one who "had been slain, having seven horns and seven eyes" (Rev 5:6),
finds its diabolical counterpart in the "great red dragon, having seven
heads and ten horns, and seven crowns upon his heads" (Rev 12:3). As
expressions of "the unity between the representative and semantic function of language,"[44] these symbols, which represented the mythical battle
between good and evil, occupied a prominent place in the discourses
of Northern Ireland evangelicalism. Examples of the semantic dualisms
which pervade the text of Revelation include the special sign of the followers of the lamb which is set in contrast to the mark of those who worship the beast, together with the heavenly city, the pure benevolent bride

42. Cooke, *Ian Paisley*, 45.

43. Juergensmeyer, *Terror in the Mind of God*, 152.

44. De Man, *Blindness and Insight*, 189.

of Christ, and its malevolent counterpart, the wicked city of Babylon, presented as a degraded harlot.[45]

The biblical passages in which this dualism is expressed in its acutest rhetorical intensity are to be found in those texts dealing with the last judgment. Passages depicting people—or "nations" (ταέθνη)—appearing before the judgment seat of Christ to be sent either to hell or to heaven (Matt 25:31–46) remind the evangelical reader of the incalculably high stakes of apocalyptic eschatology. Either one bears the mark of God and is admitted into the "eternal glory" (2 Tim 2:10) and "fullness of joy" (Ps 16:11) of God's presence in heaven or one displays the sign of the Beast and is thrown into a fiery pit (Rev 19:20; 20:15). Here the unrighteous will be sent and made to suffer for eternity in the place where "the worm dieth not, and the fire is not quenched" (Mark 9:44, 46, 48) and in which there will be "wailing and gnashing of teeth."[46] This semantic polarization found expression in Northern Ireland evangelical interpretations of apocalyptic-eschatological texts such as Revelation in which the distinction between salvation and damnation is depicted in the most vivid and contrasting terms: "While the believer will drink of the living fountains of water, the unbeliever will drink of the wine of the wrath of God. While the unbeliever will sing the new song of triumph, the smoke of the unbeliever will ascend upward forever and ever."[47] Whereas the righteous would be admitted to paradise, the damned would be cast into "that furnace of everlasting fire, that lake of brimstone and flame."[48] This polarized rhetoric depicting the ultimate fate of the "saved" and the "lost" was recognized not only by fundamentalist interpreters of apocalyptic-eschatological texts such as Revelation. Those who represented the other side of the evangelical spectrum likewise perceived the

45. The use of female imagery in Revelation, such as the Babylonian harlot and the bride of Christ, has been subject to searching criticism by feminist theologians. See Selvidge, "Powerful and Powerless," 157–67; and Pippin, *Death and Desire*. The validity of Selvidge's and Pippin's criticisms are challenged in Rossing, *Choice between Two Cities*, which contends that for the original audience the feminine-defined symbols of Revelation did not possess the gender-loaded connotations that modern feminist interpreters have ascribed to them.

46. This term recurs throughout Matthew's Gospel (8:12; 13:42; 13:50; 22:13; 24:51; 25:30) and refers to the torments of those cast into the place of "outer darkness," known in the popular imagination as "Hell." In the King James translation the term also appears in Luke 13:28.

47. Foster, *Antichrist*, 155.

48. Paisley, *Whereabouts of Mr Lostman*, 9.

absolute distinction made between the fate of the justified and the destiny of the damned, clearly articulated in the biblical texts. As one leader of ECONI put it in his exegetical study of the book of Revelation, "the reward for the saints is set in stark contrast to the destruction visited on the enemies of God."[49] He followed this remark with the observation that, "It is hard to imagine a starker contrast between the lake of fire of 20:15 and the new heaven and a new earth of 21:1."[50]

Thus, according to some interpretations of apocalyptic-eschatological discourse, there was apparently no rhetorical space in which to envision intermediate soteriological possibilities; one was either consigned to eternal destruction in the "great abyss of the damned"[51] or ordained to everlasting joy in God's presence. The lines of demarcation between the "righteous" and the "sinners" were sharply drawn.[52] In the mind of the evangelical under the sway of the dualistic worldview of apocalyptic-eschatological texts, there existed "a strict division" between "those few who are righteous and the majority who are wicked and there is no category in between."[53] As Richard Landes notes, when such people view the world "many see not a wide and nuanced spectrum of people, but a few saints and a vast sea of sinners, some redeemable, some (most) not."[54] In such a world in which "many have been created, but few will be saved" (2 Esd 8:3), notions of lukewarmness, apathy, indifference, and halfheartedness were inherently antithetical to the hermeneutic of absolute commitment demanded by the texts of apocalyptic eschatology. In the same way that their tepid dedication to his cause made Christ want to "spew out" the Laodicean church, so too did many evangelicals in Northern Ireland, taking a stand "for God and Ulster," eschew any notion of political compromise by "apostate" Protestants who were seen as embodying the Laodicean vice of concession and thereby selling Ulster's birthright. Compromise, as the political equivalent of hermeneutical lukewarmness, was perceived as something to be execrated on the grounds that it was alien to the rhetoric of total allegiance implied by apocalyptic-eschatological texts. Some interpretations of apocalyp-

49. McMillan, "Seven Beatitudes," 148.
50. Ibid., 149.
51. Paisley, *Mr Lostman*, 9.
52. Pattemore, *People of God in the Apocalypse*, 217.
53. Sim, *Apocalyptic Eschatology*, 53.
54. Landes, *Heaven on Earth*, 12.

tic eschatology thus created discursive worlds in which the Laodicean vice of compromise became a grave sin, which although not necessarily tantamount to the ultimate transgression of "blasphemy against the Holy Ghost" (Matt 12:31; Luke 12:10; Mark 3:29), was nevertheless to be repudiated as a manifestation of an underlying weakness or lack of conviction that betrayed the evangelical cause in Northern Ireland. As the biblical scholar John Gager puts it, "the category of lukewarmness has no meaning whatsoever in an apocalyptic setting where good and evil are completely unambiguous and totally opposed."[55] What Gager observed generally about "apocalyptic settings" could be said with particular truth of evangelical interpretations of apocalyptic-eschatological texts during the Troubles.

In the case of Northern Ireland evangelicalism, the semantic polarization inherent in the texts of apocalyptic eschatology generated in turn a variety of polarized hermeneutical responses on the part of their evangelical interpreters. Appealing to numerous apocalyptic-eschatological texts in his booklet about the 1641 massacre, Alan Campbell applied the apocalyptic notion of "no compromise" to address the contemporary political conflict in Northern Ireland in which he called upon Protestants not to offer concessions to the Catholic Church:

> There can be no middle ground in this struggle. . . . There is no political compromise which can resolve the present state of undeclared civil war in Ulster. . . . It can only be ultimately ended either by the victory of Roman Catholic Irish Republicanism or of Protestant British Unionism.[56]

Elsewhere he spoke out in condemnation of the alleged "spirit of compromise" that had begun to permeate throughout the "Loyal Orders."[57] Seeking to relieve his readers of any inclination to compromise with "Ulster's enemies," Campbell drew on an eclectic array of New Testament apocalyptic-eschatological extracts and passages from Exodus, Judges and Samuel, Kings and Chronicles, and concluded that "Judah enjoyed peace because God physically annihilated their enemies not because they surrendered, compromised or negotiated."[58]

55. Gager, "Attainment of Millennial Bliss," 149.

56. Campbell, *Remember 1641*, 24.

57. Campbell, *Five*, 15.

58. Campbell, *For What Should Ulster Pray?*, 19. Campbell was referring in this instance to the Judean King Jehosaphat and the genocide of the Ammonites in

It is only in the light of this uncompromising mentality that we can rightly interpret the comment of another Northern Ireland evangelical who declared that, "There will be no long lasting peace on this earth until he [Christ] returns."[59] In its locutionary aspect,[60] this statement was a simple expression of apocalyptic-eschatological hope in the *parousia*. At the illocutionary level it was a critical remark directed against those who sought for peace through political negotiation with "the enemy." Likewise according to the fundamentalist evangelicals writing for the *Protestant Telegraph* at the beginning of the Troubles, the teaching of the Scriptures was clear: peace could never be achieved through political negotiation. This conviction was often expressed explicitly and with even more rigour by fundamentalists. For instance, the following quotation from the *Protestant Telegraph*, which contains a classic example of the aforementioned juxtaposition of an explicit eschatology and an implicit soteriology, was appended with an evangelical appeal to the peace that allegedly visits an individual soul upon its conversion:

> The Bible specifically states that wars, strife, famine, pestilence, earthquakes and sorrows will continue, increase and reach a climax at the end of the age, to be settled only by the personal return of the Lord Jesus Christ in glory . . . peace cannot be obtained by world government (Isaiah 48:22), but . . . it is sure to all individuals who personally receive the Lord Jesus Christ as their Saviour (John 14:27; Romans 5:1; Ephesians 2:14).[61]

That such views could be advocated by ministers from the Church of Ireland (such as Willans), endorsed by the Orange Order,[62] and sup-

---

2 Chronicles 20:17–30.

59. Willans, *Proof the Bible is True*, 4. An indication of the popularity of Willans' book is that the Northern Ireland bookseller, Easons, placed it on their top-ten best-seller list; *Orange Standard* (October, 1987), 4.

60. The distinguishing characteristics of the locutionary, illocutionary and perlocutionary force of speech acts is expounded in Austin's classic study, *How to do things with Words*, 99–133 and *passim*.

61. *Protestant Telegraph* 10 (28 May, 1966), 10.

62. The reviewer, writing for the *Orange Standard* (October, 1987), 4, expressed his hope that Willans' book "will be read, re-read and used as a basis for Bible study." The reviewer's explicit citation of this exact same statement ("there will be no lasting peace until he [Christ] returns") in this article and his comment that this notion was "of particular relevance to our present time" is an interesting illustration of how theological texts were interpreted and which parts were emphasized by particular readers, in this instance by the Orange Order.

ported by the Free Presbyterians[63] and Baptists[64] is a clear indication of the ways in which common apocalyptic-eschatological themes continually reasserted themselves throughout the multiplicity of evangelical expressions within the churches of Northern Ireland during the Troubles. The reference to the political ramifications of apocalyptic eschatology implied in this quotation also raises the crucial issue of the ways in which apocalyptic dualistic categories fed into the political rhetoric of Northern Ireland evangelicals.

The Political Context of Uncompromising Apocalyptic Rhetoric in the Troubles, 1967–2007

In her study of religion and national identity, Claire Mitchell describes Northern Ireland as a place in which theology and politics are "mutually conditioning"[65] to the extent that an "extreme religious view often goes hand in hand with an extreme political view."[66] If we accept this observation, it is not surprising to discover that theological rhetoric in the Troubles was replicated in the political discourses in which evangelical motifs were widely employed.[67] The loose invocation of biblical texts was a common feature of the political rhetoric of Northern Ireland evangelicalism, and this was nowhere more manifest than in the case of biblical apocalyptic-eschatological language. Biblical rhetoric concerning the end times was invoked throughout the Troubles to provide a supposedly apocalyptic framework with which to interpret the political context. One of the noteworthy points about this rhetoric is the fact that it remained substantially unchanged throughout the duration of the Troubles. This point, which has been indicated throughout this study, can be illustrated with a few selected examples of how evangelicals used

63. The notion that there will be no lasting peace until the Second Coming of Christ is a theme that recurs throughout the sermons of Ian Paisley as well as the writings of other Free Presbyterians such as Ivan Foster.

64. For example, in the editorial of the December 1976 edition of the *Irish Baptist*, the writer expresses his belief that the only hope for perpetual peace lies in the prospect of the Second Coming of Christ; *Irish Baptist* (December, 1976), 2.

65. Mitchell, *Religion, Identity*, 132.

66. Thompson, *Beyond Fear*, 7.

67. The relationship between "politics" and "religion" and the apparent porosity of the borders separating them has been one of the predominant issues in the scholarly accounts of the meaning and significance of the Troubles.

apocalyptic language to interpret the political context in the thirty-year period from the beginning of the Troubles to the signing of the Belfast Agreement.

In an anti-Catholic tract which is informed throughout by an explicitly apocalyptic interpretation of the Troubles, the evangelical politician, Clifford Smyth, claimed that in 1967 he sent a letter to the *Ulster Protestant* magazine, in which he warned that the commencement of sectarian violence signalled "a watershed in history, a great spiritual conflict is taking shape."[68] Smith made this remark in order to provide his readers with a spiritual commentary on the political context of Northern Ireland in the mid- to late-1960s, which witnessed the Civil Rights Campaign (1964–72), the Derry March (5 October 1968) and the People's Democracy March (1–4 January 1969). Thus even at the beginning of the Troubles, some evangelicals perceived that the escalation of violence and civil unrest was an important development not merely in terms of its social or political implications, but also as a decisive time in the spiritual history of Northern Ireland. Speaking several years later after Smyth had prophesied about the "spiritual conflict" that was apparently unfolding in Northern Ireland, the fundamentalist preacher, Alan Campbell, in 1991, continued to make the same point about the spiritual nature of the conflict.

> It's not a war about houses. It's not a war about jobs. It's not a war about the economy. It's not a war about political parties. At root cause it is a spiritual conflict between the seed of Israel and the seed of Canaan, between the forces of Babylon and the forces of Israel, it is an attempt to exterminate God's people planted in this land and to take our inheritance from us.[69]

This commentary was provided in 1991, the first year in which substantial political progress was made in the peace process, following the unionist rejection of the Anglo-Irish Agreement in 1985. Only on 25 March 1991, had the main unionist parties (UUP and DUP) agreed to open talks with the Social Democratic and Labour Party (SDLP) and the Alliance Party of Northern Ireland (APNI) to discuss the constitutional status of Northern Ireland in the aftermath of the Anglo-Irish Agreement. These discussions, which lasted from April 1991 to November 1992 and

68. Smyth, *Rome*, 78.
69. Campbell, "A United Ireland—What Saith the Scriptures?"

which became known as the Brook-Mayhew[70] talks, indicated the ways in which unionists could be made to compromise by using the terms of the Anglo-Irish Agreement as a bargaining tactic. Although Campbell's pamphlet does not explicitly refer to these talks, it is likely that his warnings about the underlying spiritual nature of the conflict was to some extent informed by his concern about the new political situation in which some unionist politicians had indicated their willingness to accept some aspects of the Anglo-Irish Agreement.[71] Similarly in the lead up to the Belfast Agreement of 1998, Campbell employed similar tactics by invoking passages from Revelation in order to warn unionists against the alleged spiritual disaster that would ensue from any political concessions to the Republican movement. The spiritual dimension indicated by the ominous presence of Babylon in the background of the conflict raised the stakes of the Troubles and propelled the struggle into the arena of an apocalyptic-eschatological showdown between the forces of Good (i.e., "Protestantism") and Evil (i.e., "Romanism"). Ahead of the Belfast Agreement, Campbell explained that,

> Behind the Pan-Nationalist front, emerging, advising, encouraging, is the spiritual force we know as Roman Catholicism and the prophecies of the Bible call: "Mystery Babylon the Great . . . drunken with the Blood of the Saints and Martyrs of Jesus." . . . Behind every gunman, every bomber, every Nationalist politician lies the shadow of Rome.[72]

Undergirding the sectarian conflict and the violent events of the Troubles was a spiritual battle of apocalyptic dimensions, the outcome of which would decide the eschatological fate of Northern Ireland. Since the battle was of a fundamentally spiritual nature, rather than between contending factions with differing political aspirations, it would be meaningless and even harmful to attempt to compromise with the Republican movement or its alleged supporters in the Catholic Church.

This kind of attitude is to be found not merely in the sermons of evangelical pastors but also in the pamphlet literature of mainstream political parties in Northern Ireland during the Troubles. In 1977, the

70. These talks were named after the two British Secretaries of State for Northern Ireland at the time, Peter Brook and Patrick Mayhew.

71. Campbell made clear his uncompromising opposition to the Anglo-Irish Agreement in a sermon delivered in 1987; Campbell, "The Anglo-Irish Agreement."

72. Campbell, *Five Things*, 7.

year that witnessed the fiasco of a failed loyalist strike organized by the United Unionist Action Council, the Ulster Unionist Party published an election pamphlet in which we read the following pledge: "The Ulster Unionist Party will continue to press for total victory over the terrorist forces. There can be no compromise."[73] Likewise the *New Protestant Telegraph* in 1988 echoed this belligerent rhetoric, maintaining that, "This is not time for Unionists to talk the language of concession. . . . For Ulster it is a matter of LIFE OR DEATH."[74] This statement was made in a year that witnessed a series of high-profile talks between John Hume, the leader of the Social Democratic and Labour Party, and Gerry Adams, the President of Sinn Féin. At the time the British government put considerable pressure on unionist politicians to join in the talks, using the controversial Anglo-Irish Agreement as the basis for discussion. It is likely that the use of this kind of uncompromising language in the *Protestant Telegraph* was largely a response to the perceived threat that some unionists would cave into the pressure. Thus, although this rhetoric was primarily political in nature and did not draw explicitly from biblical texts for substantiation, the uncompromising tone employed corresponded to the rhetoric of absolute commitment that characterized much of the apocalyptic language used by evangelicals in the Troubles. Such extreme language was widely prevalent in evangelical texts in which such biblical corroboration was sought. Neither did the lack of an explicitly biblical citation diminish the sectarian undertones of this rhetoric of absolute commitment. As Myrtle Hill noted, in a setting such as Northern Ireland, in which "biblical language and symbols still have a steady currency, such rhetoric can also be used by those without a specific spiritual conviction to justify violent sectarianism."[75]

In contrast to the texts of the Ulster Unionist Party which did not emphasize apocalyptic-eschatological language, an explicit and overt example of such discourse can be perceived in the ethos and rhetoric of the organization known as Tara. Tara's publications, though few,[76]

73. Ulster Unionist Council, "The Unionist Way Ahead" (1977).

74. *New Protestant Telegraph* (3 December, 1988), 2.

75. Hill, *Time of the End*, 53.

76. Despite their small following, McCaughey cautions us against underestimating their influence, particularly in the cultural establishments of Northern Ireland evangelicalism: "The bizarre nature of their views and the smallness of their numbers should not necessarily lead us to imagine that they were not influential in Orange, Church and Unionist Party circles. They were"; McCaughey, *Memory and Redemption*, 43.

demonstrate the thesis of this chapter concerning the interpretation of apocalyptic-eschatological passages in such a way as to yield an un-compromising hermeneutic of absolute commitment. This unyielding hermeneutic had a bearing upon the political outlook of the texts' inter-preters. Little is known of this organization which one historian of the Troubles has described as a "shadowy and secretive Loyalist society" with alleged links to British intelligence.[77] Taking its name from the ancient residence of the Irish kings in County Meath, Tara was a self-proclaimed "national movement for the resurgence of Irish Protestantism on behalf of the British people."[78] There is also evidence to suggest a link between Tara and the Dublin government, including direct correspondence be-tween senior Tara figures and the Irish Foreign Minister of the Republic, Dr Patrick Hillary, although it should be noted that the link was between Hillary's department and the Orange lodge linked to Tara, rather than to Tara itself.[79] What is clear is that their publications contained highly emotive sentiments, many of which were couched in language inspired directly by the biblical texts of apocalyptic-eschatology which indicate that Tara "endorsed an explicitly millennial vision."[80] The juxtaposition of apocalyptic-eschatological imagery with allusions to national rebirth was a salient theme of their publications. For instance, we read the fol-lowing excerpt from the Tara publication, *Ireland Forever:*[81]

> For us the unalterable lines of history show clearly the age long struggle between good and evil, between freedom and bondage, between light and darkness, between God and Satan, and point unmistakably to the inevitable and final internal clash of arms that will herald the rebirth of the British nation.[82]

77. Wood, *Crimes of Loyalty*, 209. According to a former UVF volunteer, Roy Garland, who later wrote an MPhil dissertation on the history and ideology of the UVF, between 1966 and 1971 Tara developed a very close association with the UVF to the extent that they attended each others'' meetings; Garland, "The Ulster Volunteer Force," 35. Garland also speculated as to whether Tara was conceived and founded in London by British intelligence services; ibid., 131.

78. Tara, "Ireland Forever," 1.

79. Gribben, "Protestant Millennialism," 56.

80. Ibid., 56.

81. Unfortunately the date of this publication is not known.

82. Tara, "Ireland Forever," 10. As well as the evident dualistic rhetoric which re-curs in this and other publications, such warlike statements exhibit an adherence to an underlying belief in the efficacy of redemptive violence. In this regard a curious parallel can be discerned between the Protestant extremist of Loyalist, anti-Catholic

Anticipating "a loyalist Armageddon which would be brought on by a Catholic republican rebellion,"[83] Tara insisted that

> there can be no accommodation or compromise with the enemy which could create a viable structure of devolved government. The enemy is only interested in total surrender. . . . His philosophy and his ideology, his doctrine, will permit of no other consideration . . . the enemy has an insatiable desire for the destruction of the Protestant position, and does not possess the ability to reform.[84]

In the apocalyptic-eschatological discourses pervading this kind of language, the personification of "the enemy" as "he" could indicate the possibility of a spiritual presence (i.e., the Antichrist), a point reinforced by apocalyptic references to the "final battle" and further appeals to the imperative of Protestant people to resist "every attempt from whatever source, to unfurl the banner of the Evil One over this fair Province of ours."[85] Tara was preparing itself for "conflict on a scale never before known on this island," insisting that, "Inevitable conflict lies ahead!" Invoking the notion of Armageddon, Tara declared that this armed conflagration would "continue to grow in intensity until the final battle which will affect the life of every man and woman, boy and girl in our land."[86] Many of their pronouncements suggest that Tara wished to be involved in the active precipitation of an "apocalyptic" scenario by encouraging their followers to take up arms and to receive military

---

organizations such as Tara and some expressions of early twentieth-century expressions of Irish Republicanism. Patrick Pearse, who was executed for his role in the Easter Rising of 1916, promulgated the notion of national redemption through the violence of blood sacrifice. "Bloodshed," exclaimed Pearse, "is a cleansing and a satisfying thing and the nation which regards it as the final horror has lost its manhood . . . without the shedding of blood there is no redemption"; Pearse, quoted in Walter Wink, *Engaging the Powers*, 334. Although claiming to draw from a Christian notion of redemption through sacrifice, Pearse's expressions at a deeper level were drawn, as theologian Walter Wink has shown, from the "Myth of Redemptive Violence," which Wink argues had its origins not in the Jewish or Christian Scriptures but in ancient pagan Babylonian mythology.

83. McCaughey, *Memory and Redemption*, 43.

84. Tara, *Proclamation*. This short document is available on the University of Ulster's Northern Ireland Troubles" research website, CAIN, under http://cain.ulst.ac.uk/othelem/organ/docs/TARA73.html. This website estimates the date of the publication of the *Proclamation* to have been 1973.

85. Tara, *Tara Proclamation*.

86. Ibid.

training in preparation for Armageddon. Had they acquired sufficient munitions, Tara might well have been in a position to fulfil its own so-called "prophecy." For Tara, therefore, apocalyptic eschatology became a kind of self-fulfilling prophecy. Doomsday was not something to be awaited passively but an actual state of affairs to be implemented aggressively and energetically. Tara has thus rightly been described as a group that most explicitly represented a "genuinely millennial tradition amid the murky and ambiguous discourses of Ulster's Protestant politics."[87] Despite its grandiose rhetoric and the not inconsiderable influence it exerted on the ideology of loyalist paramilitarism, Tara's existence was abruptly and dramatically curtailed by the Kincora scandal.[88]

It is important to note that the high point of Tara's activities in the early to mid-1970s coincided with the widespread fear among unionists at that time that the British government was conspiring to hand over the sovereignty of Northern Ireland to the Irish government. These fears were particularly acute in the run up to the Sunningdale Agreement (1973),[89] which attempted to establish a Northern Ireland Executive and a cross-border Council of Ireland, which would have given the Dublin government limited powers in Northern Ireland. The apocalyptic rhetoric of Tara and the corresponding uncompromising hermeneutic that rejected political concessions out of hand undoubtedly resonated with the prevailing unionist fears that, "Dublin is just a Sunningdale away." The intransigent rhetoric of Tara in the early to mid-1970s was reflected in the language of evangelical unionist politicians at other critical periods in the course of the Troubles when not merely the constitutional status of Northern Ireland, but also the eschatological fate of "Ulster" was at stake.

One such critical period was the aftermath of the 1985 Anglo-Irish Agreement, which, like the aborted Sunningdale Agreement, proposed the creation of an Anglo-Irish Intergovernmental Conference, which would give the Dublin government an advisory role in the political,

87. Gribben, "Protestant Millennialism," 56.

88. Moore, The Kincora Scandal.

89. The Northern Ireland Executive established by the Sunningdale Agreement, which was reached on 9 December 1973, was eventually brought down by widespread loyalist intimidation, culminating in a general strike by the Ulster Workers' Council in May 1974. Unionists were particularly apprehensive about the encroachment of the Irish government in the affairs of Northern Ireland, as captured by the popular unionist slogan at the time: "Dublin is just a Sunningdale away."

legal, and security affairs of Northern Ireland. Paisley's famous declaration of rejection of the Anglo-Irish Agreement at a mass rally in Belfast in 1985 ("Never! Never! Never! Never!") bears an intriguing, if coincidental, resemblance to a well-known line from that most apocalyptic of Shakespeare's plays—*King Lear*.[90] Since his horizons were largely determined by the hermeneutic of absolute commitment through which he read the biblical apocalyptic-eschatological texts, Paisley's political opinions have been censured by his critics as being "necessarily negative and uncompromising."[91]

Since the underlying apocalyptic rhetoric of "no surrender" was common to both Tara in the mid-1970s and Paisley in the mid-1980s, it seems to be the case that the specific instances of political crisis evoked a common response. It was as if the evangelical rejection of political attempts to cede powers to the Dublin government was pre-determined as it was informed by the apocalyptic worldviews of groups such as Tara and individual evangelicals such as Paisley. According to this worldview, any attempt to compromise would not lead to peace but would merely assist the evil powers of Antichrist and his alleged agents (the Catholic Church and the Republican movement) in their aim to subdue "Protestant Ulster."

Therefore, although occupying a distinct and to some extent self-contained plot in the diverse semantic field of apocalyptic-eschatological discourse, many of the principal characteristics of Tara's language were reflected in the rhetoric of other expressions of Northern Ireland evangelicalism, such as "Paisleyism." In one sermon addressed to his congregation at Martyrs' Memorial, Paisley offered the following interpretation of contemporary religious trends based on what he called "the final conflict of the age," derived from his reading of biblical texts relating to Armageddon:

> As we survey the world situation tonight, we see the main
> forces that are involved in the evil syncretism of diverse apostate

90. Speaking of the tragic death of his sole virtuous daughter, Cordelia, Lear laments: "Why should a dog, a horse, a rat, have life / And thou no breath at all? Thou'lt come no more, / Never, never, never, never, never!" (*King Lear*, V.3.306–8). Paul Fiddes, in *Promised End*, contends that *King Lear* resonates with the salient themes of apocalyptic literature on account of the way in which the play deals with the story of how Lear "propels himself towards the nothingness of the end." "The shape of the play is dissolution to nothing," he adds, or "a journey into nothingness"; Fiddes, *Promised End*, 54–55.

91. O'Malley, *Uncivil Wars*, 199.

religions. False religions are coming together. Now we have the religion of Mohammedanism. We have the religion of the Papacy and we have the religion of Judaism. And these are the three main combatants in the religious world tonight. . . . Those three false religions are against biblical Christianity. Two great thrones at war—the throne of true religion and the throne of false religion.

In a rhetorical gesture reminiscent of Tara's insistence that "Ulster's" enemies do not "possess the ability to reform," Paisley added that, the religious systems purportedly opposed to "biblical Christianity"—Judaism, Islam, and Roman Catholicism—"are irreformable and upon them there is the curse of almighty God."[92] It is also notable that in this instance Paisley singled out Judaism and Islam alongside Catholicism as the end-times enemy of "biblical Christianity."

Alan Campbell likewise shared Paisley's anti-Islamic convictions. Using even more intemperate language and alluding to the opening verses of Revelation 9, Campbell invoked alleged scriptural proofs for his argument that the image of satanic locusts rising out of the smoke (Rev 9:3) was in fact a reference to Muslims. He further exclaimed that, "Truly Islam is a faith inspired by demon forces from the bottomless pit."[93] Foster's reading of Revelation, which warned against compromising with one's political enemies, identified the main enemy closer to home. He used texts from Revelation which seemed to stipulate against making concessions in order to articulate the deep misgivings in his mind regarding "the public 'rehabilitation' of such men as Gerry Adams and Martin McGuiness who are associated with the IRA terror campaign in Northern Ireland."[94]

The uncompromising language of apocalyptic eschatology demonstrated a deep affinity with the uncompromising mindset of some evangelicals. In political contexts this mentality was epitomized by the slogans, "No Surrender!" and "Ulster Says No!." These mottos became bywords for Protestant resistance to perceived Catholic incursions into their civil and religious liberties.[95] These liberties were seen to be sacrosanct and were to be defended vehemently by "all true Protestants"[96] in

92. Paisley, "Mohammedanism-Judaism-Romanism vs. Bible Christianity."

93. Campbell, *Islam in Prophecy*, 9.

94. Foster, *Antichrist*, 95.

95. O'Malley, *Uncivil Wars: Ireland Today*.

96. Campbell, *British-Israelism*, 22.

the name of "God and Ulster." Such political slogans, which sometimes alluded to apocalyptic-eschatological texts, were a notable feature of the evangelical rhetoric during the Troubles. For instance, an article in the *Protestant Telegraph* in 1966 covered the main points of a sermon delivered to over 2,000 people in the Ulster Hall. The text on that occasion was a passage from the book of Daniel, significantly referred to in this sermon as "Daniel's prophecy." The renaming of this key text of biblical apocalyptic eschatology is especially noteworthy considering that only approximately half of the text is apocalyptic in nature and scholars are generally agreed that Daniel is not a book of prophecy at all but belongs to the apocalyptic genre.[97] Expounding a text "in the third chapter of Daniel's prophecy"—"Be it known unto thee, O king, that we will not serve thy gods" (Dan 3:18)—the preacher interpreted Daniel's utterance in a unique way, declaring that, "to put it in the language of Ulster, that means simply, 'No Surrender.'"[98]

In the turbulent events of the Troubles, the uncompromising language of apocalyptic eschatology was thus reflected in the intransigent political rhetoric of some evangelicals. One relatively common feature of evangelical uses of biblical texts to determine their political perspectives involved the quotation of passages from apocalyptic-eschatological texts, as was the case with the preacher cited above who quoted from Daniel. Evangelicals used these texts to substantiate their uncompromising attitudes towards the "enemy" and their consequent unwillingness to make political concessions, as seen, for instance, in the evangelical resistance to the Belfast ("Good Friday") Agreement in 1998.[99] This implies that for some evangelicals context was an important factor that drove their interpretations of biblical texts. However, it was equally the case that

97. Recent biblical scholarship contends that the text of Daniel 7–12 is not prophetic in nature at all but belongs rather to the apocalyptic genre; Redditt, *Introduction to the Prophets*, 168–71. Grabbe describes Daniel 7–12 as "a quintessential apocalyptic writing"; Grabbe, "Prophetic and Apocalyptic," 120. Grabbe's article (107–33) also contains a useful discussion of the differences and similarities between the genres of "prophecy" and "apocalypse" in recent biblical scholarship.

98. *Protestant Telegraph* (5 November, 1966), 5.

99. See, for example, an article by Ian Paisley, entitled "Peace, What Peace," which was published in *Belfast Telegraph* (14 January, 1999), 16. In this article, Paisley draws on apocalyptic-eschatological themes in order to argue that Ulster's enemies will be overcome not by negotiation but by a decisive act of divine judgment. He used this reasoning to argue against the political concessions made to Sinn Fein and the IRA by the Ulster Unionist Party at the Belfast Agreement.

the apocalyptic-eschatological texts drove evangelical perceptions of the political and religious crisis. The worldviews of evangelicals and their response to instances of political and religious crises were determined by their reading of these texts. For instance, in a sermon pre-dating the Troubles, Paisley denounced the Catholic Church in the strongest terms with a rhetorical appeal to the language of the book of Revelation: "The Church of Rome is . . . the mother of harlots and the abominations of the earth. I make no apology for this statement. God calls the number of this synagogue of Satan himself in Revelation chapter seventeen."[100]

The apocalyptic-eschatological text was thus itself involved in the hermeneutical act of making an interpretive judgment concerning the signification of the "synagogue of Satan," which in this instance was as-cribed to the Catholic Church. The use of the emotive term, "synagogue of Satan,"[101] as a means to denounce rival faith communities was a recur-ring feature of Northern Ireland evangelical polemic that extended far beyond the fundamentalist rhetoric of Paisley and the Free Presbyterian Church. In like manner, a Presbyterian writing for the *Christian Irishman* sought to justify his divisive hermeneutic, which made clear distinctions between good and evil in contemporary culture, by an appeal to an apocalyptic passage in Luke's Gospel:

> Our generation prefers shades of grey rather than extremes of black and white, yet our Lord never hesitated to draw sharp dis-tinctions. . . . The end of Luke, chapter 17, presents a clear pic-ture of the tearing asunder of the closest earthly ties when Christ comes again.[102]

Another article from the *Christian Irishman* employed exactly the same intemperate term as Paisley—"synagogue of Satan"—in its attempt to set out the sequence of catastrophic events which were to portend the

---

100. Paisley, *Roman Catholic Priests*, 13.

101. The term, συναγωγή τοῦ σατανά, appears twice in the book of Revelation (2:9; 3:9). Although Northern Ireland evangelicals tended to ascribe this term to the Roman Catholic Church, this identification is not common in the field of biblical studies. Biblical scholars continue to dispute the actual identity of the members of the "synagogue of Satan." Some suggest that the term refers to Jews in Asia Minor who were persecuting Christian communities; Cohen, *Beginning of Jewishness*, 25–26. Others contend that the term refers to groups of Christians who embraced elements of Jewish practices in order to benefit from concessions permitted to Jews under the Roman Empire. See Stephen Wilson, *Related Strangers*, 162–63; Frilingos, *Spectacles of Empire*, 109.

102. *Christian Irishman* (September, 1973), 6.

end times. Suggesting an equation of the "synagogue of Satan" with a projected unholy alliance of Communism and Roman Catholicism, the Presbyterian contributor wrote:

> the nations will be in turmoil when Jesus comes again. . . . The one world church (the synagogue of Satan) will have been set up; atheistic communism and Roman Catholicism will have joined forces; the "Beast" and "False Prophet" will have done their deadly work and those who do not bear their mark will be suffering merciless persecution.[103]

Baptist minister Denis Lyle likewise denounced disagreeable developments in the church by branding them in the same immoderate terms. Commenting on Christ's appraisal of the church at Smyrna in Revelation 2:8–11, Lyle entreats his readers to think of

> the apostate churches in our land that are no more than synagogues of Satan. . . . These churches are the strong-holds of Satan. They do not preach the true Gospel of Christ. They deny the inerrancy of Scripture[;] . . . these "churches" are hellholes, instruments of the devil himself.[104]

Since these churches were perceived in light of the biblical texts as satanic in origin and utterly devoid of any capacity to reform, it would have been futile to attempt to compromise or to collaborate with them. In view of some interpretations of the "hostile dualisms"[105] read into the apocalyptic-eschatological texts, the word "compromise" became a synonym for "defeat" or even "downfall." Since the "difference between Catholics and Protestants was the difference between those who were saved and had access to the Truth and those who were damned and in Darkness,"[106] a defeat for one was perceived to involve an exactly corresponding degree of victory for the other. As the *Protestant Telegraph* put it, "Romanism will accept no peaceful compromise: it demands nothing less than a total abject submission to its authority."[107] Thus, believing themselves to be engaged in an apocalyptic struggle against a satanic

---

103. *Christian Irishman* (December, 1984), 28.

104. Lyle, *The Good*, 52.

105. Keller, quoted in Cook, *Apocalyptic Literature*, 55.

106. O'Malley, *Uncivil Wars*, 178.

107. *Protestant Telegraph* (6 June, 1981), 4.

enemy incapable of reform, some evangelicals adopted the attitude of Tara, who declared that, "This is a fight to the finish! This is total war!"[108]

Such rhetoric was used not only in evangelical pulpits or fundamentalist newspapers but also at unionist political rallies. The speech of Peter Robinson, deputy leader of the DUP, to delegates at the party's 1993 conference has been described as "apocalyptic in tone" and involved the "sense of a battle fully joined" through which he intended to "inspire in the audience recognition of the battles between light and dark in the Book of Revelations [*sic*]."[109] Robinson's senior colleague in the DUP, Ian Paisley, articulated this kind of language even more forthrightly. In the 14 January 1999 edition of the *Belfast Telegraph*, Paisley published an intriguing interpretation of a passage from John Milton's *Paradise Lost*, concerning the fallen archangel Belial. Paisley concluded with these remarks:

> we can take consolation from the fate of Belial. The conclusion of the history of salvation is the eschatological battle of the prince of luminaries against him. It ends, not in pacifying him, but with judgement upon him, his angels and people subject to him, and ushers in the cessation of wickedness and real peace achieved through the rule of truth.[110]

The notion of the "eschatological battle" was thus held up as a rhetorical mirror to the post-Good Friday political situation and was used by Paisley to persuade Protestant readers of the *Belfast Telegraph* to reject the political concessions made to the Republican movement by David Trimble's Ulster Unionist Party.

What is noteworthy about the various statements quoted in this section is that despite the fact that they were made at different points throughout the Troubles, the kind of rhetorical strategies that invoked an apocalyptic-eschatological theme in order to argue against political compromise, remained remarkably constant. The social and political context of Northern Ireland had undergone substantial change in the period between Clifford Smyth's warnings in 1967 about the spiritual dangers of the allegedly Catholic-inspired civil rights movement and the similar warnings of Ian Paisley, as cited above, about the risks of com-

---

108. Tara, *Ireland Forever*, 21.

109. Finlayson, "Contemporary Loyalist Identity," 83.

110. *Belfast Telegraph* (14 January, 1999), 16.

promising to the Republicans in the build up to the Belfast Agreement in 1998. This period had witnessed several divisive and deadly events such as Internment (1971–75), Bloody Sunday (1972), the loyalist attacks on Dublin and Monaghan (1974), the United Unionist Action Council Strike (1977), the Republican Hunger Strike (1981), the Enniskillen bombing (1987), and the Omagh bombing (1998). Moreover, this period also witnessed several attempts to make major changes to the constitutional status of Northern Ireland, as seen, for instance in the Sunningdale Agreement (1973–74), the Northern Ireland Constitutional Conven-tion (1974–76), the Anglo-Irish Agreement (1985) and the Belfast Agreement (1998). Despite the changing social and political context indicated by these events, the underlying apocalyptic-eschatological rhetoric of evangelicals remained remarkably constant throughout this period.

This point is illustrated by Ian Paisley's political "conversion," which resulted in his signing the St Andrews Agreement following talks with Sinn Fein in October 2006. Under the terms of the agreement, the Northern Ireland Executive was restored and Sinn Fein agreed to support the Police Service of Northern Ireland and the law courts.[111] The agreement led to memorable public scenes of Ian Paisley and Martin McGuinness, who had once been bitter adversaries, laughing together in front of the cameras. These images in the popular press even earned them the nickname the "Chuckle Brothers."[112] What is notable about this apparent transformation is that despite his political "conversion,"[113] Paisley's religious beliefs remained fundamentally consistent with the position he had assumed throughout the Troubles. Paisley continued to publicly air his anti-Catholic views, even after the St Andrews Agreement of 2006. During the visit of Pope Benedict XVI to the United Kingdom in September 2010, Paisley staged a protest in Edinburgh, which was attended by about sixty anti-Catholic demonstrators. One of Paisley's supporters at the protest, Ian Wilson, who was at that time the head of the Grand Orange Lodge in Scotland, remarked that 2010 marked the 450th

111. A useful summary of the terms of the St Andrews Agreement and a comparison with the provisions of the 1998 Belfast Agreement is provided in McEvoy, *The Politics of Northern Ireland*, 167–69.

112. Online: http://news.bbc.co.uk/1/hi/northern_ireland/7083818.stm.

113. The Christian magazine, *Third Way*, described Paisley's political transformation in exaggerated tones as "the unlikeliest conversion since Paul on the road to Damascus"; *Third Way* 31 (April, 2008), 17.

anniversary of Scotland's break from the Catholic Church.[114] Paisley himself maintained in an interview with a UTV journalist that it was his religious duty to resist the "Roman Antichrist": "I feel that it's my duty. I would be failing my Saviour if I allowed someone else to come and say, 'I take the place of Christ,' as the Pope claims to take the place of Christ. . . . I think that is something I must face up to."[115] Thus, in 2010 Paisley was still invoking the same text from 2 Thessalonians 2:5 to denounce the purported blasphemy of the pope, as he had done throughout the Troubles. Moreover, in another post-St Andrews Agreement television interview, Paisley continued to maintain that as someone who stood "in the historic succession of the Reformers," his position was that the Catholic Church was a "false church" and was "the church as depicted in the seventeenth chapter of the book of Revelation."[116] Therefore despite the evident change in the political context, his religious views, such as his belief that the pope was the Antichrist and the Catholic Church was the Whore of Babylon, remained unchanged. This is another indication of the ways in which apocalyptic-eschatological worldviews remained constant despite significant changes in the political context.

Semantic Dualisms in Apocalyptic-Eschatological Language in Relation to the "dialectic between the text and world"

The instances of semantic dualism and belligerent rhetoric considered above say a great deal about the world-constituting efficacy of apocalyptic-eschatological texts. New Historicists have argued that "the text is part of the process of historical change, and indeed may constitute historical change."[117] Drawing of this insight, we can perceive how apocalyptic-eschatological language became part of the process of shaping evangelical convictions during the Troubles. One of the ways texts determine these culturally modifying processes is by creating discursive fields in which certain categories, concepts, terms and words take on original connotations determined by the governing semantic field of the discourse in question. The dualistic worldview engendered by apocalyptic-eschatological discourse presents us with significant in-

114. Online: www.bbc.co.uk/news/uk-11294941.

115. This interview can be viewed at www.youtube.com/watch?v=KL9h5LFFdsU.

116. Online: www.youtube.com/watch?v=30JlJDpra7k.

117. Brannigan, *New Historicism*, 203.

sights into the socio-cultural agency of texts as living and active vectors of meaning. These texts transform their host cultures through a process which Stephen Greenblatt calls "the circulation of the social energy of texts." Greenblatt contends that texts can come to acquire a mysterious force, which he calls *energia*, through which the language encoded in the text acquires the ability to "stir the mind." The existence of this mysterious force depends upon "an irregular chain of historical transactions" which can lead back several centuries. As Greenblatt himself explains, "the "life" that literary works seem to possess long after both the death of the author and the death of the culture for which the author wrote is the historical consequence, however transformed and refashioned, of the social energy initially encoded in those works."[118] Another way of thinking about this issue would be to ask how an ancient apocalyptic-eschatological text and the rhetoric of its semantic construction could sustain "intelligibility in the exchanges and negotiations that constitute *our* reality."[119]

These considerations can be applied to our discussion of the meaning and significance of semantic dualisms in apocalyptic-eschatological language during the Troubles and their decisive role in constituting the "dialectic between the text and the world" of Northern Ireland evangelicalism. The texts of apocalyptic eschatology are examples of literary works of antiquarian origins whose signs and metaphors retained a compelling rhetorical power over interpretive communities of evangelicals several centuries after the time of their inscription. Thus it can be said that the initial inscription and subsequent interpretations of these ancient texts released a chain of signifiers which, through irregular processes of interpretation, were diffused and dispersed, becoming constitutive of various cultures, including Northern Ireland evangelical cultures, in an irregular yet unbroken succession of historical time. Moreover, the meaning of the concepts, words and phrases contained in the text were often diffused and dispersed and made to play off against dualistic categories that are set up by the logic established by the principles of signification inherent in the grammar of apocalyptic-eschatological discourses.

My claim is, therefore, that apocalyptic-eschatological rhetoric in Northern Ireland derived its *energia* not from its supposed resonance with contemporary events or "context." Rather such rhetoric acquired its

118. Greenblatt, *Shakespearean Negotiations*, 6.

119. Williams, *Wrestling with Angels*, 54 (emphasis added).

world-constituting character by being suspended in webs of textuality constituted by the biblical texts, which despite their ancient origins retained considerable shaping power over evangelical cultures in Northern Ireland. These cultures in turn were organized into interpretive communities which recognized these texts as the "Word of God," which, in the tradition of evangelical hermeneutics was held to be the Word through which, "God speaks directly to each of our souls."[120]

The Bifurcating Tendencies of Apocalyptic-Eschatological Language

The claims made in the section above raise the question of how these webs of textuality, which as we have shown tended to engender divergent interpretive responses to eschatological texts, shaped evangelical convictions in Northern Ireland during the Troubles. Taking Wittgenstein's idea that "the meaning of a word is determined by how it is used in language,"[121] we can illustrate the ways in which modes of discourse could become constitutive of worldviews by focusing on the use of particular words and the meaning these words acquired through such use. In the apocalyptic-eschatological discourses of Northern Ireland evangelicalism, there are certain words which take on notable connotations. If we follow Saussure in the assumption that linguistic signs stand in an entirely arbitrary relationship to each other, it follows that the semantic content that a particular sign is understood to signify is not determined by necessity but by discursive conventions and the ways in which words are commonly used.[122]

For instance, under the conditions of ordinary discourse, words such as "city" or "world" usually possess mundane connotations and are not commonly invested with any particular moral or spiritual undertones. In the apocalyptic-eschatological discourses of Northern Ireland evangelicalism, however, these "signifiers" ("world" and "city") were infused with substantial meaning, corresponding to their use in illustrating supposed apocalyptic-eschatological "signifieds." Take, for instance,

120. Warfield, *Inspiration and Authority*, 125.

121. "Die Bedeutung eines Wortes ist sein Gebrauch in der Sprache"; Wittgenstein, quoted in Eberhard Jüngel, *Gott als Geheimnis der Welt*, 6. For Wittgenstein's own classic statement of this notion, see his *Philosophical Investigations*, para. 43 and *passim*.

122. Badcock, *Lévi-Strauss*, 46.

this short passage from an evangelical Anglican writing in the *Belfast Telegraph*, which contains a sevenfold repetition of the word "city" or "cities":

> The human city has always failed. It is failing now. It will always fail. But all is not lost. . . . There is another city, a city not made with hands. A city with an "antistructure" which will one day supplant all earthly cities; the city that was prefigured in the dreams of the Hebrew prophets. It was the same city St John the Divine had a vision of [*sic*] on the Isle of Patinos [*sic*].

He continued to insist that, "The Christian calling is to raise here and now . . . the holy city; to establish in this evil world, islands of hope and encouragement."[123]

Similarly the city takes on particular meanings in the discursive worlds of apocalyptic eschatology. Whether warning of the threat of Gog and Magog, condemning the idolatry of Tyre and Sidon, denouncing the injustice of Nineveh, or depicting the shame and ruin of Babylon, cities assume a dominant role in the biblical narratives, from Babel to New Jerusalem. What has been said of cities in relation to the Bible in general is true to an even greater extent of biblical apocalyptic-eschatological texts, which present the further element of dualism by introducing dichotomies between the "good" city of God and the "evil" city of the world. In Revelation this dichotomy attains something of a semantic crescendo in the arresting juxtaposition of Babylon the harlot and New Jerusalem the pure bride.[124] In apocalyptic-eschatological discourses, cities can gain substantial metaphorical power by evoking "a visualisation of diverging conceptual possibilities."[125] For some Northern Ireland evangelicals the word "city" was suffused with malevolent connotations of sin and debauchery; cities were "places where crime and vice of every kind is rampant."[126]

In other interpretations, the opposite "conceptual possibilities" were represented so that the word "city" became "an extended narrative metaphor referring to the . . . evocative textual image and incentive for imagination, hope, thought, and action."[127] This was the perspective

123. *Belfast Telegraph* (19 July, 1997).

124. O'Leary, *Arguing the Apocalypse*, 71.

125. Räpple, *Metaphor of the City*, 159.

126. *Orange Standard* (March, 1982), 1.

127. Räpple, *Metaphor of the City*, 9.

of Northern Ireland Baptist, David Porter, who remarked that the city could be "a potent image of what God intends for the healing of nations and the flourishing of human experience in the New Jerusalem."[128] The eschatological city could thus become an effective metaphor which beckoned the reader to invest their imaginative powers in the temporal-spatial forms characteristic of the textual vision of apocalyptic-eschatological fulfilment.[129] Thus we can perceive the ways in which the word "city" was transformed into a compelling metaphor, evoking at once the extreme poles of lament over the depth of human sin but also stirring up a passion for the possibility of human perfection in a community of ultimate flourishing and fulfilment.

The bifurcating tendencies of apocalyptic-eschatological discourse in Northern Ireland are also to be seen in the meanings ascribed to the terms, "world" and "earth" in evangelical interpretations of biblical texts. The notion of the "evil" or "wicked" world is a prevalent motif of apocalyptic-eschatological discourses. This notion has its roots in the biblical texts, particularly the New Testament, and has continually reasserted itself in the works of countless theologians from the church fathers to the present day.[130] This notion is particularly prevalent in the Johannine texts in which salvation history seems to be conceived as a struggle between Christ and the wicked "world" together with the evil one who rules and enslaves it (cf. John 16:33; 1 John 4:3; 5:19). The negative connotations of this word in the discourses of Northern Ireland evangelicalism can be seen in its presence in the various terms used by fundamentalist evangelicals to describe the end-times enemies of "biblical Christianity," such as "the one *world* church,"[131] "the *world's* false religions,"[132] "the new *world* order,"[133] "the apostate *world* order,"[134] and "the wicked *world* system,"[135] "the One *World* Government, Economy and Religion"[136]—all

---

128. *lion & lamb* (Spring, 2008), 4.

129. This notion was at the heart of William Blake's vision of New Jerusalem (Golgonooza) in his epic poem, *Jerusalem*; Paley, *Continuing City*, 149.

130. The most notable was Augustine of Hippo's *De Civitate Dei*.

131. *Protestant Telegraph* (10 April, 1971), 5.

132. *Belfast Telegraph* (13 January, 1997), 8.

133. Campbell, *For God and Ulster*, 25.

134. Leahy, "Seeds of Secularization," 37.

135. *Ulster Bulwark* (Jan/Feb 1978), 4.

136. Campbell, *For God and Ulster*, 25.

associated with the Antichrist. Moreover, the fundamentalist enemies of ecumenism frequently used the term "the world's ecumenical system" when condemning the religious system to which they were opposed, as if to accentuate the connection of the ecumenical movement to the wicked "world."[137] The presence of the word, "world," in the ecumenical organizations with which they were in conflict, the World Council of Churches and the World Congress of Faiths, only added to the ominous connotations of the ecumenical movement in the minds of anti-ecumenical evangelical fundamentalists.[138] The word, "world," was also used to convey the system that ran counter to the rule and purposes of God. It was thus considered to be virtuous to be "out of step" with the "defiling world"[139] because to be so implied harmony with the kingdom of God. Writing of the last judgment in relation to the story of Noah (Gen 6–10), Paisley praised the patriarch on account of his being "completely out of step with the political world, the social world, the business world and the religious world of his day . . . while the whole world moved forward to its ruination."[140]

A further point to be made is that whereas the words "earth" and "world" in everyday speech are typically used unreflectively as synonyms, among Northern Ireland evangelicals the word, "earth," was not regarded as an antonym of "heaven," as was the word, "world." Rather the signifier "earth" was in fact invested with positive, hopeful connotations to the extent that the words "heaven" and "earth" were often coupled together to present a comprehensive vision of hope and consummation. It seemed that while the "world" would be destroyed, the "earth" would be redeemed. Thus one finds an abundance of references to the "world" which was "Godless," "secularised,"[141] and "fallen"[142] as well as portentous allusions to the "spiritual darkness of this world."[143] Furthermore,

---

137. Cooke, *Paisley and Mystery Babylon*, 25.

138. Interestingly the words "ecumene" and "world" have a remarkable etymological affinity; the root of the word "ecumenism" is derived from the Greek, οἰκουμένη γή, which can be translated as "inhabited world."

139. Carson, *Amazing Cross*, 75.

140. *Revivalist* (October, 1972).

141. *Orange Standard* (June, 1974), 9. The author of this article invoked 2 Timothy 3, which describes the "perilous times" which are to mark the "last days."

142. *lion & lamb* (Autumn, 2006), 5.

143. *Irish Baptist* 94 (March, 1972), 2.

since the "world" was "broken," "inadequate" and "infested by hatred and crime,"[144] it would be smitten with "great calamities."[145] By contrast, the "earth" was seen by some as the locus of millennial hope, as the site to which "the Lord Jesus will arise and return" and "establish His righteous government."[146] One evangelical even spoke of the great "earthly vision that we ... cherish," which involved praying earnestly "for the entire reformation of society in obedience to the Word of God."[147]

A clear example of the semantic disjunction between the redemptive connotations associated with the word, "earth," and the ominous meanings attached to the word, "world," in the apocalyptic-eschatological language of evangelicals is the use of these terms in the writings of F. S. Leahy. In 1986, Leahy wrote of the "world" in highly pejorative terms, insisting that it would be better to "witness faithfully to an apostate world order than capitulate to the world's demands."[148] This denunciation of the "world" is set in contrast to his redemptive conception of the destiny of the "earth," written in one of his later books: "It is this very earth itself that will be renewed. It will be purged and reborn ... there will be continuity and discontinuity between this present earth and the new earth—not a replacement earth, but a regenerated and renewed earth."[149]

The origins of this peculiarity of Northern Ireland evangelical discourses are to be found in the biblical texts of apocalyptic eschatology. Indeed it could even be claimed that the biblical semantic allocations of these terms correspond almost exactly to the way they were used in evangelical rhetoric concerning the end times.[150] This striking correspondence offers a compelling support for the notion that the apocalyptic-eschatological rhetoric of Northern Ireland evangelicals was derived not primarily from the social and political context of the Troubles, but from an ancient biblical textual tradition. As in Northern Ireland evangelical discourses, so too in the biblical texts of apocalyptic

144. *Belfast Telegraph* (19 July, 1997).

145. Paisley, *The Woman Rides the Beast*, 3.

146. Campbell, *Great Tribulation*, 42.

147. *Frontiers* (Spring, 1996), 2.

148. Leahy, "Seeds of Secularization," 37.

149. Leahy, *Victory of the Lamb*, 112.

150. A notable exception in this regard is John 3:16. Even here, however, it is the very negativity of the term "world" that gives this verse its particular impact.

eschatology, the "world" receives an almost unambiguously bad press as a place under the malevolent influence of "the rulers of the darkness" and Satan, who is described in the King James translation of John 16:11 as "the prince of this world."

The crucial point is that under the discursive conditions of apocalyptic eschatology in the Troubles, the "world" is conceived as that sphere of human and satanic activity which is hostile and at variance to the eschatological kingdom of God. The world was thus to be viewed with great suspicion and misgiving. The "wicked world system" was certainly not something to which Christians should conform (Rom 12:2). Thus the world took on the connotation as that sphere in which "humanity and the spiritual world are organized over against God."[151] This perception was reinforced by Christ's famous rebuff to Pilate in John 18:36 ("my kingdom is not of this world") and also the Johannine notion of the kind of faith which "overcometh the world" (1 John 5:4). In a manner reminiscent of the uncompromising dualism manifested in Northern Ireland apocalyptic-eschatological discourses, the apostle James was likewise adamant that "whosoever . . . will be a friend of the world is the enemy of God" (Jas 4:3). In an even more explicit denunciation of "the world," John declared that "the whole world lieth in wickedness" (1 John 5:19).

In contrast to the malevolent connotations associated with the world, the Bible's use of the word, "earth," as reflected in the Northern Ireland evangelical uses of the same term, is almost unambiguously affirmative and positive. Despite mysterious allusions in 2 Peter 3:10 to the earth "and all the works that are therein" being burned up "with fervent heat," the biblical vision of apocalyptic-eschatological hope has as its instantly-recognizable focus a redeemed earth. Alongside the depiction of the millennium kingdom of the saints in Revelation 20, which has been described as "the earthly-political moment of Christ's Reign,"[152] there are myriad references to the "new heavens and a new earth," which are the object of hope for the prophets of the Hebrew Bible as much as they are of the New Testament writers.

---

151. This is how Barrett characterizes the term "of this world" in John 18:36: "my kingdom is not ἐντευθεν." See Barrett, *Gospel according to John*, 536.

152. Zegwaart, "Apocalyptic Eschatology and Pentecostalism," 25.

Apocalyptic Language and Semantic Surplus

This chapter has analyzed the dichotomizing propensities inherent in apocalyptic-eschatological language and the corresponding interpretations by Northern Ireland evangelicals which accentuated these dualistic categories and applied them indiscriminately to a variety of social contexts. These findings have added a new dimension to the notion that interpretations are bound up with the exchanges and negotiations that determine the function of language in culture. This claim corresponds to the notion that the meaning of words is not transcendently self-evident but that systems of semantic signification are always embedded in webs of discourse, which arise from the interpretation of formative texts. The quotations from evangelical texts cited above demonstrate the principle of rhetorical surplus in language. Indeed it may even be claimed that the rhetorical excesses which characterize apocalyptic-eschatological language, both at the level of interpretation and of the texts themselves, are a function of this inherent tendency of language to exhibit what Terry Eagleton calls a "capacity for a certain lavish infringement of exact limit."[153]

In light of our foregoing theoretical reflections on the nature of language and textuality, it may be contended that such excess is a function of language in general and that we must thus recognize "the ambiguity, openness, and indeterminacy of all literature."[154] If we accept the notion that language consists of a series of signs which derive meaning from the extent to which they differentiate themselves from other signs, we can follow Derrida in asserting that language confers meaning not by conforming to a pre-supposed reality but by the diffusion and dispersion of meaning through the unleashing of arbitrary and unconnected chains of signifiers, connected only by virtue of the fact of their difference from one other.

Apocalyptic-eschatological language manifests the principle of the surplus of meaning in an exemplary way. Richard Landes rightly remarks that "no rhetoric is more powerful than apocalyptic rhetoric; no greater motivation exists in the repertoire of human behaviour than the belief that one's every action is crucial to the final destiny of the hu-

---

153. Eagleton, *William Shakespeare*, 81–82.

154. Schüssler Fiorenza, *Book of Revelation*, 186.

man race."[155] Through its creation of imaginative categories which bifurcate the cosmos into two opposing primeval forces of Good and Evil, apocalyptic-eschatological discourse floods the interpretive terrain with rhetorical excess and semantic superabundance. The rhetorical surfeit thus generated is a particular function of the dichotomizing tendencies inherent in apocalyptic-eschatological discourses, as demonstrated by this chapter's examination of how Northern Ireland evangelicals interpreted apocalyptic-eschatological texts.

155. Landes, "Millenarianism," 2.

Conclusion

Summary of Argument

As we approach the final stage of our study, it is appropriate to reca-pitulate the basic aim of the whole project. The task was to consider the ways in which apocalyptic-eschatological language contributed to the formation of evangelical worldviews during the Troubles. Through its comprehensive exploration of this issue, this study has traversed some of the most salient and pressing issues not only of millennial studies and the historiography of the Troubles but also of contemporary hermeneu-tics and critical theory. Underlying the various strands of the argument has been a unifying intention to initiate a mutually enriching conversa-tion among a variety of disciplinary approaches to the interpretation of apocalyptic-eschatological texts. In particular this work can be situated within the ongoing cooperative endeavors of theologians and literary critics to establish workable models for understanding the meaning and significance of apocalyptic-eschatological texts. In order to preclude the danger of this work degenerating into "mere theory" or an "erudite dis-cussion of inaccessible nonentities,"[1] this study has focused persistently upon specific evangelical interpretations of apocalyptic-eschatological texts arising from the turbulent, crisis-ridden backdrop of the Northern Ireland Troubles.

In addition to clarifying the key concepts, the Introduction set out the aims and scope of the study and identified its original contribution in relation to previous scholarly attempts to elucidate apocalyptic-es-chatological phenomena. Chapter 1 developed the argument spelled out in the Introduction by situating the main lines of argument in relation to ongoing scholarly endeavors to understand religion and apocalyptic

1. McClendon, *Systematic Theology*, III:398.

in Northern Ireland. The end of this chapter set out explicitly how this approach differs from previous inquiries into millennial phenomena in Northern Ireland. Crucially, this chapter identified serious shortcomings in previous treatments of the subject and was equally critical of the traditional "deprivation thesis" and more recent revisionist approaches. Whilst recognizing the significant scholarly gains made by revisionist interrogators of the "deprivation thesis," chapter 1 exposed the extent to which, despite their persistent disavowals of the "deprivation" as a necessary corollary of millennial studies, even many of the revisionist scholars have continued to operate within the theoretical frameworks bequeathed to them by the first generation, including the unexamined assumption that social context provides the key to understanding apocalyptic-eschatological phenomena. This methodological critique applies even though revisionist treatments usually place themselves at variance to the "deprivation thesis."

Chapter 2 took the descriptive task to a new level of theoretical engagement by providing a methodological prolegomenon to the project. This chapter made the case that the impact of the text has often been overlooked in favor of context and pointed out that the balance needed to be righted by giving the influence of the text more emphasis than has often been the case. This section drew on contemporary literary theory to argue for a dialectical relation between text and context. The argument was that language shapes reality since context is itself a confluence of texts. The rest of the chapter was thus devoted to formulating an alternative model for understanding apocalyptic-eschatological discourses by developing (with the aid of "New Historicism") an understanding of the text not as a passive reflection of a social milieu but as an active change-agent of contextual reality.

In the third and fourth chapters the analytical focus turned to applying these methodological insights to specific instances of evangelical interpretations of apocalyptic-eschatological texts during the Troubles. Refraining from passing critical judgments upon particular interpretations, these chapters sought to allow the primary texts to speak for themselves as much as possible. Seeking not to impose an external theoretical apparatus upon the primary material, this part of the analysis endeavored to allow these texts to organize themselves into a natural taxonomy. In terms of the apocalyptic-eschatological discourses of Northern Ireland evangelicalism, two distinctive categories of fear and hope began clearly to emerge and formed in turn the basis of chapters 3 and 4. Citing several examples of evangelical interpretations of biblical apocalyptic-eschatological text, these chapters added new levels of perception to our argument concerning the efficacy of texts as active agents in the formation of evangelical worldviews.

Chapter 5 inaugurated a reversion from an analysis of the existential aspects of apocalyptic language in terms of hope and fear and moved towards an exclusive concentration upon the polarized semantic fields that emerged from the discourses of apocalyptic eschatology. This chapter demonstrated the ways in which apocalyptic-eschatological language, instead of conveying life, vitality and hope, degenerated into a semantic graveyard of moribund dualistic categories that served the purpose of sectarian groups who sought to maintain ultimate distinctions between "them" and "us." However, this chapter also demonstrated how this effect could be countermanded by the response of hope that apocalyptic eschatology can also inspire.

Implications for Wider Scholarship

If theologians such as Karl Rahner[2] and philosophers such as Ernst Bloch[3] are right in their conviction that to be human is look beyond dominating present actualities towards new horizons of future possibility (i.e., to hope),[4] it follows that much can be learned about a community by asking the question addressed in chapter 4: "for what do these people hope?" It is also the case that as much can be learned about a community by focusing on hope's antithesis, fear, and by asking the con-

---

2. Rahner, "Theologische Prinzipien der Hermeneutik," 401–28. See especially pp. 422–23, in which Rahner spells out his anthropological conviction that the desire to conceive of a future in which all present incompleteness and discontinuities are finally resolved is a longing which belongs to the essence of what it means to be human.

3. The principle theoretical insight of Bloch's *magnum opus*, *Das Prinzip Hoffnung*, is that to be human is to evince the capacity to hope. Hudson provides a useful concise summary of the contents of Bloch's major work in his book, *Marxist Philosophy of Ernst Bloch*, 107.

4. Gadamer likewise acknowledges the unique anthropological significance of hope in his *Wahrheit und Methode*. Gadamer comments that, "Since the time of Aeschylus' Prometheus, the essence of hope has been such a distinguishing feature of human experience that we must, in light of its anthropological significance, regard as one-sided the principle of evaluating experience teleologically in terms of the degree to which it ends in knowledge"; Gadamer, *Gesammelte Werke*, I:355 (my translation).

comitant question (addressed in chapter 3): "of what are these people afraid?" When these questions are framed in evangelical contexts (such as Northern Ireland evangelicalism during the Troubles), the responses, as demonstrated throughout this book, are often framed in terms of apocalyptic eschatology, which addresses the issues of hope and fear at the deepest levels of language and human experience. It is thus important to understand how these hopes and fears were articulated in the polarized semantic fields which characterized the rhetoric of these communities, as was attempted in chapter 5. By addressing all of these vital questions in turn, I hope I have at least succeeded in raising anew the question of how literary theorists, historians, and theologians can formulate workable models for the study of apocalyptic-eschatological language and its relation to critical theory and cultural studies.

The present ripeness of the scholarly fruit in the field of millennial studies makes this a particularly auspicious time for further academic harvesting of the essence and cultural impact of apocalyptic-eschatological ideas. More than ever before, the horizons of academic engagement with apocalyptic phenomena are being expanded over a multiplicity of disciplinary perspectives. Historians, theologians, literary critics, and social scientists have all been able to establish a compelling unanimity on the point of attesting to the vital significance and critical contemporary relevance of apocalyptic eschatology. Thanks to such interdisciplinary efforts, apocalyptic eschatology is now recognized as a dynamic force that has motivated diverse world-historical individuals from Zoroaster[5] and Francis of Assisi[6] to Adolf Hitler[7] and Mao Zedong.[8] The inter-disciplinary significance of this study consists in its presentation of a theoretically engaged interdisciplinary synthesis, combining philosophical theories of hermeneutics, a historical approach to issues of textual production and reception, a literary-theoretical interpretation of the primary texts and a vigorous theology of hope.

5. Collins, *Apocalyptic Imagination*, 29.

6. Landes, "Millenarianism," 2.

7. Redles, *Hitler's Millennial Reich*.

8. Yeo, *Chairman Mao meets the Apostle Paul*.

Further Questions

Many questions requiring further elucidation arise from this study, each of which invites further discussion from a variety of perspectives. This book has demonstrated the ways in which apocalyptic-eschatological discourses can be analyzed to elucidate the relationship between theological ideas and their expression in contemporary culture. It is my hope that this book contributes something new not merely to the debate surrounding the "role of religion" in the Northern Ireland Troubles, but also to the broader discussions about the ideological negotiations and semantic exchanges which determine the reception of biblical texts into host cultures. Thus, although the previous chapters have been concerned primarily with evangelical interpretations of apocalyptic-eschatological texts during the Troubles, the foregoing analysis has also raised a broader issue of even greater significance: how evangelicals read society in light of how they read their Bibles. This study of evangelical interpretations of biblical apocalyptic-eschatological texts has indicated the formative power of biblical texts on evangelical worldviews.

Contemporary critical theory evinces an overriding concern to uncover the unspoken power interests and tacit systems of domination which govern popular conceptions of cultural consensus. This study of the ways in which people interpret apocalyptic-eschatological texts offers important insights into these negotiations and thereby contributes to our collective understanding of what has been called the "hermeneutical imperative."[9] Tradition, history and hermeneutics all negate the concept of a "plain reading." The notion of a so-called "plain reading" based on a professed "literal meaning of the text," has been exposed implicitly by our critique as a defunct category of hermeneutics, its use representing little more than a futile exercise of assuming that one's perspective is "hermeneutically innocent." Our conversation with deconstructionist approaches to interpretation has made it clear that the reader must divest her/himself of the false confidence that she or he stands in a condition of hermeneutical innocence in relation to the text. Since "the relationship between the universe of discourse and material life" is characterized by "a complex dynamic of mutual constitution and transformation,"[10] it is

9. Garfield, "Philosophy, Religion," 98–110.

10. Montrose, *Purpose of Playing*, 2.

impossible to speak of a reading subject as a hermeneutically innocent observer of a supposedly objective interpretive process.

Methodological Implications

In terms of method, I hope that this study has exemplified a sympathetic, reflective, and critical yet non-judgmental approach to evangelical communities that can serve as a standard for further explorations of millennial phenomena, whether in Northern Ireland or other settings in which apocalyptic-eschatological ideas retained a determinate shaping power on culture. Despite the critical scrutiny to which we have subjected evangelical interpretations of biblical apocalyptic-eschatological texts, it has been our aim throughout to ensure that such critiques have been based on sympathetic understandings of the convictions underpinning these readings. In the course of this inquiry we have encountered several apparently rather far-fetched interpretations of biblical apocalyptic-eschatological texts.[11] Having considered such seemingly strange, implausible, border-line racist, and downright bizarre commentaries on apocalyptic-eschatological texts offered by certain Northern Ireland evangelicals, it might well become clear what G. K. Chesterton had in mind when he wrote that, "though St. John the Evangelist saw many strange monsters in his vision, he saw no creature so wild as one of his own commentators."[12] Nevertheless, the criticism of such interpretations as "irrational," "muddle-headed," "naïve," "absurd," or "ridiculous" presupposes an objective conception of rationality against which such charges could be made. Thus in order to avoid what Quentin Skinner calls "an intrusion, a forcible imposition of our own epistemic standards on an alien 'universe of discourse' or 'form of life,'"[13] researchers of millennial phenomena must take a sympathetic approach to the apocalyptic convictions held by those whose discourses they are studying. This warning can be applied to researchers investigating all spheres of human activity, but is especially pertinent to those conducting research in the

11. Examples include the interpretation of one evangelical writing in the *Orange Standard* who predicted that "when Russia has the Middle East and North Africa under control she will invade Canada by going up over the North Pole in an attempt to dominate North America" which will be the prelude to "Armageddon" between Russia and the "White Anglo Saxon People." See *Orange Standard* (March, 1980), 5.

12. Chesterton, *Orthodoxy*, 17.

13. Skinner, *Visions of Politics*, I:38.

field of millennial studies in which the prevailing discourses are likely to be pervaded by beliefs that appear upon first view to be highly irrational, incoherent and even contradictory.

Implications for the Future of Millennial Studies

The apparent irrationality of apocalyptic-eschatological worldviews underlines the important point that researchers in the field of millennial studies take seriously the notion that apocalypticism "operates much more at an emotional than a cerebral level."[14] To take an example from another context, we can note that if the success of the *Left Behind* series has anything to teach us, it is that intellectual plausibility is not a necessary precondition to the achievement either of widespread acceptance or to the culturally-transformative impact of an apocalyptic worldview. J. Christiaan Bekker makes an important point when he notes that the neo-apocalypticism of Hal Lindsey and Jerry Falwell was popular not because it was hermeneutically rigourous or even intellectually plausible but because of its "empathy with powerful elements of the cultural climate of our time."[15]

Researchers working in millennial studies must understand that the question of whether or not millennial ideologies gain acceptance is not necessarily dependent upon the intellectual coherence or plausibility of the millennial belief in question. Millennial aspirations touch the nub not only of the specific phenomenon of apocalyptic-eschatological language in the Northern Ireland Troubles but also, more generally, of the cultural condition of our time. Sociologists today speak about this condition in terms of a general spiritual malaise in Western cultures arising out of a loss of meaning and purpose, which has generated a prevalent hopelessness about the future and a "fascination with despair."[16] It is claimed that, despite the relative material wealth of many Western nations, the signs of despair continue to manifest themselves in a culture which one theologian characterized as an "age of anxiety."[17] This despair

14. Newport, *Expecting the End*, viii.

15. Bekker, *Paul's Apocalyptic Gospel*, 20.

16. This term is attributed to William F. Lynch by Bauckham and Hart in *Hope against Hope*, 47.

17. Tillich used the term, "*Zeitalter der Angst*" and alluded to "an infiltration of the public consciousness with ideas and symbols which refer to anxiety." See Tillich, *Der Mut zum Sein*, 40.

and anxiety manifest themselves in the contemporary world in such phenomena as rising suicide rates and an unprecedented proliferation in cases of depression and other mental illnesses.[18]

These are the signs of a culture crying out for hope. If to be human is to hope, then it follows that despair, as hope's antithesis, is a dehumanizing force in human life. To lose our hope is to lose something of our humanity. Hope exerts a humanizing social and existential *energia* which combats cynicism, apathy, despondency and despair itself as well as other degenerative forces which denigrate and devalue human life by obstructing its fulfilment and flourishing. It may be hoped that the apocalyptic-eschatological vision alluded to in this study has the potential to speak prophetically to this culture, which exhibits an underlying fear of death, the threat of which no amount of technological sophistication, economic prosperity, scientific advancement or even medical innovation can confront. As demonstrated in chapter 4, many evangelicals were fully persuaded that this vision offered the genuine hope that death has been defeated and that its power, though still a reality, need not be feared. There are many Christians, in Northern Ireland and throughout the world, who believe that apocalyptic-eschatological hope can transmute the cries of despair of a dying culture into the expectant cries that accompany the hopeful birth-pangs, which will culminate in "new heavens and a new earth." This hope consists in the conviction that the "still, sad music of humanity"[19] will metamorphose into a glorious chorus of eschatological hope, a crescendo of cosmic consummation.

This book has demonstrated that apocalyptic eschatology can be used either as a convenient language arsenal from which to fire discursive epithets at one's religious and political enemies or as a living vision of hope that anticipates the "restitution of all things" and the final elimination of evil and sin, death and decay from the earth. Apocalyptic-eschatological hope points the way towards a future in which all alienation shall be overcome in the new heaven and the new earth for God's home will be with his people (Rev 21:3). From this perspective, apocalyptic eschatology can be regarded as the grammar of hope projecting an imaginative vision of hope for the unity of all unity, the reconciliation of all conflict and the restoration of all things.

18. Giroux, *Counternarratives*, 66.

19. Wordsworth, "Tintern Abbey," 37.

Millennial studies should now "come of age" by focusing its efforts not on the uncovering of the eccentric or idiosyncratic beliefs of the latest fundamentalist cult or suicide sect but by working towards the elucidation of the ways in which the apocalyptic-eschatological vision can be employed towards the renewal of culture in our age. In other words, the task of millennial studies should be to explore ways in which the "universal affirmation"[20] can find its rightful universal application. The pressing need in millennial studies scholarship today is thus for scholars who will bring apocalyptic eschatology to life by developing creative interpretive paradigms that will facilitate imaginative visions "in which text and existence are not separate entities but intrinsically related realms";[21] the urgent need is for scholars who are willing to engage in further creative explorations of the transformative and responsible application of this hope as an imaginative possibility in our world today. It is my sincere hope that this study has within it plenty of fresh insights which can guide such further explorations.

For better or worse, apocalyptic eschatology remains one of the defining themes of our times. As an area of study that leads us into an exploration of some of the most pressing and engaging issues at the intersection between cultural studies and hermeneutics, it merits serious attention from scholars across the spectrum of current research in the humanities. By exploring this theme in terms of textuality and critical theory, this study has offered an original methodological approach to the study of apocalyptic-eschatology as a decisive presence in contemporary culture.

20. Moltmann, *The Spirit of Life.*
21. Räpple, *Metaphor of the City,* 31–32.

Bibliography

Primary Sources

Newspapers and Magazines

Ballymena Times.
Battle Standard.
Belfast Telegraph.
Christian Irishman.
Combat.
Connections.
Covenant Reformed Fellowship News.
Frontiers.
Irish Baptist.
Irish News.
Larne Guardian.
lion & lamb.
New Protestant Telegraph.
Orange Standard.
Protestant Telegraph.
Revivalist.
Today.
Ulster Bulwark.
Ulster Nation.
Ulster Protestant.
Ulster Review.

Monographs

Foster, I. *Shadow of the Antichrist: A Commentary on the Book of Revelation.* Belfast: Ambassador 1996.

Garland, R. "The Ulster Volunteer Force Negotiating History". MPhil diss., Queen's University Belfast, 1991.

Gibson, A. "Gustavo Gutierrez and Northern Ireland." PhD diss., Queen's University Belfast, 2006.

Gordon, S. *Hope and Glory: Jesus is Coming Again: The Timeless Message of I & II Thessalonians.* Belfast: Ambassador, 2005.

———. *Moving On with God: Haggai: A Major Study of a Minor Prophet.* Belfast: Ambassador, 1989.

Higgins, G. "Great Expectations: The Myth of Anti-Christ in Northern Ireland." PhD diss., Queens University Belfast, 2000.

Humphries, K. *The Battleground of Truth: An Examination of the Book of Daniel*. Online: http://www.treasuredtruthtoday.org/article/khsa/Daniel.

Leahy, F. S. *The Victory of the Lamb*. Edinburgh: Banner of Truth, 2001.

Lyle, D. *Countdown to Apocalypse: Unlocking Biblical Prophecy*. Belfast: Ambassador, 1996.

McConnell, J. *A Light on a Hill*. Basingstoke, UK: Marshall Pickering, 1987.

McMillan, D. "The Role of the Seven Beatitudes in the Book of the Revelation." MPhil diss., Queen's University Belfast, 1999.

Paisley, I. *Antichrist: An Exposition*. Belfast: Martyrs Memorial Productions, no date.

———. *Christian Foundations*. Greenville, SC: Bob Jones University Press, 1971.

———. *An Exposition of the Epistle to the Romans*. London: Marshall, Morgan and Scott, 1968.

———. *A Look at Luke's Book: Four Sermons on the Gospel of Luke*. Belfast: Puritan, 1973.

———. *The Massacre of St. Bartholomew*. Belfast: Puritan, 1972.

Sermons

Campbell, A. "The Anglo-Irish Agreement." Sermon preached at Shankill Gospel Hall, 25 May 1987. Available on cassette from Open-Bible Ministries.

———. "A United Ireland—What Saith the Scriptures?" Sermon preached at Cregagh Gospel Hall, 10 July 1991. Available on cassette from Open-Bible Ministries.

———. "Zechariah's Antichrist Prophecy." Sermon preached by Alan Campbell, 13 June 1990. Available online at www.1335.com/audio.html.

Paisley, I. "Are We to Lose Our Protestant Heritage Forever." August, 2004. Online: http://www.ianpaisley.org/article.asp?ArtKey=heritage.

———. "Fundamentalism vs. Apostasy." Sermon preached at Martyrs Memorial on Saturday 2 March, 1969. Belfast: Martyrs' Memorial, 1969.

———. "Mohammedanism-Judaism-Romanism vs. Bible Christianity in the Final Conflict of the Age." Sermon preached at Martyrs' Memorial Free Presbyterian Church on 18 November 2001.

———. "The Woman Rides the Beast: A Remarkable Prophetic Fulfilment: The E.E.C. Prophetically Considered." Sermon preached on 10 June 1984. Belfast: Martyr's Memorial, 1984.

Wilson, I. "That Amazing Book." Sermon preached at Grove Baptist Church, January 2001, 3. Online: http://www.grovebaptist.co.uk/sermons/iw/iw053.htm.

Pamphlets and Booklets

Barkley, J. M. *Irish Presbyterianism and Inter-Church Relations*. Belfast: Church House, 1975.

Campbell, A. *Anti-Christ Revealed in History and Prophecy*. Belfast: Open-Bible Ministries.

———. *Five Things that Every Ulster Protestant Needs to Know*. Belfast: Open-Bible Ministries.

———. *For God and Ulster: The 90th Anniversary of the Ulster Covenant*. Belfast: Open-Bible Ministries, 2002.

———. *For What Should Ulster Pray?* Belfast: Open-Bible Ministries, 1997.

———. *The French Revolution in Prophecy*. Belfast: Open-Bible Ministries, 1989.

————. *Great Tribulation.* Belfast: Open-Bible Ministries, 1990.

————. *Islam in Prophecy.* Belfast: Open-Bible Ministries, 1985.

————. *Is the Secret Rapture Scriptural?.* Belfast: Open-Bible Ministries.

————. *Let the Orange Banner Speak.* Open Bible Ministries 1997.

————. *Light from Nahum.* Belfast: Open-Bible Ministries, 1986.

————. *Remember 1641.* Belfast: Open-Bible Ministries, 1991.

————. *The Scarlet Woman of the Apocalypse.* Belfast: Open-Bible Ministries, 1985.

————. *Why We Believe in the Millennium.* Belfast: Open-Bible Ministries, 1981.

Committee on National and International Problems. *Christians in a Situation of Conflict.* Belfast: PCI, 1973.

Committee on National and International Problems. *The Church's Comment on Political Affairs.* Belfast: PCI, 1976.

Cooke, R. *Paisley and Mystery Babylon the Great: A Defense of Paisley's Exegesis.* Hollidaysburg, PA: Manna, 1985.

ECONI. *Dreams and Visions.* Belfast: ECONI, 2003.

————. *Evangelicals and Catholics Together in Ireland.* Belfast: ECONI, no date.

————. *A Future with Hope: Biblical Frameworks.* Belfast: ECONI, 1998.

————. *Thinking Biblically, Building Peace.* Belfast: ECONI, 2002.

Elsdon, R. *The Lamb Wins: 42 Daily Readings in the Book of Revelation.* Belfast: Church of Ireland Evangelical Fellowship, 1995.

Gallagher, E. *What the Bible says about Reconciliation.* Belfast: Irish Council of Churches, 1988.

Irish Council of Churches. *What the Bible Says about Peace.* Belfast: Appletree, 1979.

Jennings, R. *Future Events.* Dun Laoghaire, Ireland: Bible Studies Institute, 1994.

Kelly, F. J. *Bible Study Guide: 1st Peter.* Belfast: The Presbyterian Fellowship, 1981.

Paisley, I. *A Call to the Protestants of Ulster.* Belfast: Martyrs" Memorial, 1975.

————. *The Myth of God Incarnate Reviewed and Refuted by Ian Paisley.* Belfast: Martyrs Memorial, 1977.

————. *Roman Catholic Priests Challenged and Answered.* National Union of Protestants: London, 1953.

————. *The Ulster Problem: A Discussion of the True Situation in Northern Ireland.* Greenville, SC: Bob Jones University Press, 1972.

————. *The Whereabouts of Mr Lostman.* Belfast: Martyrs" Memorial, no date.

Porter, N. *Ecumenism . . . Romanism . . . and Irish Baptists.* Belfast: Graham & Heslip, 1965.

Presbyterian Church in Ireland. *Our Membership in the World Council of Churches: A Report to the General Assembly.* Belfast: Church House, 1972.

Smyth, C. *Rome—Our Enemy.* Belfast: Puritan, 1974.

Smyth, W. M. *The Message of the Banners.* Belfast: Evangelical Protestant Society, no date.

Tara. *Ireland Forever.* Northern Ireland: Tara, no date.

————. *Proclamation.* Northern Ireland: Tara, no date.

Thompson, A. *Fields of Vision: Faith and Identity in Protestant Ireland.* Belfast: Center for Contemporary Christianity, 2002.

————. *The Fractured Family.* Belfast: Nelson and Knox, 1995.

Trimble, D. *The Illustrated Orange Song Book.* Belfast: Bell-Fast Graphics, no date.

Ulster Society. *The Orange Lark and Other Songs o' the Orange Tradition.* Belfast: Ulster Society, 1987.

Secondary Sources

Adorno, T. *Negative Dialektik*. Frankfurt: Suhrkamp, 1973.

Alison, J. *Living in the End Times: The Last Things Re-imagined*. London: SPCK, 1997.

Allison, D. C. "A Plea for Thoroughgoing Eschatology." *Journal of Biblical Literature* 113 (1994) 651–68.

Altizer, T. J. J. "Apocalypticism and Modern Thinking." *Journal for Christian Theological Research* 2 (1997) 1–3.

———. *The Contemporary Jesus*. Albany, NY: State University of New York, 1997.

———. *Genesis and Apocalypse: A Theological Voyage toward Authentic Christianity*. Louisville: John Knox, 1990.

———. *The Gospel of Christian Atheism*. London: Collins, 1967.

———. *The New Apocalypse: The Radical Christian Vision of William Blake*. Aurora, MI: Michigan State University Press, 2000.

Alves, R. *A Theology of Human Hope*. St. Meinrad, IN: Abbey, 1975.

Amsler, S. A. "Pedagogy against 'Dis-Utopia': From Conscientization to the Education of Desire." In *No Social Science without Critical Theory*, edited by Harry F. Dahms, 291–327. Bingley, UK: Emerald Group, 2008.

Aquinas, T. *Summa Theologiae: Volume 3: Knowing and Naming God*. Edited by Herbert McCabe. Cambridge: Cambridge University Press, 2006.

Aristotle. *Poetics*. Translated by M. Heath. London: Penguin, 1996.

Arthur, A. *The Tailor King: The Rise and Fall of the Anabaptist Kingdom of Münster*. New York: St. Martin's Press, 1999.

Aughey, A. *Under Siege: Ulster Unionism and the Anglo-Irish Agreement*. Belfast: Blackstaff, 1989.

Augustine. *The City of God against the Pagans*. Edited by R. W. Dyson. Cambridge: Cambridge University Press, 1998.

Austin, J. L. *How to Do Things with Words*. Oxford: Clarendon, 1962.

Badcock, C. R. *Lévi-Strauss: Structuralism and Sociological Theory*. London: Hutchinson, 1975.

Balthasar, H. *Das Ganze im Fragment*. Einsiedeln, Switzerland: Johannes, 1963.

———. *Theo-Drama: Theological Dramatic Theory*. Translated by G. Harrison. 5 vols. San Francisco: Ignatius, 1988–98.

Bambach, C. R. *Heidegger, Dilthey and the Crisis of Historicism*. Ithaca, NY: Cornell University Press, 1995.

Bardon, J. *A History of Ulster*. Belfast: Blackstaff, 1992.

Barkun, M., ed. *Millennialism and Violence*. London: Routledge, 1996.

Barr, D. *The Reality of Apocalypse: Rhetoric and Politics in the Book of Revelation*. Atlanta: Society for Biblical Literature, 2006.

Barr, J. *Fundamentalism*. London: SCM, 1977.

Barrett, C. K. *The Gospel according to John*. London: SPCK, 1978.

Barth, K. *Church Dogmatics*. Edited and Translated by G. W. Bromiley. 14 vols. Reprint. Edinburgh: T. & T. Clark, 2004.

———. *Der Römerbrief*. München: Kaiser, 1923.

Bauckham, R. *The Climax of Prophecy: Studies in the Book of Revelation*. Edinburgh: T. & T. Clark, 1993.

———. *God Will be All in All: The Eschatology of Jürgen Moltmann*. Edinburgh: T. & T. Clark, 1999.

———. *The Theology of the Book of Revelation*. Cambridge: Cambridge University Press, 1993.

Bauckham, R., and T. Hart. *Hope against Hope: Christian Eschatology at the Turn of the Millennium*. Grand Rapids: Eerdmans, 1999.

Beale, G. K. *The Use of Daniel in Jewish Apocalyptic Literature and in the Revelation of St John*. Lanham, MD: University Press of America, 1984.

Beardslee, W. "Hope in Biblical Eschatology and in Process Theology." *Journal of the American Academy of Religion* 38 (1970) 227–39.

Bebbington, D. W. *Evangelicalism in Modern Britain: A History from the 1730s to the 1980s*. London: Unwin Hyman, 1989.

Bekker, J. C. *Paul's Apocalyptic Gospel: The Coming Triumph of God*. Philadelphia: Fortress, 1982.

Benware, P. N. *Understanding End Times Prophecy: A Comprehensive Approach*. Chicago: Moody, 2006.

Berdyaev, N. *The Beginning and the End*. Translated by R. M. French. Santa Barbara, CA: Greenwood, 1976.

———. *Slavery and Freedom*. Translated by R. M. French. London: Scribner's Sons, 1944.

Berger, P., and T. Luckmann. *The Social Construction of Reality: A Treatise in the Sociology of Knowledge*. Garden City, NY: Anchor, 1966.

Berrio, A. G. *A Theory of the Literary Text*. Berlin: de Gruyter, 1992.

Bethea, D. M. *The Shape of Apocalypse in Modern Russian Fiction*. Princeton: Princeton University Press, 1989.

Bevans, S. B. *Models of Contextual Theology*. Maryknoll, NY: Orbis, 2005.

Birch, D. *Language, Literature, and Critical Practice: Ways of Analysing Texts*. London: Routledge, 1989.

Bloch, E. *Literary Essays*. Translated by A. Joron. Stanford: Stanford University Press, 1998

———. *Das Prinzip Hoffnung*. 5 vols. Frankfurt: Suhrkamp, 1973.

———. "Zur Ontologie des Noch-Nicht-Seins." In *Auswahl aus seinem Schriften*, 41–66. Hamburg: Fischer, 1967.

Blumenthal, D. *Facing the Abusing God: A Theology of Protest*. Bloomington, IN: Indiana University Press, 1990.

Boal, F., R. Murray, and M. Poole. "Belfast: The Urban Encapsulation of a National Conflict." In *Urban Ethnic Conflict: A Comparative Perspective*, edited by S. E. Clarke and J. L. Obler, 31–77. Chapel Hill, NC: Institute for Research in Social Science, 1976.

Bonhoeffer, D. *Ethik* .Gütersloher: Gütersloher, 2006.

Boone, K. C. *The Bible Tells Them So: The Discourse of Protestant Fundamentalism*. London: SCM, 1990.

Borg, M. "A Temperate Case for a Non-Eschatological Jesus." *Foundations and Facets Forum* 2 (1986) 81–102.

Boring, M. E. "Narrative Christology in the Apocalypse." *Catholic Biblical Quarterly* 54 (1992) 702–23.

Boxall, I. *Revelation: Vision and Insight*. London: SPCK, 2002.

Boyer, P. "666 and All That: Prophetic Belief in America from the Puritans to the Present." In *Apocalypticism and Millennialism: Shaping a Believers Church Eschatology for the Twenty-First Century,* edited by Loren L. Jones, 236–56. Scottdale, PA: Herald, 2000.

Brannigan, J. *New Historicism and Cultural Materialism.* London: Macmillan, 1998.

Brewer, J. "Sectarianism and Racism, and their Parallels and Differences." *Ethnic and Religious Studies* 15 (1992) 252–64.

Brewer, J., and G. Higgins. *Anti-Catholicism in Northern Ireland, 1600–1998: The Mote and the Beam.* London: Macmillan, 1998.

Brewer, J. "Contesting Ulster." In *Homelands: Poetic Power and the Politics of Space,* edited by R. Robin and B. Strath, 283–304. Brussels: Lang. 2003.

Brown, C. *The Death of Christian Britain: Understanding Secularisation 1800–2000.* London: Routledge, 2001.

Brown, D. *Continental Philosophy and Modern Theology.* Oxford: Blackwell, 1987.

Brown, T. *Ireland's Literature: Selected Essays.* Mullingar, Ireland: Lilliput, 1988.

Bruce, F. F. *History of the Bible in English.* Cambridge: Lutterworth, 1961.

Bruce, S. *God Save Ulster! The Religion and Politics of Paisleyism.* Oxford: Clarendon, 1986.

Bruce, S. *Fundamentalism.* Oxford: Polity, 2001.

———. "Fundamentalism and Political Violence: The Case of Paisley and Ulster Evangelicals." *Religion* 31 (2001) 387–405.

———. *Paisley: Religion and Politics in Northern Ireland.* Oxford: Clarendon, 2008.

———. *The Red Hand: Protestant Paramilitaries in Northern Ireland.* Oxford: Clarendon, 1992.

———. "The Sociology of Anti-Catholicism." *Studies: An Irish Quarterly Review* 89 (2000) 205–14.

Bruns, G. *Hermeneutics Ancient and Modern.* New Haven: Yale University Press, 1992.

Bryan, D. *Orange Parades: The Politics of Ritual, Tradition, and Control.* Sterling, VA: Pluto, 2000.

Bube, R. H. "Premillennial Pessimism, Optimism and Pessimism: Science and Eschatology." *Journal of the Evangelical Theological Society* 15 (1972) 215–29.

Buber, M. *Kampf um Israel.* Berlin: Schocken, 1933.

Buckley, A. "Uses of History among Ulster Protestants". In *The Poet's Place: Ulster Literature and Society: Essays in Honour of John Hewitt, 1907–1987,* edited by G. Dawe and J. W. Foster, 259–71. Belfast: Institute of Irish Studies, 1991.

Bulgakov, S. *The Lamb of God.* Translated by B. Jakim. Grand Rapids: Eerdmans, 2008.

Bull, M. "On Making Ends Meet." In *Apocalypse Theory and the Ends of the World,* edited by M. Bull, 1–14. Oxford: Blackwell, 1995.

———. *Seeing Things Hidden: Apocalypse, Vision and Totality.* London: Verso, 1999.

Bultmann, R. *The Gospel of John: A Commentary.* Translated by G. R. Beasley-Murray. Oxford: Blackwell, 1971.

Burke, K. "Theology and Logology." *Kenyon Review* 1 (1979) 151–85.

Burke, P. *Popular Culture in Early Modern Europe.* London: Temple Smith, 1978.

Burkett, D. *An Introduction to the New Testament and the Origins of Christianity.* Cambridge: Cambridge University Press, 2002.

Burkitt, F. C. "The Apocalypses: Their Place in Jewish History." In *Judaism and the Beginnings of Christianity,* edited by A. Cohen, 49–90. London: Routledge, 1923.

Burleigh, M. *The Third Reich: A New Study.* London: Pan, 2001.

Bynum, C. W., and P. Freedman. *Last Things: Death and the Apocalypse in the Middle Ages.* Philadelphia: University of Pennsylvania Press, 2000.

Caird, G. B. *A Commentary on the Revelation of St. John the Divine.* London: A. & C. Black, 1966.

Calvin, J. *Institutes of the Christian Religion.* Translated by F. L. Battles. London: SCM, 1961.

Caputo, J. D. *The Prayers and Tears of Jacques Derrida: Religion without Religion.* Bloomington, IN: Indiana University Press, 1997.

———. *Radical Hermeneutics: Repetition, Deconstruction, and the Hermeneutic Project.* Bloomington, IN: Indiana University Press, 1987.

———. *The Weakness of God: A Theology of the Event.* Bloomington, IN: Indiana University Press, 2006.

Caputo, J. D., and J. Derrida. *Deconstruction in a Nutshell: A Conversation with Jacques Derrida.* New York: Fordham University Press, 1997.

Carmignac, J. "Qu'est-ce que l'Apocalyptique? Son employ a Quamran." *Revue de Qumran* 10 (1979) 3–33.

Carpenter, J. A. *Revive Us Again: The Reawakening of American Fundamentalism.* Oxford: Oxford University Press, 1999.

Carpenter, M. W. *Imperial Bibles, Domestic Bodies: Women, Sexuality, & Religion in the Victorian Market.* Athens, OH: Ohio University Press, 2003.

Castell, L., and O. Ischebeck. *Time, Quantum and Information.* New York: Springer, 2010.

Chapman, M. C. *The Coming Crisis: The Impact of Eschatology on Theology in Edwardian England.* Sheffield, UK: Sheffield Academic Press, 2001.

Champagne, R. A. *Literary History in the Wake of Roland Barthes: Re-defining the Myths of Reading.* Birmingham, AL: Summa, 1984.

Charles, R. H. *Eschatology: The Doctrine of a Future Life in Israel, Judaism, and Christianity.* New York: Schocken, 1963.

Chartier, R. *On the Edge of the Cliff: History, Languages and Practices.* Translated by L. G. Cochrane. Baltimore, MD: Johns Hopkins, 1997.

Chesterton, G. K. *Orthodoxy.* Fairfield, IA: 1st World Library, 2008.

Chidester, D. *Salvation and Suicide: Jim Jones, the Peoples Temple and Jonestown.* Bloomington, IN: Indiana University Press, 2003.

Chomsky, "Symposium on Innate Ideas." In *The Philosophy of Language*, edited by J. Searle, 121–44. Oxford: Oxford University Press, 1971.

Clements, E. *Prophecy and Covenant.* London: SCM, 1965.

Cliff, B., and E. Walshe, eds. *Representing the Troubles: Texts and Images, 1970–2000.* Dublin: Four Courts, 2004.

Clouse, R. G., ed. *The Meaning of the Millennium: Four Views.* Downers Grove, IL: InterVarsity, 1977.

Cobb, J., and D. R. Griffin. *Process Theology: An Introductory Exposition.* Belfast: Westminster, 1976.

Cohen, S. *The Beginning of Jewishness: Boundaries, Varieties, Uncertainties.* Berkeley: University of California Press, 1999.

Cohn, N. *The Pursuit of the Millennium: Revolutionary Millenarians and Mystical Anarchists in the Middle Ages.* London: Random House/Pimlico, 1957.

Cohn, N. *Cosmos, Chaos and the World to Come: The Ancient Roots of Apocalyptic Faith.* New Haven: Yale University Press, 1995.

Cole, S. G. *The History of Fundamentalism.* New York: Smith, 1931.

Collingwood, R. G. *The Idea of History.* Oxford: Oxford University Press, 1946.

Collins, A. Y. *Crisis and Catharsis: The Power of Apocalypse.* Philadelphia: Westminster, 1984.

————. "Persecution and Vengeance in the Book of Revelation." In *Apocalypticism in the Mediterranean World and the Near East,* edited by D. Hellholm, 729–50. Tübingen: Mohr, 1983.

Collins, J. J. "Apocalyptic Eschatology in the Ancient World." In *The Oxford Handbook of Eschatology,* edited by Jerry Walls, 40–55. Oxford: Oxford University Press, 2007.

————. "Apocalyptic Eschatology as the Transcendence of Death." In *Visionaries and their Apocalypses,* edited by P. Hanson, 21–43. London: SPCK, 1983.

————. *The Apocalyptic Imagination: An Introduction to the Jewish Apocalyptic Literature.* New York: Crossroad, 1987.

————. "Eschatological Dynamics and Utopian Ideals in Early Judaism." In *Imagining the End: Visions of Apocalypse from the Ancient Middle East to Modern America,* edited by A. Amanat and M. Bernhardsson, 69–89. New York: St. Martin's Press, 2002.

————. "Introduction: Towards the Morphology of a Genre." *Semia* 14 (1979) 1–18.

Condorcet, M. *Sketch for a Historical Picture of the Progress of the Human Mind.* Translated by J. Barraclough. London: Weidenfeld and Nicholson, 1955.

Connolly, S. J. *The Oxford Companion to Irish History.* Oxford: Oxford University Press, 2007.

Cook, D. *Contemporary Muslim Apocalyptic Literature.* Syracuse, NY: Syracuse University Press, 2005.

Cook, S. L. *The Apocalyptic Literature.* Nashville: Abingdon, 2003.

————. *Prophecy and Apocalypticism: The Postexilic Social Setting.* Minneapolis: Fortress, 1995.

Cooke, D. *Persecuting Zeal: A Portrait of Ian Paisley.* Dingle, Ireland: Brandon, 1996.

Critchley, S. *The Ethics of Deconstruction: Derrida and Levinas.* Oxford: Blackwell, 1992.

Crookshank, C. H. *History of Methodism in Ireland.* 3 vols. London, 1886.

Cullmann, O. *Salvation in History.* Translated by S. Sowers. London: SCM, 1967.

Culpeppe, R. A. "The New Millennium in Contemporary and Biblical Perspectives." *Review and Expositor* 97 (2000) 291–99.

Daley, B. *The Hope of the Early Church: A Handbook of Patristic Eschatology.* Cambridge: Cambridge University Press, 1991.

Daschke, D. *City of Ruins: Mourning the Destruction of Jerusalem through Jewish Apocalypse.* Leiden: Brill, 2010.

Daniels, T. *Millennialism: An International Bibliography.* New York: Garland, 1992.

Deleuze, G., and F. Guattari. *What Is Philosophy?* Translated by Graham Burchell and Hugh Tomlinson. London: Verso, 1994.

Dellamora, R. ed. *Postmodern Apocalypse: Theory and Cultural Practice at the End.* Philadelphia: Pennsylvania University Press, 1995.

de Man, P. *Blindness and Insight: Essays in the Rhetoric of Contemporary Criticism.* London: Routledge, 1989.

de Saussure, F. *Course in General Linguistics.* Translated by Roy Harris. La Salle, IL: Open Court, 1983.

Derrida, J. *The Ear of the Other: Otobiography, Transference, Translation.* Lincoln, NE: University of Nebraska, 1985.

————. *Limited Inc.* Evanston, IL: Northwestern University Press, 1988.

————. "Living on: Border-Lines." In *Deconstruction and Criticism,* edited by H. Bloom et al., 62–142. New York: Seabury, 1979.

————. *Margins of Philosophy.* Chicago: University of Chicago, 1982.

————. "Of an Apocalyptic Tone Newly Adopted in Philosophy." Translated by John P. Leavy. In *Derrida and Negative Theology,* edited by H. Coward and T. Foshay, 25–71. Albany, NY: State University of New York, 1992.

————. *Of Grammatology.* Translated by G. Spivak. Baltimore: Johns Hopkins University Press, 1976.

————. "Signature Event Context." *Glyph* 1 (1977) 172–97.

————. *Spectres of Marx: The State of the Debt, the Work of Mourning and the New International.* Translated by P. Kamuf. London: Routledge, 1994.

————. *Spurs: Nietzsche's Styles.* Chicago: University of Chicago, 1978.

Detweiler, R., and K. Robbins. "From New Criticism to Poststructuralism: Twentieth-Century Hermeneutics." In *Reading the Text: Biblical Criticism and Literary Theory,* edited by S. Prickett, 225–80. Oxford: Blackwell, 1991.

Dolejšová, I. *Accounts of Hope: A Problem of Method in Postmodern Apologia.* Berlin: Lang, 2001.

Dostoevsky, F. *The Brothers Karamazov: A Novel in Four Parts and an Epilogue.* Translated by David McDuff. London: Penguin Classics, 1993.

Duff, P. B. *Who Rides the Beast? Prophetic Rivalry and the Rhetoric of Crisis in the Churches of the Apocalypse.* Oxford: Oxford University Press, 2001.

Eagleton, T. *Literary Theory: An Introduction.* Oxford: Blackwell, 1983.

————. *William Shakespeare: Rereading Literature.* Oxford: Blackwell, 1986.

Eames, R. "The Religious Factor." In *Protestant Perceptions of the Peace Process in Northern Ireland,* edited by D. Murray, 101–36. Limerick: Centre for Peace and Development Studies, 2000.

Ebeling, G. *The Nature of Faith.* Translated by R. G. Smith. Philadelphia: Fortress, 1961.

Edgar, A., and P. Sedgwick. *Cultural Theory: The Key Concepts.* London: Routledge, 2008.

Edwards, J. *The Works of Jonathan Edwards.* Edited by E. Hickman. London: Ball, 1839.

Elliott, M. "Religion and Identity in Northern Ireland." In *The Long Road to Peace in Northern Ireland,* edited by M. Elliott, 169–88. Liverpool: Liverpool University Press, 2002.

Fahlbusch, E., and G. W. Bromiley, eds. *The Encyclopaedia of Christianity.* Grand Rapids: Eerdmans, 2001.

Faragau, I. B. "New Purchase on Larger Meanings: In the Light of John's Conscious and Contextual Interlocking of Revelation 1:1—2:7 with its Old Testament Background." PhD diss., Queen's University Belfast, 2002.

Fastenrath, E. *"In Vitam Aeterna": Grundzüge christlicher Eschatologie in der ersten Hälfte des 20. Jahrhunderts.* Sankt Ottilien, Germany: Eos Verlag, 1982.

Fekkes, J. *Isaiah and Prophetic Traditions in the Book of Revelation: Visionary Antecedents and their Development.* Sheffield, UK: Sheffield Academic Press, 1994.

Fergus, J. "Eighteenth-century Readers in Provincial England: The Customers of Samuel Clay's Circulating Library and Bookshop in Warwick, 1770–72." *Papers of the Bibliographical Society of America* 78 (1984) 155–213.

Feuerbach, L. *Das Wesen des Christentums.* Stuttgart: Reclam, 1994.

Fiddes, P. S. *The Creative Suffering of God.* Oxford: Oxford University Press, 1988.

————. *Freedom and Limit: A Dialogue between Literature and Christian Doctrine.* London: Macmillan, 1991.

————. *The Promised End: Eschatology in Theology and Literature.* Oxford: Blackwell, 2000.

Finkelstein, D and McCleery, A. *An Introduction to Book History.* London: Routledge, 2005.

Fodor, J. *Christian Hermeneutics: Paul Ricoeur and the Refiguring of Theology.* Oxford: Clarendon, 1995.

Ford, A. *James Ussher: Theology, History and Politics in Early-Modern Ireland and England.* Oxford: Oxford University Press, 2007.

Foster, R. *Luck and the Irish: A Brief History of Change, 1970–2000.* London: Penguin, 2007.

Foucault, M. "Afterword: The Subject and Power." In *Michel Foucault: Beyond Structuralism and Hermeneutics,* edited by H. Dreyfus and P. Rainbow, 216–26. Chicago: Chicago University Press, 1983.

————. *Birth of the Clinic: An Archaeology of Medical Perception.* Translated by A. Sheridan. New York: Vintage, 1975.

Frilingos, C. *Spectacles of Empire: Monsters, Martyrs, and the Book of Revelation.* Philadelphia: University of Pennsylvania Press, 2004.

Frye, N. *The Great Code: The Bible and Literature.* Orlando: Harcourt, 1982.

The Fundamentals: A Testimony of the Truth. 12 pamphlets. Chicago: Testimony, 1910–15.

Fuchs, E. *Hermeneutik.* Tübingen: Mohr Siebeck, 1970.

Gadamer, H. G. *Gesammelte Werke.* 9 vols. Tübungen: Mohr, 1990.

————. *Wahrheit und Methode.* Berlin: Akademie, 2007.

Gager, J. *Kingdom and Community: The Social World of Early Christianity.* Englewood Cliffs, NJ: Prentice-Hall, 1975.

Gallagher, E., and S. Worrall. *Christians in Ulster, 1968–1980.* Oxford: Oxford University Press, 1982.

Ganiel, G. *Evangelicalism and Conflict in Northern Ireland.* New York: Palgrave MacMillan, 2008.

————. "Religious Dissent and Reconciliation in Northern Ireland." In *Ecumenics from the Rim: Explorations in Honour of John D'Arcy May,* edited by J. O'Grady and P. Scherle, 379–86. London: Transaction, 2007.

Geertz, C. *The Interpretation of Cultures.* New York: Basic, 1973.

Gelfert, H-D. *Wie interpretiert man einen Roman?.* Stuttgart: Reclam, 2006.

Georgakopoulou, A., and D. Goutsos. *Discourse Analysis: An Introduction.* Edinburgh: Edinburgh University Press, 2004.

Gerlich, F. *Der Kommunismus als Lehre vom Tausendjährigen Reich.* München: Bruckmann, 1920.

Giddens, A. *Modernity and Self-Identity.* Cambridge: Cambridge University Press, 1991.

Giroux, H. A. *Counternarratives: Cultural Studies and Critical Pedagogies in Postmodern Spaces.* New York: Routledge, 1996.

Gopin, M. *Between Eden and Armageddon: The Future of World Religions, Violence and Peacemaking.* Oxford: Oxford University Press, 2000.

Gowan, D. *Eschatology in the Old Testament.* Edinburgh: T. & T. Clark, 2000.

Grabbe, L. L. "Prophetic and Apocalyptic: Time for New Definitions and New Thinking." In *Knowing the End from the Beginning,* edited by L. Grabbe and R. D. Haak, 107–33. London: T. & T. Clark, 2003.

————. "The Social Setting of Early Jewish Apocalypticism." *Journal for the Study of the Pseudepigrapha* 4 (1989) 27–47.

Grafton, A. "The Varieties of Millennial Experience: The Latest Trends in Apocalyptic Thought." *The New Republic* (November, 1999) 76–86.

Graham B, and P. Shirlow. "The Battle of the Somme in Ulster Memory and Identity." *Political Geography* 21 (2002) 881–904.

Grant, P. "Northern Ireland: Religion and the Peace Process." In *Religion and Peacebuilding*, edited by H. G. Coward and G. S. Smith, 261–78. Albany, NY: State University of New York, 2004.

Gray, J. *Black Mass: Apocalyptic Religion and the Death of Utopia*. London: Penguin, 2007.

Green, G. *Theology, Hermeneutics, and Imagination: The Crisis of Interpretation at the End of Modernity*. Cambridge: Cambridge University Press, 2000.

Greenblat, S. *Cultural Mobility: A Manifesto*. Cambridge: Cambridge University Press, 2010.

Greenblatt, S. "The Improvisation of Power." In *The New Historicism Reader*, edited by H. Aram Veese, 46–87. London: Routledge, 1994.

Grenz, S., and R. Olson. *20th-Century Theology: God and the World in a Transitional Age*. Carlisle, UK: Paternoster, 1992.

Gribben, C. "Antichrist in Ireland—Protestant Millennialism and Irish Studies." In *Protestant Millennialism, Evangelicalism and Irish Society, 1790–2005*, edited by C. Gribben and A. Holmes, 1–30. New York, Palgrave, 2006.

———. "The Eschatology of the Puritan Confessions." *Scottish Bulletin of Evangelical Theology* 20/1 (2002) 51–78.

———. *Evangelical Millennialism in the Transatlantic World, 1500–2000*. London: Palgrave Macmillan, 2010.

———. *God's Irishmen: Theological Debates in Cromwellian Ireland*. Oxford: Oxford University Press, 2007.

———. "Protestant Millennialism, Political Violence and the Ulster Conflict." *Irish Studies Review* 15/1 (2007) 51–63.

———. *The Puritan Millennium: Literature and Theology, 1550–1682*. 2nd ed. Studies in Christian History and Thought. Milton Keynes, UK: Paternoster, 2008.

———. *Writing the Rapture: Prophecy Fiction in Evangelical America*. Oxford: Oxford University Press, 2009.

Griesinger, E. "The Shape of Things to Come: Toward and Eschatology of Literature." *Christianity and Literature* 53 (2004) 203–32.

Guess, R. *The Idea of a Critical Theory: Habermas and the Frankfurt School*. Cambridge: Cambridge University Press, 1981.

Gutierrez, C., and Schwartz, H. *The End that Does: Art, Science and Millennial Accomplishment*. Oakville, ON: Equinox, 2006.

Hammer, R. *The Book of Daniel*. Cambridge: Cambridge University Press, 1976.

Hanson, P. D. *The Dawn of Apocalyptic The Historical and Sociological Roots of Jewish Apocalyptic*. Philadelphia: Fortress, 1979.

———. *Visionaries and their Apocalypses*. London: SPCK, 1983.

Harris, H. *Fundamentalism and Evangelicals*. Oxford: Clarendon, 1998.

Hart, K. P, and A. M. Holba, eds. *Media and the Apocalypse*. New York: Lang, 2009.

Hart, T. "Imagination for the Kingdom of God?" In *God Will be All in All: The Eschatology of Jürgen Moltmann*, edited by R. Bauckham, 49–76. Edinburgh: T. & T. Clark, 1999.

Hartshorne, C. *The Logic of Perfection*. La Salle, IL: Open Court, 1962.

Hauerwas, S. *Matthew*. London: SCM, 2006.

Hayes, B. and I. McAllister. "Religious Independents in Northern Ireland: Origins, Attitudes and Significance." *Review of Religious Research* 37 (1995) 65–83.

Hayes, Z. *Visions of a Future: A Study of Christian Eschatology.* Collegeville, MN: Liturgical, 1989.

Hays, R. *The Moral Vision of the New Testament: A Contemporary Introduction to New Testament Ethics.* London: T. & T. Clark, 2004.

Heaney, S. *North.* London: Faber and Faber, 1975.

Hegel, G. W. F. *The Philosophy of History.* Translation by J. Sibtree. New York: Prometheus, 1991.

Heidegger, M. *Being and Time.* Translated by J. Macquarrie and E. Robinson. New York: Harper and Row, 1962.

———. *Introduction to Metaphysics.* Translated by K. Mannheim. Yale University Press, 1959.

———. *Kant und das Problem der Metaphysik.* Frankfurt: Klostermann, 1951.

———. *Platons Lehre von der Wahrheit, Mit einem Brief uber den Humanismus.* Bern: Francke, 1947.

———. *Was heißt Denken?* Stuttgart: Reclam, 1992.

Heist, W. W. *The Fifteen Signs of Doomsday.* East Lansing, MI: Michigan State College, 1952.

Helm, P. "Calvin, the 'Two Issues' and the Structure of the *Institutes.*" *Calvin Theological Journal* 42 (2007) 341–48.

Hempton, D. "Evangelicalism and Eschatology." *Journal of Ecclesiastical History* 31 (1980) 179–94.

Hempton, D., and M. Hill. *Evangelical Protestantism in Ulster Society, 1740–1890.* London: Routledge, 1992.

Hick, J. ed. *The Myth of God Incarnate.* London: SCM, 1977.

Hickey, J. *Religion and the Northern Ireland Problem.* Dublin: Gill and Macmillan, 1984.

Hill, M. *The Time of the End: Millenarian Beliefs in Ulster.* Belfast: Belfast Society, 2001.

Hirsch, E. D. "Three Dimensions of Hermeneutics." *New Literary History* 3 (1972) 245–61.

Hobsbawm, E. *Primitive Rebels: Studies in Archaic Forms of Social Movement in the 19th and 20th Centuries.* New York: Norton, 1965.

Hobson, M. *Jacques Derrida: Opening Lines.* London: Routledge, 1998.

Holtz, T. *Die Christologie der Apokalypse des Johannes.* Berlin: Akademischer, 1971.

———. "Sprache als Metapher: Erwägungen zur Sprache der Johannesapokalypse." In *Studien zur Johannesoffenbarung und ihrer Auslegung,* edited by F. Horn and M. Wolter, 1–10. Neukirchen-Vluyn: Neukirchener, 2005.

Horn, P. R. *Gadamer and Wittgenstein on the Unity of Language: Reality and Discourse without Metaphysics.* Aldershot, UK: Ashgate, 2005.

Hudson, W. *The Marxist Philosophy of Ernst Bloch.* London: Macmillan, 1982.

Husch, G. *Something Coming: Apocalyptic Expectation and Mid-nineteenth-century American Painting.* Lebanon, NH: New England University Press, 2000.

Idel, M. "On Apocalypticism in Judaism." In *Progress, Apocalypse, and Completion of History and Life after Death of the Person in the World Religions,* edited by Peter Koslowski, 40–74. Dordrecht: Kluwer, 2002.

Idinopulos, T. "Nazism, Millenarianism and the Jews." *Journal of Ecumenical Studies* 40 (2003) 296–302.

Irvine, M. *Northern Ireland: Faith and Faction.* London: Routledge, 1991.

Jakobson, R., and M. Halle. *Fundamentals of Language*. The Hague: Mouton, 1971.

Jakobson, R., and F. de Saussure. "L'arbitraire du Signe et la Substance Phonique du Langage." In *Proceedings of the Sixth International Congress of Phonetic Sciences*, edited by B. Hala *et al.*, 599–603. Prague: Academia, 1972.

Jameson, F. *Archaeologies of the Future: The Desire Called Utopia and Other Science Fictions*. London: Verso, 2005.

Jaspers, K. *Die Atombombe und die Zukunft des Menschen: Politisches Bewusstsein in unserer Zeit*. München: Piper, 1958.

Jauhiainen, M. *The Use of Zechariah in Revelation*. Tübingen: Mohr, 2005.

Jay, M. "Should Intellectual History Take a Linguistic Turn? Reflections on the Habermas-Gadamer Debate." In *Modern European Intellectual History: Reappraisals and New Perspectives*, edited by Dominick LaCapra and Steven L. Kaplan, 86–110. Ithaca, NY: Cornell University Press, 1982.

Jeanrond, W. *Text and Interpretation as Categories of Theological Thinking*. Translated by Thomas Wilson. Dublin: Gill and Macmillan, 1988.

———. *Theological Hermeneutics: Development and Significance*. London: Macmillan, 1991.

Jenkins, F. *The Old Testament in the Book of Revelation*. Grand Rapids: Baker, 1976.

Johnson, C. *System and Writing in the Philosophy of Jacques Derrida*. Cambridge: Cambridge University Press, 1993.

Johnson, D. "Contemporary Hopes: Evangelical Christianity and the Decline of Narrative." In *Future of Hope: Christian Tradition amid Modernity and Postmodernity*, edited by M. Volf and W. Katerberg, 27–48. Grand Rapids: Eerdmans, 2004.

Jonas, H. *The Gnostic Religion*. Boston: Beacon, 1963.

Jones, A. "Teleology and the Hermeneutics of Hope." In *Proceedings of the Fifteenth International Congress for Analytical Psychology*, 402–16. Cambridge: Cambridge University Press, 2001.

Juergensmeyer, M. *Terror in the Mind of God: The Global Rise of Religious Violence*. Berkeley: University of California Press, 2001.

Jüngel, E. *Gott als Geheimnis der Welt: Zur Begründung der Theologie des Gekreuzigten im streit zwischen Theismus und Atheismus*. Tübingen: Mohr, 1978.

Kabbani, M. H. *The Approach of Armageddon? An Islamic Perspective*. Fenton, MI: Islamic Supreme Council of America, 2003.

Kallenberg, B. *Ethics as Grammar: Changing the Postmodern Subject*. South Bend, IN: University of Notre Dame Press, 2001.

Kant, I. *Grundlegung zur Metaphysik der Sitten*. Riga, Latvia: Hartknock, 1797.

Kaplan, J. "Absolute Rescue: Absolutism, Defensive Action and the Resort to Force." In *Millennialism and Violence*, edited by M. Barkun, 128–63. London: Routledge, 1996.

Käsemann, E. "Die Anfänge christlicher Theologie." *Zeitschrift für Theologie und Kirche* 57 (1960) 162–85.

Kearney, R. "Eschatology of the Possible God." In *The Religious*, edited by J. Caputo, 175–96. Oxford: Blackwell, 2002.

———. *On Paul Ricoeur: The Owl of Minerva*. Aldershot, UK: Ashgate, 2004.

Kehl, M. *Eschatologie*. Würzburg: Echter, 1986.

Keller, C. *Apocalypse Now and Then: A Feminist Guide to the End of the World*. Minneapolis: Fortress, 2005.

———. "Eyeing the Apocalypse." In *Postmodern Interpretations of the Bible: A Reader*, edited by A. K. M. Adam, 253–77. St. Louis: Chalice, 1985.

Keller, C., and S. Moore. "Derridapocalypse." In *Derrida and Religion: Other Testaments,* edited by Y. Sherwood and K. Hart, 189–208. London: Routledge, 2005.

Kelly, T. A. F. *Language, World and God: An Essay in Ontology.* Dublin: Columba, 1996.

Kermode, F. *The Sense of an Ending: Studies in the Theory of Fiction.* Oxford: Oxford University Press, 1968.

Kesser, A. *Ernst Blochs Ästhetik: Fragment, Montage, Metapher.* Würzburg: Königshausen & Neumann, 2006.

Key, A. "Marx's Messianic Faith." In *Messianism Through History,* edited by W. Beuken, S. Freyne, and A. Weiler, 101–13. London: SCM, 1993.

King, W. S. A. *The War between the Two Beasts and the Two Witnesses: A Chiastic Reading of Revelation 11.1—14.5.* London: T. & T. Clark, 2005.

Kippenberg, H. G. "Die Geschichte der Mittelpersischen Apokalpytischen Traditionen." *Studia Iranica* 7 (1978) 49–80.

Klausner, J. *The Messianic Idea in Israel from Its Beginning to the Completion of the Mishnah.* Translated by W. F. Stinespring. London: Allen and Unwin, 1956.

Knipe, D. M. "Zur Rolle des provisorischen Körpers für den Verstorbenen in hinduistischen Bestattungen." In *Der Abschied von den Toten: Trauerrituale im Kulturvergleich,* edited by J. Assmann, F. Maciejewski and A. Michaels, 62–81. Göttingen: Wallstein, 2001.

Koch, K. *Apocalyptic Literature and Testaments.* Garden City, NY: Doubleday, 1983.

———. *Ratlos vor der Apokalyptik. Eine Streitschrift über ein vernachlässigtes Gebiet der Bibelwissenschaft und die schädlichen Auswirkungen auf Theologie und Philosophie.* Gütersloh: Mohn, 1970.

———. "What is Apocalyptic? An Attempt at a Preliminary Definition." In *Visionaries and their Apocalypses,* edited by P. Hanson, 16–36. London: SPCK, 1983.

Kraybill, J. N. *Imperial Cult and Commerce in John's Apocalypse.* Sheffield, UK: Sheffield Academic Press, 1996.

Krüger, A. *Verstehen als Geschehen: Wissenschaftliche Zuständigkeitsbegrenzung und hermeneutische Erkenntnis.* Erlangen, Germany: Wehrhahn, 2007.

Kuhn, T. *The Structure of Scientific Revolutions.* Chicago: University of Chicago Press, 1962.

Kyle, R. *The Last Days are Here Again: A History of the End Times.* Grand Rapids: Baker, 1998.

Kysar, R. *John, the Maverick Gospel.* Louisville: Westminster John Knox, 2007.

Lachenmann, H. *Entwicklung und Endzeit.* Hamburg: Wittig, 1967.

Ladd, G. E. *A Commentary on the Revelation of John.* Grand Rapids: Eerdmans, 1972.

Lamont, W. "Richard Baxter, the Apocalypse, and the Mad Major." *Past and Present* 55 (1972) 68–90.

Landes, R. "The Fear of an Apocalyptic Year 1000: Augustinian Historiography Medieval and Modern." In *The Apocalyptic Year 1000: Religious Expectation and Social Change, 950–1050,* edited by R. Landes, 243–70. Oxford: Oxford University Press, 2003.

———. *Heaven on Earth: The Varieties of Millennial Experience.* Oxford: Oxford University Press, 2011.

———. "Millenarianism and the Dynamics of Apocalyptic Time." In *Expecting the End: Millennialism in Social and Historical Context,* edited by C. Gribben and K. Newport, 1–24. Waco, TX: Baylor University Press, 2006.

————. "Roosters Crow, Owls Hoot: On the Dynamics of Apocalyptic Millennialism." In *War in Heaven/Heaven on Earth: Theories of the Apocalyptic*, edited by S. O'Leary and G. McGhee, 19–46. London: Equinox, 2005.

Langenberg, H. *Die Prophetische Bildsprache der Apokalypse.* Würzburg: Metzingen, 1959.

Lawrence, D. H. *Apocalypse.* London: Heinemann, 1931.

Leahy, F. S. "The Seeds of Secularization." *Reformed Theological Journal* (November, 1986) 21–32.

Leavis, F. R. "The Responsible Critic: or the Functions of Criticism at any Time." *Scrutiny* 19 (1953) 162–83.

Lévi -Strauss, C. *The Elementary Structures of Kinship.* London: Penguin, 1969.

————. *Structural Anthropology.* Translated by C. Jacobson and B. G. Schoepf. New York: Basic, 1963.

————. *Tristes Tropiques.* London: Penguin, 1992.

Levitas, R. "The Imaginary Reconstitution of Society: Utopia as Method." In *Utopia Method Vision: The Use Value of Social Dreaming*, edited by T. Moylan and R. Baccolini, 47–68. Bern: Lang, 2007.

Lindbeck, G. *The Nature of Doctrine: Religion and Theology in a Post-Liberal Age* Philadelphia: Fortress, 1984.

Lindsey, H. *The Late Great Planet Earth.* New York: Bantam, 1973.

Livingstone, D. N., and R. A. Wells. *Ulster-American Religion: Episodes in the History of a Cultural Connection.* South Bend, IN: University of Notre Dame Press, 1999.

Lohse, E. *Die Offenbarung des Johannes.* Göttingen: Vandenhoek & Ruprecht, 1960.

Löwith, K. *Meaning in History: The Theological Implications of the Philosophy of History.* Chicago: Chicago University Press, 1949.

Lücke, F. *Versuch einer vollständigen Einleitung in die Offenbarung Johannis und in die gesamte apokalyptische Literatur.* Bonn: Weber, 1832.

Lukács, G. *Essays on Thomas Mann.* Translated by S. Mitchell. London: Merlin, 1964.

————. *Geschichte und Klassenbewusstsein.* Neuwied, Germany: Luchterhand, 1968.

MacDonald, M. *Children of Wrath: Political Violence in Northern Ireland.* Oxford: Blackwell, 1986.

MacIntyre, A. "Epistemological Crises, Narrative and the Philosophy of Science." In *Why Narrative? Readings in Narrative Theology*, edited by S. Hauerwas and L. G. Jones, 138–57. Grand Rapids: Eerdmans, 1989.

————. *A Short History of Ethics: A History of Moral Philosophy from the Homeric Age to the Twentieth Century.* London: Routledge, 1967.

MacIver, M. A. "A Clash of Symbols in Northern Ireland: Divisions between Extremist and Moderate Protestant Elites." *Review of Religious Research* 30 (1989) 360–74.

————. "Ian Paisley and the Reformed Tradition." *Political Studies* 35 (2006) 359–78.

————. "Militant Protestant Political Ideology: Ian Paisley and the Reformation Tradition." PhD diss., University of Michigan, 1984.

Macquarrie, J. *Christian Hope.* London: Mowbray, 1978.

————. *An Existentialist Theology.* London: SCM, 1960.

————. *In Search of Humanity: A Theological and Philosophical Approach.* London: SCM, 1982.

————. *Martin Heidegger.* London: Lutterworth, 1968.

Manoussaki, J. P. *After God: Richard Kearney and the Religious Turn in Continental Philosophy.* New York: Fordham University Press, 2006.

Marcus, J., and M. Soards, eds. *Apocalyptic and the New Testament: Essays in Honour of J. Louis Martyn*. Sheffield, UK: Sheffield Academic Press, 1989.

Marcuse, H. *Ideen zu einer kritischen Theorie der Gesellschaft*. Frankfurt: Suhrkamp, 1969.

Marrinan, P. *Paisley: Man of Wrath*. Tralee, Ireland: Anvil, 1973.

Marsden, G. "Fundamentalism as an American Phenomenon. A Comparison with English Evangelicalism." *Church History* 36/2 (1977) 215–32.

Marsden, G. *Understanding Fundamentalism and Evangelicalism*. Grand Rapids: Eerdmans, 1991.

Martinet, A. *Elements of General Linguistics*. Translated by Elisabeth Palmer. Chicago: Chicago University Press, 1960.

Mayer, A. C. *Sprache der Einheit im Epheserbrief und in der Ökumene*. Tübingen: Mohr Siebeck, 2002.

Martyn, J. L. "Apocalyptic Antinomies in Paul's Letter to the Galatians." *New Testament Studies* 31 (1985) 410–24.

McAllister, I., and B. C. Hayes. "Ethnonationalism, Public Opinion and the Good Friday Agreement." In *After the Good Friday Agreement: Analysing Political Change in Northern Ireland*, edited by J. Ruane and J. Todd, 30–48. Dublin: University College Dublin Press, 1999.

McBride, I. *Scripture Politics: Ulster Presbyterians and Irish Radicalism in the Late Eighteenth Century*. Oxford: Clarendon, 1998.

McCaughey, T. *Memory and Redemption: Church, Politics and Prophetic Theology in Ireland*. Dublin: Gill and MacMillan, 1993.

McClendon, J. *Systematic Theology: Volume I: Ethics*. Nashville: Abingdon, 1986.

———. *Systematic Theology: Volume II: Doctrine*. Nashville: Abingdon, 1994.

———. *Systematic Theology: Volume III: Witness*. Nashville: Abingdon, 2000.

McCutchan, G. "The Irony of Evangelical History." *Journal for the Scientific Study of Religion* 20 (1981) 309–26.

McDowell, J. *Hope in Barth's Eschatology: Interrogations and Transformations Beyond Tragedy*. Aldershot, UK: Ashgate, 2000.

McElroy, D. D. *Existentialism and Modern Literature: An Essay in Existential Criticism*. New York: Philosophical Library, 1963.

McEvoy, J. *The Politics of Northern Ireland*. Edinburgh: Edinburgh University Press, 2008.

McGarry, J., and B. O'Leary. *Explaining Northern Ireland: Broken Images*. Oxford: Blackwell, 1995.

McGinn, B. *Antichrist: Two Thousand Years of the Human Fascination with Evil*. New York: Columbia University Press, 2000.

———. *Apocalyptic Spirituality: Treatises and Letters of Lactantius, Adso of Montier-En-Der, Joachim of Fiore, the Franciscan Spirituals, Savonarola*. Mahwah, NJ: Paulist, 1979.

———. "The End of the World and the Beginning of Christendom." In *Apocalypse Theory and the Ends of the World*, edited by Malcolm Bull, 62–89. Oxford: Blackwell, 1995.

———. *Visions of the End: Apocalyptic Traditions in the Middle Ages*. New York: Columbia University Press, 1979.

McGinn, B., S. Stein, and J. J. Collins, eds. *The Encyclopaedia of Apocalypticism*. 3 vols. New York: Continuum, 1998.

McGrath, A. E. *Christian Theology: An Introduction*. Oxford: Blackwell, 1994.

————. *The Genesis of Doctrine: A Study in the Foundation of Doctrinal Criticism.* Oxford: Blackwell, 1990.

————. *The Blackwell Encyclopaedia of Modern Christian Thought.* Oxford: Blackwell, 1993.

McIntosh, G. *The Force of Culture: Unionist Identities in Twentieth-Century Ireland.* Cork: Cork University Press, 1999.

McManners, J. *The Oxford History of Christianity.* Oxford: Oxford University Press, 1993.

Mesle, C. R. *Process Theology: A Basic Introduction.* Danvers, MA: Chalice, 1993.

Meyer, H. "Das Papstum bei Luther und in der lutherischen Bekenntnisschriften." In *Lehrverurteilungen - kirchentrennend?,* edited by K. Lehrmann and W. Pannenberg, 306–28. Freiburg: Herder, 1996.

Migliore, D. *Faith Seeking Understanding: An Introduction to Christian Theology.* Grand Rapids: Eerdmans, 2004.

Milbank, J. *Theology and Social Theory: Beyond Secular Reason.* Oxford: Blackwell, 2006.

Millar, D. *Queen's Rebels: Ulster Loyalism in Historical Perspective.* Dublin: Gill and Macmillan, 1978.

Miller, J. H. *The Ethics of Reading: Kant, de Man, Eliot, Trollope, James, and Benjamin.* New York: Columbia University Press, 1987.

Minear, P. *I Saw a New Earth: An Introduction to the Visions of the Apocalypse.* Washington, DC: Corpus Books, 1968.

Mitchel, P. *Evangelicalism and National Identity in Ulster, 1921–1998.* Oxford: Clarendon, 2003.

————. "Unionism and the Eschatological 'Fate of Ulster', 1921–2005." In *Protestant Millennialism, Evangelicalism and Irish Society, 1790–2005,* edited by C. Gribben and A. Holmes, 202–27. London: Palgrave Macmillan, 2006.

Mitchell, C. "Behind the Ethnic Marker: Religion and Social Identification in Northern Ireland." *Sociology of Religion* 66 (2005) 3–21.

————. *Religion, Identity and Politics in Northern Ireland: Boundaries of Belonging.* Aldershot, UK: Ashgate, 2006.

Moltmann, J. *The Church in the Power of the Spirit: A Contribution to Messianic Ecclesiology.* Translated by M. Kohl. London: SCM, 1977.

————. *The Coming of God.* Translated by M. Kohl. Minneapolis: Fortress, 1996.

————. *The Crucified God: The Cross of Christ as the Foundation and Criticism of Christian Theology.* Translated by R. A. Wilson and J. Bowden. London: SCM, 1974.

————. *The Experiment Hope.* Translated by M. D. Meeks. Philadelphia: Fortress, 1975.

————. *Im Gespräch mit Ernst Bloch.* München: Kaiser, 1976.

————. *In the End—the Beginning: The Life of Hope.* Translated by M. Kohl. London: SCM, 2003.

————. *Kirche in der Kraft des Geistes: Ein Beitrag zur messianischen Ekklesiologie.* München: Kaiser, 1975.

————. *Das Kommen Gottes: Christliche Eschatologie.* München: Kaiser, 1995.

————. "Das Prinzip der Hoffnung und die christliche Zuversicht." *Evangelische Theologie* 23 (1963) 537–57.

————. *The Spirit of Life: A Universal Affirmation.* Translated M. Kohl. London: SCM, 1992.

————. *Theologie der Hoffnung.* München: Kaiser, 1964.

Montefiore, A. "Preface." In *Neutrality and Impartiality: The University and Political Commitment*, edited by A. Graham and A. Montefiore, vii–x. Cambridge: Cambridge University Press, 1975.

Montrose, L. "New Historicisms." In *Redrawing the Boundaries: The Transformation of English and American Literary Studies*, edited by S. Greenblatt and G. Gunn, 392–418. New York: Modern Language Association, 1992.

———. *The Purpose of Playing: Shakespeare and the Cultural Politics of the Elizabethan Theatre*. Chicago: University of Chicago Press, 1996.

Moore, C. *The Kincora Scandal: Political Cover-up and Intrigue in Northern Ireland*. Dublin: Marino, 1996.

Morrow, D. "'Suffering for Righteousness' Sake'? Fundamentalist Protestantism and Ulster politics." In *Who Are the People? Unionism, Protestantism and Loyalism in Northern Ireland*, edited by P. Shirlow and M. McGovern, 55–71. London: Pluto, 1997.

Mounce, R. *The Book of Revelation*. Grand Rapids: Eerdmans, 1997.

Mowinckel, S. *He that Cometh*. Oxford: Oxford University Press, 1975.

Mühling, M. *Grundinformation Eschatologie: Systematische Theologie aus der Perspektive der Hoffnung*. Göttingen: Vandehoeck & Ruprecht, 2007.

Müller, H. P. *Ursprünge und Strukturen alttestamentlicher Eschatologie*. Berlin: de Gruyter, 1969.

Murphy, F. A. *God is Not a Story: Realism Revisited*. Oxford: Oxford University Press, 2007.

Nelson-Pallmeyer, J. *Is Religion Killing Us?*. Harrisburg, PA: Trinity, 2003.

Newport, K. *Apocalypse and Millennium: Studies in Biblical Eisegesis*. Cambridge: Cambridge University Press, 2000.

———. *The Branch Davidians of Waco: The History and Beliefs of an Apocalyptic Sect*. Oxford: Oxford University Press, 2006.

Nida, E. A. "The Role of Context in the Understanding of Discourse." In *Discourse Analysis and the New Testament: Approaches and Results*, edited by S. Porter and J. Reed, 20–27. Sheffield, UK: Sheffield Academic Press, 1999.

Niebuhr, R. *Faith and History: A Comparison of Christian and Modern Views of History*. New York: Scribner, 1957.

———. *The Nature and Destiny of Man*. 2 vols. London: Nisbet, 1946.

Nietzsche, F. *Die Geburt der Tragödie, oder Griechenthum und Pessimismus*. Berlin: de Gruyter, 1972.

Nolan, S. L. "Communicative Success in Political Wall Murals in Northern Ireland: A Critical Discourse Analysis." PhD diss., Queen's University Belfast, 2003.

Northcott, M. *An Angel Directs the Storm: Apocalyptic Religion and American Empire*. London: I. B. Tauris, 2004.

O'Callaghan, P. *The Christological Assimilation of the Apocalypse: An Essay on Fundamental Eschatology*. Dublin: Four Courts, 2004.

Odermatt, M. *Der Fundamentalismus: Ein Gott—eine Wahrheit—eine Moral?* Zürich: Benziger, 1991.

O'Donnell, E. E. *Northern Ireland Stereotypes*. Dublin: College Of Industrial Relations, 1977.

O'Donovan, O. "The Political Thought of the Book of Revelation." *Tyndale Bulletin* 37 (1986) 61–94.

———. *Resurrection and the Moral Order: An Outline for Evangelical Ethics*. Grand Rapids: Eerdmans, 1994.

O'Farrell, P. "Millennialism, Messianism and Utopianism in Irish History." *Anglo-Irish Studies* 2 (1976) 45–68.

O'Leary, S. *Arguing the Apocalypse: A Theory of Millennial Rhetoric.* Oxford: Oxford University Press, 1994.

Olson, R. *The Story of Christian Theology: Twenty Centuries of Tradition and Reform.* Downers Grove, IL: InterVarsity, 1999.

O'Maier, H. "The President's Revelation: The Apocalypse, American Providence, and the War on Terror." *Word and World* 25 (2005) 294–307.

O'Malley, P. *Uncivil Wars: Ireland Today.* Belfast: Blackstaff, 1983.

Osbourne, G. R. *The Hermeneutical Cycle: A Comprehensive Introduction to Biblical Interpretation.* Downers Grove, IL: InterVarsity, 2006.

Paley, M. D. *The Continuing City: William Blake's Jerusalem.* Oxford: Oxford University Press, 1983.

Pannenberg, W. *The Basic Questions in Theology.* 3 volumes. London: SCM, 1970.

———. "Constructive and Critical Functions of Christian Eschatology." *The Harvard Theological Review* 77 (1984) 119–39.

———. "Hermeneutics and Universal History." Translated by P. J. Achtemaier. In *History and Hermeneutic: Journal for Theology and the Church* 4, 122–52. New York: Harper and Row, 1967.

———. *Systematic Theology.* Translated by G. Bromiley. Grand Rapids: Eerdmans, 1998.

Pablo R. *Apocalypse: A People's Commentary on the Book of Revelation.* Maryknoll, NY: Orbis, 1995.

Parfitt, T. *The Lost Tribes of Israel: The History of a Myth.* London: Weidenfeld and Nicolson, 2002.

Parushev, P. "Walking in the Dawn of the Light: On the Salvation Ethics of the Ecclesial Communities in the Orthodox Tradition from a Radical Reformation Perspective." PhD diss., Fuller Theological Seminary, 2006.

Pattemore, S. *The People of God in the Apocalypse: Discourse, Structure, and Exegesis.* Cambridge: Cambridge University Press, 2004.

Peillon, M., and M. Corcoran, eds. *Ireland Unbound: A Turn of the Century Chronicle.* Dublin: Institute of Public Administration, 2002.

Phelan, J. E. "Revelation, Empire and the Violence of God." *Ex Auditu* 20 (2004) 65–84.

Pijatigorskij, A. M. "Nekotorye obščie zamečanija otnositel "no rassmotrenija teksta kak raznovidnosti signale." In *Teksty Sovetskogo Literaturovedceskogo Strukturalizma,* edited by K. Eimermacher, 78–88. Munich: Fink, 1971.

Pilnei, O. *Wie entsteht christlicher Glaube?* Tübingen: Mohr Siehbeck, 2007.

Pippin, T. *Apocalyptic Bodies: The Biblical End of the World in Text and Image.* London: Routledge, 1999.

———. *Death and Desire: The Rhetoric of Gender in the Apocalypse of John.* Louisville: Westminster John Knox, 1992.

Plato. *Statesman.* Translated by R. Waterfield. Cambridge: Cambridge University Press, 1995.

Plöger, O. *Theokratie und Eschatologie.* Neukirchen: Neukirchener Verlag, 1959.

Polkinghorne, D. *Narrative Knowing and the Human Sciences.* Albany, NY: State University of New York, 1988.

Preuss, H. D. *Jahwehglaube und Zukunftserwartung.* Stuttgart: Kohlhammer, 1968.

Prickett, S. *Origins of Narrative: The Romantic Appropriation of the Bible.* Cambridge: Cambridge University Press, 1996.

Porter, F. *Changing Women, Changing Worlds: Evangelical Women in Church, Community and Politics.* Belfast: Blackstaff, 2002.

Pyman, A. "The Prism of the Orthodox Semisphere." In *Dostoevsky and the Christian Tradition,* edited by George Pattison and Diane Oenning Thompson, 103–15. Cambridge: Cambridge University Press, 2001.

Rahner, K. *Grundkurs des Glaubens: Einführung in den Begriff des Christentums.* Freiburg: Herder, 1984.

———. *Schriften zur Theologie.* Koln: Benziger, 1961.

———. *Theological Investigations* 4. Baltimore: Helicon, 1966.

Randall, I. *What a Friend We Have in Jesus: The Evangelical Tradition.* London: Darton, Longman and Todd, 2005.

Räpple E. M. *The Metaphor of the City in the Apocalypse of John.* New York: Lang, 2004.

Rapport, N. and Overing, J. *Social and Cultural Anthropology: The Key Concepts.* London: Routledge, 2000.

Ratzinger, J. *Eschatologie: Tod und ewiges Leben.* Regensburg: Pustet, 1977.

Raval, S. *The Art of Failure: Conrad's Fiction.* London: Allen & Unwin, 1986.

Redditt, P. *Introduction to the Prophets.* Grand Rapids: Eerdmans, 2008.

Redles, D. *Hitler's Millennial Reich: Apocalyptic Belief and the Search for Salvation.* New York: New York University Press, 2005.

Reynolds, B. E. *The Apocalyptic Son of Man in the Gospel of John.* Tübingen: Mohr Siebeck, 2008.

Reynolds, J., and J. Roffe, eds. *Understanding Derrida.* London: Continuum, 2004.

Richard, P. *Apocalypse: A People's Commentary on the Book of Revelation.* Maryknoll, NY: Orbis, 1995.

Richardson, N., ed. *A Tapestry of Beliefs: Christian Traditions in Northern Ireland.* Belfast: Blackstaff, 1998.

Ricoeur, P. *Figuring the Sacred: Religion, Narrative, and Imagination.* Translated by David Pellauer. Minneapolis: Augsburg Fortress, 1995.

———. "Freiheit im Licht der Hoffnung." In *Hermeneutik und Strukturalismus: Der Konflikt der Interpretationen I.* Translated by Johannes Rütsch, 199–226. München: Kösel, 1973.

———. *From Text to Action: Essays in Hermeneutics II.* Translated by Kathleen Blamey and John Thompson. Evanston, IL: Northwestern University Press, 1991.

———. *Interpretation Theory: Discourse and the Surplus of Meaning.* Fort Worth, TX: Texas Christian University Press, 1976.

———. "The Hermeneutics of Symbols and Philosophical Reflection: II." Translated by C. Freilich. In *The Conflict of Interpretations: Essays in Hermeneutics,* edited by Don Ihde, 315–34. Evanston, IL: Northwestern University Press, 1974.

———. "The Question of the Subject: The Challenge of Semiology." Translated by K. McLaughlin. In *The Conflict of Interpretations: Essays in Hermeneutics,* edited by Don Ihde, 236–66. Evanston, IL: Northwestern University Press, 1974.

———. *Time and Narrative.* Translated by Kathleen McLaughlin and David Pellauer. 2 vols. Chicago: Chicago University Press, 1985.

———. "What is a Text?" In *Hermeneutical Inquiry: Volume 1: The Interpretation of Texts.* Edited by David E. Klemm. Atlanta: Scholars, 1986.

Rigby, S. H. *Marxism and History: A Critical Introduction.* Manchester: Manchester University Press, 1998.

Roberts, J. "Myth versus History: Relaying the Comparative Foundations." *Catholic Biblical Quarterly* 38 (1976) 1–13.

Robbins, T., and S. J. Palmer, eds. *Millennium, Messiahs and Mayhem: Contemporary Apocalyptic Movements*. London: Routledge, 1997.

Robinson, J. A. T. *Redating the New Testament*. Philadelphia: Penn, 1976.

Rollins, W. G. "The New Testament and Apocalyptic." *New Testament Studies* 17 (1970–71) 454–76.

Rorty, R. *Consequences of Pragmatism*. Minneapolis: University of Minnesota Press, 1982.

———. *Philosophy and the Mirror of Nature*. Princeton: Princeton University Press, 1979.

Rose, R. *Governing without Consensus: An Irish Perspective*. London: Faber and Faber, 1971.

Rossing, B. *The Choice between Two Cities: Whore, Bride and Empire in the Apocalypse*. Harrisburg, PA: Trinity, 1999.

Routledge, R. *Old Testament Theology: A Thematic Approach*. Nottingham, UK: InterVarsity, 2008.

Rowland, C. *Blake and the Bible*. New Haven: Yale University Press, 2010.

———. *The Open Heaven: A Study of Apocalyptic in Judaism and Early Christianity*. 1982. Reprint. Eugene, OR: Wipf and Stock, 2002.

Rückert, F. *Die Weisheit des Brahmanen*. Leipzig: Hirzel, 1868.

Ruiz, J. P. *Ezekiel in the Apocalypse: The Transformation of Prophetic Language in Revelation 16:17—19:10*. Berlin: Lang, 1989.

Rüsen, J. "Sense of History: What Does It Mean? With an Outlook onto Reason and Senselessness." In *Meaning and Representation in History*, edited by J. Rüsen, 40–64. Oxford: Berghahn, 2008.

Russell, D. S. *The Method & Message of Jewish Apocalyptic*. London: SCM, 1964.

Sabatier, P. *Life of St. Francis of Assisi*. New York: Cosimo, 2007.

Sacchi, P. *Jewish Apocalyptic and Its History*. Sheffield, UK: Sheffield Academic Press, 1996.

Sacchi, M. E. *The Apocalypse of Being: The Esoteric Gnosis of Martin Heidegger*. South Bend, IN: St. Augustine's, 2002.

Sadler, I. A. *Mystery, Babylon the Great*. Trowbridge, UK: Cromwell, 1999.

Sagovsky, N. *Ecumenism, Christian Origins and the Practice of Communion*. Cambridge: Cambridge University Press, 2000.

Said, E. W. *Beginnings: Intention and Method*. New York: Columbia University Press, 1985.

Sandeen, E. *The Roots of Fundamentalism: British and American Millenarianism, 1800–1930*. Chicago: University of Chicago Press, 1970.

Sanders, E. P. "The Genre of Palestinian Jewish Apocalypses." In *Apocalypticism in the Mediterranean World and the Near East*, edited by D. Hellholm, 447–59. Tübingen: Mohr, 1983.

Sartre, J. P. *Being and Nothingness: An Essay on Philosophical Ontology*. Translated by H. Barnes. New York: Philosophical Library, 1956.

———. *Notebooks for an Ethics*. Translated by David Pallauer. Chicago: Chicago University Press, 1992.

Sauter, G. *What Dare We Hope? Reconsidering Eschatology*. Harrisburg, PA: Trinity, 1999.

Sawyer, J. F. A. ed. *The Blackwell Companion to the Bible and Culture*. Oxford: Blackwell, 2006.

Scheppard, C. "End Times Hermeneutics: An Overview." In *Brethren Life and Thought* 46 (2001) 5–10.

Schlier, H. *Die Zeit der Kirche*. Freiburg: Herder, 1956.

Schmithals, W. *The Apocalyptic Movement: Introduction and Interpretation*. Nashville: Abingdon, 1975.

Schneiders, S. M. *The Revelatory Text: Interpreting the New Testament as Sacred Scripture*. Collegeville, MN: Liturgical, 1999.

Scholem, G. *The Messianic Idea in Judaism: And Other Essays on Jewish Spirituality*. New York: Schocken, 1995.

Schreiter, R. *Constructing Local Theologies*. Maryknoll, NY: Orbis, 1985.

Schüssler-Fiorenza, E. *The Book of Revelation: Justice and Judgement*. Philadelphia: Fortress, 1985.

———. "The Phenomenon of Early Christian Apocalyptic: Some Reflections on Method." In *Apocalypticism in the Mediterranean World and the Near East*, edited by D. Hellholm, 295–316. Tübingen: Mohr, 1983.

———. *Revelation: Vision of a Just World*. Minneapolis: Fortress, 1991.

Schwarz, H. *Eschatology*. Grand Rapids: Eerdmans, 2000.

Schwambach, C. *Rechtfertigungsgeschehen und Befreiungsprozess: Die Eschatologien von Martin Luther und Leonardo Boff im kritischen Gespräch*. Göttingen: Vandenhoeck & Ruprecht, 2004.

Schweitzer, A. *The Mysticism of Paul the Apostle*. Translated by W. Montgomery. London: Black, 1931.

———. *Von Reimarus zu Wrede: Eine Geschichte der Leben-Jesu-Forschung*. Tübingen: Mohr, 1906.

Scott, N. A., and R. A. Sharp. *Reading George Steiner*. Baltimore: Johns Hopkins University Press, 1994.

Searle, J. R., ed. *The Philosophy of Language*. Oxford: Oxford University Press, 1971.

———. *Speech Acts: An Essay in the Philosophy of Language*. Cambridge: Cambridge University Press, 1969.

Searle, J. T. "The Biblical and Social Ethical Grounds for a Theology of Peacemaking in Resolving Violent Conflicts." MTh essay, International Baptist Theological Seminary, 2008.

———. "Is the Sermon on the Mount Too Unrealistic to Serve as a Resource for Healthy Discipleship and Spiritual Formation?" *Journal of European Baptist Studies* (January, 2009) 38–50.

———. "Ideology, Convictions and Eschatology: Towards a Theological Critique of Ideology from an Eschatological Perspective." *Baptistic Theologies* 3 (2011) 99–115.

———. "Romantismus, Fantasie a Utopie: Teologické Zhodnocení." In *Křesťanství a Romantismus*, edited by Ivana Noble and Jiří Hanuš, 32–46. Brno, Czech Republic: CDK, 2011.

Searle, J. T., and K. Newport, eds. *Beyond the End: The Future of Millennial Studies*. Sheffield, UK: Sheffield Phoenix, 2012.

Selby, P. "Christianity in a World Come of Age." In *The Cambridge Companion to Dietrich Bonhoeffer*, edited by J. W. de Grunchy, 226–45. Cambridge: Cambridge University Press, 1999.

Selvidge, M. J. "Powerful and Powerless Women in the Apocalypse." *Neotestamentica* 26 (1992) 157–67.

Shantz, D. H. "Millennialism and Apocalypticism in Recent Historical Scholarship." In *Prisoners of Hope? Aspects of Evangelical Millennialism in Britain and Ireland, 1800–*

1880, edited by C. Gribben and T. Stunt, 18–43. Paternoster, UK: Milton Keynes, 2004.

Sheehan, T. *Karl Rahner: The Philosophical Foundations*. Athens, OH: Ohio University Press, 1987.

Shirlow, P., and M. McGovern, eds. *Who are the People? Unionism, Protestantism and Loyalism in Northern Ireland*. London: Pluto, 1997.

Shupe, A. "Christian Reconstructionism and the Angry Rhetoric of Neo-Postmillennialism." In *Millennium, Messiahs and Mayhem: Contemporary Apocalyptic Movements*, edited by T. Robbins and S. J. Palmer, 195–206. London: Routledge, 1997.

Silverman, H. *Textualities: Between Hermeneutics and Deconstruction*. London: Routledge, 1994.

Sim, D. C. *Apocalyptic Eschatology in the Gospel of Matthew*. Cambridge: Cambridge University Press, 1996.

Skinner, Q. *The Foundations of Modern Political Thought: Volume 2: The Reformation*. Cambridge: Cambridge University Press, 1978.

———. "Meaning and Understanding in the History of Ideas." *History and Theory* 8 (1969) 3–53.

———. *Reason and Rhetoric in the Philosophy of Hobbes*. Cambridge: Cambridge University Press, 1996.

———. *Visions of Politics: Volume 1: Regarding Method*. Cambridge: Cambridge University Press, 2002.

Smith, D., and G. A. Chambers. *Inequality in Northern Ireland*. Oxford: Clarendon, 1991.

Smylie, J. H. "A New Heaven and New Earth: Uses of the Millennium in American Religious History." *Interpretation* 53 (1999) 143–57.

Snodgrass, K. *Stories with Intent: A Comprehensive Guide to the Parables of Jesus*. Grand Rapids: Eerdmans, 2008.

Soper, J. C. *Evangelical Christianity in the United States and Great Britain: Religious Beliefs, Political Choices*. London: Macmillan, 1994.

Southern, N. "The Democratic Unionist Party and the Politics of Religious Fundamentalism." PhD diss., Queen's University Belfast, 2001.

———. "Strong Religion and Political Viewpoints in a Deeply Divided Society: An Examination of the Gospel Hall Tradition in Northern Ireland." *Journal of Contemporary Religion* 26 (2012) 433–49.

Spiegel, G. M. "History, Historicism, and the Social Logic of the Text in the Middle Ages." *Speculum* 65 (1990) 59–86.

Stegemann, H. "Die Bedeutung der Qumranfunde für die Erforschung der Apokalyptik." In *Apocalypticism in the Mediterranian World and the Near East,* edited by D. Hellholm, 495–530. Tübingen: Mohr, 1983.

Steiner, G. *After Babel: Aspects of Language and Translation*. Oxford: Oxford University Press, 1992.

Stemberger, G. *Geschichte der Jüdischen Literatur: Eine Einführung*. München: Beck, 1977.

Stewart, D. "In Quest of Hope: Paul Ricoeur and Jürgen Moltmann." *Restoration Quarterly* 13 (1970) 31–52.

Stewart, J. "The Symbol Model vs. Language as Constitutive Articulate Contact." In *Beyond the Symbol Model: Reflections on the Representational Nature of Language*, edited by J. Stewart, 9–68. Albany, NY: State University of New York Press, 1996.

Stiver, D. R. *The Philosophy of Religious Language: Sign, Symbol and Story.* Oxford: Blackwell, 1996.

———. "Theological Method." In *The Cambridge Companion to Postmodern Theology,* edited by K. Vanhoozer, 170–85. Cambridge: Cambridge University Press, 2003.

———. *Theology After Ricoeur: New Directions in Hermeneutical Philosophy.* Louisville: Westminster John Knox, 2001.

Strozier, C. *Apocalypse: On the Psychology of Fundamentalism in America.* Boston: Beacon, 1994.

Tanner, M. *Ireland's Holy Wars: The Struggle for a Nation's Soul, 1500–2000.* New Haven: Yale University Press, 2001.

Taylor, C. *Philosophy and the Human Sciences: Philosophical Papers 2.* Cambridge: Cambridge University Press, 1985.

Taylor, M. C. *Deconstructing Theology.* New York: Crossroad, 1982.

Tertullian. *The Shows or De Spectaculis.* Whitefish, MT: Kessinger, 2004.

Thatcher, A. *The Savage Text: The Use and Abuse of the Bible.* Oxford: Wiley-Blackwell, 2008.

Theunissen, M. "Negativität bei Adorno." In *Adorno-Konferenz 1983,* edited by Jürgen Habermas and Ludwig von Friedeburg, 41–65. Frankfurt: Suhrkamp, 1983.

Thiselton, A. C. *The Hermeneutics of Doctrine.* Grand Rapids: Eerdmans, 2007.

———. *New Horizons in Hermeneutics.* London: Harper Collins, 1992.

———. *Thiselton on Hermeneutics.* Aldershot, UK: Ashgate, 2006.

Thompson, D. *The End of Time: Faith and Fear in the Shadow of the Millennium Faith and Fear in the Shadow of the Millennium.* London: Vintage, 1999.

Thompson, E. P. *The Making of the English Working Class.* Harmondsworth, UK: Penguin, 1968.

Thompson, L. L. *Revelation: Apocalypse and Empire.* Oxford: Oxford University Press, 1990.

———. "A Sociological Analysis of Tribulation in the Apocalypse of John." *Semia* 36 (1986) 147–74.

Tillich, P. *Der Mut Zum Sein.* Stuttgart: Furche-Verlag, 1952.

———. *Systematic Theology.* 3 vols. London: Nisbet, 1953.

Tompkins, J. ed. *Reader-Response Criticism: From Formalism to Post-Structuralism.* London: Johns Hopkins University Press, 1980.

Todd, J., and J. Ruane. *The Dynamics of Conflict in Northern Ireland: Power, Conflict and Emancipation.* Cambridge: Cambridge University Press, 1996.

Tonge, J. *Northern Ireland: Conflict and Change.* Harlow: Pearson Education, 2002.

Tonstad, S. K. *Saving God's Reputation: The Theological Function of Pistis Iesou in the Cosmic Narratives of Revelation.* London: T. & T. Clark, 2006.

Tozer, A. W. *This World: Playground or Battleground.* Carlisle, UK: Paternoster, 1989.

Travis, S. H. *Christian Hope and the Future of Man.* Leicester, UK: InterVarsity, 1980.

Trible, P. *Texts of Terror: Literary Feminist Readings of Biblical Narratives.* Philadelphia: Fortress, 1984.

Upton, C. *Legends of the End: Prophecies of the End Times, Antichrist, Apocalypse, and Messiah From Eight Religious Traditions.* Hillsdale, MI: Sophia Perennis/TRSP, 2005.

Vanhoozer, K. J. *Is There a Meaning in This Text? The Bible, the Reader and the Morality of Literary Knowledge.* Leicester, UK: Apollos, 1998.

Vanhoye, A. "L'utilisation du livre d'Ezéchiel dans l'Apocalypse." *Biblica* 43 (1962) 436–76.

Veelenturf, K. "Visions of the End and Irish High Crosses." In *Apocalyptic and Eschatological Heritage: The Middle East and Celtic Realms,* edited by M. McNamara, 144–73. Dublin: Four Courts, 2003.

Volf, M. *Exclusion and Embrace: A Theological Exploration of Identity, Otherness, and Reconciliation.* Nashville: Abingdon, 1994.

Volf, M., and W. Katerberg, eds. *The Future of Hope: Christian Tradition amid Modernity and Postmodernity.* Grand Rapids: Eerdmans, 2004.

Wainwright, A. W. *Mysterious Apocalypse: Interpreting the Book of Revelation.* Nashville: Abingdon, 1993.

Wallis, R., S. Bruce, and D. Taylor. "Ethnicity and Evangelicalism: Ian Paisley and Protestant Politics in Ulster." *Comparative Studies in Society and History* 29 (1987) 293–313.

Walliss, J. *Apocalyptic Trajectories: Millenarianism and Violence in the Contemporary World.* New York: Lang, 2004.

Walker, B. *Past and Present: History, Identity and Politics in Northern Ireland.* Belfast: Queen's University Belfast, 2000.

Walker, G. *A History of the Ulster Unionist Party: Protest, Pragmatism and Pessimism.* Manchester: Manchester University Press, 2004.

Ward, G. *Barth, Derrida and the Language of Theology.* Cambridge: Cambridge University Press, 1995.

————. *Cultural Transformation and Religious Practice.* Cambridge: Cambridge University Press, 2005.

————. *Theology and Contemporary Critical Theory.* London: Macmillan, 2000.

Ward, K. *What the Bible Really Teaches: A Challenge for Fundamentalists.* London: SPCK, 2004.

Weber, E. *Apocalypses: Prophecies, Cults and Millennial Beliefs throughout the Ages.* London: Hutchinson, 1999.

Weber, M. *Die protestantische Ethik und der Geist des Kapitalismus.* Weinheim: Beltz, 2000.

————. *The Sociology of Religion.* Translated by E. Fischoff. Boston: Beacon, 1963.

Weber, T. *Living in the Shadow of the Second Coming: American Premillennialism 1875–1982.* Grand Rapids: Academic Books, 1983.

Weiss, J. *Die Predigt Jesu vom Reiche Gottes.* Göttingen: Vandenhoeck & Ruprecht, 1892.

Wessinger, C. ed. *Millennialism, Persecution, and Violence.* Syracuse, NY: Syracuse University Press, 2000.

————. "Millennialism in Cross-cultural Perspective." In *The Oxford Handbook of Millennialism,* edited by Catherine Wessinger, 3–26. Oxford: Oxford University Press, 2011.

————. "Millennialism with and without the Mayhem." In *Contemporary Apocalyptic Movements,* edited by T. Robbins and S. J. Palmer, 47–59. London: Routledge, 1997.

Wheeler-Robinson, H. *The Christian Experience of the Holy Spirit.* London: Fontana, 1962.

Whelan, I. *The Bible War in Ireland.* Madison, WI: University of Wisconsin Press, 2005.

White, H. *The Content of the Form: Narrative Discourse and Historical Representation.* Baltimore: The Johns Hopkins University Press, 1990.

Whitehead, A. N. *Process and Reality: An Essay in Cosmology.* New York: Free, 1978.

Whyte, J. H. Y. *Interpreting Northern Ireland.* Oxford: Clarendon, 1990.

Wichert, S. *Northern Ireland since 1945.* London: Longman, 1999.

Wilcox, C., S. Linzey, and T. G. Jelen. "Reluctant Warriors: Premillennialism and Politics in the Moral Majority." *Journal for the Scientific Study of Religion* 30 (1991) 245–58.

Wiles, M. "What Christians Believe." In *The Oxford History of Christianity,* edited by J. McManners, 571–86. Oxford: Oxford University Press, 1993.

Williams, R. *Wrestling with Angels: Conversations in Modern Theology.* London: SCM, 2007.

Williams, S. "Anti-Catholicism: A Theological Consideration." *Studies: An Irish Quarterly Review* 89 (2000) 227–33.

Williamson, A. H. *Apocalypse Then: Prophecy and the Making of the Modern World.* Westport, CT: Praeger, 2008.

Wilson, R. R. "The Biblical Roots of Apocalyptic." In *Imagining the End: Visions of Apocalypse from the Ancient Middle East to Modern America,* edited by A. Amanat and M. Bernhardsson, 56–66. London: I. B. Tauris, 2002.

Wilson, S. *Related Strangers: Jews and Christians, 60–170.* Minneapolis: Fortress, 1995.

Wink, W. *Engaging the Powers: Discernment and Resistance in a World of Domination.* Minneapolis: Fortress, 1989.

———. *The Powers that Be: Theology for a New Millennium.* New York: Random House, 1998.

Wittgenstein, L. *Philosophical Investigations.* Translated by G. E. M. Anscombe. Oxford: Blackwell, 1953.

———. *Zettel.* Translated by G. E. M. Anscombe. Oxford: Blackwell, 1967.

Wood, I. S. *Crimes of Loyalty: A History of the UDA.* Edinburgh: Edinburgh University Press, 2006.

Wright, F. "Protestant Ideology and Politics in Ulster." *European Journal of Sociology* 14 (1973) 213–80.

Yoder, J. H. "Armaments and Christian Eschatology." In *Studies in Christian Ethics* 1 (1988) 41–63.

———. *For the Nations: Essays Public and Evangelical.* Grand Rapids: Eerdmans, 1997.

———. *The Original Revolution: Essays on Christian Pacifism.* Scottdale: Herald, 1977.

Zachman, R. C. "What Kind of Book Is Calvin's *Institutes?*" *Calvin Theological Journal* 35 (2000) 238–61.

Zegwaart, H. "Apocalyptic Eschatology and Pentecostalism: The Relevance of John's Millennium for Today." *The Journal of the Society for Pentecostal Studies* 10 (1988) 3–25.

Zimmerli, W. "Promise and Fulfilment." Translated by J. L. Mays. In *Essays on Old Testament Interpretation,* edited by C. Westermann, 89–112. London: SCM, 1963.

Zakzouk, M. "The Islamic Doctrine of the Eschatological Completion of History and Eternal Life." In *Progress, Apocalypse, and Completion of History and Life after Death of the Person in the World Religions,* edited by P. Koslowski, 89–100. Dordrecht: Kluwer, 2002.

Žižek, S. *Living in the End Times.* London: Verso, 2010.